LIBRARY OF HEBREW BIBLE/ OLD TESTAMENT STUDIES

622

Formerly Journal for the Study of the Old Testament Supplement Series

Editors
Claudia V. Camp, Texas Christian University, USA
Andrew Mein, Durham University, UK

Founding Editors
David J. A. Clines, Philip R. Davies and David M. Gunn

Editorial Board
Alan Cooper, Susan Gillingham, John Goldingay,
Norman K. Gottwald, James E. Harding, John Jarick, Carol Meyers,
Daniel L. Smith-Christopher, Francesca Stavrakopoulou,
James W. Watts

THE PERFORMATIVE DIMENSIONS OF RHETORICAL QUESTIONS IN THE HEBREW BIBLE

Do You Not Know? Do You Not Hear?

Jim W. Adams

LONDON • NEW YORK • OXFORD • NEW DELHI • SYDNEY

T&T CLARK
Bloomsbury Publishing Plc
50 Bedford Square, London, WC1B 3DP, UK
1385 Broadway, New York, NY 10018, USA
29 Earlsfort Terrace, Dublin 2, Ireland

BLOOMSBURY, T&T CLARK and the T&T Clark logo
are trademarks of Bloomsbury Publishing Plc

First published in Great Britain 2020
This paperback edition published in 2022

Copyright © Jim W. Adams, 2020

Jim W. Adams has asserted his right under the Copyright, Designs and Patents Act, 1988, to be identified as Author of this work.

For legal purposes the Acknowledgments on p. xi constitute an extension of this copyright page.

All rights reserved. No part of this publication may be reproduced or transmitted in any form or by any means, electronic or mechanical, including photocopying, recording, or any information storage or retrieval system, without prior permission in writing from the publishers.

Bloomsbury Publishing Plc does not have any control over, or responsibility for, any third-party websites referred to or in this book. All internet addresses given in this book were correct at the time of going to press. The author and publisher regret any inconvenience caused if addresses have changed or sites have ceased to exist, but can accept no responsibility for any such changes.

A catalogue record for this book is available from the British Library.
Library of Congress Control Number: 2019956638.

ISBN:	HB:	978-0-5675-5323-2
	PB:	978-0-5676-9789-9
	ePDF:	978-0-5676-9558-1

Series: Library of Hebrew Bible/Old Testament Studies, volume 622

ISSN 2513-8758

Typeset by: Forthcoming Publications Ltd

To find out more about our authors and books visit www.bloomsbury.com
and sign up for our newsletters.

In Loving Memory of John E. Hartley
(9 May 1940–6 August 2019)
מי כמוך

Contents

List of Tables and Figures	ix
Acknowledgments	xi
List of Abbreviations	xiii
INTRODUCTION	1
Chapter 1	
SPEECH ACT THEORY AND INDIRECT SPEECH ACTS	21
Basic Philosophical Notions of Speech Act Theory	29
Indirect Speech Acts	40
Conclusions	107
Chapter 2	
ANALYSIS OF RHETORICAL QUESTIONS	
AND OTHER SIMILAR TYPES OF INTERROGATIVES	126
Ilie's Five Characteristics of Rhetorical Questions	129
Ilie's Three Misconceptions of Rhetorical Questions	144
Rhetorical Questions as Indirect Speech Acts	145
Proposed Theoretical Framework for the Analysis	
of Rhetorical Questions	166
Conclusion	187
Chapter 3	
THE PERFORMATIVE DIMENSIONS	
OF RHETORICAL QUESTIONS IN THE HEBREW BIBLE	188
Genesis 30:2	188
Genesis 50:19 and Other Interrogatives in Genesis	192
Exodus 3:11	201
Exodus 5:2	205
Exodus 15:11 and Four Psalmic Interrogatives	
Conveying Yahweh's Incomparability	207
Psalm 88:11–13 (vv. 10–12)	220
Psalm 8:5 (v. 4)	227

  Psalm 144:3–4 and Job 7:17–18   241
  Psalm 27:1   245
  Isaiah 40:12–31   248

CONCLUSION   261

Bibliography   268
Index of References   284
Index of Authors   289

Tables and Figures

Tables
1.1 Searle's Rules/Conditions for Successful
      and Felicitous Assertions   32
1.2 Searle's Rules/Conditions for Successful
      and Felicitous Questions   38
1.3 Searle's Rules/Conditions for Successful
      and Felicitous Directives and Commissives   64
1.4 Van Eemeren/Grootendorst's General Inference Scheme
      for Direct and Indirect Speech Acts   95
2.1 Ilie's Illocutionary Acts Conveyed by Rhetorical Questions   147
2.2 Ilie's Theoretical Frame for the Analysis
      of Rhetorical Questions   149
2.3 Slot's General Inference Scheme for Rhetorical Questions   158
2.4 Proposed Theoretical Framework for the Analysis
      of Rhetorical Questions   167

Figures
2.1 Stenström's Degrees of Addresser Assumptions
      and Strength of Belief   141
2.2 Spectrum of Degrees of Informativity of Rhetorical Questions   180

Acknowledgments

I have been working on this manuscript for close to ten years and without the patience and support of my wife, Audry, and our three children it would not have been realized. Much of the reason for this lengthy span of time is because of the extensiveness and denseness of the research involved, but other reasons include several broken arms due to skateboarding; two for my youngest son Parker and one for me.

I am deeply grateful to Claudia Camp, Andrew Mein, and Dominic Mattos for their patience as well, who graciously extended numerous deadlines to me. I also sincerely thank Duncan Burns for his exceptional and conscientious editorial work which has greatly improved the final version of my manuscript.

I want also to thank Gary Merriman and Michaela Allen of the LPU library for their consistent assistance in locating and retrieving obscure books and journal articles for my research, without whom and which I could not have completed this project.

Lastly, I want to thank John E. Hartley, to whom I have dedicated this book. My professor and friend slipped into eternity just before he could review my last chapter. He had been working with me on this manuscript and we were playing phone and email tag during the last couple of months of his life and I regrettably missed his last phone call. I was fortunate to present some of my initial conclusions in a paper during a regional SBL session dedicated to him in 2016. I was anxious for him to review my final chapter as much of the material reflects his own teaching and research, but I was too late. I take comfort in the fact that I will see him again and perhaps then we can talk over my interpretive conclusions about rhetorical questions in the Hebrew Bible, but I am fairly certain that they won't really matter at that point!

ABBREVIATIONS

AB	Anchor Bible
ABD	David Noel Freedman (ed.), *The Anchor Bible Dictionary*. New York: Doubleday, 1992
ACCS	Ancient Christian Commentary on Scripture
AJSL	*American Journal of Semitic Languages and Literature*
BBET	Belträge zur biblischen Exegese und Theologie
BCOT	Baker Commentary on the Old Testament
BETL	Bibliotheca ephemeridum theologicarum lovaniensium
BHS	*Biblia hebraica stuttgartensia*
Bib	*Biblica*
BibInt	*Biblical Interpretation: A Journal of Contemporary Approaches*
BRS	Biblical Resource Series
BSac	*Bibliotheca Sacra*
BT	*The Bible Translator*
BZAW	Beihefte zur *ZAW*
CBQ	*Catholic Biblical Quarterly*
CBQMS	*Catholic Biblical Quarterly*, Monograph Series
CLS	*Chicago Linguistic Society*
ConBOT	Coniectanea biblica, Old Testament
CRBS	*Currents in Research: Biblical Studies*
ECC	Eerdmans Critical Commentary
FOTL	The Forms of the Old Testament Literature
GKC	*Gesenius' Hebrew Grammar*. Edited by E. Kautzsch, revised and trans. A.E. Cowley. Oxford: Clarendon Press, 1910
HALOT	Koehler, L., W. Baumgartner, and J. J. Stamm, *The Hebrew and Aramaic Lexicon of the Old Testament*. Translated and edited under the supervision of M. E. J. Richardson. 5 vols. Leiden: Brill, 1994–2000
HCOT	Historical Commentary on the Old Testament
HS	*Hebrew Studies*
HSM	Harvard Semitic Monographs
HTR	*Harvard Theological Review*
IBHS	*An Introduction to Biblical Hebrew Syntax*. B. K. Waltke and M. O'Connor. Winona Lake: Eisenbrauns, 1990.
ICC	International Critical Commentary
Int	*Interpretation* (journal)
Int	Interpretation (series)

ISBL	Indiana Studies in Biblical Literature
JANESCU	*Journal of the Ancient Near Eastern Society of Columbia University*
JBL	*Journal of Biblical Literature*
JNES	*Journal of Near Eastern Studies*
JNSL	*Journal of Northwest Semitic Languages*
Joüon-Muraoka	Paul Joüon and T. Muraoka, *A Grammar of Biblical Hebrew*. Subsidia Biblica 27. Rome: Editrice Pontificio Istituto Biblico, 2008
JP	*Journal of Pragmatics*
JPSTC	JPS Torah Commentary
JR	*Journal of Religion*
JSOT	*Journal for the Study of the Old Testament*
JSOTSup	*Journal for the Study of the Old Testament*, Supplement Series
JSS	*Macmillan Journal of Semitic Studies*
LCC	Library of Christian Classics
LHBOTS	Library of Hebrew Bible/Old Testament Studies
LXX	Septuagint
MLBS	Mercer Library of Biblical Studies
NCB	New Century Bible
NCBC	New Cambridge Bible Commentary
NIBCOT	New International Bible Commentary on the Old Testament
NICOT	New International Commentary on the Old Testament
NIDOTE	Willem A. VanGemeren, ed. *New International Dictionary of Old Testament Theology and Exegesis*. 5 vols.; Grand Rapids: Zondervan, 1997
NIVAC	NIV Application Commentary
OBT	Overtures to Biblical Theology
OTL	Old Testament Library
PhQ	*Philosophical Quarterly*
PhR	*Philosophical Review*
PTMS	Princeton Theological Monograph Series
RelS	*Religious Studies*
RevExp	*Review and Expositor*
SBLMS	SBL Monograph Series
SBLSS	SBL Symposium Series
SR	*Studies in Religion*
Syr	Syriac
TynBul	*Tyndale Bulletin*
Vg	Vulgate
VT	*Vetus Testamentum*
VTSup	*Vetus Testamentum*, Supplements
WBC	Word Biblical Commentary
ZAW	*Zeitschrift für die alttestamentliche Wissenschaft*

Introduction

The rhetorical tactic of posing questions that do not expect verbal responses has long been utilized and analyzed.[1] The origins of conceptualizing the nature and function of Rhetorical Questions (RQs) is found in the writings of Greek rhetoricians. In ancient Greece a public speaker, attorney, or teacher was identified as a ῥήτωρ "rhetor" who used ῥητορική "rhetoric" in her/his argumentation or teaching. According to E. M. Cope, Aristotle identified three broad τόποι "places" and/or στοιχεῖον "elements" wherein lies a collection of stock rhetorical arguments of the same kind.[2] Questions and answers played an essential role for Greek rhetoricians and are a preferred device used in a public assembly and law courts when interrogating an adversary. Aristotle distinguished four specific τόποι or "occasions of using" such rhetorical instruments. In his descriptions, Aristotle sees interrogatives functioning much more than merely asking a question as the object of this type of interrogation

> is to enforce an argument; or to take the adversary by surprise and extract from her/him an unguarded admission; or to place her/him in an awkward dilemma, by shaping your question in such a way, that she/he must either by avowing it admit something which her/his antagonist wishes to establish, or by refusing seem to give consent by her/his silence to that which the questioner wishes to insinuate; or to gain some similar advantage. It may be made therefore in this way subservient to proof.[3]

Latin *oratoria* "rhetoric" built on such Greek concepts with Cicero and Quintilian expanding and sharpening prior descriptions of RQs. Both these rhetoricians designate RQs as *figurae sententiarum* "figures of thought" as the interrogative sentence form of the expression does not

---

1. Jane Frank, "You Call That a Rhetorical Question?" *JP* 14 (1990): 723.
2. E. M. Cope, *An Introduction to Aristotle's Rhetoric* (London: Macmillan, 1867), 124–29.
3. Ibid., 362 (pronouns revised); see the fuller descriptions of the four types of interrogation on pp. 363–65.

correspond with its function. Quintilian appears to take it upon himself to present a fuller description of these figures than Cicero and other rhetoric specialists. In doing so he begins by reflecting on two terms for questioning: *interrogare* "to ask" or *percontari* "to inquire." Both terms are used indifferently, yet the latter appears to imply a desire for knowledge whereas the former suggests a desire to prove something. More exacting, a question involving a figure is not employed to acquire information, but is used to function figuratively.[4] Quintilian spends quite a bit of time describing his view of *figurae*[5] and in the end they all involve "a rational change in meaning or language from the ordinary and simple form."[6] In short, *figurae* "do not mean quite what they say."[7] Quintilian also observed diverse uses of *figurae* which included:

- ask to emphasize a point
- pose a question which cannot be denied
- ask something which is difficult to reply
- ask to throw odium on the addressee
- ask to provoke pity
- ask to embarrass an opponent
- ask to express indignation
- ask to express wonder
- ask to express a command
- ask oneself
- to ask as an answer a question
- to ask to provoke laughter
- to ask and answer oneself
- to ask without waiting for a reply
- to ask involving a comparison
- to ask with hesitation to express a truth[8]

Although more observational in approach, Quintilian's descriptions of RQs provide foundational insight and, as I will discuss further below, he points to their self-involving nature. Yet, as Cornelia Ilie highlights, Quintilian views RQs from primarily an addresser-oriented perspective

---

4. Quintilian, *The Institutio Oratoria of Quintilian*, trans. H. E. Butler (Cambridge, MA: Harvard University Press, 1943), 3:377.
5. See ibid., 348–63.
6. Ibid., 353.
7. Donald L. Clark, *Rhetoric in Greco-Roman Education* (Morningside Heights, NY: Columbia University Press, 1957), 90.
8. Quintilian, *Oratoria of Quintilian*, 3:376–85.

and thus neglects to include their multiple effects within the interaction between addressers and addressees.[9]

Contemporary language specialists (i.e., linguists, philosophers of language, pyscholinguists, pragmatists, semanticists) continue to explore the nature and function of RQs with biblical scholars employing this research in their own current analyses. It has long been acknowledged that the Latter Prophets and Wisdom literature regularly utilize RQs as a key verbal and literary device.[10] This correlates with many language specialists focusing their examination of RQs in argumentative type contexts. Yet, RQs are used extensively throughout the entirety of the biblical literature and for multiple different intentions. For the vast majority of all language specialists, the intention of RQs is the *rhetorical* or *persuasive* effect on addressees. For both past and present biblical interpreters, this intent remains the primary grid for interpreting RQs. Where language specialists diverge with this rhetorical purpose is exactly *how* this persuasive effect occurs which is often dependent upon the particular contextual setting of the respective RQs analyzed (e.g., the classroom, the courtroom, public speeches, formal argumentation, etc.).

It is undeniable that certain RQs possess an overarching persuasive or challenging goal, but as with any type of linguistic expression RQs are much more diverse, complex, versatile, and multifunctional as Quintilian observes. For instance, a singer opens Psalm 27 with:

Yahweh, my light and my salvation!	יהוה אורי וישעי
From among whom should I fear?	ממי אירא
Yahweh, protector of my life!	יהוה מעוז־חיי
From among whom should I be afraid?	ממי אפחד:

The two confessionary assertions about Yahweh provide contextual clues that with the two interrogatives the psalmist does not pose real or genuine questions.[11] Because of this, these positive interrogatives indirectly imply that the psalmist should fear no one. As such, these

---

9. Cornelia Ilie, *What Else Can I Tell You? A Pragmatic Study of English Rhetorical Questions as Discursive and Argumentative Acts*, AUS 82 (Stockholm: Almqvist & Wiksell, 1994), 11–12.

10. E.g., Ernst Wendland, "Linear and Concentric Patterns in Malachi," *BT* 36 (1985): 109. For some of Jeremiah's use of RQs, see Walter Brueggemann, "Jeremiah's Use of Rhetorical Questions," *JBL* 92 (1973): 358–74; for the wisdom tradition see Gerhard von Rad, *Wisdom in Israel*, trans. J. D. Martin (Valley Forge: Trinity Press International, 1972).

11. All translations mine.

interrogatives appear to intentionally operate as RQs. From this brief and basic analysis, a question arises as to how do such positive interrogatives convey negative answers? Within a cooperative communicative interchange, addressers typically direct RQs in one way or another to addressees, but in this instance the addressee and addresser are one and the same. The persuasive interpretive angle typically centers on the effect of RQs on other addressees, but how does this focus work in this instance? Most language specialists and biblical scholars understand the inferred answer as an assertion or statement, but is this true with these RQs? This self-addressed type is also not unique to the biblical text, but does raise the question of how such RQs function? For what purpose does the psalmist use such interrogatives?

A fairly straightforward RQ is found in the fourth servant passage (Isa 53:1):

Who could have believed what we have heard?	מי האמין לשמעתנו
And upon whom has the arm of Yahweh revealed itself?	וזרוע יהוה על־מי נגלתה׃

These parallel interrogatives introduce the confession and testimony of an anonymous first plural voice which ends at v. 11aα. There are no linguistic or contextual clues to identify these interrogatives as RQs, but they do not readily appear to seek for an informative answer. As with the previous example, these positive interrogatives indirectly convey the answers, *No one!* No person could have anticipated or believed the implausible exaltation of this unlikely suffering servant and how Yahweh's power is uncharacteristically manifested. As RQs who, though, are the addressers as well as the addressee(s)? How do they persuade (a) possible addressee(s)? What is the purpose of these parallel RQs?

Among the languages of the world, three basic sentence types are typically distinguished: (1) declarative; (2) interrogative; and (3) imperative.[12] In broad terms, with declaratives addressers make statements or assertions, with interrogatives addressers ask questions, and with imperatives addressers issue requests or commands. To ask a question, addressers employ a specific syntactical structure identified as an interrogative form.

---

12. See Jerrold M. Sadock and Arnold M. Zwicky, "Speech Act Distinctions in Syntax," in *Language Typology and Syntactic Description, Volume 1: Clause Structure*, ed. T. Shopen (Cambridge: Cambridge University Press, 1985), 160–62; Ekkehard König and Peter Siemund, "Speech Act Distinctions in Grammar," in *Language Typology and Syntactic Description, Volume 1: Clause Structure*, ed. T. Shopen, 2nd ed. (Cambridge: Cambridge University Press, 2007), 276–84.

This form also has a particular semantic conception as well as a speech act function of requesting information.[13] Robert Fiengo observes that interrogative forms are in themselves purposefully incomplete to reveal ignorance or a lack in an addresser's understanding that she/he is eliciting relief from.[14]

Language specialists use multiple different descriptors for the manifold types of interrogatives employed by addressers with each falling into two general categories: Open and Closed. Within these two broad categories, theorists often identify three main types of interrogatives. Closed, Polar, or Yes–No Interrogatives normally contain a closed interrogative clause with a pair of polar opposites of answers, often either *Yes* or *No*. With these types, addressers inquire about the truth or falsity expressed in the proposition such as *Is it breathing?* Open, Constituent, Information, Variable, or *wh*-Interrogatives typically begin or front with a constituent interrogative (e.g., *which, who, when, where, why, what, how*) and are constructed with an open propositional content. Addressers issue such forms to elicit variable possible information to complete the openness of the sentence signaled by interrogative term such as *Why isn't it moving?* Alternative Interrogatives fall within the Closed category as they occur in closed interrogative clauses, but differ from this specific classification with the inclusion of the coordinate *or* which then cannot be answered simply with a *Yes* or *No*, such as *Is it a boy or a girl?* Addressers use such interrogative forms to inquire of which of the possible alternatives is true or false.[15]

---

13. James Higginbotham, "The Semantics of Questions," in *The Handbook of Contemporary Semantic Theory*, ed. S. Lappin, BHL (Oxford: Blackwell Publishers, 1996), 361.

14. Robert Fiengo, *Asking Questions: Using Meaningful Structures to Imply Ignorance* (Oxford: Oxford University Press, 2007), cf. 1–10.

15. Rodney Huddleston, "Clause Type and Illocutionary Force," in *The Cambridge Grammar of the English Language*, ed. Rodney Huddleston and G. K. Pullman (Cambridge: Cambridge University Press, 2002), 867. Some language specialists often incorporate Alternative Questions with Polar Questions due to their similarity in syntactical form and pragmatic function, but as Peter Siemund observes such categorization disregards the fact that Alternative Interrogatives cannot be answered simply by *Yes* or *No* ("Interrogative Constructions," in *Language Typology and Language Universals, Volume 2*, ed. M. Haspelmath et al. [Berlin/New York: de Gruyter, 2001], 1012). Interestingly, König and Siemund recognize the uniqueness of Alternative Questions, but see no "striking typological variation" from Polar Questions and thus view these interrogative forms as "coding strategies for polar questions" ("Speech Act Distinction," 292).

RQs generally fall within the category of Closed interrogatives and more narrowly within the Biased interrogative type in distinction to Neutral interrogatives. With the former, addressers use interrogatives to express their belief and thus only accept one particular answer as the correct one whereas with the latter addressers have no bias, but remain neutral towards an answer in line with the Open category.[16] RQs are identical in form to that of genuine questions, but differ in how they function. In other words, on the sentence level both match as linguistic interrogatives whereas on the pragmatic level they differ. The intended function of RQs does not match their linguistic form. In biblical Hebrew, the same interrogative particles (e.g., הֲ, מִי, מָה, לָמָה, הֲלֹא, אִם) mark all types of interrogatives, but not exclusively. Further, unmarked sentences can be understood as expressing any type of interrogative (e.g., Gen 27:24a; Job 2:10; 10:9).[17] Beyond any syntactical markers, intonation certainly plays a role towards distinguishing any interrogative in modern languages;[18] however, with any written work, and even more so ancient ones, literary context and genre play crucial interpretive roles. Along with their typical syntactical interrogative form, questions on the semantic level are also distinguished by the fact that they define a set of logically possible answers (e.g., *Where did you go? Who was there?*).[19] Questions also express illocutionary force to one degree or another and in general that of a Directive or request. A large number of language specialists agree that genuine questions typically *request* or *seek* unknown information whereas RQs *provide* information.[20] Bible translators John Beekman and John Callow representatively view RQs in this sense as they "serve the purpose of *imparting* or *calling attention to* information, not eliciting it. They are thus semantically

---

16. See Sadock/Zwicky, "Speech Act Distinctions," 180; see also Huddleston, "Clause Type," 879–81.

17. See further GKC §150a; Lénart J. de Regt, "Discourse Implications of Rhetorical Questions in Job, Deuteronomy and the Minor Prophets," in *Literary Structure and Rhetorical Strategies in the Hebrew Bible*, ed. Lénart J. de Regt et al. (Winona Lake: Eisenbrauns, 1996), 53–54.

18. See, e.g., Atissa Banuazizi and Cassandre Creswell, "Is that a Real Question? Final Rises, Final Falls and Discourse Function in Yes–No Question Intonation," *CLS* 35 (1999): 1–14; König/Siemund, "Speech Act Distinctions," 292–94.

19. Huddleston, "Clause Type," 865.

20. E.g., Martin Bell, "Questioning," *PhQ* 25 (1975): 209; Felix S. Cohen, "What Is a Question?" *The Monist* 39 (1929): 352; John E. Llewelyn, "What Is a Question?" *The Australasian Journal of Philosophy* 42 (1964): 70; Jürgen Schmidt-Radefeldt, "On So-Called 'Rhetorical' Questions," *JP* 1 (1977): 377–78.

equivalent to statements."²¹ Bruce Waltke and M. O'Connor also follow this line of thought by claiming that RQs "aim not to gain information but to give information with passion."²² More recently J. Kenneth Kuntz also distinguishes RQs as providing information and concurs with these specialists while using speech act terminology to claim that "the 'illocutionary force' of rhetorical questions is not to inquire but to assert."²³ As I will discuss in my second chapter, there are obviously numerous *information-providing* RQs, but unquestionably there are *uninformative* RQs as well.²⁴ Two consistent characteristics of RQs, though, are clear: they do not elicit a verbalized answer nor seek information.²⁵ Thus, they are non-information eliciting interrogatives.²⁶

Language specialists usually consider imperatives as primarily requests for some type of *nonlinguistic* behavior whereas questions are primarily concerned with *linguistic* responses while, conversely, RQs do neither.²⁷ Fiengo follows this line of thinking with his two types of interrogatives that normally function as RQs: (1) unanswerable (a question that has no answer) and (2) insultingly obvious (questions with answers so well known or obvious that it would appear insulting to even ask them so as to get answers). Thus, one who asks a RQ "intends to be taken as not wanting an answer."²⁸ Yet, as I will explore later, RQs do in fact expect

---

21. John Beekman and John C. Callow, *Translating the Word of God* (Grand Rapids: Zondervan, 1974), 238.

22. *IBHS* §18.2g. Similarly, E. A. Nida et al. state that RQs "are expressions which have the form of a question but are not designed to elicit information. The intent, therefore, is not to ask for a response but to make an emphatic declaration" (E. A. Nida et al., *Style and Discourse: With Special Reference to the Text of the Greek New Testament* [Cape Town: Bible Society, 1983], 39).

23. J. Kenneth Kuntz, "Making a Statement: Rhetorical Questions in the Hebrew Psalter," in *Probing the Frontiers of Biblical Studies*, ed. J. H. Ellens and J. T. Greene, PTMS (Eugene: Pickwick, 2009), 157.

24. Cf. Hannah Rohde, "Rhetorical Questions as Redundant Interrogatives," *San Diego Linguistics Papers* 2 (2006): 134–68.

25. See, e.g., Ann Borkin, "Polarity Items in Questions," *CLS* 7 (1971): 53–62; Chung-hye Han, "Interpreting Interrogatives as Rhetorical Questions," *Lingua* 112 (2002): 201–29; Jerrold M. Sadock, "Queclaratives," *CLS* 7 (1971): 223–31.

26. Ilie, *What Else Can I Tell You?*, 81.

27. E.g., Wallace L. Chafe, *Meaning and the Structure of Language* (Chicago: University of Chicago Press, 1970), 309 (italics mine). Such a definitive categorization does not properly represent the complexity of language and questions in particular; see Ilie, *What Else Can I Tell You?*, 72–77.

28. Fiengo, *Asking Questions*, 62.

a response and specifically addressers expect and inferentially elicit a mental assent to obvious and exclusive answers that can lead to or request particular behavioral changes and/or actions. As such, RQs possess an inherent *indirectness* which obviously differs from genuine questions. Edwin Black puts it this way:

> A question becomes unequivocally rhetorical when it acquires the hue of benign deception: a declarative statement posing as an interrogative. It is no more deceptive than other ironies that feint in one direction and move in another, but it has abandoned the beckoning innocence of a real question—one that is seeking an answer rather than sponsoring one.[29]

RQs continue to occupy the attention among contemporary scholars of the Hebrew Bible (e.g., Kenneth M. Craig Jr., Kuntz, Dennis R. Magary, Adina Moshavi, and Lénart J. de Regt[30]), with a number of them appealing to the more current philosophical and linguistic research as well as Speech Act Theory (SAT) descriptions of RQs (especially Kuntz, Moshavi, and de Regt). Ilie's work stands out among this research since she is regularly utilized and cited by biblical scholars, and for good reason as she has carefully and insightfully detailed the characteristic semantic and pragmatic nature of RQs including their multifunctionality and intended function. Along with Ilie, a number of other language specialists also incorporate aspects of SAT in their descriptions of RQs. More specifically, many of these same theorists identify RQs as a type of Indirect Speech Act (ISA),[31] but do not take much time explaining the complex nature of ISAs while only a few describe the performative nature of RQs beyond

---

29. Edwin Black, *Rhetorical Questions: Studies of Public Discourse* (Chicago/London: University of Chicago Press, 1992), 2.

30. See the Bibliography for the work of each of these authors on interrogatives and RQs.

31. E.g., Gloria I. Anzilotti, "The Rhetorical Question as an Indirect Speech Device in English and Italian," *The Canadian Modern Language Review* 38 (1982): 290–302; Penelope Brown and Stephen Levinson, *Politeness: Some Universals in Language Usage*, SIS 4 (Cambridge: Cambridge University Press, 1987), 132; Cornelia Ene (Ilie), "Rhetorical Questions within the Theory of Speech Acts," *Cahiers de linguistique théorique et appliqué* 20 (1983): 35–54; idem, "Text Analysis of Rhetorical Questions," *Révue Roumaine de Linguistque* 28 (1983): 307–16; idem, *What Else Can I Tell You?*; Jörg Meibauer, *Rhetorische Fragen* (Tübingen: Max Niemeyer Verlag, 1986); François Récanati, *Literal Meaning* (Cambridge: Cambridge University Press, 2004), 77–78; Stanimir Rakić, "Serbo-Croatian Yes/No-Questions and Speech Acts," *JP* 8 (1984): 693–713; Pauline Slot, *How Can You Say That? Rhetorical Questions in Argumentative Texts*, SLLU 2 (Amsterdam: IFOTT, 1993);

a persuasive type force which has in turn impacted how biblical scholars interpret these interrogatives.

I will present detailed descriptions of ISAs in the following chapter, but I will begin here with some initial ideas. Theoretically, with direct speech acts *speaker-meaning* matches explicitly and exactly the *sentence-meaning*.[32] In other words, the illocutionary force of an utterance is explicitly identified from the linguistic sentence construction or named by the finite verb such as *I promise to*…. In contrast, nonliteral and indirect utterances do not have an explicit correspondence between the sentence type and illocutionary force. Put another way, the semantic content of *what is said* fails to express the force and content of the addresser's *use* of the sentence. As such, an *indirect illocution* is somewhat a contradiction in terms. Still, as Stephen C. Levinson points out, the majority of language use is indirect and moreover when one makes a request it is typically through an indirect expression.[33]

Nonliteral expressions and ISAs have similar characteristics, but remain distinct utterance types. The former includes expressions such as irony, metaphor, and figures of speech. Addressers use these types of sentences to mean something else entirely different from the semantic meaning of the words. More specifically, when one speaks *ironically* she/he does not simply intend something else from what the sentence means, but conveys the opposite of the linguistic form. When one speaks *metaphorically* she/he does not intend what the sentence means, but does not mean the opposite either. In a basic sense, ISAs are single linguistic sentences that contain two meanings simultaneously with one being intended. As I introduced above, the problem raised by both nonliteral and ISAs is the relation between *sentence-meaning* and *speaker-meaning*; between the *literal meaning* of a sentence (semantics) and how addressers *use* that sentence to express a different meaning (pragmatics).

ISAs generally consist of an interrogative used to make an assertion, request, etc., not to ask a question for information. Among theorists, classic indirect utterances include *Can you pass the salt?* and *It is hot in here!* The former could be a request to pass the salt while the latter could

---

Frans H. van Eemeren et al., *Fundamentals of Argumentation Theory: A Handbook of Historical Backgrounds and Contemporary Developments* (New York/London: Routledge, 1996), 13–14.

32. I will consistently use "addresser" and "addressee" to refer to communicative participants while retaining the phrases "sentence-meaning" and "speaker-meaning" due to the technical use of these phrases in the literature.

33. Stephen C. Levinson, *Pragmatics*, CTL (Cambridge: Cambridge University Press, 1983), 264–65.

be a request to turn on the air-conditioner. In analyzing such expressions there is both (a) a sentence-meaning and (b) a speaker-meaning. In other words, an addresser uttering *Can you pass the salt?* means both that she/he (a) would like to *know* whether the addressee has the ability to reach the salt (semantics) and (b) if the addressee would pass the salt to her/him (pragmatics). That said, in most communicative contexts an addresser uttering such a sentence does not *inquire* as to a person's ability, but rather makes a *request*. Thus, ISAs attempt to do *more than* what is expressed linguistically. With ISAs addressers' intentions are linguistically hidden; rather than uttering requests explicitly with imperative type sentences, addressers instead use interrogative sentences as if they ask questions. So, as a beginning point, ISAs are identified when addressers express interrogative sentences to make assertions or requests for addressees to do something.

With these basic distinctions in place, sometimes addressers use expressions to simultaneously express nonliteral and indirect ideas. For example, one might utter, *I love the sound of your voice* to tell someone in an ironic, sarcastic and nonliteral way that she/he cannot stand the sound of her/his voice while at the same time *indirectly* asks her/him to stop singing.[34] Thus, an indirect sentence contains a literal direct aspect and an indirect aspect and in certain instances also a nonliteral dimension. Both of these sentence types are typical instances when the semantic content of a sentence *underdetermines* the full force and content of the sentence. Taking all this together, the central interpretive problem with ISAs is as follows: an addresser can use a single linguistic sentence in one communicative context to ask a *question* and in another make an *assertion* or a *request*. How, then, can an addresser use a linguistic sentence in a particular context and intentionally mean something different that is incompatible to its literal meaning? From the perspective of the addressee, how does she/he know to go beyond the literal meaning of a sentence and indirectly recognize the addresser's intended illocutionary force?

RQs are formed and function virtually identically to ISAs. Both expressions are composed as interrogatives that do not typically function according to their linguistic form. Both indirectly and pragmatically imply something beyond their sentence-meaning. In a preliminary sense, ISAs and RQs correspondingly express two Illocutionary Acts (IAs) simultaneously:

---

34. Kent Bach, "Speech Acts and Pragmatics," in *Blackwell Guide to the Philosophy of Language*, ed. M. Devitt and R. Hanley (Oxford: Blackwell, 2006), 156.

ISAs
1. Literal interrogative
2. Indirect assertion, request, etc.

RQs
1. Literal interrogative
2. Indirect answer

These observations would not likely cause much disagreement among theorists, but how meaning actually transpires between addressers and addressees remains one of the central points of debate. Regarding ISAs in particular, a number of theorists endorse John R. Searle's interpretive scheme where "one illocutionary act is performed indirectly by way of performing another."[35] The dual illocutionary ISA expresses (a) an intended non-literal illocution by way of (b) a literal illocution. Searle's descriptions here appear logical enough, but do not come without some challenges and critiques along with numerous adaptations and alternative suggestions proposed by other theorists. Because ISAs and RQs intentionally communicate more than is actually expressed they necessitate pragmatic interpretive aspects in direct connection with the semantics of the sentence to one degree or another. With ISAs, Searle suggests that addressees must employ inferential strategies to establish (a) that the intended illocution point departs from the literal one and (b) what the intended illocutionary point is. Theorists, along with Searle, adopt either wholesale or a version of the inferential scheme proposed by Paul Grice, and specifically his notion of "conversational implicatures"[36] which has become one of the principal and most influential tenets within the discipline of pragmatics.[37]

I will also present the essential notions of Grice's communicative scheme in the following chapter. These are not only crucial to any engagement within the theory of meaning, but they are also at the center of the longstanding debate on what exactly constitutes *what is said*. In connection to this, as Ilie has pointed out, a number of those endorsing SAT for analyzing RQs also recognize its limitations.[38] For instance, Jane

---

35. John R. Searle, *Expression and Meaning: Studies in the Theory of Speech Acts* (Cambridge: Cambridge University Press, 1979), 30.
36. Ibid., 32.
37. Levinson concurs that "conversational implicature is one of the single most important ideas in pragmatics" (*Pragmatics*, 97).
38. Ilie, *What Else Can I Tell You?*, 25.

Frank concludes that the chief difficulty with identifying RQs from the perspective of SAT is "reliance on analysts' ability to discern speaker's intentions accurately and identify the forces carried by utterances in language 'as it is actually used.' For, as they stand in form, and as they function in usage, RQs are not so neatly describable nor attributable to speakers' intentions."[39] Contrary to Searle, I agree that SAT is unable to independently identify the illocutionary force of each and every sentence with definitive certainty. Yet in all fairness, with ISAs Searle clearly acknowledges the necessity of an inferential component to discern intention. Thus, Frank's observations have merit, but as I will discuss later, they do not appear limited to defining RQs within a SAT account. Rather, her concerns represent the larger problem of language itself and how addressers *use* language; more technically, the issue of the *semantics/pragmatics interface* which is essentially centered on Grice's implicature notions.

Due to the clear linguistic and pragmatic parallels between RQs and ISAs, I will argue that in order to grasp the nature and function of RQs one must understand the nature and function of ISAs. This will also help towards conceiving RQs as speech acts. What has not been considered among speech act theorists as well as biblical interpreters with RQs is their function in performative terms and specifically as self-involving speech acts.[40] Towards the development of these ideas, Ilie argues that the *challenging force* is the common characteristic of all RQs while *addresser-commitment* to an implied, exclusive answer is the distinctive feature of RQs which is not found with other interrogatives. Generally with RQs, an addressee is challenged to compose an alternative answer which is ultimately dismissed by the addresser right from the beginning. The addresser indirectly implies her/his commitment to the exclusive answer to the RQ while excluding all other possible answers with the expectation that the addressee recognizes and agrees with this inferred commitment.[41] Examining interrogatives in Serbo-Croatian, Stanimir Rakić similarly states that with RQs "the speaker presumes some proposition, and challenges the addressee to deny it."[42] Rakić also sees RQs

39. Frank, "Rhetorical Question?" 725.
40. I presented some similar, but quite brief and rudimentary ideas on RQs in my previous work which I generally still agree with, while in some specific instances my descriptions are imprecise (*The Performative Nature and Function of Isaiah 40–55*, LHBOTS 448 [New York/London: T&T Clark, 2006], 136–39).
41. Ilie, *What Else Can I Tell You?*, 56, 59.
42. Rakić, "Serbo-Croatian," 701.

expressing various forces (e.g., demand, reproach, surprise, protest, etc.). With a RQ the addresser is not looking for information, but "what she or he really wants is to induce H[*earer*] to accept the speaker's belief" which occurs indirectly.[43] Gloria Italiano Anzilotti categorizes RQs as ISAs expressing the possible illocutionary forces of declarative, imperative, or exclamatory while also implicitly recognizing their self-involving nature.[44] RQs are attention-arousers, "invitations for cooperation, involvement—all rhetorical questions seek participation of the sort that is sought in conversation."[45] While RQs do not request for information, they do ask "for some type of agreement, positive or negative. Not only is it an underlying affirmative or imperative utterance, but also it requires outside confirmation or execution to be felicitous. Therefore, it may justifiably be considered a performative in function."[46]

In my previous research in SAT, I described in some detail the concept of self-involvement with IAs as well as being a speech act category itself.[47] This notion originates with Donald Evans and specifically in his work *The Logic of Self-Involvement*[48] wherein he examines how certain types of language are self-involving, in other words, the logical connections between a person's utterances and her/his practical commitments, attitudes, and feelings. Anthony C. Thiselton and Richard S. Briggs[49] have utilized, expanded, and sharpened Evans's work in the development of a hermeneutic of self-involvement. Thiselton presents the essence of his hermeneutic of self-involvement by stating that

> the speaker "stands behind" the words giving *a pledge and personal backing* that he or she is prepared to undertake commitments and responsibilities that are entailed in extra-linguistic terms by the proposition which is asserted.[50]

---

43. Ibid., 709.
44. Anzilotti, "Rhetorical Question," 290.
45. Ibid., 298.
46. Ibid., 300.
47. Adams, *Performative Nature*, 45–63.
48. Donald D. Evans, *The Logic of Self-Involvement: A Philosophical Study of Everyday Language with Special Reference to the Christian Use of Language about God as Creator* (London: SCM, 1963).
49. Richard S. Briggs, *Words in Action: Speech Act Theory and Biblical Interpretation: Toward a Hermeneutic of Self-Involvement* (Edinburgh: T. & T. Clark, 2001).
50. A. C. Thiselton, *New Horizons in Hermeneutics: The Theory and Practice of Transforming Biblical Reading* (Grand Rapids: Zondervan, 1992), 617 (italics original).

Expressed within Evans' and Thiselton's hermeneutic of self-involvement, two dimensions of a self-involved utterance are expressed: *stance* and *entailment*. Following Evans, while the sentences *I am six feet four inches tall* and *I am a Christian* have identical surface grammar, their logical grammar is very different. Both sentence-types are assertions and in both instances the addresser takes responsibility for the truthfulness of the statement and thereby adopt a particular stance to the current states of affairs. However, the former assertion would be considered weak whereas the latter strong. The difference between the two sentences centers entirely upon the matter of the scope of the entailments. Thus in uttering the above strong sentence, "I take a *stance* in the public domain which *commits* me to certain forms of (positive and negative) behavior," which is in fact "strongly self-involving" language.[51] Thus, the assertion *It is raining* is a weak assertion as it does not express any consequential entailments of the stance taken whereas with *God is creator* the stance related to this assertion logically includes entailments and thus constitutes a strong self-involving speech act. This assertion functions as a confession whereby the addresser *involves* her/him*self* by uttering the particular propositional content and thereby takes a *stance* in the public arena concerning her/his relationship to God (Austin/Evans' Behabitive or Searle's Expressive) which then *entails* lifestyle implications that normatively accompany the confession (Commissive).[52]

A few biblical scholars have described RQs in similar self-involving terms. For instance, in his classic work, C. J. Labuschagne discusses the importance of RQs in the Hebrew Bible that bear similar language to the concept of self-involvement:

> The rhetorical question is one of the most forceful and effectual ways employed in speech for driving home some idea or conviction. Because of its impressive and persuasive effect the hearer is not merely listener [*sic*]: she/he is forced to frame the expected answer in her/his mind, and by doing so she/he actually becomes a *co-expressor* of the speaker's conviction.

In connection with this premise, he identifies and analyzes specific RQs expressing Yahweh's incomparability (Exod 15:11; Pss 35:10; 71:19; 77:14; 89:9; 113:5; Mic 7:18; Job 36:22; also including Deut 3:24; 4:7). These particular RQs for Labuschagne are "confessions expressing a conviction. Their primary intention is a confession of faith, the driving

---

51. Briggs, *Words in Action*, 151 (italics mine).
52. See further ibid., 187.

home of a conviction."⁵³ Similarly, Wilfred G. E. Watson remarks that RQs are generally "used *for dramatic effect*: it *involves* the audience directly, if they are addressed, or it creates tension which then requires resolution."⁵⁴ In his work on Second Isaiah, Kuntz claims that RQs "persuasively *invite* the listener or reader *to share* in the prophet's own assumption."⁵⁵ In his research in the Psalms, while also reflecting on both Labuschagne and Ilie's work, Kuntz states that the RQ "may *induce* in the addressee a *commitment* to the implicit answer that is on par with the speaker's own *commitment*."⁵⁶ Raymond E. Johnson observes in Qoheleth that a RQ "is a sentence whose *form* is interrogative, but whose intention is to assert or deny something either by implication or by anticipation in such a manner as to evoke *audience or reader involvement*."⁵⁷ Moshavi also recognizes that an RQ "is used to *indirectly* express an assertion" and "is in essence an intensifier, deriving its *force*…from the *implication* of obviousness."⁵⁸ Further, RQs have a "strengthening effect" as shown by both Labuschagne and Johnson. Additionally RQs generally express a challenging force used to confront, elicit a confession, accuse, advise, demand, etc.⁵⁹

Looking again at the RQs expressing Yahweh's uniqueness, Labuschagne focuses his analysis primarily on semantics and linguistic form along with comparative type interrogatives in ANE literature to draw the conclusion that such RQs function in a confessionary sense. I agree with this interpretation, but how exactly do these types of interrogatives transform into confessions? In regards to Labuschagne's "co-expressor" idea, recall the parallel RQs in Ps 27, the addressee does not become a co-expressor as the addresser and the addressee are one and the same.

---

53. C. J. Labuschagne, *The Incomparability of Yahweh in the Old Testament*, POS 5 (Leiden: Brill, 1966), 23 (italics mine; pronouns revised).

54. W. G. E. Watson, *Classical Hebrew Poetry*, JSOTSup 26 (Sheffield: Sheffield Academic, 1986), 341 (the italicization of "*involves*" is mine).

55. J. Kenneth Kuntz, "The Form, Location, and Function of Rhetorical Questions in Deutero-Isaiah," in *Writing and Reading the Scroll of Isaiah, Volume 1*, VTSup 70, ed. C. C. Broyles and C. A. Evans (Leiden: Brill, 1997), 131 (italics mine).

56. Kuntz, "Making a Statement," 158 (italics mine).

57. Raymond E. Johnson Jr., "The Rhetorical Question as a Literary Device in Ecclesiastes" (PhD diss., The Southern Baptist Theological Seminary, 1986), xvii (italics mine).

58. Adina Moshavi, "What Can I Say? Implications and Communicative Functions of Rhetorical 'WH' Questions in Classical Hebrew Prose," *VT* 64 (2014): 93 (italics mine).

59. See ibid., 93–108.

Still, when a contemporary sincere reader/singer utters the RQs in this psalm she/he does in fact become a *co-expresser* along with the psalmist; but this appears quite different from what Labuschagne has in mind[60] while more in line with Watson's observations and Johnson's reader-involvement notion.

Like ISAs and in direct connection with the notion of self-involvement, what is interpretively significant about RQs is their hybrid nature as they simultaneously express both a literal interrogative and an illocutionary answer. This dual nature of RQs is highlighted by SAT and specifically ISAs as I have briefly displayed above. As Ilie observes, since a RQ "functions as a cross-bread between a question and a statement, it shares certain features with each of these utterance types: on the one hand, it can be followed by a verbalized answer like any other question, and, on the other, it indirectly conveys an assertion or a denial like any statement."[61] RQs "*are meant to be heard as questions and understood as statements.*"[62] It is this hybrid aspect that allows in many instances addressees to either accept the implied, indirect answer of the interrogative and/or offer a contrary opinion. For these reasons, Jürgen Schmidt-Radefeldt identifies RQs as "pseudo-statements" and analyzes these expressions from both a semantic and pragmatic point of view. For Schmidt-Radefeldt, because

> of the somewhat undefinable nature of rhetorical questions with regard to their classification as questions and/or statements, the other dialogue-partner can "answer the question" and/or "contradict the statement"—in as much as opportunity is given her/him. Thus pragmatically it can be up to the addressee whether she/he accepts a rhetorical question as an assertion (as it is intended by the speaker) or, contrary to the speaker's expectation, takes up the interrogative element in the rhetorical question as an opportunity for intervention.[63]

From my observations, it is this very hybrid nature that initiates and implores the self-involvement of addressees as the interrogative prompts contemplative dialogue and the answer dimension challenges addressees to assent to or confirm the exclusive answer which addressers are already committed to. Ilie also recognizes that due "to their specific structure as interrogative sentences functioning as indirect statements, rhetorical

---

60. Labuschagne does not explicitly identify the "hearer" and "listener" of his incomparability RQs.
61. Cornelia Ilie, "Rhetorical Questions," in *The Routledge Pragmatics Encyclopedia*, ed. Louse Cummings (London/New York: Routledge, 2013), 406.
62. Ilie, *What Else Can I Tell You?*, 130.
63. Schmidt-Radefeldt, "Rhetorical Questions," 381 (pronouns revised).

questions emphatically focus on the interaction between the addresser and the addressee."⁶⁴ Along with above theorists, Schmidt-Radefeldt identifies an aspect of self-involvement with RQs as he claims that they function "to highlight certitude and incertitude (they serve to communicate doubt, perplexity, uncertainty, contingency, or deliberation); or they may contain an evaluation." In any case, RQs "express a propositional attitude of the speaker (e.g., reproach, indignation, protest, wonder, perplexity or dismay, or emphasis). When a speaker makes use of rhetoricity in her/his utterance, she/he always expresses that *she/he personally* is engaged or concerned."⁶⁵

In contrast to most language specialists, Robert van Rooy argues that RQs "are really information-seeking,"⁶⁶ thus viewing these interrogatives more along the lines of real questions. However, as I presented above, one of the key distinctive characteristics of RQs is how they do not expect or elicit a verbal response. Still, RQs are obviously linguistically formed as interrogatives that on a semantic surface level would appear to elicit a response.⁶⁷ Anna-Brita Stenström proposes that the degree of *elicitative force* conveyed provides a criterion for discerning between the various types of interrogatives. According to Stenström,

> Different types of Q[uestions] have different "elicitative force," which implies that whether or not R[esponses] follows is more noticeable with some Q*s* than with others. If no *R* follows a request for information, such as *What's the time?*, the absence will be noticed, but if no R follows a request for acknowledgement, *eg This I think is a lovely picture, isn't it?*, it would hardly be noticed by all. I suggest that the degree of elicitative force is related to the form of Q, which in turn is related to its specific function, and can be registered by the presence/absence and shape of R.⁶⁸

Accordingly, the more an interrogative is information-seeking the higher its degree of elicitative force, whereas the less information-seeking the lower its degree of elicitative force. For Ilie, this "is why a question

---

64. Ilie, *What Else Can I Tell You?*, 98.

65. Schmidt-Radefeldt, "Rhetorical Questions," 389 (pronouns revised).

66. Robert van Rooy, "Negative Polarity Items in Questions: Strength and Relevance," *Journal of Semantics* 20 (2003): 239.

67. Richard A. Hudson states that RQs "are ones that don't expect an answer; but so far as I know, there is never anything in their FORM that tells the hearer whether or not she/he is supposed to offer an answer" (The Meaning of Questions," *Language* 51 [1975]: 16 [pronouns revised]).

68. Anna-Brita Stenström, *Questions and Responses in English Conversation*, LSE (Lund: Liber Förlag Malmö/CWK Gleerup, 1984), 46.

displaying a high degree of information-elicitation puts a greater pressure on the addressee to supply an answer than a question displaying a lower degree of information-elicitation."[69] Applying this notion to RQs, this type of interrogative expresses "close to a zero degree of verbalized response elicitation."[70] So, when one sees or hears an interrogative, the degree of elicitative force conveyed can provide an interpretive criterion for identifying the type of interrogative employed. As most theorist agree, RQs, although containing an interrogative dimension, do not intend to elicit information, but rather invite addressees to engage with the expression and either confirm the inferred answer/assertion or to provide an alternative or counter claim and thus reject the intended answer. A dissenting answer, though, is not one addressers imply; rather, addressers are ultimately seeking agreement with and assent to their intended answer.[71]

Do you not know? Do you not hear? As I was deliberating about the most appropriate title for this monograph, I imagined that these two interrogatives would best prompt contemplation on whether or not they are true questions, RQs, or another type of interrogative. I have isolated these parallel interrogatives from the literary unit of Isa 40:12–31 which directly follows the Prologue for chs. 40–55 (vv. 1–11). I will explore this literary section in more detail in my final chapter, but for introductory purposes I will focus here on these two interrogatives. In this section the prophet's display of his strategic and artful use of interrogatives is most evident. Here the prophet encourages while also interrogates and confronts his exilic audience about Yahweh's sovereignty over creation and history as well as his superiority to idol-gods (cf. chs. 40–48). Within this larger literary unit, actually two pairs of these parallel interrogatives of knowing and hearing occur. The first instance (v. 21a) occurs with plural imperfect verbs:

Do you not know?	הלוא תדעו
Do you not hear?	הלוא תשמעו

While the second occurs (v. 28a) with singular perfects:

Have you not known?	הלוא ידעת
Or have you not heard?	אם־לא שמעת

---

69. Ilie, *What Else Can I Tell You?*, 81.
70. Ibid.
71. Similarly Rikic, "Yes/No-Questions," 708.

Along with other interrogatives in this literary unit, scholars are divided on how these parallel expressions function and typically viewed as either real questions or RQs.

In the book of Isaiah, eyes and ears are naturally necessary to see, listen, and comprehend, but in chs. 40–48 servant Jacob-Israel is self-inflicted with *blindness* and *deafness* (42:19) and has *no knowledge* due to its worship of idol-gods (cf. 45:20; see also e.g., 40:18–20; 42:17; 44:9–20; 45:20; 46:1–7). Most Isaianic scholars identify these parallel interrogatives of knowing and hearing as RQs. Kuntz representatively follows this line of thought, but in a seemingly hesitant way claims that they "manifest a rhetorical cast. They are giving information, not seeking it. Israel *has* heard. It *has* been told."[72] Considering the overall context of 40:12–31, the tone of the prophet's interrogative discourse is confrontational, challenging Jacob-Israel to recall what it does or is supposed to have known and heard. Yet, Yahweh's blind and deaf servant (cf. 42:19) does not apparently possess the capacity to know and hear. I agree that these interrogatives do not convey much information-elicitative force, but taken as RQs implying a positive, obvious answer is not readily convincing either. So, perhaps these interrogatives are functioning somewhat similarly to a RQ, but as a different type of question altogether?

With these *knowing/hearing* interrogatives, I have intended to highlight whether or not we truly *know* a RQ when we *hear* or *see* one? One of my goals in this work is to provide some additional criteria for identifying an interrogative as a RQ along with other similar types of interrogatives. I suggest that a central way for making such an interpretive decision will occur by viewing RQs as types of ISAs which will also provide additional interpretive criteria for understanding such expressions as performative utterances.

With all this in mind, I have organized this study as follows. In the initial section of Chapter 1 I briefly rehearse some of the basic notions of SAT that selectively relates to understanding the nature of ISAs. Following this, I present the main proposals on ISAs revolving around several questions raised by the literature that also relate to RQs. This section centers on providing a framework for understanding RQs as types of ISAs while at the same time presents some of the primary ways language specialists conceptualize the nature of ISAs and how addressees interpret them. With this analysis, my additional hope is that this chapter will provide ways for understanding indirect sentences in general for the purpose of identifying and interpreting such expressions within the biblical

---

72. Kuntz, "Rhetorical Questions," 133.

text. Chapter 2 concentrates on explaining the nature of RQs along with other similar types of interrogatives while primarily utilizing the work of Ilie. I present her basic ideas on RQs here which I critically interact with and provide supplement research. Because of the focus and denseness of my analysis of ISAs in Chapter 1, the reader may wish to start with my conclusion to this chapter and then proceed to my second chapter while referring back to the first when necessary. In my final chapter I apply my analysis to particular RQs while including other types of interrogatives within the Hebrew Bible. As I indicated previously, biblical scholars have focused their attention on the rhetorical dimension of RQs and specifically in argumentative ways which have provided much interpretive insight. My goal here is to add to this research while primarily exploring the performative nature and function of RQs. My analysis is nowhere near exhaustive, but I have selected specific salient RQs to highlight this interpretive angle of these expressions as well as to lay the ground work for myself and perhaps others to examine further the potential performative dimensions of the numerous RQs and other types of interrogatives spread throughout Scripture.

Chapter 1

SPEECH ACT THEORY AND INDIRECT SPEECH ACTS

In cooperative communicative contexts addressers desire addressees to recognize their intended meanings expressed through diverse types of sentences regarding specific states of affairs while addressees make a serious effort to recognize such intended meanings. In other words, during communicative interchanges the discourse participants assume that each does what they do, express what they express, on purpose, intentionally, and for a reason.[1] Recognizing and understanding *what is said* is theoretically more readily available with direct or explicit speech acts, but with ISAs such intended recognition becomes more difficult because of the increased necessity of inferential mechanisms involved. In this chapter I set out to describe the various proposals for conceptualizing the nature and interpretation of ISAs.[2] I will begin my descriptions by briefly summarizing the essential aspects of SAT with the selective purpose of setting a framework for understanding ISAs.[3]

1. Georgia M. Green, *Pragmatics and Natural Language Understanding*, 2nd ed. (New York: Routledge, 1996), 97.
2. From my research, the concept of ISAs has not been described in any detailed way among biblical scholars while at the same time being applied only in a limited way to the biblical text. I am only aware of two specific biblical applications of ISAs. Kristofer Holroyd examines ISAs from a Searlian view while implementing that analysis to Jer 50–51 (*A [S]word Against Babylon: An Examination of the Multiple Speech Acts Layers within Jeremiah 50–51*, Siphrut 22 [Winona Lake: Eisenbrauns, 2017]). Much earlier Richard A. Young describes ISAs as well as Gricean pragmatics and applies his research to certain NT conditional expressions ("A Classification of Conditional Sentences Based on Speech Act Theory," *Grace Theological Journal* 10 [1989]: 29–49). Young also briefly introduces how RQs are ISAs (49).
3. My following description of SAT assumes while also expands upon my explanations found in Adams, *Performative Nature*, 18–63. For more recent summaries of SAT see Y. Huang, "Speech Acts," in *The Encyclopedia of Language and*

Research on speech acts falls within the larger enterprise of the Philosophy of Language which primarily concerns itself with the relationship between words and the world; how language represents how things are or might be. The study of meaning within this field centers on the fact that what *speakers* mean when uttering a linguistic form can be quite distinct, and variously so, from what that uttered *sentence* means semantically. More technically, the linguistically encoded meaning of a sentence often drastically underdetermines the propositional content addressers express when uttering sentences; often referred to as the *linguistic underdeterminacy thesis*.[4] From another angle, the *null hypothesis* posits that there is always some pragmatic explanation for how any sentence-meaning can underdetermine what speakers mean.[5] This gap between *sentence-meaning* and *speaker-meaning* arises from a variety of factors. Sentences can be elliptical, indeterminate, ambiguous, vague, semantically underdetermined, etc. Indexicals (*person deixis*, e.g., "I," "you"; *spatial deixis*, e.g., "here," "there"; *temporal deixis*, e.g., "now," "then") used by addressers may not explicitly determine the intended referent. Addressers say things that are implicit such as non-literal, ISAs, ironic, and metaphorical type sentences. At the center of concern for theorists is how to determine *what is said* as it relates to what is actually communicated. To start and in very simplistic terms, for semanticists *what is said* refers to the propositional and truth-conditional content expressed by addressers that is linked entirely or to a large degree to the literal semantic meaning of a sentence; whereas for pragmaticists *what is said* represents more of intended speaker-meaning which involve inferential processes to determine meaning in more indirect type utterances. Thus, primary questions in the study of language include what exactly constitutes the content of *what is said* as well as how addressees understand *what is said*. Relatedly, what is the relationship between sentence-meaning and the use of sentences, i.e., speaker-meaning? Additionally, how much do addressees rely on the output of semantics *as* the input into pragmatics or how much do addressees rely on *pragmatic intrusion* into the semantic

---

Linguistics, ed. K. Brown, 2nd ed. (New York: Elsevier Science, 2006), 11:656–65; Jerrold Sadock, "Speech Acts," in *The Handbook of Pragmatics*, ed. L. R. Horn and G. Ward (Malden, MA: Blackwell, 2004), 53–73; Tim Wharton, "Speech Act Theory," in *The Routledge Pragmatics Encyclopedia*, ed. L. Cummings (London/New York: Routledge, 2010), 452–56.

4. Yan Huang, *Pragmatics*, OTL (Oxford: Oxford University Press, 2007), 5–6.

5. Kent Bach, "The Semantics–Pragmatics Distinction: What It Is and Why It Matters," in *The Semantics/Pragmatics Interface from Different Points of View*, ed. K. Turner (Oxford: Elsevier, 1999), 66–67.

and truth-conditional content to understand *what is said* by addressers? Theorists generally agree that the above concerns represent the focus of the Philosophy of Language; however, there is a wide disparity on exactly how to describe the relationship between semantics and pragmatics, if it is even possible, and which methodology best addresses this as well as other central issues that can best account for all the different ways communication transpires.[6]

The Philosophy of Language technically refers to the field of analytical philosophy which began in the early twentieth century.[7] Towards the middle of the century two opposing camps arose within this field of study. Gottlob Frege and Bertrand Russell are typically identified as the pioneering developers of the Ideal Language Philosophy which saw a close connection, if not equation, between meaning and truth-conditions. In other words, meaning derives from the conventional assignment of words with worldly entities. This particular position focuses on semantics to determine meaning: utterances derive from the literal meaning of words and sentences as determined by the semantic rules of language. This method is the traditional approach within analytical philosophy and has also given rise to contemporary *formal semantics*. Ordinary

---

6. Carlo Penco and Filippo Domaneschi claim that the current debate on *what is said* includes three core aspects: "(i) the definition of truth-conditional content, (ii) the role of context dependence and (iii) clarification of the explicit/implicit distinction." They go on to say that any "semantic or pragmatic theory must show how these topics are connected to one other, and the main challenge is to demonstrate how each aspect depends on semantics or on pragmatics" ("What Is Said: A Short History in Quotes," in *What Is Said and What Is Not: The Semantics/Pragmatics Interface*, ed. Carlo Penco and Filippo Domaneschi, CSLILN 207 [Stanford: CSLI, 2013], 1).

7. The following is based on Kent Bach, "Pragmatics and the Philosophy of Language," in *The Handbook of Pragmatics*, ed. L. R. Horn and G. Ward (Oxford: Blackwell, 2004), 463–87; María J. Frápolli and Robyn Carston, "Introduction: Representation and Metarepresentation," in *Saying, Meaning and Referring*, ed. M. J. Frápolli, PSPLC (New York: Palgrave Macmillan, 2007), 1–17; Brian Loar, "Language, Thought, and Meaning," in Devitt and Hanley, eds., *The Blackwell Guide to the Philosophy of Language*, 77–90; Alice ter Meulen, "Linguistics and the Philosophy of Language," in *Linguistics: The Cambridge Survey, Volume 1: Linguistics Theory: Foundations*, ed. F. J. Newmeyer (Cambridge: Cambridge University Press, 1988), 430–46; Penco/Domaneschi, "What Is Said," 1–12; François Récanati, "Contextualism and Anti-Contextualism in the Philosophy of Language," in *Foundations in Speech Act Theory*, ed. S. L. Tsohatzidis (London: Routledge, 1994), 156–66; idem, "Pragmatics and Semantics," in Horn and Ward, eds., *The Handbook of Pragmatics*, 442–62; Scott Soames, *Philosophy of Language*, Princeton Foundations of Contemporary Philosophy (Princeton: Princeton University Press, 2010).

Language Philosophy as proposed by Ludwig Wittgenstein, J. L. Austin, and Peter Strawson opposed such a framework. Meaning, rather, occurs through the natural pragmatic *use* of sentences.[8] Context and language use are the primary vehicles for meaning to transpire. This approach has given rise to contemporary *pragmatics*. Consequently, twentieth-century theory of meaning essentially divides into two: *truth* theories and *use* theories.[9] Generally speaking, these two philosophical camps provide the current dividing line for understanding the relationship between sentence-meaning (semantics) and speaker-meaning (pragmatics). Determining exactly how these two relate is typically referred to as the "semantics–pragmatics interface."[10] At the center of this discussion is defining what the technical expression *what is said* actually refers to in relation to semantics and pragmatics,[11] which for the last decade has prompted one of the most heated points of debate among language specialists.[12] In broad terms, semantics concerns itself with the literal meaning of words and sentences as predetermined by the rules of language whereas pragmatics deals with how speakers express meaning through the use of words and sentences.[13] François Récanati additionally identifies these two historic schools of thought as Anti-contextualists and Contextualists respectively.

---

8. For example, Wittgenstein asserts that "the meaning of a word is its use in language" (*Philosophical Investigations*, trans. G. E. M. Anscombe, 3rd ed. [Englewood Cliffs: Prentice-Hall, 1958], §43); see further James Conant, "Wittgenstein on Meaning and Use," *Philosophical Investigations* 21 (1998): 222–50. Nathan Salmon states that many regard Wittgenstein's use and meaning "identification as one of the deepest philosophical insights of the twentieth century" ("Two Conceptions of Semantics," in *Semantics versus Pragmatics*, ed. Z. G. Szabó [Oxford: Clarendon Press, 2005], 317).

9. Loar, "Language, Thought, and Meaning," 85.

10. Soames, *Philosophy of Language*, 3.

11. Huang identifies four different ways the expression *what is said* is used by theorists and thus ends up quite ambiguous as to what it is exactly referencing (see *Pragmatics*, 217 n. 8); see also, e.g., K. M. Jaszczolt, "Default Semantics, Pragmatics, and Intentions," in Turner, ed., *The Semantic/Pragmatics Interface*, 200–3.

12. Penco/Domaneschi, "What Is Said," 1.

13. A large amount of material is currently being produced describing the interface between semantics and pragmatics. For helpful introductions see, e.g., C. Bianchi, ed., *The Semantics/Pragmatics Distinction* (Stanford, CA: CSLI, 2004); Horn and Ward, eds., *The Handbook of Pragmatics*; Szabó, ed., *Semantics versus Pragmatics*; Turner, ed., *The Semantics/Pragmatics Interface*. For specific essays see, e.g., Bach, "The Semantics-Pragmatics Distinction," 65–84; idem, "Pragmatics and the Philosophy of Language," 475–78; Récanati, "Contextualism"; idem, "Pragmatics and Semantics"; idem, *Literal Meaning*, 3; Soames, *Philosophy of Language*, 145–73.

According to Récanati, the debates between these two positions have all but disappeared with now a new situation centering on the debate between Literalism and Contextualism with the former closely paralleling the Ideal Language position.[14]

At the heart of the current discussion for language specialists is defining specific roles and boundaries of semantics and pragmatics for determining *what is said*. Towards this goal, drawing a distinct line between semantics and pragmatics has played an important methodological factor for both linguists and philosophers. Most language specialists agree that semantics and pragmatics are two subdisciplines within the study of meaning; however, that is where any agreement begins and ends. The distinctions between sentence-meaning and speaker-meaning can function as entry points into the discussion for theorists, but in no way captures the complexity of the issues at stake. According to Yan Huang, linguists and philosophers of language have been and remain puzzled over the roles of semantics and pragmatics for determining meaning. Some questions that have caused such bewilderment include "what constitutes the domain of semantics, and what constitutes that of pragmatics? Can semantics and pragmatics be distinguished? Are they autonomous, or do they overlap with each other? To what extent and how do they interact with each other?"[15] The chief concern centers on determining what constitutes *what is said* and to what degree does pragmatic intrusion play with *what is said* and then establishing the interpretive domains of semantics and pragmatics. These issues are difficult enough, but the numerous proposals over the last sixty years to answer the questions at hand have only further complicated the discussion.[16] Kent Bach attempts to simplify matters by first observing that the manifold proposals tend to fall into three main types:

- linguistic conventional meaning versus use.
- truth-conditional versus non-truth-conditional.
- context-independent versus context-dependent.[17]

According to Bach, though, each of these types ultimately fail in one way or another to comprehensively define the semantic-pragmatic distinction.[18]

---

14. See Récanati, "Contextualism"; idem, *Literal Meaning*, 1–4.
15. Huang, *Pragmatics*, 209.
16. For a brief summary of the main suggested distinctions see, e.g., ibid., 211–12.
17. Huang follows this threefold categorization as well (ibid., 212–16).
18. See Bach, "Philosophy of Language," 475–78; idem, "Speech Acts and Pragmatics," 158–60.

Bach proposes, then, broader definitions: semantic information pertains to linguistic expressions while pragmatic information pertains to utterances and facts surrounding them.[19]

Maintaining a distinction between semantics and pragmatics remains fruitful while at the same time acknowledging their interrelatedness and inseparability. To their distinction, semantics obviously provides an essential independent component to determine the meaning of a linguistic expression, but does not provide all the necessary data.[20] Nonlinguistic contextual factors provide essential information over and above linguistic properties for meaning to actually transpire. With this in mind, Nathan Salmon describes the distinction and connection between these two ideas by observing that the

> distinction is typically explained in terms of the concept of *use*: pragmatics is the study of the way signs or symbols are used in context, whereas semantics concerns the meaning of a symbol in abstraction from its use. But this is more of a slogan than a clarification or explanation. How are we supposed to understand the difference between semantics and pragmatics when the meaning of an expression is so closely bound to the manner in which that expression is used? An expression is used a certain way because of its meaning, and yet the expression came to have the meaning it does through usage. Each of meaning and use seems to be a direct product of the other.[21]

Moreover, some linguistic expressions convey their literal meaning in direct relation to use and thus a simple division between conventional versus nonconventional meaning cannot be sustained. Further, with certain utterances nonlinguistic context can play a factor in semantics as well as pragmatics.[22]

The semantic/pragmatic distinction may have initially surfaced in the 1960s and implicitly evidenced in Austin's contrast between locutionary

---

19. Bach, "Semantics–Pragmatics Distinction," 74; for Bach these two broader descriptions accommodate the following facts: only literal contents are semantically relevant; some expressions, as a matter of meaning, are context-sensitive; narrow context is relevant to semantics, broad context to pragmatics; non-truth-conditional, use-related information can be linguistically encoded; rules for using expressions do not determine their actual use; and that a sentence is actually uttered is a pragmatic fact (ibid., 73).

20. Bach identifies two common, but different, conceptions within the study of semantics: (1) linguistic meanings of expressions (words, phrases, sentences) and (2) the truth-conditional contents of sentences ("Philosophy of Language," 475).

21. Salmon, "Two Conceptions of Semantics," 317.

22. Bach, "Semantics-Pragmatics Distinction," 70–71; see further Huang, *Pragmatics*, 211–16.

and illocutionary acts.[23] Yet, the now "classic" or "traditional" understanding of the semantic/pragmatic interface has been traced back to Paul Grice who is the first theorist to formally present a system for understanding how addressers mean something different from the meaning of sentences used. The traditional understanding of this interface is based in Grice's distinction between *what is said* and *what is implicated*.[24] For Grice, these two elements essentially constitute "the total signification of an utterance" and ultimately *what is meant* by a speaker.[25] Within this general framework, then, semantics constitutes *what is said* and pragmatics concerns *what is implicated* (implicature), with both providing the interpretive components to determine *what is meant*.[26] The classic picture of the interface, then, is that semantics provides *what is said* as the input to pragmatics while the latter focuses on what is done with language beyond *what is said*.[27]

I will describe Grice's pragmatic system in much more detail below, but for introductory purposes the example of a motorist (A) whose car has become immobilized and is approached by a passerby (B) is often regarded as an ideal paradigm of what Grice identifies as implicature. In this scenario, the following exchange takes place:

A: *I am out of petrol.*
B: *There is a garage round the corner.*

B *says* that a garage is located around the corner while *implicates* that the garage is open or at least may be open and sells fuel.[28] The Gricean implicature in this example is that B intends to get A to understand that the garage may be open and contains fuel while A operates under the assumption that B is conversationally cooperating appropriately for A to believe

---

23. So Bach, "Semantics-Pragmatics Distinction," 68–69. Isabel C. Hungerland observes this distinction utilized in philosophy beginning in the 1950s (see "Contextual Implication," *Inquiry* 3 [1960]: 211–58).

24. Récanati views Grice as unique in his thinking that both schools of thought in language philosophy "were not incompatible but complementary" ("Pragmatics and Semantics," 462 n. 2).

25. H. P. Grice, *Studies in the Way of Words* (Cambridge, MA: Harvard University Press, 1989), 41, 118.

26. Zoltán G. Szabó, "Introduction," in Szabó, ed., *Semantics versus Pragmatics*, 3.

27. Kepa Korta and John Perry, "How to Say Things with Words," in *John Searle's Philosophy of Language: Force, Meaning and Mind*, ed. S. L. Tsohatzidis (Cambridge: Cambridge University Press, 2007), 170.

28. Grice, *Way of Words*, 32.

this is the case. From this formula, the conventional semantic meaning of a sentence provides for the content of *what is said* and functions as the input to pragmatics. Put another way, *what is conversationally implicated* is distinct from the truth-conditional propositional content, but is at the same time interpretively calculated on the basis of *what is said*.[29]

In general terms, the Traditional view based on Gricean principles, then, recognizes three different components involved in the interpretation of meaning: *what is said*, *what is implicated*, and *what is meant*. *What is said* refers to the conventional, linguistic meaning of words and phrases which is the concern of semantics. *What is implicated* is the focus of pragmatics which primarily refers to an aspect of speaker meaning distinct from *what is said* while also includes the inferential operations utilized by addressees to interpret the intended meaning of addressers. *What is meant* refers to the interpretation of the intended meaning of addressers' utterance which involves both semantics and pragmatics. For a number of theorists, this Gricean framework provides for understanding the essence of the semantics/pragmatics interface; however, for many others the relationship between these two ideas are far more complex and thus Gricean pragmatics needs further refining or for some should be abandoned entirely. In fact, theorists are not unanimously convinced that even Grice himself fully ascribed to these ideas. As Zoltán Szabó observes, Grice does not actually employ the terms "semantics" and "pragmatics" in his explanations on utterance meaning. More importantly, though, Grice acknowledges that the conventional linguistic meaning contributing to the total signification of the sentence fails to belong in totality to *what is said*.[30] Consequently, for Grice semantics alone does not provide all the necessary interpretive data to determine *what is said*; more contextual factors need to be invoked as the above example highlights such as who is A and when did she/he say it. According to Kepa Korta and John Perry, the above scenario represents "a fundamental dilemma for the Gricean picture, which has shaped discussion of 'the semantics-pragmatics interface' from the 1960's until the present." This dilemma raises two central questions for these two theorists: "Do we stick to the narrow conception of semantics? Then pragmatics has to take over before we get to what is said. Or do we stick to the conception of semantics as giving us what is said? Then we must abandon the conception of semantics as computing according to rules of language associated with types."[31]

29. Huang, *Pragmatics*, 187–88.
30. Szabó, "Introduction," 3.
31. Kepa Korta and John Perry, "Three Demonstrations and a Funeral," *Mind & Language* 21 (2006): 168.

Récanati admits that the current situation among linguists and philosophers is very confusing, but at the same time clear. On the one hand, something is considered semantic to the extent that it concerns the conventional, linguistic meaning of words and phrases. The less descriptive or truth-conditional as well as the more contextual an aspect of meaning is the less tempted one is to identify it as semantic. Interestingly, though, Récanati observes that the semantics-pragmatics distinction lends itself more readily to languages in which the conventional meaning of a sentence can be equated with its truth conditions (i.e., Carnapian languages), but with Natural languages this distinction becomes strained and less and less applicable.[32] With these basic issues outlined, I will now turn to describing the basic tenets of SAT.

Basic Philosophical Notions of Speech Act Theory

Performative Utterances

Austin and his student John R. Searle have been identified as the principal linguistic philosophers providing the foundational understanding of SAT proper as it is known today. The ideas of these two theorists remain central in the ongoing discussions and debates on SAT as well have significantly impacted the contemporary research in linguistics, semantics, and the philosophy of language.

Austin, in his William James Lectures at Harvard University in 1955 and subsequently published in the small book *How To Do Things with Words*,[33] set out to re-focus the then-current study of language from words to sentences. He challenged the so-called descriptive fallacy as espoused by logical positivism. The overarching assumption within this school of thought was "that the business of a 'statement' can only be to 'describe' some state of affairs, or to 'state some fact,' which it must do either truly or falsely."[34] Austin acknowledged the existence of such statements, but other utterances may not be statements at all, i.e., "pseudo-statements." Hence, Austin made a distinction between two types of utterances that he identified as *constatives* and *performatives*. The former are descriptive statements whereas the latter are utterances that *count as* doing. This leads Austin to formulate his simple, yet complex, thesis: "to *say* something is to *do* something; or in which *by* saying or *in* saying something we are doing

---

32. Récanati, "Pragmatics and Semantics," 461.
33. J. L. Austin, *How To Do Things With Words*, 2d ed, ed. J. O. Urmson and Marina Sbisà (Cambridge, MA: Harvard University Press, 1975).
34. Ibid., 1.

something."³⁵ Austin's classic example of a performative is when one says *I do* during the course of a marriage ceremony she/he does not report on a marriage, i.e., "we are marrying." Rather, it is an action performed by the one uttering it that indulges in the act that actually realizes the marriage relationship, i.e., "marrying."

For Austin, the total speech act consists of three kinds of acts:

- Locution: to say something *is* to do something (e.g., he said to me, "Shoot her!" meaning by "shoot" shoot and referring by "her" to her)
- Illocution: *in* saying something one does something (e.g., he urged [or advised, ordered, etc.] me to shoot her)
- Perlocution: *by* saying something one does something (e.g., he persuaded me to shoot her).³⁶

It has been predominantly Searle who has built upon, refined, and advanced Austin's understanding of speech acts. Following Austin's lead, Searle further diminishes any distinction between performatives and constatives.³⁷ Searle also approves of Austin's conception of Illocutionary Acts (IAs), but he does not accept his distinction between locutions and illocutions. Searle's adjustments of Austin led him to compose an alternative conception of the total speech act containing four elements:

- *Utterance acts*: include Austin's phonetic and phatic acts that entail uttering words and sentences.
- *Propositional acts*: referring and predicating.
- *Illocutionary acts*: statements, questions, promises, or commands.
- *Perlocutionary acts*: the consequences of an utterance that entail effects on the actions, feelings, attitudes, beliefs, and behavior of addressees.

Searle's distinction between Propositional acts and IAs is central to his entire speech act scheme. In fact, "the character of the whole illocutionary act is entirely determined by the nature of its illocutionary force and propositional content."³⁸ With this emphasis, Searle departs from Austin's notions and specifically his focus on use and speech acts. In his early

---

35. Ibid., 12.
36. See ibid., 94–120.
37. See, e.g., John R. Searle, *Speech Acts: An Essay in the Philosophy of Language* (Cambridge: Cambridge University Press, 1969), 16.
38. John R. Searle and Daniel Vanderveken, *Foundations of Illocutionary Logic* (Cambridge: Cambridge University Press, 1985), 8.

work, Searle makes a clear distinction between the propositional indicator and the illocutionary force indicator. These two acts form for Searle the bipartite syntactical structure, but combined create the total speech act. The Propositional Act, denoted as p, expresses the proposition while the Illocutionary Force Indicating Device (IFID), symbolized as the variable F, determines the literal force of the utterance. Searle's chief example of an IA is that of a promise, which can be configured as:

I promise (F) that I will come (p).

The performative prefix (F) plays a primary role for Searle because the main verb *names* the IA and "shows how the proposition is to be taken."[39] This formulation exposes Searle's tendency to isolate the semantic dimension of the IFID for explicitly identifying and ensuring the specific IA intended. Searle does acknowledge that there is no single element in every sentence which marks its IA and in fact that there are a variety of devises that can operate in this capacity;[40] however, as David Holdcroft observes, Searle does not provide other specific IFIDs and thus theoretically undermines his entire SAT program, reducing it to semantics.[41]

According to Searle, "speaking a language is performing acts according to rules." These rules are the conventional correspondence between a particular type of action and the socially determined results of that action.[42] Searle identifies these rules or conditions as *constitutive rules* which find parallels with the rules for playing football or chess that do not merely regulate the game (*regulative rules*), they actually create or constitute the activity of the game. In other words, they function as the rules of the game. In the same way, to perform a speech act occurs by following particular conventional rules that are *constitutive* of that type of act. This conventional IA is conceptualized as "X *counts as* Y." As a particular move in chess *counts as* checkmate so making a promise *counts as* an obligation.[43]

These constitutive rules are intimately associated with the conditions of a felicitous and successful IA. Following Austin's lead on felicitous conditions,[44] Searle claims that constitutive rules are determined by the conditions of a felicitous and successful IA. Moreover, such conditions are

39. Searle, *Speech Acts*, 30.
40. See ibid., 30–31, 64.
41. David Holdcroft, "Indirect Speech Acts and Propositional Content," in *Foundations of Speech Act Theory: Philosophical and Linguistic Perspectives*, ed. S. L. Tsohatzidis (London: Routledge, 1994), 350–54.
42. See Searle, *Speech Acts*, 36–37.
43. See ibid., 33–37.
44. See Austin, *Things with Words*, 12–15.

not simply rules for a happy performative, but for Searle they also *constitute* the illocutionary force itself, e.g., they create the successful speech act. To identify the felicitous use of an IFID, Searle applies his theory to various types of IAs while identifying five semantic rules and conditions:

>   Rule 1: Propositional Content
>   Rules 2 and 3: Preparatory
>   Rule 4: Sincerity
>   Rule 5: Essential

Searle works his theory extensively with promises which he claims provide a "general application" for other types of IAs.[45] For promising Searle proposed the following rules and conditions:

Rule 1: *Pr* (IFID for promising) is to be uttered only in the context of a sentence (or larger stretch of discourse) T, the utterance of which predicates some future act A of the speaker S.
Rule 2: *Pr* is to be uttered only if the hearer H would prefer S's doing A to his not doing A, and S believes H would prefer S's doing A to his not doing A.
Rule 3: *Pr* is to be uttered only if it is not obvious to both S and H that S will do A in the normal course of events.
Rule 4: *Pr* is to be uttered only if S intends to do A.
Rule 5: The utterance of *Pr* counts as the undertaking of an obligation to do A.[46]

Searle applies these rules and conditions to other types of IAs, such as Assertions:

Table 1.1 Searle's Rules/Conditions
for Successful and Felicitous Assertions

Rules/Conditions	*Assertions*
Propositional Content	Any proposition p
Preparatory	1. S has evidence (reasons, etc.) for the truth of p
	2. It is not obvious to both S and H that H knows (does not need to be reminded of, etc.) p
Sincerity	S believes p
Essential	Counts as an undertaking to the effect that p represents an actual state of affairs[47]

---

45. Searle, *Speech Acts*, 54.
46. Ibid., 63.
47. Ibid., 66; see also Sadock, "Speech Acts," 61.

Searle highlights the propositional content condition and consequently this condition becomes seemingly primary as "rules 2–5 apply only if rule 1 is satisfied."[48] In other words, meaning is determined principally with the linguistic form of an utterance. This is confirmed with his Principle of Expressibility which is "whatever can be meant can be said."[49] As will be discussed in greater detail below, Searle is aware of the gap between *what is said* and *what is meant* with utterances. For Searle, this gap is closed because "it is always in principle possible for" a speaker "to say exactly what she/he means."[50] The linguistic meaning of an utterance corresponds exactly to and determines the content and force of a speech act. The "study of the meaning of sentences is not in principle distinct from a study of speech acts. Properly construed, they are the *same study*."[51] Searle clearly recognizes that what is communicated occurs through a combination of a linguistic, semantic form and background assumptions for speaker-meaning to transpire.[52] Yet, he maintains that there is nothing inconsistent between his Principle of Expressibility and his notion of the "relativity of literal meaning that there are meanings that are inherently *inexpressible*."[53] Still, as Récanati observes, Searle's explanations of his Principle are often vague and perhaps can be interpreted in different ways, but at face value these two theses run counter to each other.[54] The apparent way Searle sees these two ideas working together is his claim that addressers know "how to apply the literal meaning of a sentence only against a background of other assumptions."[55] With this claim and by maintaining his Expressibility Principle without deviation, Searle further betrays his focus on linguistic, semantic meaning over against contextual factors for speaker-meaning. Searle thus distinguishes himself from Austin's contextual view of language.[56] In particular, Searle makes a clear distinction between IAs and perlocutionary acts as the latter are derived from the former and thus meaning derives from the IA, not the perlocutionary effect (PE).[57]

48. Ibid., 63.
49. Ibid., 19.
50. Ibid., 18 (pronouns revised).
51. Ibid., 18 (italics mine).
52. See, e.g., J. R. Searle, "The Background of Meaning," in *Speech Act Theory and Pragmatics*, ed. J. R. Searle, F. Kiefer, and M. Bierwisch (Dordrecht: Springer Netherlands, 1980), 221–32.
53. Searle, *Expression and Meaning*, 134 (italics mine).
54. Récanati, "The Limits of Expressibility," in *John Searle*, ed. B. Smith, Contemporary Philosophy in Focus (Cambridge: Cambridge University Press, 2003), 194.
55. Searle, *Expression and Meaning*, 134.
56. See Récanati, "Limits of Expressibility," 189–213.
57. See further Adams, *Performative Nature*, 39.

Illocutionary Acts

Taxonomy of Illocutionary Acts

A major issue among speech act theorists concerns the IA classifications offered preliminarily by Austin[58] and the numerous and ongoing proposals attempting to improve upon Austin[59] with Searle's taxonomy enduring as the most influential.[60] Theorists generally utilize three different types of criteria when constructing their taxonomies: (1) formal/grammatical features, (2) semantic/pragmatic features, or (3) a combination of the above two criteria.[61] Although a host of typologies have been proposed, it is important to highlight Sadock's observation that "in almost all of the schemes that have been put forward, the imprint of Austin's original, highly intuitive compartmentalization is clearly visible. Austin's class of commissives, for example, seems to survive intact on everyone's list of basic illocutionary types."[62]

In formulating their taxonomies, Austin and Searle employ a semantic/pragmatic mode. These two also present similar classifications that both consist of five types of utterances (Austin: Verdictive, Exercitives, Commissives, Bahabitives, Expositives; Searle: Assertives, Directives, Commissives, Expressives, Declarations).[63] Although Sadock, along with numerous others, have suggested useful alternative schemes and formal classifications,[64] it remains profitable to maintain both Austin's and Searle's taxonomies simultaneously while considering both functional and neither as definitive.[65] In addition, as Sadock demonstrates,[66] illocutionary forces are not independent or disassociated one from another,

---

58. See Austin, *Things with Words*, 151–64.

59. For a summary of some of the dominant proposals see, e.g., Michael Hancher, "The Classification of Cooperative Illocutionary Acts," *Language in Society* 8 (1979): 1–14; for a more recent discussion see Sadock, "Speech Acts," 64–66.

60. See Searle, *Expression and Meaning*, 1–29.

61. See Sadock, "Speech Acts," 65.

62. Ibid., 66.

63. For critiques of these taxonomies see Dieter Wunderlich, "Methodological Remarks on Speech Act Theory," in Searle, Kiefer, and Bierwisch, eds., *Speech Act Theory and Pragmatics*, 291–312; Jerrold M. Sadock, "Toward a Grammatically Realistic Typology of Speech Acts," in Tsohatzidis, ed., *Foundations of Speech Act Theory*, 393–406.

64. See Sadock, "Typology of Speech Acts," 395–402; see also Briggs's discussion of Sadock in *Words in Action*, 56–58.

65. So also Briggs, *Words in Action*, 57–58; Thiselton, *New Horizons*, 296; see also Levinson, *Pragmatics*, 240.

66. See Sadock, "Typology of Speech Acts," 396–99.

but rather the various dimensions of other forces are often incorporated into a single utterance with one force typically being primary. Thus, IAs are often, if not always, multidimensional utterances, as Searle's own assertive-declarative hybrid category exemplifies.[67] Further, Searle, in his work with Daniel Vanderveken, recognize that "sometimes by performing one illocutionary act a speaker can be committed to another illocution."[68]

Nature of Illocutions
Neither Austin nor Searle ever actually defined the nature of or what *counts as* an IA. In fact, Searle believed that the viability of his own analysis would "provide the basis for a definition."[69] Within biblical studies this lack of clear definitions concerning the nature and stratification of illocutionary acts has resulted in two major issues: (1) every locution is considered an illocution and/or (2) illocutions are analyzed in perlocutionary terms. In response to these issues, Anthony C. Thiselton[70] and Richard S. Briggs[71] appeal to G. J. Warnock's analysis of Austin's suggestions on performative utterances and his observation that Austin identified two sub-classes of this special class: *conventionally "operative" utterances* and *explicit performative utterances*.[72] With this in view, these two biblical interpreters propose viewing illocutions operating along a spectrum of strengths ranging from weak to strong. Lying at each end of this spectrum is the constative (weak) and performative (strong). With certain adjustments and clarifications,[73] I remain convinced that this conceptual framework is insightful and interpretively valuable.

---

67. See Searle, *Expression and Meaning*, 19–20; Briggs, *Words in Action*, 52, 68.

68. Searle/Vanderveken, *Foundations of Illocutionary Logic*, 23. Earlier in this work they claim that a "theory of illocutionary logic of the sort we are describing is essentially a theory of *illocutionary commitment* as determined by illocutionary force. The single most important question it must answer is simply this: Given that a speaker in a certain context of utterance performs a successful illocutionary act of a certain form, *what other illocutions* does the performance of that act *commit her/him to?*" (ibid., 6).

69. Searle, "What Is a Speech Act?" in *The Philosophy of Language*, ed. J. R. Searle (Oxford: Oxford University Press, 1971), 39.

70. A. C. Thiselton, "Communicative Action and Promise in Interdisciplinary, Biblical, and Theological Hermeneutics," in *The Promise of Hermeneutics*, ed. R. Lundin, C. Walhout, and A. C. Thiselton (Grand Rapids: Eerdmans, 1999), 236.

71. Briggs, *Words in Action*, 63–65.

72. G. L. Warnock, "Some Types of Performative Utterance," in *Essays on J. L. Austin*, ed. I. Berlin et al. (Oxford: Clarendon, 1973), 69–89.

73. See Adams, *Performative Nature*, 33–37.

William P. Alston builds on Austin and Searle's work while attempting to sharpen the nature of illocutions with his concept Illocutionary Act Potential (IAP).[74] Alston's basic thesis is: "A sentence's having a given meaning consists in its having a certain illocutionary act potential."[75] To arrive at this thesis, Alston highlights the fact that addressers can use an invariable linguistic form to perform different types of IAs and conversely they can utter a specific illocutionary force with various types of IAs. Moreover, addressers frequently express an IA without making that force explicitly clear or even also which action is in question. With this in mind, an addresser can use the sentence *That dog bites* with one and the same literal meaning to perform various IA types:

- Asserting that a particular dog bites
- Warning that a particular dog bites
- Admitting that a particular dog bites
- Suggesting that a particular dog might bite
- Complaining that a particular dog bites and so on.

Yet, addressers cannot use *any* one sentence to perform *any* IA because a single linguistic form does not express all possible meanings and convey expected actions. Sentences, therefore, operate within a *potential range* of IA types that thereby excludes other types of forces.

As shown above, to identify illocutionary type sentences Searle among others tends to focus their descriptions on explicit action type verbs that specify a particular illocutionary force. For Alston, any utterance possesses the potential to express an illocutionary force of a certain type. Although verbs have the capacity to indicate a force type, most sentences do not contain such explicit illocutionary identifiers.[76] What converts a simple utterance (Alston's "Sentential act" which reduces Austin's

---

74. William P. Alston's primary descriptions of his IAP theory include: "Sentence Meaning and Illocutionary Act Potential," *Philosophical Exchange* 2 (1977): 17–35; "Matching Illocutionary Act Types," in *On Being and Saying*, ed. J. J. Thompson (Cambridge, MA: MIT Press, 1987), 151–63; "Searle on Illocutionary Acts," in *John Searle and his Critics*, ed. E. Lepore and R. Van Gulick (Oxford: Blackwell, 1991), 57–80; "Illocutionary Acts and Linguistic Meaning," in Tsohatzidis, ed., *Foundations of Speech Act Theory*, 29–49; *Illocutionary Acts and Sentence Meaning* (Ithaca: Cornell University Press, 2000).

75. Alston, "Illocutionary Acts," 29.

76. Verbal criterion for identifying IA types has been a major issue discussed among theorists; see Adams, *Performative Nature*, 30–32; Briggs, *Words in Action*, 98–102; Thiselton, "Communicative Action," 233–34.

locution to his simple "phatic act"[77]) to a certain IA includes the rules of language which involve a sentence's linguistic form and its conventional or standard semantic status in the language, the particular circumstances involved, and most importantly the addresser's relation to the sentence. According to Alston, whatever "turns my utterance into an assertion that p must connect *me* with p; it must be some 'stance' I have or take *vis-à-vis* p."[78] This condition is Alston's central feature or condition of an IA which he coins as the speaker "*taking responsibility*." Here Alston builds on and sharpens Searle's essential condition of obligation with a promise illocution. For Alston, though, this condition does not simply apply to IAs such as with a promise, but is the *key* characteristic of all IA forces. The addresser's "taking responsibility for the satisfaction of various conditions is not only necessary but also sufficient for an utterance's counting as the performance of an illocutionary act of a certain type."[79] Alston further defines this condition as follows:

> The utterance is made the illocutionary act it is, apart from any conventional effect production that is essentially involved,[80] not by any "natural" facts about the speaker—her/his beliefs, perlocutionary intentions, or whatever—but by a "normative" fact about the speaker—the fact that she/he has changed her/his normative position in a certain way by laying her/himself open to the possibility of censure, correction, or the like in case the conditions in question are not satisfied. What a speaker does…to make her/his utterance a token of a certain illocutionary act type, is to "stick her/his neck out" in this way, making her/himself the one who is to "respond" if the conditions in question are not satisfied…. An utterance is most basically made into an illocutionary act of a certain type by virtue of a normative stance on the part of the speaker.[81]

It is important to note that throughout his work, Alston only intermittingly touches on indirect speech while he contrasts his IAP scheme with Gricean pragmatics, which he identifies as "perlocutionary-act-potential."[82] That said, with the above sentence *That dog bites* as well as other examples Alston presents (e.g., *It* [a bull] *is going to charge,*

---

77. See Alston, *Illocutionary Acts*, 18.
78. Alston, "Illocutionary Acts," 39.
79. Ibid., 43 (see 40–45); see further idem, *Illocutionary Acts*, 54–71.
80. Alston defines "conventional effect" as what a particular utterance brings about or produces. For example, orders engender an obligation on the addressee to do what she/he was ordered to do; see further Alston, "Illocutionary Acts," 43–44.
81. Alston, *Illocutionary Acts*, 70–71 (pronouns revised).
82. See, e.g., Alston, "Illocutionary Acts," 33–36; *Illocutionary Acts*, 37–40.

The gate is unlocked) in specific communicative contexts I would argue function as ISAs.[83]

Questions

Neither Austin nor Searle dealt with RQs in any significant way, but they did classify questions. For Austin, verbs of asking and questioning fall under the category of Expositives which involve the "expounding of views, the conducting of arguments, and clarifying of usages and of references." Such illocutions engage in "conversational interchange."[84] Looking ahead, Austin interestingly included in this illocutionary category verbs of affirming, denying, and doubting which can relate to RQs. For Searle, Directives have the illocutionary point in addressers attempting to get addressees to do something. Questions are a subclass of Directives because addressers attempt to get addressees to answer, i.e., perform a speech act.[85] With genuine questions, Searle restricts his analysis to two types: *real* and *exam* questions which request some type of informative answer. He claims that "certain kinds of illocutionary acts are really special cases of other kinds; thus asking questions is really a special case of requesting, viz., requesting information (real questions) or requesting that the hearer display knowledge (exam question)." Requesting for Searle expresses at least two different aspects as evidenced with the verb to ask: *She asked me do some*thing (request) and *He asked me why* (question).[86] Searle also includes verbs of *dare*, *defy*, and *challenge* (specific terms in Austin's *Behabitive* class) belong here.[87] As presented above with his semantic rules and conditions for IAs, Searle presents his scheme for Questions:

Table 1.2. Searle's Rules/Conditions for Successful and Felicitous Questions

Rules/Conditions	*Questions*
Propositional Content	Any proposition or propositional content
Preparatory	1. S does not know "the answer"
	2. It is not obvious to both S and H that H will provide the information at that time without being asked
Sincerity	S wants this information
Essential	Counts as an attempt to elicit this information from H[88]

83. So also Sadock, "Speech Acts," 62.
84. Austin, *Things with Words*, 161–62.
85. Searle, *Expression and Meaning*, 13.
86. Searle, *Speech Acts*, 69.
87. Searle, *Expression and Meaning*, 14.
88. Searle, *Speech Acts*, 66.

This formal analysis descriptively works with his specific two types of questions; however, there are obviously many more diverse types of questions in English as well as among the world's languages. Specifically, as I will present in the next chapter, Searle's above rules for Questions, except for the first one, do not correspondingly apply to RQs. In his essay on ISAs, Searle proposes examples of indirect requests and other Directives while briefly including some interrogatives that for all intents and purposes function as RQs such as *How many times have I told you (must I tell you) not to eat with your fingers?*[89] Thus and significantly for this study, Searle identifies certain RQs as indirect requests. That said and as I will discuss in much detail in my next chapter, RQs violate most of Searle's semantic rules for questions which in turn provide criteria for identifying such expressions while at the same time eliminating them from being categorized as genuine questions.

Illocutionary Acts and Perlocutionary Effects

As seen above with Austin's and Searle's speech act stratifications, theorists include in their discussion on speech acts the aspect of PEs; however, the central feature within SAT is the illocutionary force. In general, language specialists typically base their theory of meaning in either psychological effects or IAs. For speech act theorists, IAs are the locus for determining sentence-meaning. This is supported by various facts and first, PEs depend upon IAs, not vice versa.[90] An evidence of this fact is that an IA becomes manifest at the point of the utterance whereas a PE becomes apparent only until after the IA. Second, IAs are intended by addressers whereas PEs are not always intended by the addresser. Third and relatedly, addressers control IAs, but cannot ultimately control PEs. Finally, IAs are conventionally linguistic in form whereas perlocutions are not.[91] For speech act theorists, then, meaning is found in the linguistic form whereas the perlocution occurs outside of language and concerns the nonlinguistic psychological effects of IAs occurring with the addressee. Kent Bach observes that we need to distinguish between illocutions and perlocutions

> because utterances are generally more than just acts of communication. They have two levels of success: considered merely as an illocutionary act, a request (for example) succeeds if your audience recognizes your desire that

---

89. Searle, *Expression and Meaning*, 38.
90. See in particular Alston, "Illocutionary Acts," 33–36; *Illocutionary Acts*, 33–80.
91. See also Huang, *Pragmatics*, 103–104.

they do a certain thing, but as a perlocutionary act it succeeds only if they actually do it. You can express your desire without getting compliance, but your one utterance is the performance of an act of both types.[92]

Although PEs are intended and prompted by an IA, they only actually transpire within addressees. Yueguo Gu provides a sound and accessible way of understanding this relationship between IAs and PEs.[93] According to Gu, addresser and addressee engage in a communicative "transaction" with IAs playing a "triggering role" in this transaction. Thus, addressers utter IAs with the intention to trigger specific PEs, but addressees remain the active agent of the intended effects.[94] Addressers utter IAs with intended PEs which are dependent upon and prompted by those utterances; however, these effects are ultimately *caused* by addressees not by the illocution itself. Further, the IA trigger may remain the same, but the response varies based on the addressees involved.

Indirect Speech Acts

Introduction

The above descriptions will prove important for my analysis of ISAs which will then provide for understanding the nature and function of RQs. My discussion here will explore the nature and function of ISAs while focusing on how such sentences express illocutionary force.

Because ISAs intentionally communicate *more than* is actually expressed these sentence types necessitate a pragmatic interpretive aspect in combination with semantics. To recall, in a general sense the study of sentence-meaning belongs to the realm of semantics whereas speaker-meaning falls within pragmatics. As I introduced above, theorists often identify intended, inferential meaning with Grice's term *implicature*. Laurence Horn provides a helpful definition of this key notion as

> a component of speaker meaning that constitutes an aspect of what is meant in a speaker's utterance without being part of what is said. What a speaker intends to communicate is characteristically far richer than what she directly expresses; linguistic meaning radically underdetermines the message conveyed and understood. Speaker S tacitly exploits pragmatic principles to bridge this gap and counts on hearer H to invoke the same principles for the purposes of utterance interpretation.[95]

---

92. Bach, "Speech Acts and Pragmatics," 151.
93. Yueguo Gu, "The Impasse of Perlocution," *JP* 20 (1993): 405–32.
94. See ibid., 422–28; see further Adams, *Performative Nature*, 37–44.
95. Horn, "Implicature," in Horn and Ward, eds., *The Handbook of Pragmatics*, 3.

Because the intended meaning of ISAs goes beyond the linguistically encoded utterance, most language specialists include some aspect of implicature to describe how such meaning transpires.

The problem raised with ISAs and meaning centers on addresser implicature and addressee inference. This problem can be highlighted by the following sentences:

1. *Pass the salt!*
2. a. *Can you pass the salt?*[96]
   b. *Are you able to pass the salt?*
   c. *Do you have the ability to pass the salt?*

The request uttered with sentence (1) can be indirectly conveyed by using the interrogative (2a), but not with (2b) and (2c). All three interrogatives are virtually synonymous, but only (2a) can be used to express the imperative force as with sentence (1). According to Horn, the disappearance of the implicature from (2b) and (2c) normally attached to (2a) ends up a mystery.[97] It is this mystery that has prompted numerous theorists to attempt to solve. Further and according to Nicholas Asher and Alex Lascarides, linguists "consider questions and requests as not only distinct, but *incompatible* semantic types. Questions denote a set of propositions (i.e., its direct answers), whereas requests denote a relation between worlds and actions." As (2a) "has the linguistic hallmarks of both questions and requests, its semantic type must be distinct from, but related to, both of these; but it's unclear what its semantic type is." They go on to say that many "other ISAs also behave linguistically as if they're 'two speech acts in one,' involving other kinds of incompatible semantic types."[98] Similarly, Sadock observes that sentence types are associated with a certain IAP and to "count as a type within such a system, the formal features defining the types must be mutually exclusive: A sentence cannot be simultaneously of the declarative and interrogative type, or of the interrogative and imperative type or of the interrogative and imperative type."[99]

Correlated with this, an additional problem arises with (2a) as addressers can use this sentence as either a question to provide some information (direct speech act) *or* to request that an addressee pass the salt (ISA).

---

96. This sentence is the typical ISA example utilized in the literature and will be designated throughout as "(2a)."
97. Laurence R. Horn, "Pragmatic Theory," in Newmeyer, ed., *Linguistics*, 138.
98. Nicholas Asher and Alex Lascarides, "Indirect Speech Acts," *Synthese* 128 (2001): 184.
99. Sadock, "Speech Acts," 71–72.

The central question here concerns how addressees are able to *recognize* the specific intended force of addressers in each instance of such a sentence? I will present some of the primary solutions to these problems and specifically the nature of indirect and nonliteral utterances and how they convey meaning while focusing on the former in order to begin to describe the nature and function of RQs. From this study three central and interrelated questions arise that will guide my descriptions and will also serve as a grid for my summary conclusions:

- What is the relationship between implicatures and speech acts?
- How many illocutionary forces are expressed with a single indirect type utterance?
- How does a literal linguistic form express an indirect illocutionary force and how do addressees successfully recognize that force?

To begin, SAT and Pragmatics are often depicted as two independent disciplines when examining the nature of sentence-meaning and speaker-meaning. This is especially true for a number of speech act theorists when explaining the nature of explicit performative type utterances as they tend to focus on semantics (cf. Searle's IFID); however, with ISAs and non-literal utterances such theorists incorporate pragmatics into their explanations. Searle, Ferenc Kiefer, and Manfred Bierwisch explain their understanding of the relationship between pragmatics and ISAs as follows:

> Insofar as the illocutionary potential of a sentence is determined by its context-free, literal meaning, then it is part of its semantic structure, and its study is in the domain of semantics. Insofar as its illocutionary potential depends on the context of [the] utterance, including intentions of the speaker, its study belongs to the domain of pragmatics. A typical example of the distinction would arise in the study of indirect speech acts. In an indirect speech act, the speaker says one thing, means what she/he says, but she/he also means something more. A speaker might, for example, say to a hearer, "You are standing on my foot." And she/he might mean "You are standing on my foot," but in most contexts, she/he would likely mean something more, such as "Please get off my foot." In such an utterance, the direct speech act expressed by the literal meaning of the sentence lies in the domain of semantics. The indirect speech act, expressed in the speaker's utterance meaning insofar as it differs from the literal meaning of the sentence, lies within the domain of pragmatics.[100]

---

100. Searle, Kiefer, and Bierwisch, "Introduction," in Searle, Kiefer, and Bierwisch, eds., *Speech Act Theory and Pragmatics*, x (pronouns revised).

Within the Philosophy of Language, two primary questions arise from the study of ISAs: (1) what is the illocutionary nature of an ISA (speech act theory)? And (2) how do addressers intentionally express a speech act indirectly so that addressees know that addressers are saying more than the literal sentence meaning (pragmatics)?

Before moving forward, I must also address one final issue which concerns the assumption that ISAs even exist. The distinction between direct and ISAs fundamentally depends on the fact that certain sentences actually express a literal direct force. Levinson identifies this as the Literal Force Hypothesis (LFH): a direct and evident correlation between linguistic form and force.[101] Levinson identifies several problems with this view. Specifically, the problem of force and sentence form correspondence which also has affinities with the issue of verbal criterion for identifying performatives. The problem here particularly concerns the failure of the assumed predictability of performative verbs directly naming a force (e.g., Searle's IFID) as such verbs may be *used* to identify a different force than expressed by the verb's meaning.[102] For instance, the performative verb *promise* in *I promise to fire you if you don't finish your work* names or identifies the force of a threat or warning rather than a declarative promise.[103] A second major problem is the fact that most utterances are indirect. This is especially true with request speech acts which rarely occur in English with the imperative. Moreover, there are an infinite variety of ways to express a request indirectly. One solution to these problems is to simply reject the LFH and assume that illocutionary force is entirely pragmatic along with the denial that any correlation between form and force exists.[104] The obvious difficulty with assigning all speech acts to pragmatics is the clear existence of certain sentence types matching illocutionary forces. It is also undeniable that semantics play a role towards determining speech act types and with this approach sentence meaning only plays a minor role, if any; speaker-meaning determines force.[105] Despite these real difficulties and complexities with sentence-meaning, most theorists acknowledge the irrefutable existence of ISAs (even Levinson identifies nineteen ways of asking someone to

---

101. Levinson, *Pragmatics*, 263–68; see also Gerald Gazdar, "Speech Act Assignment," in *Elements of Discourse Understanding*, ed. A. K. Joshi et al. (Cambridge: Cambridge University Press, 1981), 64–83, cf. 75–79.
102. See Adams, *Performative Nature*, 30–32; Briggs, *Words in Action*, 98–102.
103. Huang, *Pragmatics*, 111.
104. See, e.g., Gazdar, "Speech Act Assignment."
105. See further Levinson, *Pragmatics*, 274–76.

shut the door as "indirectly requesting").[106] Further, Alston's IAP notion alleviates the rigidity of Searle's IFID rule and thus performative verbs and sentences should be viewed with a range of IAs while also excluding others. The question, though, that arises with the LFH is: How and why can literal linguistic forms seemingly express syntactically inherent indirect forces?[107]

Interpretive Models Introduction

There are a number of approaches to ISAs. These methods, though, fall into two general categories: Ambiguity models and Inference approaches. These methods all have in common that an indirect meaning derives to one degree or another from a linguistic form. My focus will be on the approaches consistently referenced in the literature as the leading suggestions offered by theorists. I will summarize the main ideas of these various proposals while drawing certain conclusions concerning the nature of ISAs and how such utterances convey meaning with my above central questions in mind.

Ambiguity Models

Idiom Model. Jerrold M. Sadock is the primary proponent of this approach who understands utterances like (2a) as semantically ambiguous with the request dimension considered a *direct* speech act idiom which does not include any inferential interpretative processes at all.[108] To demonstrate his thesis, Sadock begins by showing how individual, single lexical items such as "great" and "brilliant" are idioms.[109] From here he analyzes multi-word sentences expressing two distinct meanings: (a) literal and (b) idiomatic. For example the phrase *Kick the bucket* means either "to kick the bucket" (literal) or "to die" (idiomatic). Yet, the expression in any given context cannot convey its literal and idiomatic senses simultaneously; the expression unambiguously means one or the other. Thus, the sentence has two senses, two syntactic meanings. From here, Sadock turns to ISAs. Similar to the above expression the indirect utterance, *You bet it's cold* can either be an assertion or an expression of strong

---

106. See Levinson's list of ways to indirectly request someone to shut the door (*Pragmatics*, 264–65; see also Rod Bertolet, "Are There Indirect Speech Acts?" in Tsohatzidis, ed., *Foundations of Speech Act Theory*, 343; Huang, *Pragmatics*, 111).

107. Levinson, *Pragmatics*, 268.

108. Jerrold M. Sadock, "Speech Act Idioms," *CLS* (1972): 329–39; idem, *Toward a Linguistic Theory of Speech Acts* (New York: Academic Press, 1974), 73–146; idem, "Speech Acts," 69.

109. Sadock, "Speech Act Idioms," 330–32.

agreement. Yet, in specific contexts the sentence is a speech act idiom when the addresser expresses the latter. In this instance the semantic meaning of "bet" is replaced with an abstract performative speech act type expressing strong agreement, e.g., *I agree*. Thus, the expression is understood through its conventional meaning rather than the semantic meaning of the sentence. With this in place, Sadock turns to the utterance *Is it cold in here?* As the IA of the former sentence can be one of agreement, this sentence cannot be formed into an unambiguous request and thus only expresses the illocution of inquiring.[110] For instance, in contrast to (2a) one cannot felicitously say in idiomatic English *Isn't it **please** cold in here*. When the sentence *Is it cold in here?* is uttered, then, to make a request it conventionally functions as a speech act idiom. Therefore, one should analyze the nature of ISAs in their intended effect as directly illocutionary rather than as an indirect PE.[111]

Although Sadock's idiom model can account for some specific types of ISAs, it has not gained much support among theorists. Searle as well as Kent Bach and Robert Harnish take particular exception to this theory due to the ambiguous encumbrance and unnecessary complexity of *two* literal, simultaneous meanings associated with the utterances in question.[112] In other words, addressees are challenged to respond to an ambiguous sentence with simultaneously two different literal meanings: a literal interrogative and a historically conventionalized idiom request.[113] In addition, addressees typically use the linguistic, literal meaning of sentences to various degrees to interpret indirectness, which this theory appears to dismiss wholesale.[114] To handle the different types of indirect sentences, as Levinson highlights, Idiom models require a pragmatic inference theory to bridge the gap between *what is said* and what is intentionally meant during typical discourse exchange.[115] Consequently, the

---

110. Ibid., 335.

111. Sadock, "Speech Acts," 69.

112. For this reason Bach/Harnish identify Sadock's theory as "The Ambiguity Thesis."

113. Kent Bach and Robert M. Harnish, *Linguistic Communication and Speech Acts* (Cambridge, MA: MIT Press, 1979), 174–83; Searle, *Expression and Meaning*, 40–41, 49–50; see also Bertolet, "Are There Indirect Speech Acts?" 337–38; Huang, *Pragmatics*, 114–15; Levinson, *Pragmatics*, 268–70.

114. So, e.g., Huang, *Pragmatics*, 115.

115. Levinson applies this critique solely to Sadock's Idiom model (*Pragmatics*, 269–70), but this critique also reasonably applies to the notion of *conversational postulates* which I will discuss next. See also Jerry L. Morgan, "Two Types of Convention in Indirect Speech Acts," in *Syntax and Semantics 9: Pragmatics*, ed. P. Cole (New York: Academic Press, 1978), 278.

ambiguity thesis cannot stand on its own to adequately deal with all the diverse types of indirect utterances. Further, as both Levinson and Huang have observed, idioms are idiosyncratic to speech communities whereas ISAs translate linguistically across numerous languages and thus cannot be considered idioms in a proper sense.[116]

Conversational Postulates. David Gordon and George Lakoff propose a type of convention of meaning as with Sadock, but in a quite different way with their notion of "conversational postulates."[117] Gordon/Lakoff understand a sentence like (2a) as *ambiguous* and thus simultaneously conveying both a literal question about ability and a literal request to pass the salt. Similar to Sadock, this sentence type is not indirect, but direct with two literal expressions and meanings. For Sadock, most interrogatives are speech act ambiguous between their request and question sense. Thus, he identifies this type of sentence as a "requestion."[118] Conversely, what disambiguates an intended illocutionary act for Gordon/Lakoff is the "systematic relation" between sentence type and the conversational or meaning postulate along with context.[119] Identifying such conversational postulates are predictable and thus reduce the amount of inference required to determine the intended indirect illocutionary force. With this, Gordon/Lakoff isolate two specific and typical strategies to express a request: (a) asserting an addresser-based sincerity condition or (b) questioning an addressee-based sincerity condition. The basic sincerity condition is defined as:

116. Levinson, *Pragmatics*, 270; cf. Huang, *Pragmatics*, 114.

117. Gordon/Lakoff, "Conversational Postulates," in Cole and Morgan, eds., *Syntax and Semantics 3*, 83–106. Levinson (*Pragmatics*, 271–73) followed by Huang (*Pragmatics*, 113–14) categorizes Gordon/Lakoff's conversational postulate model as an Inference theory. Gordon/Lakoff do reference Grice and "conversational principles" at the beginning of their essay and naturally discuss inference in association with indirect utterances, but they do not employ Grice's notions in a detailed sense when describing conversational postulates and indirect requests (so also William G. Lycan, *Logical Form in Natural Language* [Cambridge, MA: MIT Press, 1984], 159–60). While there are contrasts between conversational postulates and Sadock's Idiom theory there are also clear parallels and so I am placing this approach here as both approaches understand indirect utterances in a *convention of meaning* sense while not depending much upon Grice's pragmatic notions (so also, e.g., Bertolet, "Indirect Speech Acts?" 337–38; Michael L. Geis, *Speech Acts and Conversational Interaction: Toward a Theory of Conversational Competence* [Cambridge: Cambridge University Press, 1995], 125).

118. Sadock, "Speech Act Idioms," 337.

119. For Gordon/Lakoff's general conversational postulates, see "Conversational Postulates," 85.

If *a* sincerely requests of *b* that *b* do *R*, then *a* wants *b* to do *R*, *a* assumes that *b* can do *R*, *a* assumes that *b* would be willing to do *R*, and *a* assumes that *b* will not do *R* in the absence of the request.[120]

These conditions characterize particular conversational postulates. With these ideas in place, an addresser-based sincerity condition type sentence is a sentence such as (2a) with the conversational postulate conceptualized as: $SAY(a,b,WANT(a,Q))^* \rightarrow REQUEST(a,b,Q)$. An addressee-based sincerity condition type sentence would be like (2a). This indirect utterance questions the ability or preparatory condition of the addressee with the intended effect that the addresser assumes that the addressee does in fact possess the ability. The conversational postulate is conceptualized as: $ASK(a,b,Can(b, Q))^* \rightarrow REQUEST(a,b,Q)$.[121] So in this instance, the above utterance corresponds to the utterance on the left-hand side of the arrow which implicates the form on the right-hand side with the asterisk signaling the dependence of these postulates on the mutual understanding of the addresser and addressee that the literal meaning of the illocutionary content is not the intended meaning of the utterance. This mutual understanding is connected to the sincerity, preparatory condition that if an addresser in a certain context questions an assumed ability of the addressee, the addressee then thereby knows the utterance is not a question. Thus, the utterance (2a) directly functions as an illocutionary request equivalent to the utterance *I request you to pass the salt*.

Gordon/Lakoff's thesis has come under numerous attacks and not least of all because of the unclear meaning of the phrase "conversational postulate."[122] Theorists have also leveled similar criticisms against this postulate theory as with Sadock's idiom model.[123] For instance, J. L. Morgan observes that if Gordon/Lakoff are correct then when a speaker intends *Can you open the door?* to *convey* "I request that you open the door" and not also to *convey* a request for information then it appears that the interrogative is truly ambiguous between two senses. Consequently, the request is not a conversational implicature of the interrogative, but

---

120. Ibid.
121. Ibid., 86.
122. See, e.g., J. L. Morgan, "Conversational Postulates Revisited," *Language* 53 (1977): 277–78.
123. Searle in particular finds Gordon/Lakoff's scheme to be problematic (see *Expression and Meaning*, 30–57); see further, e.g., Levinson, *Pragmatics*, 272–73; Sadock, "Speech Acts," 69–70; Lycan, *Logical Form*, 160–61; see also the essays by Sadock, Peter Cole, Alice Davison, Georgia M. Green, John R. Ross in Cole and Morgan, eds., *Syntax and Semantics 3*.

a second literal meaning of the surface form of the interrogative in the Sadockian sense.[124] Thus, again we are left with sentence ambiguity with this conversational postulates idea. Following along these lines, Sadock himself finds the postulate suggestion providing some insight, but he also raises the real problem with Gordon/Lakoff not identifying which actual grammatical forms disambiguate an intended illocutionary effect.[125] These two theorists also tend to blend the terms "can convey" and "convey" when describing inferential addresser-meaning[126] and explain conversational postulates in terms of automatic inference.[127] It is clear that indirect utterances do not typically contain inherently predictable inferences and thus this model cannot address all of the possible types of indirect utterances.[128] Moreover, as with idioms, the proposed meaning postulates are not universally cross-linguistic.[129] Despite these serious deficiencies, their primary thesis remains significant that with certain indirect utterances (e.g., [2a]) a high level of predictability exists with the combination of linguistic content, addresser/addressee-based sincerity conditions, and its speech act function.[130] Thus, addressers *can* use a particular interrogative with the predictable result to *convey* a type of IA.

Inference Approaches

Those who find the ambiguity thesis or convention of meaning approach inadequate, develop various inference models utilizing some form of Grice's pragmatic program and specifically his notion of *conversational implicatures*. As I pointed out above, Grice is known as the seminal developer in the study of contemporary pragmatics primarily expressed in his own William James lectures at Harvard on "Logic and Conversation" (1967) containing his most influential understanding on the subject.[131] Although there have been a number of critiques and alternative

---

124. Morgan, "Conversational Postulates Revisited," 282.
125. Sadock, "Speech Acts," 69.
126. See, e.g., Gordon/Lakoff, "Conversational Postulates," 87.
127. See Morgan, "Conversational Postulates Revisited," 278–82.
128. So Geis, *Conversational Interaction*, 127; Alice Davison, "Indirect Speech Acts and What To Do with Them," in Cole and Morgan, eds., *Syntax and Semantics 3*, 180, and, in the same volume, Georgia M. Green, "How To Get People To Do Things with Words: The Whimperative Question," 118–20; Sadock, "Speech Acts," 69.
129. See, e.g., Green, "Get People to Do Things," 138–40.
130. See Levinson, *Pragmatics*, 271–72.
131. See Grice, *Way of Words*, 22–40.

suggestions to Gricean pragmatics,[132] his work and concepts remain the most widely recognized and utilized while they also continue to play a prominent role in the discussions of contemporary pragmatics. As Yan Huang asserts, "Since its inception, the Gricean paradigm has revolutionized pragmatic theorizing and to date remains one of the cornerstones of contemporary thinking in linguistic pragmatics and the philosophy of language."[133] More specific for my study here, Grice's scheme is utilized in one way or another by most theorists for describing speech acts in general and especially with ISAs.[134] Unfortunately, Grice is not exactly clear in his pragmatic descriptions; in addition, his work reflects a certain amount of incompleteness. These facts alone have created a whole host of diverse debates concerning Gricean principles.[135]

Paul Grice and Conversational Implicatures. Grice's notion of conversational implicature directly relates to indirect utterances as this idea focuses on what addressers intentionally *implicate* with particular sentences. According to Grice, he chose the noun "implicature" in relation to the verb *implicate* to convey the idea of *implying, what is implied* when

---

132. According to Yan Huang two neo-Gricean theories on conversational implicatures stand out as the most influential alternatives to Grice's scheme: Laurence R. Horn's two-principled theory and Stephen C. Levinson's three-principled theory; see the Bibliography and Huang, *Pragmatics*, 36–54. Another neo-Gricean theory is proposed by Jay D. Atlas, *Logic, Meaning, and Conversation: Semantical Underdeterminacy, Implicature, and their Interface* (New York: Oxford University Press, 2005).

133. Huang, *Pragmatics*, 23. Deirdre Wilson and Dan Sperber similarly state that "it seems no exaggeration to say that most recent theories of utterance-interpretation are a direct result of Grice's William James Lectures" ("On Grice's Theory of Conversation," in *Pragmatics: Critical Concepts, Volume 4: Presupposition, Implicature, and Indirect Speech Acts*, ed. A. Kasher [London/New York: Routledge, 1998], 347).

134. For an example of a typical Gricean chain of interpretation of ISAs, see Sadock, "Speech Acts," 70.

135. For instance, Georgia M. Green affirms the ongoing importance of Grice's work while also confesses the interpretive problems with his descriptions: "Now, I have read 'Logic and Conversation' a number of times over the last 23 years. Since I have been unable to arrive at a coherent, consistent literal interpretation, my strategy has been to assume that Grice's ability to say clearly what he meant just did not match his vision, and therefore, to interpret problematic terms [e.g., *purpose* and *goal*; *conversation* and *talk exchange*] in such a way as to arrive at a consistent and explanatory theory" ("The Universality of Gricean Interpretation," *Berkeley Linguistic Society* 16 [1990]: 416).

one makes an utterance.[136] As presented above, Grice's central tenet for determining the meaning of an utterance transpires through the distinction between *what is said* and *what is implicated*. So *what is implicated* is determined in contrast to *what is said* yet at the same time calculated on the basis of *what is said*. *Conversational* implicatures contrast *conventional* implicatures as the latter are arbitrarily attached by convention to lexical items and/or linguistic, grammatical constructions. Conversely, conversational implicatures are deduced from what is communicated, not necessarily from sentence-meaning.[137]

Conversational implicatures are directly connected to what Grice identifies as the Cooperative Principle (CP) that assumes people in a conversation naturally cooperate with each other by providing the proper amount of information as well as being truthful, relevant, and perspicuous. Grice defines his CP as follows:

> Make your conversational contribution such as is required, at the stage at which it occurs, by the accepted purpose or direction of the talk exchange in which you are engaged.[138]

In connection to his CP, Grice identifies four major maxims of cooperative conversation with no privileged status:

1. *Quantity*
   - Make your contribution as informative as is required (for the current purposes of the exchange), i.e., don't say too little.
   - Do not make your contribution more informative than is required, i.e., don't say too much.
2. *Quality*: Be truthful
   - Do not say what you believe to be false.
   - Do not say that for which you lack adequate evidence.
3. *Relation*: Be relevant (each dialogue partner expects her/his contribution to be appropriate to the immediate needs at each stage of the transaction)

---

136. Grice, *Way of Words*, 24.
137. Ibid., 25–26; see further, e.g., Huang, *Pragmatics*, 54–57; Levinson, *Pragmatics*, 127–31; George Yule, *Pragmatics*, Oxford Introductions to Language Study (Oxford: Oxford University Press, 1996), 45–46.
138. Grice, *Way of Words*, 26.

4. *Manner*: Be perspicuous
- Avoid obscurity of expression.
- Avoid ambiguity.
- Be brief (avoid unnecessary prolixity).
- Be orderly.[139]

These maxims are directly related to the CP, but they do not constitute this general principle of communication. Rather, for Grice the maxims are rational ways of operating in accordance with the CP with specific maxims playing more prominent roles depending upon the cooperative conversational needs.[140] Some have argued that Grice's maxims are rules or norms that *must be learned* in order to successfully communicate,[141] but rather it appears that the maxims for Grice are simply intuitive ways of being conversationally cooperative.[142] Although for many language specialists the role of the maxims continues to be a source of contention,[143] these maxims *define* conversational implicatures for Grice. His general depiction of conversational implicatures follows along these lines: A person utters a sentence in a particular context that semantically expresses a certain proposition identified with *what is said*. The propositional content of the sentence does not fully express or exhaust the semantic meaning of the sentence. With a sentence the addresser also conversationally implicates something else. For Grice, anything communicated in an utterance that closely corresponds to its linguistic form counts as *what is said* while any other information expressed counts as being *implicated*.[144]

---

139. Ibid., 26–27 (pronouns revised). Grice also acknowledges that there are "of course, all sorts of other maxims (aesthetic, social, or moral in character), such as 'Be polite,' that are also normally observed by participants in talk exchanges, and these may also generate nonconventional implicatures" (ibid., 28).

140. For Grice, conversational participants would ideally include all of the major maxims, but "the observance of some of these maxims is a matter of less urgency than is the observance of others" (ibid., 27). See further Green, "Gricean Interpretation," 413; idem, *Pragmatics*, 96.

141. Cf., Dan Sperber and Deirdre Wilson, *Relevance: Communication and Cognition* (Cambridge, MA: Harvard University Press, 1986), 162.

142. So Green, "Gricean Interpretation," 414; idem, *Pragmatics*, 96; see Grice, "Logic and Conversation," 22–40.

143. E.g., Sperber/Wilson, *Relevance*, 36. See further Horn, "Implicature," 7–8; Green, "Gricean Interpretation," 413–15; idem, *Pragmatics*, 95–98.

144. See Kent Bach, "Conversational Impliciture," *Mind and Language* 9 (1994): 142–43.

Grice envisions his maxims functioning with his cooperative principle to explain normal communicative interchange with the participants in full compliance with these principles. Grice assumes that "talk exchanges" are "cooperative efforts" with each participant recognizing to some extent "a common purpose or set of purposes, or at least a mutually accepted direction."[145] Thus, these maxims are mutually assumed and shared ways participants converse. For this reason, Georgia M. Green identifies the maxims more "like default instantiations of the CP,"[146] or as Horn classifies them, "default settings,"[147] or as Bach/Harnish identify, as "conversational presumptions."[148]

Grice also sees in "characteristic talk exchanges, there is a common aim...namely, that each party should, for the time being, identify her/himself with the transitory conversational interests of the other."[149] Following Grice here, Green describes the purposes of the CP as "mutually modelled." For "any communication to occur, for each participant to understand what the other meant, each must make assumptions about the other's goals." "This is the sense in which participants recognize a common goal."[150]

The relationship between addressers and Grice's maxims includes simply to observe the maxims or to deliberately flout or infringe on a maxim.[151] Regarding the latter and first, addressers can *opt out* of a maxim such as with *hedges* (an expression indicating the possible inaccuracy of a statement, e.g., *as far as I know*...). Second, a *clash* between two maxims can occur such as when it may appear that addressers opt out when they do not provide enough information with a sentence (maxim of Quantity),

---

145. Grice, *Way of Words*, 26.
146. Green, "Gricean Interpretation," 411.
147. Horn, "Implicature," 8.
148. Bach/Harnish, *Linguistic Communication*, 103–107.
149. Grice, *Way of Words*, 29.
150. Green, *Pragmatics*, 97, 98 (pronouns revised). Some theorists relate this notion to SAT; see, e.g., Philip R. Cohen and Hector J. Levesque, "Speech Acts and the Recognition of Shared Plans," in *Proceedings of the Third Biennial Conference of the Canadian Society for Computational Studies of Intelligence* (Victoria, BC: University of Victoria, 1980), 263–71; idem, "Rational Interaction as the Basis for Communication," in *Intentions in Communication*, ed. P. R. Cohen et al. (Cambridge, MA: MIT Press, 1990), 221–55, cf. 229–31; C. Raymond Perrault, "An Application of Default Logic to Speech Act Theory," in Cohen et al., ed., *Intentions in Communication*, 161–85.
151. Huang identifies the former as Conversational Implicature$_O$ and the latter Conversational Implicature$_F$ (*Pragmatics*, 27–29).

but by providing more information they would infringe the maxim of Quality.[152] Third, addressers can *violate* a maxim such as with deliberately telling a lie. Finally, addressers can *flout* or *exploit* a maxim as with tautology, figures of speech, irony, etc.[153]

The failure to cooperate with these maxims in one way or another is important for the study of ISAs. In each instance and especially with the final category, addressers infringe on a maxim on the sentence-meaning level, but observes it on the level of what is implicated. By intentionally violating a maxim addressers thereby generate or trigger implicatures. For instance, Grice sees the maxim of Quality exploited with the metaphor, *My memory is a bit cloudy*, as at the sentence level the utterance is false, but succeeds at the implicature level because the addresser obviously means more than what she/he says. Faced with the above sentence, the interpretive process goes something like this: The addressee is left to determine whether the addresser has either (a) abandoned the CP or (b) remains conversationally cooperative despite the apparent failure of such cooperation. The addressee characteristically and naturally chooses the latter and decides that the addresser is still cooperating and because of the CP recognizes that the addresser has intentionally exploited the Quality maxim to express something beyond the literal linguistic meaning of the utterance and thereby is cooperating conversationally at a deeper level. The addresser utters this type of sentence knowing full well that the addressee will interpretively calculate her/his implicated message.

Grice considers implicatures deriving from the violation of Relation rare. Grice admits that his definition of this maxim "be relevant" is terse while posing a number of difficult questions needing to be answered.[154] He does, though, offer an example of such an occurrence:

> At a genteel tea party, A says *Mrs. X is an old bag.* There is a moment of appalled silence, and then B says *The weather has been quite delightful this summer, hasn't it?* B has blatantly refused to make what he says relevant to A's preceding remark. He thereby implicates that A's remark should not be discussed and, perhaps more specifically, that A has committed a social gaffe.[155]

---

152. For an example see Grice, *Way of Words*, 32–33; see also Bach/Harnish, *Linguistic Communication*, 167–68.

153. These instances are under Grice's "Group C" examples (*Way of Words*, 33–37).

154. Ibid., 27.

155. Ibid., 35. For another description of Grice's CP and the maxims see Green, *Pragmatics*, 89–95.

Significantly, and as I will describe below, a number of contemporary theorists and specifically argued by Relevance theorists consider the violation of this maxim as the singular way addressers trigger inferential data.

Grice also distinguishes between *particularized* and *generalized* conversational implicatures. The implicature of the former type relies on "special features of the context" in order for addressees to interpret addressers' conveyed meaning. The implicature of the latter type is conveyed by "the use of a certain form of words in an utterance."[156]

Grice additionally identifies four major features or properties[157] of conversational implicatures:

- *Cancelability*: Conversational implicatures may not materialize depending on certain linguistic or nonlinguistic contexts.[158] Implicatures are either *explicitly cancelable* (through the addition of a clause) or *contextually cancelable* (the context of the conversation makes it clear that the addresser is opting out of the implicature).[159]
- *Nondetachability*: Conversational implicatures derive from speaker-meaning not sentence-meaning. Thus, implicatures can be conveyed through any linguistic form as they are attached to semantic content, not sentence form.
- *Nonconventionlity*: Implicatures depend on but are not included in the conventional linguistic meaning of an expression.
- *Calcuablity*: The presence of a conversational implicature must be able to be calculably worked out which occurs through the CP and its maxims.[160]

---

156. Grice, *Way of Words*, 37–38.

157. Grice actually presents six points in his description of conversational implicature properties (see ibid., 39–40), but four properties arise from his discussion that most pragmatic and linguistic specialists also recognize (see, e.g., Levinson, *Pragmatics*, 114–19).

158. Specialists also identify this property as "defeasibility"; see, e.g., Huang, *Pragmatics*, 32; Levinson, *Pragmatics*, 114.

159. For possible linguistic and nonlinguistic contexts see Huang, *Pragmatics*, 32–33.

160. Jerrold M. Sadock critiques Grice's conversational implicatures and identifies a number of problems that Grice himself is not unaware of (Jerrold M. Sadock, "On Testing for Conversational Implicature," in *Syntax and Semantics 9: Pragmatics*, ed. P. Cole [New York: Academic Press, 1978], 281–97). Following his critique, Sadock proposes an additional property of *reinforceability*: conversational implicatures can be made explicit without creating redundancy ("Testing," 294–95).

With all this in place, Grice describes the essence of conversational implicatures[161] and how an implicature is identified and calculably interpreted:

> The presence of a conversational implicature must be capable of being worked out; for even if it can in fact be intuitively grasped, unless the intuition is replaceable by an argument, the implicature (if present at all) will not count as a conversational implicature; it will be a conventional implicature. To work out that a particular conversational implicature is present the hearer will rely on the following data: (1) the conventional meaning of the words used, together with the identity of any references that may be involved; (2) the Cooperative Principle and its maxims; (3) the context, linguistic or otherwise, of the utterance; (4) other items of background knowledge; and (5) the fact (or supposed fact) that all relevant items falling under the previous headings are available to both participants and both participants know or assume this to be the case.

From here Grice presents his formulaic pattern for the working out a conversational implicature:

> She/He has said that p; there is no reason to suppose that she/he is not observing the maxims, or at least the Cooperative Principle; she/he could not be doing this unless she/he thought that q; she/he knows (and knows that I know that she/he knows) that I can see that the supposition that she/he thinks that q is required; she/he has done nothing to stop me thinking that q; she/he intends me to think, or is at least willing to allow me to think, that q; and so she/he has implicated that q.[162]

From Grice's descriptions, two ideas come to the forefront towards conceptualizing how he understands the distinction between conversational

---

Levinson recognizes the validity of this property while also suggesting another property, *universality*: standard, universal conversational implicatures should be expected (*Pragmatics*, 120–21; *Presumptive Meanings: The Theory of Generalized Conversational Implicature* [Cambridge, MA: MIT, 2000], 15). Huang also recognizes both of these properties (*Pragmatics*, 34–35).

161. In contrast to conversational implicatures, conventional implicatures would be non-cancellable, detachable, not calculable, and obviously conventional (cf. Horn, "Pragmatic Theory," 123; see also, e.g., Huang, *Pragmatics*, 56–57; Levinson, *Pragmatics*, 127–290. On the issue of even the existence of conventional implicatures, see Bach, "Conversational Impliciture," 144–49; idem, "Philosophy of Language," 474–75; idem, "Speech Acts," 157.

162. Grice, *Way of Words*, 31 (pronouns revised).

implicatures from semantic meaning and how addressers use and addressees interpret linguistic forms. First, a conversational implicature is a piece of information conveyed beyond *what is said*, but is *closely related* to the linguistic content. Second, addressers use sentences in a particular way within a specific context with the goal of addressees *recognizing* this intention. This recognition occurs through the calculable data of the semantic meaning of the utterance, the conversational maxims, the context of the utterance, and other background knowledge.

To expand upon these two points, Grice conceives speaker-meaning as a matter of intentions, meaning-intentions, which he identifies as "M-intentions." These ideas stem from Grice's early and seminal essay entitled "Meaning" (1957).[163] In this particular essay, which has produced much debate and various interpretations, Grice proposed how addressers mean something with an utterance:

> "*A* meant something by *x*" is (roughly) equivalent to "*A* intended the utterance of *x* to produce some effect in an audience by means of the recognition of this intention."[164]

In other words, an utterance (which for Grice here is any form of communication), is successful only if the addressee recognizes that she/he is intended to recognize this purpose and thereby compute the addresser's communicative intentions. This set of intentions is typically identified by theorists as "the Gricean mechanism."[165] Here Grice views meaning as going from speaker-meaning to sentence-meaning. As I stated above, this specific aspect of Grice's program is what Alston identifies as a "perlocutionary-act-potential" theory of speaker-meaning which he particularly finds problematic due to his own view of that perlocutionary intentions depend entirely upon and derive from IAs and not vice versa.[166] As presented above, Grice does acknowledge a connection between speaker-meaning and the linguistic meaning of an utterance. Grice remains quite cautious, though, when he describes the exact nature of the relationship between literal sentence-meaning and conversational implicatures. That said, Grice does claim that *what is said* is "closely related to the conventional meaning of the words (the sentence) she/he has uttered."[167] He

---

163. H. P. Grice, "Meaning," *PhR* 66 (1957): 377–88 (= *Way of Words*, 213–23).
164. Grice, *Way of Words*, 220.
165. See, e.g., Loar, "Language," 81.
166. Alston, "Illocutionary Acts," 34–36; idem, *Illocutionary Acts*, 37–40, 162–73.
167. Grice, *Way of Words*, 25 (pronouns revised).

expands upon this in a subsequent essay entitled "Further Notes on Logic and Conversation":

> For in order that a nonconventional implicature should be present in a given case, my account requires that a speaker shall be able to utilize the conventional meaning of a sentence. If nonconventional implicature is built on what is said, if what is said is closely related to the conventional force of the words used, and if the presence of the implicature depends on the intentions of the speaker, or at least on his assumptions, with regard to the possibility of the nature of the implicature being worked out, then it would appear that the speaker must (in some sense or other of the word *know*) know what is the conventional force of the words which she/he is using.[168]

Further, *what is said* corresponds to the "particular meanings of the elements of [the sentence], their order, and their syntactical character."[169] Grice never explains exactly *how* "closely" these two are related and, as Levinson points out, his definition of *what is said* is quite complex and by no means straightforward.[170] Nevertheless, it does appear that Grice sees inferred speaker-meaning deriving in one way or another from sentence-meaning with perhaps a greater degree of connection occurring with generalized implicatures than with particularized implicatures. As many theorists have observed, the Gricean implicature program, then, is a two-fold sequentially, hierarchical interpretive procedure for deciphering the total signification of an utterance:

1. Addressers use a semantic linguistic form which addressees initially utilize to interpret an additional piece of information, an implicature (sentence-meaning).
2. Contrasted from as well as calculated on the basis of the propositional content and Gricean principles addressees recognize and infer addressers' implicated, intentional meaning (speaker-meaning).

---

168. Ibid., 49 (pronouns revised).
169. Ibid., 87.
170. See Levinson, *Presumptive Meanings*, 170. Levinson presents a rough description of Grice's explanation of *what is said* as follows:
U said that p by uttering x iff ["iff" is an abbreviation for "if and only if"]:
    a. x conventionally means p
    b. U speaker meant p
    c. p equals the conventional meaning of x minus any conventional implicature (*Presumptive Meanings*, 170; see further Huang, *Pragmatics*, 216).

Yet, as I described above, some caution is in order here because there is evidence that even Grice himself did not fully ascribe to the so-called Classic or *Gricean* view of the semantic/pragmatic interface. The above scheme may be more representative with Grice's conventional implicatures notion and not as much with conversational ones. Clearly Grice emphasizes the implicature or pragmatic dimension of meaning over linguistic input throughout his descriptions, but at the very least his entire program intuitively or naturally appears to assume the initial reliance of implicatures on the semantic meaning of utterances.

Grice also claims that one can implicate without saying "or making as if to say," which he distinguishes from saying or meaning something. In these instances an addresser does not mean what she/he appears to be saying as with irony and metaphor.[171] Put more directly, instances of "as if to say" occur when an addresser says something but not intending to mean that (the literal linguistic meaning) and at the same time meaning something else instead. With all this in mind, Searle's and Alston's critique of Grice's theory of meaning and specifically his "M-intentions" as a perlocutionary theory of meaning is well taken; however, Grice's implicature notion clearly locates meaning in one way or another in the linguistic form of a sentence. Thus, I am not entirely convinced that Grice's program should be considered a purely perlocutionary (pragmatic) theory of meaning, but one that involves pragmatics as well as semantics.[172]

Another significant and related issue with the above discussion concerns how Grice understands the relationship between *implicature* and *assertion*. Grice defines implicatures as something "implied," "suggested," or "meant" as derived from an utterance;[173] they are something conveyed without literally saying or asserting it. Importantly, implicatures are not actual or real assertions; rather, the assertion precedes the implicature.

---

171. Grice, *Way of Words*, 30, 34.

172. So, e.g., Szabó, "Introduction," 3. In his essays on IAP, Alston does not explicitly engage with Grice's essay "Logic and Conversation" and thus his explanation and critique of conversational implicatures does not appear to include Grice's comprehensive theory of meaning. This seems to be the same with Searle's critique of Grice (see Searle, *Speech Acts*, 42–50) which explicitly centers on Grice's "Meaning" essay (see Grice, *Way of Words*, 213–23). I did not include Grice in my earlier treatise on SAT in *Performative Nature* (18–63), and I also failed to nuance my description of Alston's or Searle's understanding of perlocutionary acts (*Performative Nature*, 40–41), which does impact to a degree on my initial thoughts on the relationship between IAs and perlocutionary intentions.

173. Grice, *Way of Words*, 24.

In fact, addressers typically use indirect utterances to purposefully avoid asserting something. Grice illustrates this with several examples. One in particular deals with the flouting of the maxim of Quantity. An instructor is writing a recommendation for a student applying for a philosophy job which reads:

> Dear Sir, Mr. Smith's command of English is excellent and his attendance in class sessions has been consistent. Yours truly.

With this the instructor implicates that the student does not have any skill in philosophy whatsoever. How is this so? The instructor is cooperating conversationally due to the fact that she/he wrote at all. She/he knows the student and thus has enough information to write more and consequently there must be some good reason why more was not provided. Further, the instructor could have expressed some positive information being in such a position. The reader deduces that the instructor is providing additional information that she/he is reluctant to actually write down. Therefore, the recommendation is a negative one; not explicitly stated, but implicated indirectly.[174] Clearly in this instance as well as throughout Grice's descriptions, *classic* implicatures are not assertions themselves, but rather derive from assertions.[175]

Before moving forward, it is important to highlight one of Grice's own concerns with his theory and the potential and real dispute over how one decides which part of meaning derives from propositional content and which part is implicated. He voices this worry with a paradox deriving from his own theory:

> If we, as speakers, have the requisite knowledge of the conventional meaning of sentences we employ to implicate, when uttering them, something the implication of which depends on the conventional meaning in question, how can we, as theorists, have difficulty with respect to just those cases in *deciding where conventional meaning ends and implicature begins?* If it is true, for example, that one who says *that A or B* implicates the existence of non-truth-functional grounds for A or B, how can there be any doubt whether the word "or" has a strong or weak sense?[176]

---

174. Adapted from ibid., 33.
175. See further Scott Soames, *Philosophical Essays, Volume 1: Natural Language: What it Means and How We Use It* (Princeton: Princeton University Press, 2009), 300–303, 320.
176. Grice, *Way of Words*, 49 (italics mine).

Grice's own proposals attempt to solve this paradox, but the controversy remains and continues to demand the attention of theorists to solve as will be evident below.

Searle's Dual Illocutionary Conventional Approach. As for the speech act analysis of ISAs, Austin only briefly touches on these types of utterances. Austin identifies his "rhetic act" as an ISA. Such an utterance is used as an indirect means to perform another act as in *I bid three clubs* in the game of bridge. The success of such an utterance occurs through extralinguistic conventions.[177] Searle follows closely to Austin, but with a far more comprehensive rationale supporting his conclusions which has become the most influential view of ISAs among contemporary theorists.[178] Searle's notions of ISAs are based upon and directly relate to his own SAT as described above. He also incorporates aspects of Grice's notion of conversational implicatures while wholesale rejecting the necessity of Gordon/Lakoff's conversational postulates.[179] In Searle's discussion, two ideas come to the forefront:

- the dual illocutionary nature of ISAs
- the convention of usage dimension of ISAs

Regarding the former notion, indirect utterances express two IAs simultaneously. For Searle "a sentence that contains the illocutionary force indicators for one kind of illocutionary act" is "uttered to perform, *in addition*, another type of illocutionary act." As I introduced earlier, "one illocutionary act is performed indirectly by way of performing another."[180] Indirect utterances are speech acts, but because they communicate more than expressed within the propositional content they rely on "mutually shared background information, both linguistic and nonlinguistic, together with the general powers of rationality and inference on the part of the hearer."[181] Still, ISAs are not explicit declar-

---

177. See Austin, *Things with Words*, 96–97, 130–31.
178. Searle, *Expression and Meaning*, 30–57; see also Searle/Vanderveken, *Foundations of Illocutionary Logic*, 10–11.
179. Searle, *Expression and Meaning*, 32. Grice's essay "Logic and Conversation" was originally published in the same volume as Searle's essay "Indirect Speech Acts," namely Cole and Morgan, eds., *Syntax and Semantics 3*.
180. Searle, *Expression and Meaning*, 30, 31.
181. Ibid., 31–32.

ative/performatives[182] due to the fact that performatives are literal and direct sentences as in the case of a promissory utterance.

The dual illocutionary ISA expresses (a) a primary non-literal illocution by way of (b) a secondary literal illocution. Addressees must employ an inferential strategy that establishes (a) that the primary illocution point departs from the secondary literal one and (b) what the primary illocutionary point is.[183] In certain instances the utterance (2a) is not a literal question about an addressee's ability, but is an illocutionary directive for her/him to pass the salt. Applying general Gricean inferential processes, "the speaker intends to produce in the hearer the knowledge that a request has been made to her/him, and she/he intends to produce this knowledge by means of getting the hearer to *recognize* her/his intention to produce it."[184] Thus with (2a) the addressee must *recognize* that the primary IA is not literal, but she/he is indirectly being requested to pass the salt. Searle presents a simplified procedure for inference and ISA which closely resembles Grice's two-fold sequential inference process:

First, the hearer must have some device for recognizing that the

> utterance might be an indirect speech act. This requirement is satisfied by the fact that in the context, a question about the hearer's ability lacks any conversational point. The hearer, therefore, is led to seek an alternative meaning. Second, since the hearer knows the rules of speech acts, she/he knows that the ability to pass the salt is a preparatory condition on the speech act of requesting her/him to do so. Therefore, she/he is able to infer that the question about her/his ability is likely to be a polite request to perform the act.[185]

Searle's felicity conditions also play an important role towards recognizing the presence of an ISA. Searle's "bare-bones reconstruction" of the interpretive process for ISAs is as follows:

---

182. Searle, "How Performatives Work," in *Essays in Speech Act Theory*, ed. D. Vanderveken and S. Kubo, P&BNS 77 (Amsterdam: John Benjamins, 2002), 90, 92–93.
183. Searle ("Indirect Speech Acts," 34–35) describes this reconstruction of the literal illocution from the primary illocution as occurring in ten sequential steps.
184. Searle, *Expression and Meaning*, 30–31 (pronouns revised; italics mine).
185. Ibid., 113–14 (pronouns revised). For a more detailed procedure see ibid., 34–35, 46–47.

Step 1: Y has asked me a question as to whether I have the ability to pass the salt (fact about the conversation).

Step 2: I assume that she/he is cooperating in the conversation and that therefore her/his utterance has some aim or point (principles of conversational cooperation).

Step 3: The conversational setting is not such as to indicate a theoretical interest in my salt-passing ability (factual background information).

Step 4: Furthermore, she/he probably already knows that the answer to the question is yes (factual background information). (This step facilitates the move to *Step 5*, but is not essential.)

Step 5: Therefore, her/his utterance is probably not just a question. It probably has some ulterior illocutionary point (inference from *Steps 1, 2, 3, and 4*). What can it be?

Step 6: A preparatory condition for any directive illocutionary act is the ability of H to perform the act predicated in the propositional content condition (theory of speech acts).

Step 7: Therefore, X has asked me a question the affirmative answer to which would entail that the preparatory condition for requesting me to pass the salt is satisfied (inference from *Steps 1 and 6*).

Step 8: We are now at dinner and people normally use salt at dinner; they pass it back and forth, try to get others to pass it back and forth, etc. (background information).

Step 9: She/he has therefore alluded to the satisfaction of a preparatory condition for a request whose obedience conditions it is quite likely she/he wants me to bring about (inference from *Steps 7 and 8*).

Step 10: Therefore, in the absence of any other plausible illocutionary point, she/he is probably requesting me to pass her/him the salt (inference from *Steps 5 and 9*).[186]

With this procedure in place, Searle supplements his SAT with the idea of *convention of usage* and specifically claims that ISAs are not imperative idioms, but do function as idiomatic requests. It is important to quote Searle at length here:

---

186. Ibid., 46–47 (pronouns revised).

> The theory of speech acts and the principles of conversational cooperation do indeed, provide a framework within which indirect illocutionary acts can be meant and understood. However, within this framework certain forms will tend to become conventionally established as the standard *idiomatic* forms for indirect speech acts. While keeping their literal meanings, they acquire conventional uses as, e.g., polite forms for requests.
>
> It is by now, I hope, uncontroversial that there is a distinction to be made between meaning and use, but what is less generally recognized is that there can be *conventions of usage* that are not *meaning conventions*. I am suggesting that "can you," "could you," "I want you to," and numerous other forms are conventional ways of making requests (and in that sense it would be *incorrect* to say they are *idioms*), but at the same time they do not have an imperative meaning (and in that sense it would be *incorrect* to say they are *idioms*). Politeness is the most prominent motivation for indirectness in requests, and certain forms naturally tend to become the conventionally polite ways of making indirect requests.[187]

Here Searle identifies, without providing much clarification and explanation, two types of conventions: (a) convention of meaning and (b) convention of usage. Searle categorizes idioms as conventions of meaning in the Sadockian sense and idiomatic expressions as conventions of usage. For Searle, ISAs are not idioms, but idiomatic. In fact, in order to be a "plausible candidate for an utterance as an indirect speech act, a sentence has to be idiomatic to start with." Searle goes on from here and adds a maxim to Grice's conversational implicatures and specifically the *maxim of Manner*: "Speak idiomatically unless there is some special reason not to."[188] Regarding illocutionary point, Searle identifies (2a) as a genuine indirect Directive because it requests addressees to perform an action. In this instance or with the sentence *I would appreciate it if you could make less noise* the addresser issues a Directive by way of asking a question or making a statement. Along with indirect Directives Searle recognizes ISAs conveying the Commissive force. For example, the utterance *Can I help you?* is again not a question of ability, but is an indirect offer from an addresser to help an addressee.[189] Searle also applies his felicity conditions to indirect Directives and Commissives as follows:

---

187. Ibid., 49 (italics mine).
188. Ibid., 50.
189. Ibid., 54–56.

Table 1.3. Searle's Rules/Conditions for Successful and Felicitous Directives and Commissives

Rules/Conditions	Directive (Request)
Preparatory	H is able to perform A
Sincerity	S wants H to do A
Propositional Content	S predicts a future act A of H
Essential	Counts as an attempt by S to get H to do A

Rules/Conditions	Commissive (Promise)
Preparatory	S is able to perform A
	H wants S to perform A
Sincerity	S intends to do A
Propositional Content	S predicts a future act A of S
Essential	Counts as the undertaking by S of an obligation to do A[190]

It is important for my subsequent descriptions of RQs to highlight here that Searle does not include a perlocutionary aspect in his explanatory framework of ISAs. As I presented above, he understands ISAs expressing two IAs, not an IA and a PE; or more specifically not an intended IA with an accompanied PE by way of a literal IA. Perhaps he assumes an inclusion of this effect from his direct speech act descriptions, but this is not explicit with his explanations of ISAs.

Before moving forward, I need to briefly describe Searle's understanding of metaphor. For Searle, "metaphorical meaning is always speaker's utterance meaning."[191] In other words, the meaning of a metaphor does not derive from sentence-meaning, but solely from speaker-meaning. Searle further distinguishes the literal, ISA, ironic, and metaphorical aspects of a single utterance. For instance, a speaker can utter *It's getting hot in here* to assert that is in fact getting hot (literal), to request that someone open a window (ISA), to complain about how cold it is (irony), or to remark on the vituperation of an argument in progress (metaphor). With literal sentences the sentence-meaning and speaker-meaning match. With ironic sentences the meaning is opposite of its literal sentence-meaning. With metaphors there is "never a change of meaning," but one is derived from going through the literal sentence-meaning as the speaker says "S is P, but means metaphorically that S is R."[192] According to Searle, there is a

---

190. Ibid., 44.
191. Ibid., 77.
192. Ibid., 86, 115.

"radical difference" between ISAs and irony and metaphor as with the former type a speaker means what she/he says and in addition something more. Sentence-meaning forms part of the speaker-meaning whereas with irony and metaphor meaning derives solely from speaker-meaning.[193]

Searle's approach to decipher between the literal and the primary illocution occurs through the implementation of Grice's implicatures and his view that indirect utterances are conventional and idiomatic in nature. The use of Grice helps Searle bridge the gap between sentence- and speaker-meaning that the ambiguity model needs. Also, Searle's approach demonstrates a clear connection between the use of an utterance and its linguistic form to identify various IAPs. However, Searle limits potential ISAs as *idiomatic* in nature and forms expressing *politeness*[194] which remains a problem as only linguistic form specific utterances have ISA potential.[195] Huang also interestingly observes that although Searle denounces the need for conversational postulates, his two-fold illocutionary thesis comes quite close to Gordon/Lakoff's model. According to Huang, it is the amount of inference and conventionality involved when computing an ISA that differentiates these theories rather than conceptual divergence.[196]

Theorists have raised a number of issues with Searle's indirect scheme, but three stand out as the most serious which also relate to my three central questions stated above. One question concerns Gricean inferential processes and two specifically deal with ISAs. Regarding the former,

- why does the interpretive process of an ISA require beginning with the literal semantic IA?

In other words, Searle, closely resembling Grice, proposes that one identify the literal sentence-meaning first then the intended indirect meaning second. Numerous language specialists have problems with this procedure in general, but vary when considering ISAs.

Regarding the latter two additional issues arise and first,

- how does an utterance with one IFID express an additional IA with a completely different meaning from its literal meaning?

---

193. Ibid., 113.
194. See Geis, *Conversational Interaction*, 130.
195. So also ibid., 139.
196. Huang, *Pragmatics*, 113–14.

Very closely related to this question,

- how can an indirect meaning constitute the semantic property of an IA?

Second,

- how does a single utterance successfully meet the felicity conditions of two distinct IAs?

Put a different way, Searle suggests that an utterance can simultaneously meet the conditions of a direct IA and an indirect IA which he obviously treats as exclusive types of speech acts. Alice Davison discusses these issues by observing that ISAs

> are not all alike, and not all members of just one class of linguistic structures. In SOME sense, indirect speech acts are the speech acts suggested by their surface forms, in addition to being some other speech act. The question that now plagues linguists is whether indirect speech acts are two illocutionary acts, simultaneously, or whether they are primarily one illocutionary act, and secondarily or relatedly some other act. If the former possibility is the case, it must be explained how one illocutionary component determines the surface form and some emotional value, and the other the semantic aspect of its actual illocutionary force. If the latter is the case, then it must be demonstrated that one illocutionary act is primary and that the other can be related to it in some general way.[197]

Because of these specific issues as well as others a number of theorists consider Searle's view as quite confusing[198] if not completely unnecessary and incomprehensible.[199] I will address these issues initially through my descriptions of how other theorists work through them while drawing some specific conclusions at the end of this chapter.

One final difficulty that I will elaborate on here concerns the fact that addressers do in fact use sentences to express indirection and figurativeness simultaneously which Searle's view does not appear to allow for. Savas L. Tsohatzidis further exposes the problems with Searle's proposals that metaphorical meaning is a special type of nonliteral,

---

197. Davison, "Indirect Speech Acts," 157.
198. E.g., Geis, *Conversational Interaction*, 132.
199. Cf. Geoffrey N. Leech, *Principles of Pragmatics* (London/New York: Longman, 1983), 38–39.

speaker-meaning and that metaphors are functions of speaker-meaning and not sentence-meaning.[200] According to Tsohatzidis, on the one hand, addressers can utter sentences ironically and metaphorically simultaneously. For example, an addresser can say, *He is a real lion, of course!* and thereby express that a certain person is not brave at all (irony) while also describing that person as a lion (metaphor). On the other hand, addressers can speak indirectly and figuratively simultaneously. For instance, an addresser can utter *Your baby has become a piglet* and thereby express that the baby in question needs a bath (ISA) while also comparing the baby to a piglet (metaphor). Tsohatzidis goes a step further and shows how metaphorical meaning does in fact derive from sentence-meaning by utilizing Grice's Cancellability test. To recall, conversational implicatures are either explicitly (adding a clarifying clause) or contextually (the context of the utterance) cancellable.[201] Tsohatzidis focuses on the former to show how certain metaphorical sentences cannot be cancelled without oddity. Using one of Searle's prime examples, *My wife Sally is a block of ice*, Tsohatzidis claims that if the meaning of this sentence derives solely from speaker-meaning then addressers should be able to explicitly cancel without oddity all metaphorical interpretations to ensure that Sally is literally a block of ice and nothing else by stating something like: *My wife Sally is a block of ice—please put her in the refrigerator before she melts.* However, this is obviously not the case as either the utterance is cancelled as odd or accepted because the metaphor has not been cancelled by the added clause. Therefore, the Cancellability test demonstrates that it is sentence-meaning rather than speaker-meaning that cannot be prevented without oddity. The metaphorical meaning of the above sentence derives from what it means rather than from what any addresser might have intended it to mean. With all this and important for this chapter, there are clearly utterances that involve indirection and figurativeness simultaneously.

Short-Circuited Implicatures. Jerry L. Morgan attempts to expand and sharpen Searle's notions and solve the paradoxical nature of utterances such as (2a).[202] For Morgan, such a sentence is not an idiom, but conventional in how the expression is used. Morgan examines two different approaches to ISAs: (a) natural approach and (b) conventional approach.

200. Tsohatzidis, "Speaker Meaning, Sentence Meaning, and Metaphor," in Tsohatzidis, ed., *Foundations of Speech Act Theory*, 365–73.
201. See above and Grice, *Way of Words*, 39, 44–46.
202. Morgan, "Two Types of Convention," 261–80.

The latter approach treats the above utterance in a Sadockian sense which operates within a *convention of meaning* as the sentence expresses a literal implicature, a request. The former approach falls within the category of *convention of usage* as the above sentence is understood as a literal Yes–No question, but *naturally* conveys a request as a consequence of Grice's maxims. A paradox arises from this analysis as this sentence has both a natural and conventional meaning.[203] The most appropriate approach for Morgan lies with Searle's *conventions of usage* thesis. As with Searle, sentence (2a) is not an idiom, but only has the obvious literal meaning of a question about an addressee's abilities (convention of language/meaning), but through Grice's maxims the sentence is implicated as a request. In fact, to use the expression this way has become conventional (convention of usage). Yet, because of this phenomenon a wholesale Gricean interpretation does not adequately address such utterance types. For Morgan, the apparent calculable implicature becomes "short-circuited" as the literal, conventional usage of an indirect utterance is "in some way latent, rather than the basis for an inference." Utterance (2a) is calculable in theory as with all implicatures, but is not actually calculated by addressees operating within the relevant conventions of usage.

Grice's conversational implicatures is short-circuited as addressees *directly* understand the intended meaning because of the usage conventions.[204] Thus, it is conventional to use the literal interrogative meaning of (2a) to convey *Pass the salt!*

Morgan's proposals underscores how theorists generally view, to one degree or another, implicatures as conventionalized; either as conventions of meaning or conventions of use.[205] The strengths of Morgan's view mirror those of Searle's, but have the additional advantage that particular utterances are conventionally used that greatly reduce the necessity of inferential calculation. This strength, however, is also its weakness in the sense of its narrow applicability. There are very few utterances that have reached the level of such standard idiomatic conventionality.[206] Thus, this model is limited to certain types of indirect utterances. Other legitimate

---

203. Ibid., 262–63.
204. See further Laurence R. Horn and Samuel Bayer, "Short-Circuited Implicature: A Negative Contribution," *Linguistics and Philosophy* 7 (1984): 397–414; Horn, "Pragmatic Theory," 113–45.
205. So, e.g., Geis, *Conversational Interaction*, 125.
206. See Lycan, *Logical Form*, 178–81; Geis, *Conversational Interaction*, 128–29.

types of indirect utterances would need to be understood as nonconventional as well as non-short-circuited implicatures.[207] What is important, though, is to highlight Morgan's understanding of the conventions of usage:

> the language learner's task is to discover or reconstruct the details of the connection between occasion and purpose, on the one hand, and linguistic means—the sentence used—on the other.[208]

In other words, when deciphering the meaning of any sentence, especially expressing indirectness, one must take into account the contextual setting of the utterance (pragmatics) as well as its linguistic meaning (semantics).

Illocutionary Standardization. Kent Bach and Robert M. Harnish reject Sadock's idiom model while finding Morgan's thesis on the right track, but is in need of refinement.[209] In the development of their entire SAT program these two language philosophers contrast Austin's view of IAs as conventional while also completely rejecting Searle's SAT proposals due to his emphasis on constitutive rules. Bach/Harnish's Intention-and-Inference Approach employs and intends to refine P. F. Strawson's intention communication-centered theory[210] while also explicitly incorporating Grice's implicature notions. In brief, they formalize a Speech Act Schema (SAS) with its basis consisting of Austin's three-fold speech act stratification along with a version of Searle's initial Utterance Act.[211] They identify each component of this four-fold scheme as an act that function intimately together for linguistic communication to transpire which is essentially an *inferential* process. With this in place, the simple version of their SAS is as follows:

1. S is uttering e.
2. S means such-and-such by e.
3. S is saying to H that so-and-so.
4. S is doing such-and-such.

---

207. So also Sadock, "Speech Acts," 71.
208. Morgan, "Two Types of Convention," 272.
209. Bach/Harnish, *Linguistic Communication*.
210. P. F. Strawson, "Intention and Convention in Speech Acts," in Searle, ed., *The Philosophy of Language*, 23–38.
211. See Bach/Harnish, *Linguistic Communication*, 3.

A derived inference follows from each phase of the scheme sequentially along with supplemental general rules.[212] The IA operates as the locus of the inferential process that expresses addressers' attitudes which correspond to the specific type of illocutionary intent. Here they acknowledge the importance of Grice's M-intentions theory, but interpret this idea as "reflexive in character" (based chiefly on Grice's notion that an addresser intends "to produce some effect in an audience by means of the recognition of *this intention*") and thus categorized as "R-intentions."[213] Linguistic communication, then, is an inferential process of recognizing the R-intention of an utterance. The locutionary act constitutes the linguistic content of *what is said*, but is often ambiguous and underdetermined. Addressees interpret *what is said* through the meaning of the words and through intentional reflexive and recognizable inference based on Mutual Contextual Beliefs (MCBs) shared by both addresser and addressee.[214] A successful IA occurs when addressees reflexively recognize both the illocutionary intention to produce a certain effect as well as the effect itself.[215] According to Bach/Harnish, types of IAs are distinguished by types of illocutionary intents. These types derive from a selective use of both Austin and Searle's taxonomies: Constatives, Directives, Commissives, and Acknowledgments.[216] With all of this, for Bach/Harnish the "SAS represents the pattern of inference a hearer follows in identifying a speaker's illocutionary intent" while "linguistic communication essentially involves the speaker's issuing an utterance with an R-intention whose fulfillment consist in its recognition."[217] According to Bach/Harnish, the utterance, locutionary, and illocutionary acts are all intentional "and are generally performed with the primary intention of achieving some perlocutionary effect."[218] More specifically, IAs are characteristically the means to PEs and not vice versa which correlates with the perlocutionary notions of Searle and Alston.[219]

---

212. See ibid., 4–8; see also Sadock, "Speech Acts," 63–64.
213. See Bach/Harnish, *Linguistic Communication*, xiv, 15–16, 39–40. Bach continues to maintain this notion (see his "Speech Acts," 153; "Pragmatics," 469–70, 485 n. 7).
214. See Bach/Harnish, *Linguistic Communication*, 5–7.
215. See ibid., 15.
216. The final classification replaces Austin's Behabitive and Searle's Expressive. See ibid., 39–55; see also Bach, "Philosophy of Language," 466–67.
217. Bach/Harnish, *Linguistic Communication*, 84.
218. Ibid., 17.
219. See ibid., 81–83.

The notion of *standardization* corresponds to Grice's *generalized* conversational implicatures in distinction from *particularized* implicatures.[220] Bach defines standardization as follows:

> A form of words is standardized for a certain use if this use, though regularized, goes beyond literal meaning and yet can be explained without special conventions. In each case, there is a certain core of linguistic meaning attributable on compositional grounds but a common use that cannot be explained in terms of linguistic meaning alone. The familiarity of the form of words, together with a familiar inference route from their literal meaning to what the speaker could plausibly be taken to mean in using them, streamlines the process of identifying what the speaker is conveying. The inference is compressed by precedent.[221]

Independently while following along similar lines of Morgan's thesis, standardization also involves MCBs that *short-circuit* the SAS. In short, the standardization thesis proposes that an addresser's performative intention is inferable in Gricean fashion, but the precedent for the performative use of an utterance streamlines or short-circuits the inference required on the part of the addressee.[222]

Here is where Bach/Harnish definitively separate themselves from Searle. These two theorists understand performatives operating along the same lines as ISAs. A performative consists of two IAs; they are both *doings* and *statings*.[223] Performatives are true or false statements because "they are literally and directly statements and only *indirectly* promises, pronouncements, etc."[224] Thus, addressers utter literal statements which addressees infer through Gricean principles and precedent to be a second, indirect IA. Bach/Harnish's basic account of performatives is as follows:

> a performative sentence when used performatively is used literally, *directly* to make a statement and *indirectly* to perform the further speech act of the type (an order, say) named by the performative verb ('order').[225]

They specify their thesis by stating:

---

220. For Bach/Harnish, Gricean particularized implicatures are "indirect constatives" (ibid., 170).
221. Kent Bach, "Standardization Revisited," in Kasher, ed., *Pragmatics*, 713.
222. Ibid., 715.
223. Bach/Harnish, *Linguistic Communication*, 203.
224. Kent Bach and Robert M. Harnish, "How Performatives Really Work: A Reply to Searle," *Linguistics and Philosophy* 15 (1992): 93.
225. Ibid., 98 (italics mine).

Performatives are but a special case of indirect speech acts, in which the audience identifies one communicative intention by way of identifying another. They are special only insofar as the direct statement explicitly specifies which type of act (e.g., a promise) is being performed indirectly. But the fact that this is explicitly specified plays no special role in the performance of the act, in the making of the promise. Explicitly specifying the act type merely facilitates the audience's inference by eliminating the need to search for a plausible candidate.[226]

Bach/Harnish also distinguish between conventionalized and nonconventionalized performatives as "conventions provide a substitute for inference." Performatives involving convention are utterances directly associated with specific institutional situations along with specific form of words designating the performance of the act such as adjourning a meeting, christening a ship, etc. Thus, conventional IAs require a different description from their SAS theory. Yet, "precedents without conventions compress inferences"; the inference is short-circuited because of standardization of form or precedent in use. There is "a wide variety of forms of words which have come standardized for specific indirect uses, forms which serve to streamline or compress the audience's inference process" in the same way as the ISA (2a) operates.[227] Ultimately, performatives do not succeed by conformity to convention, but by the recognition of R-intentions.[228] For Bach/Harnish, even an addressee unaware of the standardized performative formula could inferentially discern the intention of an addresser as in the case of the utterance *I order you to leave* with the following steps:

1. She/He is saying *I order you to leave.*
2. She/He is stating that she/he is ordering me to leave.
3. If her/his statement is true, then she/he must be ordering me to leave.
4. If she/he is ordering me to leave, it must be her/his utterance that constitutes the order (what else could it be?).
5. Presumably, she/he is speaking the truth.
6. Therefore, in stating that she/he is ordering me to leave, she/he is ordering me to leave.[229]

---

226. Ibid., 103–104.
227. Ibid., 98.
228. See Bach/Harnish, *Linguistic Communication*, 108–34.
229. Ibid., 208; idem, "How Performatives Really Work," 99 (pronouns revised).

Bach/Harnish's understanding of the nature of ISAs matches closely to Searle's view as an indirect IA is performed subordinately to another (usually literal) IA with its success tied to the first act. In his later work, Bach correspondingly claims that with ISAs "a single utterance is the performance of one illocutionary act by way of performing another."[230] That said, Bach/Harnish view ISAs operating along the same lines as their inferential scheme for direct speech acts which completely contrasts Searle's program. Another difference from Searle is the inclusion of both literal and nonliteral utterances in their description of ISAs.[231] Thus, for Bach/Harnish one can perform a speech act (a) directly or indirectly, by way of performing another speech act, (2) literally or non-literally, depending on how we are using our words, and (3) explicitly or inexplicitly, depending on whether the speaker spell outs what she/he is doing. With regards to indirection

> a single utterance is the performance of one speech act by way of performing another. For example, by way of asking a question we can make a statement ('Are you kidding?') or a request ('Do you have a quarter?'), and by way of making a statement we can give permission ('The door is open') or refuse an invitation, as when Garbo said 'I want to be alone'). Strictly speaking, what is indirect is not the refusal (e.g.) but its means of communicative success. That is, the intended inference route from the utterance to the refusal is by way of the statement.[232]

Regarding how ISAs express meaning, Bach/Harnish recognize that the Idiom/Ambiguity Thesis correctly points to formalized expressions, but the insurmountable weakness is its failure to show how indirect acts relate to direct acts evidenced by sentences expressing two meanings which for them standardization overcomes. Searle's Conventionality Thesis (i.e., convention of usage) heads in the right direction, but its main weakness centers on the fact that the variety of linguistic forms expressing ISAs are too open-ended for a restricted conventional explanation. "A wide variety of relations between sentences and illocutionary acts can constitute their indirect illocutionary act potential."[233] Drawing a line between these two proposals, (2a) is a *standardized* request. In this instance, the SAS

---

230. Bach, "Pragmatics," 468.
231. Bach/Harnish, *Linguistic Communication*, 70–81; see also Bach, "Philosophy of Language," 468–69.
232. Bach/Harnish, "How Performatives Really Work," 96–97.
233. Bach/Harnish, *Linguistic Communication*, 192; see also Bach, "Standardization Revisited," 714–15.

process of inference is short-circuited and thus the addressee does not have to first rule out the literal intent as primary and then second infer the addresser's indirect intent. Rather, the utterance itself as well as the context activate the mutual belief that addressers and addressees share so that addressers can reasonably intend and addressees can recognize that illocutionary intention. "Standardized indirect acts are like literal acts in that the identity of the speaker's illocutionary intent is the first candidate to be arrived at in the process of inference."[234]

ISAs, Sentence Types, and Illocutionary Forces. As I described above, because direct and indirect utterances operate along the same inferential route, Bach/Harnish claim that ISAs are in fact a type of performative which also directly contrasts Searle's claims.[235] Here is where Bach/Harnish's program provides another angle for understanding the performative function of ISAs in relation to the spectrum of strengths paradigm suggested by Thiselton and Briggs. To recall, Warnock observed that Austin identified two sub-class performative utterances. Each of these types are in fact performatives, but remain distinct, as the former type of utterances count as doing by virtue of *nonlinguistic convention* whereas the latter are all by definition of a certain verbal form—first person present indicative active—and count as doing solely on the level of *linguistic convention*. Thus, although all utterances can rightly be categorized as speech acts, there still remains "a legitimate *sub-class* of utterances called 'performative'" and, in fact, there are "at least two such special sub-classes."[236]

Warnock's analysis finds very close parallels with Searle's reexamination of his understanding of performative utterances in his essay "How Performatives Work."[237] In this essay Searle directly responds to Bach/Harnish's notions on the nature of performatives and specifically their claim that these types of utterances are also statements or assertions. In this later work, Searle also makes a clear distinction between performatives and other IAs which still find antecedents in his earlier

---

234. Bach/Harnish, *Linguistic Communication*, 174, 193, 195–96.
235. Bach/Harnish, "How Performatives Really Work," 98.
236. Warnock, "Performative Utterance," 87.
237. Searle, "How Performatives Work," *Linguistics and Philosophy* 12 (1989): 535–58. This essay was reprinted in Vanderveken and Kubo, eds., *Essays in Speech Act Theory*, 85–107, 288–89 (see the full bibliographic information above and in the Bibliography). I will use Searle's original essay here as this is the work with which Bach/Harnish specifically interact.

IFID criterion. For Searle, "every utterance is indeed a *performance*," but "only a very restricted class are *performatives*" which essentially corresponds to Austin's *explicit performative* category.[238] Thus, performatives are typically "self-referential" sentences as "their meaning encodes the intention to perform the act named in the sentence by the utterance of that very sentence."[239] In direct connection to this notion, these types of utterances are also "self-guaranteeing" as the presence of the intention is inherent in the sentence.[240] The sole illocutionary force that meets these criteria is the Declarative point as such utterances alone "create a new fact corresponding to the propositional content" due to their double directional fit.[241]

Searle's self-referential notion highlights the connection between semantic meaning and performatives in line with his IFID notion. However, as he approaches the end of his analysis he discloses that performatives are *not* designated by some special semantic property. "Performative speaker meaning includes sentence meaning but goes *beyond* it."[242] What truly distinguishes the performative from all other speech acts is social conventional and institutional rules that enable an utterance to bring about actual changes in the world as represented in the propositional content.[243] In contrast to supernatural declarations made by God, human speakers have a "quasi-magical power" derived from "human agreement" that enables a performative to change the world.[244] Searle further identifies within his performative/declarative two types which come quite close to Warnock's observation of Austin's notions: *extralinguistic declarations* and *linguistic declarations*. Both are speech acts and are "performed by way of performative utterances." The former create new facts through extralinguistic conventions such as adjourning a meeting, pronouncing a couple man and wife, or declaring war whereas the latter create new speech acts such as promises, statements, or orders. Because of this special restricted type of utterance, Searle then claims that performative utterances are *not* ISAs.[245]

238. Searle, "How Performatives Work," 536.
239. Ibid., 552.
240. See ibid., 539–43.
241. Ibid., 549, 541. Searle initially posed this conclusion in his work with Vanderveken (*Foundations of Illocutionary Logic*, 3).
242. Searle, "How Performatives Work," 552.
243. See ibid., 554–55.
244. Ibid., 549.
245. Ibid., 540.

What Warnock's and Searle's studies demonstrate is that there are at least two types of performative utterances. Bach/Harnish, though, contend that there is nothing theoretically special about a so-called performative. "They are special only insofar as the direct statement explicitly specifies which type of act (e.g., a promise) is being performed indirectly."[246] As even Searle acknowledges, these two theorists present a strong case initially because addressers can express a performative type sentence without a specific verb naming that performance (e.g., *I will go to lunch with you*).[247] Second, the performative verb naming the act thesis falls prey to the semantic or linguistic underdeterminacy thesis. For Searle, though, performative verbs are unambiguous,[248] but Bach/Harnish among others demonstrate the fact that a so-called performative verb can be used in a non-performative sense as in reporting *I promise* rather than actually promising.[249] A performative utterance is rather identified through Gricean inferential principles. As shown above, Bach/Harnish acknowledge that a so-called explicit performative plays a theoretical special role, though not in the performance of the act of promising, but in its communication. Thus, any utterance can function as a performative or a strong IA; however and importantly, not every utterance is a performative. This latter fact is exactly what Thiselton and Briggs are trying to correct within biblical studies which I also think is fundamental to the interpretive significance of SAT.

Jennifer Hornsby's reciprocity thesis adds an important dimension here.[250] For Hornsby, the "true significance of *illocution* is shown when speech act theory is located in a broader, social context."[251] Agreeing with Warnock and Strawson, Hornsby criticizes Austin, as well as Searle and Daniel Vanderveken, that illocutions are solely marked by nonlinguistic convention.[252] For Hornsby, although IAs "require consequences of a sort," "they require no specific conventions beyond the locutionary ones which (arguably) are presupposed to them." Thus, the only element Hornsby sees as necessary for successful illocutions is what she calls "reciprocity," which replaces convention as the key to illocution. The "speaker relies only on a certain receptiveness on her audience's part for her utterance to

---

246. Bach/Harnish, "How Performatives Really Work," 103.
247. Ibid., 97; Searle, "How Performatives Work," 554.
248. Searle, "How Performatives Work," 540.
249. Bach/Harnish, "How Performatives Really Work," 98.
250. Jennifer Hornsby, "Illocution and Its Significance," in Tsohatzidis, ed., *Foundations of Speech Act Theory*, 187–207.
251. Ibid., 187.
252. See ibid., 191–92, 202.

work for her as illocutionarily meant: the audience takes her to have done what she meant to."²⁵³ Reciprocity, then, occurs through (a) the semantic content (i.e., locution) of the utterance and (b) the linguistic receptiveness of language users within a society.

With all this, I want to highlight the language Hornsby uses to describe her understanding of reciprocity as "normal linguistic exchange" and especially as it closely corresponds to the above ideas of Bach/Harnish as well as Grice. First, her goal to demonstrate that an idea of illocution reveals the *use* of words to be communicative action highlights pragmatics for listeners to decipher the meaning of a speech act. Second, in line with the former theorists, "one speech act can arise from another, more basic one" as illustrated by the statement *There's a bull*. Third, reciprocity includes addressees drawing inferences from addressers' utterances. Hornsby claims that when "reciprocity obtains between people, they are such as to *recognize* one another's speech as it is meant to be taken."²⁵⁴ Further, "whatever the particular language, it is a condition of its normal successful use—of speakers' intended communicative acts actually being done—that people be sufficiently in harmony, as it were, to provide for *recognition* of what speakers are up to."²⁵⁵ Here Hornsby's language has affinities with Grice's M-intentions and Bach/Harnish's R-intentions, which to recall refers to addressers' utterances intending to produce some effect for addressees to inferentially *recognize* the intended meaning of the utterance. Reciprocity provides this *intention recognition* which occurs through both the linguistic form and the social assumptions of language users. Hornsby more explicitly talks in terms of pragmatic processes when she describes how "speakers can *exploit*, in addition to their knowledge of a language, the existence of reciprocity."²⁵⁶ Here she implicitly points to Grice's maxims and the exploitation of such to generate intended implicatures.

Although Hornsby does not explicitly appeal to Grice or Bach/Harnish to develop or support her conclusions, as I have attempted to illustrate above her descriptions of reciprocity correlates with basic, fundamental pragmatic notions which both compliments as well as supplements Gricean principles. Hornsby's suggestion of reciprocity provides an important aspect to the interpretive grid for addressers and addressees to successfully engage in communicative action. Perhaps Hornsby's reciprocity thesis shows how Gricean notions are more intuitive than typically

253. Ibid., 192.
254. Ibid.
255. Ibid., 193 (italics mine).
256. Ibid. (italics mine).

considered by language specialists. More importantly, reciprocity helps to conceive ISAs *counting as* IAs as understood by addressers and addressees. Much earlier, Dennis W. Stampe argued along similar lines as Hornsby.[257] He also finds problems with Austin and Searle's focus on conventionalism and in particular Searle's semantic rules and IFID criterion, which in the end for Stampe proves "Inessential."[258] According to Stampe, it is simply addressers intending an utterance as a warning, promise, assertion, remark, suggestion, report, or request that makes it such an expression while addressees inferentially determine which IA addressers intend. Noun Phrases illustrate well how addressers can intend any linguistic form to express an IA. Green highlights such expressions to support the fact "that illocutionary force is conveyed as an inference the addressee is expected to make from the utterance of a form with some ostensible literal meaning and the mutually assumed context in which it is uttered."[259] Noun Phrases such as *Police!*, *Lunchtime!*, and *My car!* can convey an intended IA in a particular communicative context. During a bank robbery an addresser shouts *Police!* which implicates a warning to the thieves that they need to hurry and finish the task and/or immediately start running! Yet, the same Noun Phrase shouted by a robber additionally implicates an unintended announcement to the employees and patrons that could convey a sense of relief and/or further anxiety. Apart from a specific communicative context, though, such an expression possesses numerous possible IAs. Green illustrates this with the expression *The laundry!*

That thunderstorm is wetting my laundry that's hanging out to dry!

I/You have to pick up the laundry before the cleaner closes in 15 minutes!

I/You have to remember to do the laundry today.

I forgot to do the laundry!

What have you done to the laundry!?

Green concludes that the "noun phrase itself has no inherent illocutionary force, but as long as the hearer assumes that the speaker is behaving rationally, uttering a noun phrase will implicate that its referent is relevant to the speaker's and/or addressee's goals (whether or not these goals correspond to goals of the ongoing conversation)."[260] Thus, the use of

---

257. Dennis W. Stampe, "Meaning and Truth in the Theory of Speech Acts," in Cole and Morgan, eds., *Syntax and Semantics 3*, 1–39.
258. Ibid., 3.
259. Green, *Pragmatics*, 114.
260. Ibid., 115 (see pages 113–16).

specific verbs as well as other semantic indicators can explicitly enhance an addressees recognition of an intended IA, but all types of linguistic forms have the capacity to convey diverse types of illocutionary forces.[261] In line with this, Green concludes that

> the number of potential illocutionary forces is not limited (to around four) by the number of basic sentence types, or (to a couple of thousand) by the number of verbs in a language that can be used "performatively," but only by the number of different kinds of intentions which a speaker might have (in saying what she says) and which an addressee assuming that the speaker is abiding by the Cooperative Principle could be intended and expected, given the utterance in its context, to infer that the speaker has. Probably there are an infinite number of such intentions.[262]

Alston's notion that a sentence has a specific IAP based on the primary condition of taking responsibility compliments Stampe's and Green's conclusions concerning addresser intentions. Although addressers can use any expression to convey numerous intentions, it appears incontrovertible that not any one sentence has the capacity to express any IA as Alston, as well as Sadock above, argues with his IAP thesis. For instance, an addresser would not normally announce *Police!* to make a promise. Thus, linguistic form and semantic meaning provides some specific interpretive boundaries for potential IAs of specific utterance types. Still, Alston like Searle places the onus of meaning on the semantics of a sentence, but the cooperative communicative context as well as mutual background assumptions and reciprocity play equally, and in numerous instances more vital, interpretive roles for meaning to transpire. Regarding ISAs, Alston does not explicitly apply his IAP notion to such expressions, but his examples (e.g., *That dog bites*, *It* [a bull] *is going to charge*, *The gate is unlocked*) along with Green's *The laundry!* in particular communicative contexts function as ISAs accompanied with specific IAPs.

To draw all this together, Bach/Harnish's performative thesis highlights the fact that every sentence possesses an inherent interpretive dimension, which for me is ultimately undeniable. Explicit performative type sentences that name the act performed reduce the interpretive dimension required while also involve less inferential processing. Yet, as Bach/Harnish demonstrate, such sentences still need interpreting whether or

---

261. For expressions which do not nicely fit into conventional categories that express illocutionary force see Don Larkin and Michael H. O'Malley, "Declarative Sentences and the Rule-of-Conversation Hypothesis," *CLS* 9 (1973): 306–19.

262. Green, *Pragmatics*, 114.

not they *counts as* performative. So, the linguistic content can provide an essential criterion to determine the specific IA type, yet it still remains with addressees to then match the IA type intended by addressers.

It seems quite clear from my research that every speech act theorist includes a dimension of interpretive inference with her/his system; it is often a matter of how much one acknowledges and/or admits to. Searle, as well as Alston, obviously emphasize semantics and nonlinguistic convention over any other criteria when determining IAs; whereas Bach/Harnish center their program on inference to determine the force of a sentence which proposes other problems for how to exactly determine IAs.[263] Significantly, with Searle's restricted performative/declarative category extra-linguistic context becomes a major factor along with mutual agreement within society and background assumptions. Searle is critical of Grice's system of meaning, while at the same time finds his scheme displaying some merit[264] and vice-versa.[265] That said, Searle, as well as Austin, focus their version of SAT on how we do things with words that go *beyond* words.[266] For Searle, what goes *beyond saying* is the intended IA meaning as well as the derived intended PE while for Grice his focus is on *what is implicated*, yet, as I have presented above, although implicature extends *beyond* it also *derives* from *what is said* to one degree or another.[267]

I also find it quite significant that Searle's conception of ISAs directly conflict with his SAT linguistic emphasis as clearly the intended ISA goes beyond *what is said*, but he still *counts* the intended meaning of the indirect utterance *as* an IA. Addressees use and calculate from the linguistic content of the indirect saying to derive from and interpret the intended meaning. To recall, Searle's criteria for a performative is identified by the performative sentence token, the performative verb (e.g., *I promise*), which constitutes the act named by the performative expression in the sentence. It is the literal meaning of the sentence uttered

---

263. So, e.g., Sadock, "Speech Acts," 64.

264. Cf. Searle, *Speech Acts*, 42–50.

265. Grice confesses that he is "in sympathy with the general character of Searle's method of dealing with linguistic phenomena," but is "not entirely happy about the details of his position" (*Way of Words*, 15).

266. Korta/Perry, "Things with Words," 169.

267. See further Marcelo Dascal's analysis of how Searle and Grice's schemes compliment and need each other as well as how they contrast ("Speech Act Theory and Gricean Pragmatics: Some Differences of Detail that Make a Difference," in Tsohatzidis, eds., *Foundations of Speech Act Theory*, 323–34).

and the institutional fact created by its utterance, e.g., *I promise* creates a promise. Yet, the act of creating the new facts or changes in the world only occurs when successful communication between addresser and addressee transpires.[268] In line with my above conclusions, this extralinguistic necessity also allows, then, for any other type of linguistic form to potentially and pragmatically *count as* performative.

'Indirect' Illocutionary Standardization. Bach/Harnish's standardization program has not gained much support among speech act theorists as well as other language specialists, especially due to its central dependence upon Gricean inferential program and thus producing a quite complicated interpretive system.[269] Their thesis also requires difficult grammatical forms for standardized ISAs. For example, these two theorists consider utterances such as *Can you **please** pass the salt* or *Will you **please** pass the salt?* as "not fully grammatical"; "they are not grammatical interrogatives and cannot be used as literal questions,"[270] which for Sadock and others seems quite improbable to demonstrate.[271] However, Bach/Harnish's short-circuit standardized indirection paradigm provides similar insight as with communicative felicity conditions highlighted by Gordon/Lakoff as well as with Morgan's short-circuit implicature notion.

Despite the problems of the standardization thesis for theorists, Rod Bertolet finds aspects of their basic notions compelling and applies it specifically to ISAs.[272] In short, ISAs such as questions that are also requests do not exist; to ask without asking is as paradoxical as it sounds. Addressers uttering "indirect" type sentences only express one "direct" force. Thus, addressers issue a single intended meaning indirectly; not two different IAs. Bertolet supports his thesis with two interconnected ideas: (a) the standardization of beliefs and/or desires, not standardized illocutionary forces and (b) Grice's understanding of the property of implicatures. Regarding the former, Bertolet rejects Sadock's Idiom model, Searle-Morgan's convention of usage concept, as well as Bach/Harnish's illocutionary standardization thesis as an answer. All that is required to express a request with utterance (2a) is the beliefs and/or desires lying behind the utterance in the Gricean sense. "The implicature

---

268. Searle, "How Performatives Work," 555.
269. See, e.g., Sadock, "Speech Acts," 63–64.
270. Bach/Harnish, *Linguistic Communication*, 199.
271. Sadock, "Speech Acts," 70; *pace* Laurence R. Horn, "Postscript (1995): Neg-Raising: Tinkering with the Short-Circuit," in Kasher, ed., *Pragmatics*, 678.
272. Bertolet, "Indirect Speech Acts?" 335–49.

that the speaker would like to have the salt is all that is required."[273] The suggestions offered by Searle and Morgan as well as Bach/Harnish do not work due to Levinson's observation that there exists numerous ways to indirectly request someone to shut the door. Put another way, because certain types of sentences like (2a) are more amenable to indirection it should not be deduced that such typically used sentences are *exclusively* suitable for such purposes.[274] Thus, because most requests are expressed indirectly such notions of standardization and/or conventional usage do not comprehensively account for the vast array of ISAs.

Concerning the nature of implicatures, Bertolet takes issue with Searle's dual illocutionary force concept and specifically the problem I raised above concerning inferred information possessing the semantic property of an IA. Whereas Searle and Morgan as well as Bach/Harnish accuse the Idiom model of postulating unnecessary meanings Bertolet in turn accuses these theorists of positing unnecessary IAs. "Speakers have no need to perform second non-literal illocutionary acts to make points that they already made clear."[275] Bertolet's dismissal of Searle's ISA theory is based in Grice's own understanding of conversational implicatures. As discussed above, he notes that Grice does not consider implicatures as *additional* literal assertions. One indirectly implies something through an assertion, but an implicature is not an indirect assertion.

What is standardized, then, for Bertolet is the beliefs and/or desires that lie behind an utterance, not a second indirect IA. Thus, (2a) expresses the force of a request, but in terms of the "'practical effect' rather than 'illocutionary force.'"[276] The utterance functions *as if* it was a request, but *is not an actual* request. According to Bertolet, we "may need something like standardization, as characterized by Bach/Harnish, to explain the short-circuiting that 'Can you…?' formulations seem to exhibit, but this need only involve a standardized way of indicating that one has a certain desire, and not a standardized way of making a request."[277] The difference here with Bach/Harnish along with Searle is that only one so-called direct intention is uttered: the implicated force calculated through Gricean pragmatics. Because of Bertolet's understanding of standardization it is simply unnecessary to incorporate a second IA in order to explain how addressers interpret an indirect utterance. Sentence (2a) is standardly used

---

273. Ibid., 340.
274. Ibid., 343–44.
275. Ibid., 344.
276. See ibid., 346.
277. Ibid., 347.

to request the passing of salt when accompanied with the mutual belief of such desired action and additionally the literal force of the utterance violates the Gricean CP.[278]

Although Bertolet slightly differs from Bach/Harnish, his thesis falls under the same criticism leveled against the standardization concept.[279] That said, Bertolet presents some important conclusions concerning the central questions of this study. First, it is incorrect to assume that only standardized or conventional types of utterances can express intended meanings distinct from their linguistic form. Rather, addressers can employ a variety of indirect type utterances which addressees can successfully decipher through general Gricean principles. Second, Bertolet observes that Grice typically views implicatures as implied information, not actual assertions. In conjunction with this, he also points out the conceptual problem raised above with Searle of treating an implicature as possessing the actual property of an IA when it is simply an inferred meaning derived from a literal utterance; thus an indirect type utterance should be considered *as if* it had that semantic property rather than possessing that actual property. Bertolet's dismissal of the ISA phenomenon, though, is problematic due to the fact that certain utterances like (2a) contain a literal linguistic form that does not semantically correspond to its indisputable *use* as a request which the majority of theorists acknowledge and even Bertolet cannot ultimately escape in his own articulation of these types of utterances. Clearly (2a) has a literal interrogative element as well as an implied meaning and thus it remains legitimate to distinguish between as well as identify a direct speech act and an ISA within a certain type of utterance. Thus, the basic Searlian dual illocutionary force notion remains viable; however, the question of how indirect information can be legitimately considered an IA still remains to be answered. In a preliminary way, one could begin by employing Searlian notions to Bertolet's critique and propose that (2a) does not have the property of a request, but in certain contexts *counts as* a request[280] which I will explore in more detail below.

Daniel Vanderveken and Non-Literal Speech Acts. Vanderveken has produced a large body of work on SAT[281] with some of his research done in collaboration with Searle while his own work often closely correlates with this same theorist. His research on nonliteral utterances

---

278. See ibid., 341–42.
279. So Sadock, "Speech Acts," 70.
280. Bertolet briefly talks in these terms ("Indirect Speech Acts?" 337).
281. See the Bibliography.

and ISAs is quite similar to Searle's, but also differs in significant ways. Vanderveken's basic thesis regarding these two types of utterances and ordinary conversations is as follows:

> Firstly, the primary illocutionary act of the utterance is different from the literal speech act in the cases of metaphor, irony and indirect speech acts. Secondly, the speaker often means to perform secondary non literal illocutionary acts such as conversational implicatures.[282]

Before heading into any specifics, I need to make several observations from these lines. First and similar to Searle, Vanderveken understands nonliteral utterances and ISAs containing two IAs; a literal and nonliteral. Second and different from Searle, the terms "secondary" and "primary" refer to the inferred IA. Third and also distinctly he treats nonliteral utterances and ISAs very similarly.[283] Fourthly, he employs Gricean conversational principles, but not without certain qualifications and revisions which I will present below. Finally and relatedly, Vanderveken talks in terms of nonliteral IAs as implicatures.[284]

An important aspect to Vanderveken's entire SAT program and as expected his description of nonliteral speech acts is the notion of direction of fit. A successful performance of an IA depends upon the condition of satisfaction and specifically the success of fit between language and the

---

282. Vanderveken, "Universal Grammar and Speech Act Theory," in Vanderveken and Kubo, eds., *Essays in Speech Act Theory*, 51 (Vanderveken italicizes these lines); see also idem, "Non-Literal Speech Acts and Conversational Maxims," in Lepore and Van Gulick, eds., *John Searle and his Critics*, 371. Vanderveken sees his work on nonliteral utterances and ISAs as expanding upon his work with Searle in *Foundations of Illocutionary Logic*.

283. As evidenced above, Vanderveken treats nonliteral utterances and ISAs in the exact same way while he often uses the terms "nonliteral" and "indirect speech act" interchangeably. That said, it does appear he wants to differentiate to some degree between how the nonliteral utterance derives from the literal sentence-meaning and how an ISA stems from the literal sentence-meaning (see Vanderveken, "Universal Grammar," 57–59). For this reason I hesitate to present Vanderveken's descriptions of these two types of utterances exactly in the same way. What is clear, though, is that Vanderveken sees nonliteral utterances and ISAs deriving from the literal linguistic form of a sentence.

284. Although Vanderveken describes ISAs in conversational implicature terms he also claims that "Grice purely and simply confuses the primary non-literal speech acts and the conversational implicatures" ("Non-Literal Speech Acts," 376). However, Vanderveken does not explicitly explain how Grice confuses these ideas.

world. When such a fit does not occur this is a result of either a failure of the utterance or an intentional violation or exploitation of the conversational background of the utterance.[285]

To develop his basic ideas, Vanderveken first claims that the proper task of pragmatics "is to explain our capacity to perform and understand non literal illocutionary acts."[286] Pragmatics must answer two fundamental questions:

1. How do addressers succeed in getting addressees to understand that what they mean is not identical with what the sentence that they use means in the context of the utterance?
2. Once addressees have understood that, how do they succeed in identifying non-literal speech acts?[287]

For Vanderveken, in order to answer these questions both the theory of speaker-meaning as well as the theory of sentence-meaning are equally necessary within the larger task of pragmatics. The latter is accomplished through SAT which also addresses the first question and the former through Gricean principles which answers the second. Thus, in order for addressers to successfully express nonliteral utterances they rely on: (a) addressees' knowledge of the meaning of the used sentence as well as their ability to understand the success and satisfaction conditions of the literal IA; (b) their mutual knowledge of certain facts in the conversational background; and (c) addressees' ability to make inferences based on the hypothesis of the respect of conversational maxims. With this, Vanderveken concurs with Grice's hierarchical framework of implicatures deriving from linguistic sentences as "it is not possible to understand the primary non-literal speech act without having *first* identified the literal speech act and without having understood that this literal act cannot be the primary speech act in the context of the utterance, given that the speaker respects the conversational maxims in that context."[288]

---

285. Ibid., 380, 373. For the concept of direction of fit, see Searle, *Expression and Meaning*, 12–20; see also Daniel Vanderveken, "A Complete Formulation of a Simple Logic of Elementary Illocutionary Acts," in Tsohatzidis, ed., *Foundations of Speech Act Theory*, 105–106; see also Adams, *Performative Nature*, 28–29.
286. Vanderveken, "Universal Grammar," 52.
287. Vanderveken, "Non-Literal Speech Acts," 372 (pronouns revised).
288. Ibid., 372 (italics mine); see also idem, "Universal Grammar," 52–53.

With all this in mind, Vanderveken uses while also revises Grice's maxims of Quality and Quantity. Regarding the former, an IA of *perfect quality* is felicitous when it is successful, nondefective, and satisfied. Vanderveken's maxim of Quality is: *Let the illocutionary act that you mean to perform be felicitous in the context of your utterance!* This generalized version allows for all types of IAs, not restricted to simply assertions or true and false statements as in Grice's account.[289] Thus, Vanderveken includes specific sub-maxims of Quality for each possible illocutionary force such as for promises, commands, etc. In particular, Vanderveken describes the sub-maxim of Quality for assertions as: *Let your assertion represent how things are in the world. Let it be an assertion supported by evidence, sincere and true!* With the maxim of Quantity, an IA of *perfect quantity* is an utterance expressed as strong as required. Particular IAs are naturally stronger than others and thus require more felicity conditions to achieve their intended linguistic purposes. With this in mind, Vanderveken's generalized maxim of Quantity is: *Let the illocutionary act that you mean to perform be as strong as required (neither too strong nor too weak)!* And as with the Quality maxim, this maxim includes specialized sub-maxims in contrast to Grice's isolated assertive cases which solely function as informative.[290]

Vanderveken also finds Grice's properties of Cancelability and Nondetachability important for his framework to discover when addressers say more than the literal linguistic form. Because nonliteral utterances are cancelable, in order for addressers to mean more than the literal sentence then certain felicity conditions must be achieved. With the failure of these conditions the sentence-meaning can only be literal. Because nonliteral speech acts are nondetachable, certain conditions relative to the linguistic form and the conversational background must be sufficient for the speaker-meaning to differ from sentence-meaning. With the failure of these conditions the speaker-meaning cannot match sufficiently with the literal sentence-meaning.[291]

All this in place, Vanderveken expands upon his above thesis in more pragmatic terms:

---

289. Vanderveken, "Universal Grammar," 53.

290. See ibid., 53–54. The above maxims represent Vanderveken's most recent versions which differ slightly from his earlier descriptions, but are conceptually the same (see "Non-Literal Speech Acts," 376–79).

291. See Vanderveken, "Universal Grammar," 57; idem, "Non-Literal Speech Acts," 374.

First, a speaker means to perform a primary nonliteral speech act when she/he exploits conversational maxims and second she/he implies conversationally that she/he performs a secondary nonliteral illocution when she/he uses such maxims in the context of her/his utterance.[292]

Vanderveken explains his claims here by describing what transpires with the exploitation of his maxims. In general, when addressers exploit a maxim an apparent violation of the maxim occurs at the literal sentence-meaning level whereas the primary, nonliteral IA is felicitous. Addressers exploit the maxim of Quality when they intend addressees to recognize the incompatibility between the conversational background facts and the felicity conditions of the literal speech act. Addressers exploit the maxim of Quantity when they intend addressees to recognize that the literal speech act is not strong enough to achieve their intended linguistic purposes. With the exploitation of a maxim addressers are prevented from performing the literal speech act.

Irony for Vanderveken is a prime case of the exploitation of the maxim of Quality whereby the speaker-meaning is in opposition to the sentence-meaning. For instance, an addresser can ironically complain *Thank you very much for your help!* whereby she/he wants the addressee to recognize that she/he is very dissatisfied with the lack of help. At the literal level the sincerity conditions are violated, but at the nonliteral level the opposite felicity conditions are satisfied. An ISA is a premier instance of exploiting the maxim of Quantity. For example, with the understatement in a particular conversational context *That painting is not bad!* an addresser exploits the maxim of Quantity; however, the felicity conditions are met as the addresser indirectly means to convey a stronger assertion than the literal one which she/he intends the addressee to recognize that she/he is obviously quite impressed by the painting.

What is significant about Vanderveken's work is his revisionary use of Gricean principles when describing ISAs and nonliteral utterances that necessarily broadens the maxims applicability. It is important to highlight again that Vanderveken views both nonliteral and ISAs containing two IAs. An ironic utterance comprises of a primary nonliteral IA as well as a literal IA. Irony is expressed through an ironic illocutionary force (primary speech act) and an ironic propositional content (literal speech act). With ISAs addressers perform an indirect speech act by way of performing the literal speech act; "speaker-meaning is always an extension of sentence

---

292. Vanderveken, "Universal Grammar," 57 (Vanderveken italicizes these lines; pronouns revised).

meaning."²⁹³ With both of these types of utterances, speaker-meaning derives from sentence-meaning; the primary ironic act and indirect illocutionary act stem from a literal speech act. Thus, nonliteral utterances and ISAs both have a literal IA and a nonliteral, primary IA and both components are necessary for addressers to convey their intended meaning that differs in one way or another from the literal sentence-meaning. Although Vanderveken does not explicitly deal with metaphorical language, his treatment of nonliteral IAs appears to fall more in line with Tsohatzidis's conclusions and critique of Searle's notion that metaphor is always an instance of speaker-meaning.

Vanderveken's ISA dual IA descriptions retain the same problems raised with Searle's scheme while also displaying insight. The latter is especially true with his felicity condition descriptions which extend further than Searle's and Gordon/Lakoff's as he explicitly links these to Grice's conversational maxims. In short, when the felicity conditions in question fail with the literal sentence-meaning then the addresser cooperating conversationally is intentionally exploiting a maxim while also fulfilling the necessary conditions with the nonliteral, primary IA. Along these lines, Vanderveken claims that "a speaker *means to perform a primary non-literal speech act* if and only if she/he *exploits one or several conversational maxims* and second that she/he *means to implicate conversationally* something if and only if she/he uses one or several maxims in the context of her/his utterance."²⁹⁴ Also important for my purposes, Vanderveken includes a sincerity condition as well as directional fit with his sub-maxim of Quality for assertions. Yet, like Searle, Vanderveken does not explicitly include PEs with his ISA descriptions.

Indirect Speech Acts and Direction of Fit. David Holdcroft's proposal for interpreting ISAs incorporates Searle's concept of directional fit as well as Gricean conversational principles.²⁹⁵ Whereas Vanderveken more so assumes the necessity of direction of fit, Holdcroft centralizes this criterion for identifying ISAs. Towards the development of his ideas, Holdcroft concentrates on Searle's speech act program. Holdcroft initially finds problems with his basic theory and specifically his IFID concept due to the typical indeterminacy of sentence-meaning apart from a communicative context. In particular, Declaratives meet other propositional content conditions and thus can be used to express a variety of forces

---

293. Vanderveken, "Universal Grammar," 59.
294. Vanderveken, "Non-Literal Speech Acts," 380 (pronouns revised).
295. Holdcroft, "Indirect Speech Acts," 350–64.

while without a context such an utterance cannot express a force at all. Holdcroft also finds problems with Searle's ISA scheme; it is correct in principle and is "the right explanation" with certain types of utterances, but it remains difficult to sustain with every type.[296] For example, with the utterance *I want you to VP* Searle's scheme understands its direct use determined by its IFID whereas its indirect use is inferred through Gricean principles and not determined by its IFID.[297] Here Holdcroft addresses the second issue I raised with Searle's ISA scheme and specifically the problem of a conflict of conditions of satisfaction. Searle's theory in this instance requires "the joint satisfaction of felicity conditions which are meant to be exclusive." An equally difficult problem raised by Searle's scheme is his inferential procedure that corresponds to Grice's which requires the initial identification of the direct IA before the subordinate indirect IA. Sentences like *I want you to VP* represent a standardized way of making a request and does not necessitate identifying a prior assertive; it can be "non-deviantly used to request without asserting anything at all" and thus there is no recoverable direct act underlying the indirect one; only the indirect act is expressed with such types of sentences.[298] Consequently, an utterance is *either* direct or indirect; *not both simultaneously*. Moreover, no difference in kind exists between Searle's direct and indirect utterances as "in *both* cases identification involves inferences in an assumed context."[299]

Holdcroft's answer to these two issues consists of an interdependent interpretive procedure that combines the propositional content of an utterance and the direction of fit between language and the world along with the overall communicative context. Within Searle's system, Assertives have a words-to-world (↓) fit; Directives and Commissives have world-to-words (↑) fit; Expressives do not have a directional fit; and Directives have both directional fits (↕).[300] This interdependence for Holdcroft results from the fact that in order for a certain type of act there must be an appropriate direction of fit and in order to have such a language-world match there must be a suitable content clause.[301] Thus, in order for a direction of fit to occur items must match, which consists of possible states of affairs and representatives of them which are referentially or indexically linked

296. Ibid., 359.
297. Ibid., 357.
298. Ibid., 358.
299. Ibid., 361.
300. See Searle, *Expression and Meaning*, 12–20.
301. Holdcroft, "Indirect Speech Acts," 362.

to them. What makes an utterance have "the word-to-world fit," though, "is not its content p, but the fact that S [speaker] accepts that if not-p, then there is a compelling reason to retract."[302] For example, an addresser utters *You will be there* with the linguistic content allowing for both word-to-world and world-to-word directions of fit. If uttered as an assertion and the person in question at the appropriate time is not there, then a word-to-world mismatch occurs and the addresser must retract the utterance. Yet, if uttered as a request then the world-to-word fit occurs. In a Searlian sense, this sentence as an assertion is in a certain way primary, but because of its linguistic content it can also function as a request; however, an assertive interpretation is no more direct than the Directive one. The particular communicative context of the utterance ultimately determines the most plausible directional fit.[303]

Holdcroft raises an important point with speech acts in general and specifically ISAs. As I presented above, addressers can use an utterance like (2a) to ask for some information (a direct speech act) *or* to make a request for the addressee to do something (an ISA) simultaneously. The question is how do addressees recognize the intended force? Holdcroft addresses this central dilemma with this type of utterance as an addresser has *one* intended meaning which the addressee is supposed to recognize. Further, within a particular communicative context an utterance only meets the felicity conditions of one IA—a direct one or an indirect one— and Holdcroft's interdependent procedure help towards understanding how addressees recognize the intended meaning. This procedure also alleviates in some ways the assumed necessity of Gricean hierarchal inferential processes; the utterance is either direct or indirect depending upon the communicative context.

Holdcroft confirms how literal linguistic sentence-meaning in the sense of Searle's IFID, as well as Levinson's LFH, provide vital data for identifying potential IAs. Yet, semantic content alone cannot sufficiently provide the sole criterion for determining the meaning of an utterance due to the fact of the semantic vagueness and the diverse uses of IAs. Rather, the interdependent combination of propositional content and direction of fit along with the specific communicative context provide an interpretive grid for determining the specific use of particular utterances. Holdcroft's interpretive proposal, though, does not comprehensively address each type of utterance as some utterances will prove more difficult to determine. His interdependent procedure works well with utterances that include

---

302. Ibid., 363.
303. Ibid.

both Assertive and Directive or Directive and Declarative dimensions (which end up functioning as his prime examples). However, utterances like (2a) that contain a simple interrogative (a question for information) and a Directive dimension do not readily comply with his proposal and interestingly, although he extensively deals with (2a), he does not apply his interpretive solution for such sentence types. That said, this felicity condition of directional fit remains significant within the calculable process as Holdcroft, as well as Vanderveken, demonstrates and below I will explore ways of applying this procedure to ISAs like (2a).

Pragma-Dialectical Approach to Argumentation. Frans H. van Eemeren and Rob Grootendorst focus their research on developing tools for argumentative dialogical discourse while explicitly incorporating SAT as well as Gricean pragmatics. These two specialists find much of Searle's notions insightful, but needing adjustments and revisions in a general sense and specifically for implementing them to argumentative discourse. Van Eemeren/Grootendorst define argumentation as follows:

> Argumentation is a speech act consisting of a constellation of statements designed to justify or refute an expressed opinion and calculated in a regimented discussion to convince a rational judge of a particular standpoint in respect of the acceptability or unacceptability of that expressed opinion.[304]

Similar to the notions of Bach/Harnish, these two authors also observe that the use of IAs "in colloquial speech depends strongly on pragmatic conventions. One indication of this is that *implicit* and *indirect* IAs are as a rule understood perfectly and the addresser can also assume in principle that they will be understood, so that it is plausible that other conventions besides strictly semantic ones will (also) play a role."[305] Towards developing their argumentation thesis, they integrate Searlean notions concerning SAT and Gricean concepts on conversational maxims. In short, van Eemeren/Grootendorst revise Grice's CP to develop an understanding of speech acts.

According to van Eemeren/Grootendorst, developing argumentation as a speech act clashes with Searle's SAT in three specific ways. First, unlike asserting, requesting, or promising, with argumentation more than

---

304. Frans H. Van Eemeren and Rob Grootendorst, *Speech Acts in Argumentative Discussions: A Theoretical Model for the Analysis of Discussions Directed towards Solving Conflicts of Opinion*, PDA 1 (Dordrecht-Holland/Cinnaminson: Foris Publications, 1984), 18.

305. Ibid., 22.

one proposition is *always* involved: one explicit and the other implicit or "unexpressed premises."[306] Second, the sentence uttered in an argumentation expresses two illocutionary, or as they prefer, *communicative forces* simultaneously.[307] The utterance functions in an argumentative sense and also as an assertion, question, advice, proposal etc. This adjustment of Searle's parallels Sadock's and others observations that utterances are often multidimensional IAs. Finally, argumentative speech acts do not stand alone as isolated speech acts as Searle typically analyzes, but they occur in a constellation of interrelated speech acts[308] which does have some affinities, though, with Searle/Vanderveken's observations (see n. 68). Van Eemeren/Grootendorst suggest that to resolve these differences, a distinction must be made between the communicative forces at the *sentence* and *textual* levels. The sentence level consists of minimal communicative units which contain *elementary speech acts*. The textual level is where communication between language users occurs which only has the communicative force of argumentation expressed by illocutionary complexes. *Complex speech acts* aim "at convincing another person of the acceptability of a standpoint."[309]

Van Eemeren/Grootendorst conceive the total speech act containing two distinct aspects: (1) the IA relating to the communicative aspect expressed in the attempt to achieve understanding and (2) the perlocutionary act relating to the interactional aspect expressed in the attempt to achieve acceptance.[310] These two specialists see the acceptance of an argumentative standpoint as a perlocutionary, or as they prefer, *interactional effect* of the complex speech act. They also recognize that speech act theorists have paid very little attention to perlocutionary acts. PEs in a Searlean sense directly derive from IAs as the latter bring about specific effects on the actions, thoughts, beliefs, etc. upon addressees. Consequently, the addressee "is always deemed to play a purely *passive role* and no account is taken of the *interactional aspect* of language." However, addressees interactionally engage in conversations and thus actively participate in the perlocutionary dimension of a speech act. For van Eemeren/Grootendorst, most conversations between language users and certainly with discussions

---

306. See ibid., 32, 119–49.

307. Van Eemeren/Grootendorst do not see this dual illocutionary force paralleling ISAs (ibid., 32–33).

308. See ibid., 33.

309. Frans H. Van Eemeren and Rob Grootendorst, "Speech Act Conditions as Tools for Reconstructing Argumentative Discourse," *Argumentation* 3 (1989): 368–69.

310. Van Eemeren/Grootendorst, *Argumentative Discussions*, 51.

designed to resolve disputes, the addressee "is expected to decide on rational grounds whether or not she/he should allow the perlocutionary effect desired by the speaker to be brought about."[311] These theorists also see two aspects of interactional effects: *Inherent* perlocutionary effects and *Consecutive* perlocutionary consequences. The former consist exclusively of the *acceptance* of the speech act by addressees whereas the latter comprise *all other consequences* of the speech act. Addressers consciously attempt to achieve both of these perlocutionary goals with a speech act. Van Eemeren/Grootendorst further identify *Inherent* perlocutionary effects as *Minimal* and *Consecutive* perlocutionary consequences as *Optimal*. Addressers *minimally* set out to achieve the PE of *acceptance* by addressees while as a rule complete success of the speech act is completely satisfied *optimally* when the other intended consequences are achieved which lie in the extension of *acceptance*.[312] They also distinguish between consequences which occur accidentally and effects intended by addressers while reserving the phrase perlocutionary act to exclusively refer to the latter.[313]

For van Eemeren/Grootendorst, the illocution and perlocution are two distinct aspects of the total speech act. Thus, these two specialists identify a direct speech act as an "illocutionary perlocution." For example, when an addresser expresses a threat the threat aspect constitutes the illocution while the perlocution constitutes the intimidation of the addressee. Van Eemeren/Grootendorst recognize that illocutionary perlocutions appear to resemble ISAs, but a crucial difference between these two expressions

> is that indirect speech acts are performed by means of *two illocutions*, whereas illocutionary perlocutions are performed by means of *one illocution* and *one perlocution*. The only consequence that is required for the 'happiness' of an indirect speech act (as an illocution) is that the listener should recognize both of the two illocutionary forces (and the propositional content) and thus *understand* the illocutions.[314]

Thus, adopting Searle's ISA scheme (2a) expresses a *secondary* illocutionary force of an interrogative and a *primary* illocutionary force of a request.[315] Interestingly, though, van Eemeren/Grootendorst also follow Searle by not explicitly incorporating PEs with their analysis of ISAs.

311. Ibid., 28.
312. Ibid., 24.
313. Ibid., 26–27.
314. Ibid., 53.
315. See ibid., 33, 52–53.

Towards articulating their understanding of speech acts, these two specialists begin by redefining Grice's CP with a more general and succinct phrase *Principle of Communication* that language users be *clear, honest, efficient*, and *to the point*.[316] With this in place, they alternatively describe Grice's four maxims within a speech act account containing five rules of communication:

1. Do not perform any *incomprehensible* speech acts.
2. Do not perform any *insincere* speech acts.
3. Do not perform any *unnecessary* or *superfluous* speech acts.
4. Do not perform any *pointless* or *futile* speech acts.
5. Do not perform any speech acts that *do not appropriately connect to* preceding speech acts.[317]

Rule 1 implements the communication requirement of *Be clear* which roughly corresponds to Searle's Propositional Content and the Essential conditions. Addressers intentionally formulate the speech act in such a way that addressees readily recognize its communicative force and the propositions expressed. Rule 2 implements *Be honest* which corresponds to the conditions of correctness and consists in addressers held responsible for having undertaken the commitments directly associated with the particular speech act uttered. The implication of this honesty requirement corresponds with Searle's Sincerity conditions which Van Eemeren/Grootendorst rename as the *responsibility conditions* to remove any mental aspect to this condition. Rules 3 and 4 implement *Be efficient* which also address the condition of correctness in that the correct performance of a speech act must not be either unnecessary or pointless. These rules correspond to Searle's Preparatory conditions. Rule 5 implements *Keep to the point* and has no parallel with any speech act condition. This relevance requirement concerns the appropriate relation of sequential speech acts as well as the function of a speech act in a particular speech event. This sequence of speech acts includes the original addresser and addressee who may change roles from addresser to addressee.[318]

---

316. Van Eemeren/Grootendorst, "Speech Act Conditions," 371; idem, *Argumentation, Communication, and Fallacies: A Pragma-Dialectical Perspective* (Hillsdale: Lawrence Erlbaum, 1992), 50.

317. Van Eemeren/Grootendorst, *Argumentation*, 50–52; idem, "Speech Act Conditions," 371.

318. Van Eemeren/Grootendorst, "Speech Act Conditions," 371–72; idem, *Argumentation*, 50–52.

With this synthesis framework in place, van Eemeren/Grootendorst propose an inference scheme for both direct speech acts and ISAs:

Table 1.4. Van Eemeren/Grootendorst's General Inference Scheme
for Direct and Indirect Speech Acts

1.
The addresser A has uttered U

2.
If U is taken literally,
A has performed speech act 1,
with communicative function 1
and propositional content 1.

Direct Speech Acts

3a.
In Context C, speech act 1 observes the rules of communication.

4a.
Therefore: Speech act 1 is a correct interpretation of U.

ISAs

3b.
In context C, speech act 1 is a violation of communication rule i.

4b.
In context C, speech act 2 observes rule i and all other communicative rules.

5.
Speech act 1, speech act 2 and the context C can be linked by means of rule j.

6.
Therefore: Speech act 2 is a correct interpretation of U.[319]

Along with this scheme, van Eemeren/Grootendorst highlight the importance of context for the proper inferential understanding of ISAs. These two theorists identify weakly conventionalized ISAs operating in well-defined communicative contexts and strongly conventionalized ISAs not occurring in well-defined communicative contexts. Concerning the latter and using (2a) as an example, such expressions are strongly

---

319. Van Eemeren/Grootendorst, *Argumentation*, 55.

conventionalized and appear as if the speech act is not indirect at all, but as a direct request. However, the former comes in to view when an addresser asks *Where can I get a new toaster?* with the addressee responding *Woolworth's toasters are the best!* In this specific, well-defined communicative context the response naturally expresses a piece of advice; however, taken in isolation this exact same response could function as a type of assertion making a claim. Van Eemeren/Grootendorst see ISAs on a type of continuum with strong and weak contextual conventionalization lying at the extreme ends while many others lying between these.[320]

Looking specifically at ISAs, van Eemeren/Grootendorst combine Searle's dual illocutionary force view with their revised Gricean inference scheme. As with Grice, van Eemeren/Grootendorst's Principle of Communication assumes that language users generally try to ensure that their communication goes as smoothly as possible and while performing speech acts they observe certain rules which further this purpose.[321] Also similar to the flouting of Grice's maxims, with ISAs the literal interpretation of the implicit speech act performed involves some violation of a rule of communication. "With the help of the rules of communication, it can also be shown what kind of connection there is between the indirect speech act and the literal utterance." These rules also provide for establishing that the literal interpretation of the speech act is incorrect as well as how the correct interpretation is inferred. The violation of a certain rule, though, is only an *apparent* violation which becomes nullified when the correct interpretation is inferred. For van Eemeren/Grootendorst, the inference of ISAs "can always be accounted for by a fixed scheme of analytical steps. The only thing that varies is the exact rule that is violated and the kind of link between the literal utterance and the indirect speech act."[322]

To illustrate this, van Eemeren/Grootendorst schematically analyze the utterance *Can you get a move on?* As with (2a), taken literally this is a question for information about the physical abilities of the addressee. Based on the assumed contextual knowledge of the addresser about the addressee the literal interpretation of the interrogative violates Rule 3 (no superfluous speech acts) as the addresser already knows the answer. However, if the utterance is interpreted as an indirect request *to move on* then no violation has occurred. Further, Rule 4 (no pointless speech act) enables one to correctly recognize the link between the literal utterance to the ISA. The request has the preparatory condition that the addresser

---

320. See ibid., 56–59.
321. Ibid., 50.
322. Van Eemeren/Grootendorst, "Speech Act Conditions," 377.

knowingly assumes that the addressee is able to comply with the request. If this is not the case then the addresser violates Rule 4 by asking a pointless speech act.[323]

Although concentrating on argumentative discourse, van Eemeren/ Grootendorst's proposals provide a helpful framework for understanding speech acts and specifically ISAs. In their own words, on the one hand compared to Grice's maxims their rules "are more *specific* as a consequence of their connection with the Searlean conditions." While on the other hand, "they are more *general* because they are no longer restricted to assertions, as they are with Grice"[324] which does address the consistent criticism that Gricean principles are too specific to deal with the complexity of language. Van Eemeren/Grootendorst also claims that the conditions for different speech acts are specifications of more general rules of communication. These two specialists also provide a more systematized and accessible integration of Gricean insights into SAT than Bach/Harnish while retaining the seminal notions of both Searle and Grice as well as providing complimentary descriptions to Vanderveken's revisions. Further, their Principle of Communication with its communication requirements and rules/maxims are more precise at points than those offered by Grice as well as Vanderveken while general enough for broader applicability which corresponds with Vanderveken's goals. Van Eemeren/Grootendorst renaming Searle's Sincerity condition as the *responsibility condition* is also helpful while displaying correlations with Alston's *taking responsibility* criterion. They also confirm how PEs ultimately depend upon addressees with their *interactional effect* notion. Further, their understanding of PEs also bears very close affinities with Gu's communicative *transactional* idea and that IAs trigger PEs which are ultimately caused by addressees.[325] Further, their notion that ISAs vary in degree from strongly conventionalized to weakly conventionalized properly highlights the inferential importance of communicative context for interpreting most of these types of expressions.

One general point of critique is that van Eemeren/Grootendorst follow wholesale Searle's five-fold taxonomy.[326] They do define the Searlean taxonomy in argumentative terms which may work for their intended

---

323. For their complete analysis see ibid., 377–78.
324. Ibid., 373 (italics mine).
325. Van Eemeren/Grootendorst do not explicitly engage with Gu's work nor vice versa.
326. See van Eemeren/Grootendorst, *Argumentation*, 37–40; idem, *Argumentative Discussions*, 22–23, 104–18; idem, "Speech Act Conditions," 370.

purposes, but as I described above, communication between language users is far too complex to reduce it to simply five utterance types. They also adopt wholesale Searle's ISA scheme and do not critically engage with the problems raised by Bertolet and others. As I touched on above, as with Searle as well as Vanderveken, van Eemeren/Grootendorst do not explicitly incorporate PEs within their understanding of ISAs. Another issue arises with their analysis of the ISA *Can you get a move on?* Not only is Rule 3 violated, but also Searle's Sincerity condition is flouted, which corresponds to their Rule 2 as well as generally related to the Gricean maxim of Quality (do not say something false). This highlights how more than one rule of communication can be violated to provide criteria for identifying ISAs. Thus, as Pauline Slot suggests, van Eemeren/Grootendorst need to adjust their scheme to allow for such multiple violations because it "is important for the critical analysist to determine exactly which rule(s) is (are) violated, so that he or she can make sure that all violations are rectified with the reconstruction of the intended speech act."[327]

François Récanati and Primary Pragmatic Processes. Récanati has produced a substantial amount of research on the Philosophy of Language over the last thirty years and in particular concerning semantics, pragmatics, SAT, and ISAs. In his initial work on pragmatics and SAT, Récanati approves of and implements Grice's notions on implicatures. However, in his later work he rejects these same Gricean principles. Because his earlier work utilizes Grice's program Récanati's approach would naturally fall within the Inferential approach to ISAs; however, his later work would exclude him from such a category. That said, Récanati's specific approach to ISAs retains some of the basic ideas of Gricean conversational implicatures.

---

327. Slot, *How Can You Say That?*, 72. Slot has other points of critique of van Eemeren/Grootendorst's scheme with one being that their analysis does not properly address embedded ISAs in another ISA or what she identifies as *"multiply indirect speech acts"* such as the sentence *Can I ask if you could move over a bit?* (see ibid., 73–75). Another concerns the function of the literal speech act with ISAs. For Slot, van Eemeren/Grootendorst's inferential scheme for ISAs and specifically the final sixth step "suggests that only the second possibility is accounted for in the scheme." However, both the literal and inferred speech acts are possible and thus their sixth step needs rephrasing to account for this (ibid., 73). What Slot observes is true, but in all fairness van Eemeren/Grootendorst clearly emphasize the interpretive necessity of communicative context in their inferential scheme itself as well as with their elaborative descriptions of ISAs as I presented above (see also van Eemeren/Grootendorst, "Speech Act Conditions," 378).

In his earlier conceptual analysis of ISAs, Récanati explicitly combines the concepts of SAT and Grice's cooperative principles. In these initial descriptions Récanati tends to be a bit perplexing and thus difficult to systematize. In his book *Meaning and Force*, Récanati appears to agree with Searle's notion that ISAs express *two* illocutions.[328] Conversely, in a previously published essay on ISAs he finds such a two-illocutionary account inadequate and argues that only *one* illocution is actually expressed.[329] In this instance, Récanati asserts that as direct performative utterances do not express two different illocutionary acts[330] so also with ISAs it "is much more likely that *only* the indirect illocutionary act is performed."[331] If I understand him correctly, Récanati in both treatises claims in the end that ISAs ultimately express a single intentional indirect illocutionary act *disguised* in a literal illocution.

In his essay, Récanati arrives at this latter conclusion by appealing to Austin's tripartite scheme and specifically his locutionary and illocutionary dimensions. An ISA includes two dimensions: (a) the literal locution indicated by the sentence and (b) the intended illocution actually performed. The literal aspect of the utterance is the *illocutionary act indicated* by the sentence while the intended illocution aspect is the *illocutionary act performed* in uttering the sentence. Thus, with (2a) the addresser performs the *locutionary act* of "asking whether" the addressee can pass the salt (*illocutionary act indicated*) and she/he performs the IA of requesting her/him to do so (*illocutionary act performed*). With this sentence, "the illocutionary act of issuing a directive is performed *indirectly*."[332]

In *Meaning and Force*, Récanati does not engage with Austin's locutionary/illocutionary distinctions. For Récanati here, the problem with ISAs lies with how addressers communicate a hidden intentional force. The way addressees decipher that an indirect utterance expresses a request in certain contexts is determined through Grice's conversational implicatures. On the literal level of an indirect utterance addressers have *violated* the conversational maxims and the only plausible way to reconcile that

---

328. François Récanati, *Meaning and Force: The Pragmatics of Performative Utterances* (Cambridge: Cambridge University Press, 1987), 117–34, cf. 126.

329. Récanati, "Some Remarks on Explicit Performatives, Indirect Speech Acts, and Locutionary Meaning and Truth-Value," in Searle, Kiefer, and Bierwisch, eds., *Speech Act Theory and Pragmatics*, 205–20.

330. On the claim that performatives issue two illocutions see Récanati, "Explicit Performatives," 205–206.

331. Ibid., 206 (emphasis mine).

332. Ibid., 210 (pronouns revised).

they have in fact *obeyed* the maxims is to assume that she/he intends to convey more than literally uttered.[333] Récanati views the reconstruction of the non-literal illocutionary intention of an utterance as follows:

> If the speaker intended to perform *only* the illocutionary act literally indicated by the sentence, her/his utterance would constitute a *violation* of the conversational maxims. But she/he *abides* by these maxims; so she/he *must* intend to perform a *second* illocutionary act such that the utterance that serves to perform this act does indeed *conform* to the maxims. The violation therefore is only apparent.

Récanati goes on to claim that the

> speaker's superficially inexplicable violation of the maxims is a *signal* that they are being obeyed on another level than that of literal communication. It is this *signal* that allows us to recognize that an illocutionary intention has been "disguised," and the assumption that the speaker has obeyed the conversational maxims provides us with a criterion for identifying the intention behind its disguise: The indirect illocutionary act that the hearer attributes to the speaker is the act whose performance, together with that of the literal act, would reconcile the utterance with the conversational maxims.[334]

Grice's conversational maxims thus provide the grid for Récanati to claim that indirect utterances are identifiable, intentional, and IAs.[335] Récanati lays out an addressee's inferential reasoning in the following five steps:

Step 1: S has performed the illocutionary act F(p).

Step 2: S respects the conversational maxims.

Step 3: By performing F(p) in this context, S is violating a conversational maxim M, unless she/he intends to perform, in addition to F(p), another illocutionary act such that M is after all respected.

Step 4: Therefore, S intends to perform, in addition to F(p), a second illocutionary act such that the conversational maxim M, which S would have violated if she/he had intended to perform only F(p), is respected.

---

333. See Récanati, *Meaning and Force*, 125.
334. Ibid., 126 (emphasis mine; pronouns revised).
335. Ibid., 125–26. Récanati cites Grice's "Group C" conversational implicatures as examples for his discussion on ISAs (see Grice, "Logic and Conversation," 33–37).

Step 5: Given the context, the illocutionary act in question must be the act G(q).[336]

From this reasoning, then, addressees inferentially determine which IA addressers intend to perform. Important also for Récanati is that ISAs differ from implying something; ISAs *overtly imply* something and this intentional implication is *mutually manifest* to both addresser and addressee. Thus, it is the context of the utterance that allows addressees to infer that addressers intentionally communicate more than is literally said.

In his later work, Récanati rejects a Gricean approach to speaker-meaning which he identifies as "secondary pragmatic processes" wherein addressees subsequently infer *what is said* from the first identified explicit content of the utterance.[337] Récanati identifies such an approach as Minimalism which sees only a *minimal* distance between sentence-meaning and speaker-meaning. In other words, speaker-meaning departs from the conventional meaning of the sentence only when it is necessary to complete the meaning and make it propositional, i.e., *saturation* (the sole and linguistically mandated contextual process whereby the meaning of a sentence is completed or filled to make it propositional). This approach views *what is said* as part of the literal meaning of the sentence in distinction to speaker-meaning. Conversely, the Maximalist or Non-minimalist position stresses the commonality between sentence-meaning and speaker-meaning which views *what is said* and *what is implicated* as part of speaker-meaning in distinction to the literal sentence-meaning.[338] Relatedly, Récanati adopts a Contextual approach over what he identifies as an Anti-Contextual one, i.e., Gricean pragmatics.[339] For the latter, speaker-meaning derives independently from the context of

---

336. Récanati begins his numerated scheme with direct illocutionary intentions and thus these steps are actually 5–9 (*Meaning and Force*, 129; pronouns revised).
337. Récanati's latest work on speaker-meaning can be found in his book *Literal Meaning*; see also idem, "The Pragmatics of What Is Said," *Mind & Language* 4 (1989): 295–329; idem, *Direct Reference: From Language to Thought* (Oxford: Blackwell, 1993); idem, "The Alleged Priority of Literal Interpretation," *Cognitive Science* 19 (1995): 207–32; idem, *Oratio Obliqua, Oratio Recta: An Essay on Metarepresentation* (Cambridge, MA: MIT Press, 2000); idem, "What Is Said," *Synthese* 128 (2001): 75–91; idem, "Literal/Nonliteral," *Midwest Studies in Philosophy* 25 (2001): 264–74; idem, "Does Linguistic Communication Rest on Inference," *Mind & Language* 17 (2002): 105–26; idem, "Pragmatics and Semantics," 442–62.
338. See Récanati, "What Is Said," 77–79; idem, *Literal Meaning*, 5–6.
339. Cf. Récanati, "Contextualism," 156–66.

the utterance whereas the former views speaker-meaning completely dependent upon context. These approaches represent the two different schools of thought which I described in the beginning of this chapter: Ideal Language Philosophers (meaning derives from semantics: linguistic convention) and Ordinary Language Philosophers (meaning derives from pragmatics: contextual language use).[340] For Récanati, Contextualism, in line with the latter approach, is much preferred over Anti-contextualism or Literalism because it correctly "holds that *speech acts* are the primary bearers of content. Only in the context of a speech act does a sentence express a determinate content."[341] According to Contextualism

> the contrast between what the speaker means and what she/he literally says is illusory, and the notion of 'what the sentence says' incoherent. What is said (the truth-conditional content of the utterance) is nothing but an aspect of speaker's meaning. That is not to deny that there *is* a legitimate contrast to be drawn between what the speaker says and what he or she merely implies. Both, however, belong to the realm of 'speaker's meaning' and are pragmatic through and through.[342]

Récanati's underlying assumptions for his entire program are as follows: (a) sentence-meaning is something more abstract and theoretical than *what is said* and (b) we have "intuitions" concerning *what is said* that serve as a starting point in the process of determining the linguistic meaning of the sentence.[343] The chief problem with the Literalist position is "the assumption that semantic interpretation can deliver something as determinate as a complete proposition"; at best, "it delivers only semantic schemata."[344] With these ideas in place, Récanati appeals to "primary pragmatic processes" that contrasts Gricean minimalist secondary pragmatic processes. Primary processes also involve a two-step process, but does not "*need to antecedently compute the proposition literally expressed.*"[345] In other words, the interpretation of the literal sentence-meaning does not need to be processed first. Interpreting *what is said* derives from primary processes whereas implicatures derive from secondary processes. Secondary processes are inferentially, reflectively,

---

340. See ibid.; idem, *Literal Meaning*, 1–4.
341. Here Récanati understands "speech act" in an Austinian sense rather than a Searlian.
342. Récanati, *Literal Meaning*, 3, 4 (pronouns revised).
343. Récanati, "Pragmatics of What Is Said," 309.
344. Récanati, *Literal Meaning*, 56.
345. Ibid., 27.

and consciously accessible whereas primary processes are non-inferential, unreflective, and not conscious. "Secondary pragmatic processes are 'post-propositional'" whereas "primary pragmatic processes are 'pre-propositional.'"[346] For Récanati, rather than construing *what is said* as the "nonpragmatic property of a sentence, independent of speaker's meaning," he suggests starting "with the pragmatic notion of *what is said*, and define the semantic notion in terms of it."[347] In general, primary processes view the computation of the literal and derived interpretations as "processed in parallel." These two interpretations actually compete in the computation process and with nonliteral utterances some derived meaning is retained (based on the context of the discourse) while the literal interpretation suppressed. Similar to Grice, the derived meaning does theoretically proceed *from* the literal meaning; however and against Grice, "the derived interpretation is *associatively derived* from the literal interpretation, but is not *inferentially* derived."[348]

With all this in place, Récanati describes his preferred approach entitled as the Availability Hypothesis or Principle which he defines as:

> In deciding whether a pragmatically determined aspect of utterance meaning is part of what is said, that is, in making a decision concerning what is said, we should always try to preserve our pre-theoretic intuitions on the matter.[349]

This principle understands *what is said* determined by the "intuitive truth-condition content" of the utterance no matter how distant from the semantic meaning of the utterance.[350] A "normal interpreter" intuitively understands *what is said* as she/he "knows which sentence was uttered, knows the meaning of that sentence, knows the relevant contextual facts" despite the fact that the "minimal proposition literally expressed by the sentence exists in semantic heaven" and "plays no role in the actual process of communication."[351] In short, the pragmatically enriched dimension of *what is said* is consciously available to both addresser and addressee.[352]

---

346. Ibid., 23.
347. François Récanati, "'What Is Said' and the Semantics/Pragmatics Distinction," in Bianchi, ed. *Semantics/Pragmatics Distinction*, 57 (italics mine).
348. Récanati, *Literal Meaning*, 28–29.
349. Récanati, *Direct Reference*, 248; idem, "Pragmatics," 310.
350. See Récanati, *Literal Meaning*, 8–17; idem, *Direct Reference*, 246–51.
351. Récanati, *Literal Meaning*, 19, 96.
352. Huang, *Pragmatics*, 226; see Récanati, *Direct Reference*, 246–57.

What Récanati addresses here in his latest work is a main criticism with Gricean pragmatics and specifically that implicature categorically accounts for the vast majority of the pragmatically determined aspect of sentence-meaning. Language specialists have explored a middle phenomenon or area that lies between *what is said* and *what is implicated* particularly evidenced by what is often coined as "loose talk."[353] According to Bach, utterances such as *sentence non-literality* which are literal (non-metaphorical) sentences with words left out of the proposition (e.g., *I haven't eaten*) and *semantic underdetermination* which are sentences failing to express a complete proposition (e.g., *Steel isn't strong enough*).[354] In the former case, *expansion* is needed with minimal propositions to deliver a more elaborate proposition whereas in the latter case *completion* is needed just to deliver a proposition. In short, "with sentence non-literality a minimal proposition is fleshed out [expansion]; with semantic underdetermination a propositional radical is filled in [completion]."[355] For critics of Grice, he overlooked, for example, expansion and completion and within his theory these two phenomena would be incorrectly categorized as implicature. Thus, Grice's distinction between *what is said* and *what is implicated* should not be considered definitive as he appears to convey in his writings.[356]

For Récanati, the main problem with Grice centers on his implicit assumption that there are two and *only two* approaches to *prima facie* ambiguities, (a) the semantic approach (sentence-meaning) and (b) the pragmatic approach (speaker-meaning) that both fall under the broader notion of implicature.[357] This distinction between sentence-meaning and speaker-meaning is far too simplistic, and so two equally important distinctions must be identified: (a) the distinction between the linguistic, sentence-meaning and *what is said* and (b) the distinction between *what is actually said* and what is merely "conveyed" by the utterance.[358] As stated above, Minimalists see a close connection between sentence-meaning and *what is said* whereas Maximalists or Contextualists stress the commonality between *what is said* and what is implicated.

---

353. See Sperber/Wilson, *Relevance*, 231–37; idem, "Loose Talk," *Proceedings of the Aristotelian Society* 86 (1985–86): 153–71.
354. See Kent Bach, "Semantic Slack: What Is Said and More," in Tsohatzidis, ed., *Foundations of Speech Act Theory*, 267–69.
355. Ibid., 269.
356. See ibid., 269–71.
357. See Récanati, "Pragmatics," 297–302.
358. Récanati, *Literal Meaning*, 5.

Récanati's Availability Principle contrasts the traditional Minimalist view as well as an intermediate position which he identifies as the Syncretic View represented by Kent Bach, Nathan Salmon, Jonathan Berg, and Scott Soames.[359] These theorists see two equally legitimate notions of *what is said*: (a) a purely semantic notion corresponding to the minimal proposition resulting from saturation and (b) a pragmatic or psychological notion corresponding to the content of the speech act actually performed by uttering the sentence.[360] This literalist picture of meaning produces a four-level paradigm of *what is said*: literal meaning (sentence-meaning and what is said$_{min}$) and speaker-meaning (what is said$_{max}$ and what is implicated).[361] The primary problem with the Syncretic Approach, insofar as it is based in the literalist view of meaning, is that "semantic interpretation by itself is powerless to determine *what is said*, when the sentence contains a semantically underdeterminate expression."[362] In contrast, Récanati's approach contains three basic levels: (a) the linguistic meaning of the sentence; (b) *what is said* in the pragmatic sense; and (c) what is implied or otherwise conveyed by the utterance.[363] Although he retains a semantic and pragmatic dimension for *what is said*, the latter plays the dominant role.

Despite his criticism of the Gricean program and with these distinctions in place, Récanati relates ISAs to conversational implicatures. For Récanati, more often than not, nonliteral meaning is *secondary* meaning; "meaning derived from some more basic, primary meaning which it presupposes."[364] The commonality between ISAs and conversational implicatures is this *secondary character*: the interpretation of both "involves an inference from the utterance's primary meaning to its derived meaning." Very similar to Récanati's original procedure as he describes in *Meaning and Force*, when computing ISAs the interpreter first determines the utterance's *primary* or literal meaning then second infers some additional and dependent meaning. Also in line with Searle, ISAs are performed indirectly "via the performance of another speech act which falls within the illocutionary-act potential of the uttered sentence

---

359. See the Bibliography.
360. See Recaanti, "Semantics/Pragmatics Distinction," 55; idem, *Literal Meaning*, 21, 54–55.
361. Récanati, "What Is Said," 80.
362. Récanati, *Literal Meaning*, 58 (italics mine).
363. Récanati, "Semantics/Pragmatics Distinction," 62.
364. Récanati, *Literal Meaning*, 70.

and is said to be performed directly."³⁶⁵ This process, though, also necessitates the other aspects of primary processes (e.g., enrichment, loosening) because all conventional meanings of words need some interpretive adjustment.³⁶⁶ Thus, Récanati views secondary meaning determined by the primary or literal semantic meaning of a sentence plus an aspect of Gricean conversational maxims, i.e., secondary pragmatic processes.

Récanati sees, though, a difference between conversational implicatures and ISAs. The former "are pragmatic implications of *an act of speech*" whereas the latter, as in line with his earlier suggestions working with Austinian categories, occurs "where the speaker's intention *to perform the indirect speech act* is conversationally implicated by his performance of the direct speech act."³⁶⁷ In other words, conversational implicatures and ISAs possess a common secondary characteristic, but an implicature is merely something inferred from a speech act whereas an ISA is an additional inferred speech act as with (2a). Récanati also includes the Relevance theoretic notion of *explicature* with conversational implicatures which I will describe in more detail below.

Récanati's work is important and illuminating, especially towards understanding the vast complexities within the Philosophy of Language. I agree with many of Récanati's critics and his semantic contextualist approach that he tends to polarize all sentence types as semantically indeterminate. His proposals do provide insight into short, idiomatic sentences, but not for all sentence types. Further, Récanati places the onus of meaning for determining *what is said* on speaker-meaning while leaving little to no importance on linguistic, semantic value as such meaning resides in *semantic heaven*. The obvious problem with assigning all speech acts to speaker-meaning is the clear existence of linguistic sentence types matching illocutionary forces. It seems undeniable that semantics play a role in determining speech act types whereas for Récanati speaker-meaning determines force. Further, it is not exactly clear when and why primary and secondary processes are applied along with the blending of and distinction between these processes with nonliteral utterances. That said, what remains specifically important for this study is Récanati's notions concerning ISAs and implicatures and especially his description of the common and distinct characteristics of each. It is also noteworthy to highlight the fact that although Récanati rejects Gricean "secondary pragmatic processes" he retains these basic principles when discussing "secondary" nonliteral utterances, at least in a general sense.

365. Ibid., 70–71.
366. Ibid., 74–75.
367. Ibid., 70–71 (italics mine in the second quote).

Conclusions

Before answering my three guiding questions I need to initially address two issues. First, within SAT itself and as evidenced in the above descriptions, theorists do not employ consistent language when describing sentence types and the elements therein. Thus, in order to move forward I suggest the following descriptors. Theorists characteristically use the term "direct" to refer to the literal linguistic form of an utterance and "indirect" for the nonliteral, inferred meaning of a sentence. As with most theorists, the term "literal" refers to the linguistic form of a sentence and "indirect" identifies the inferred meaning derived from a sentence. With ISAs, the term "secondary" for Searle typically refers to the literal meaning of a sentence whereas for Vanderveken and Récanati this term usually identifies the inferred nonliteral meaning. Both Searle and Vanderveken along with others use the term "primary" to identify the nonliteral or indirect expression whereas Récanati uses this term to refer to the literal meaning of a sentence. To avoid confusion I suggest that the terms "intention" or "intentional" refer to the intended meaning of an indirect or nonliteral utterance. I will use the term "intended" to refer to the inferred nonliteral IA meaning and the term "literal" I will use to identify the linguistic sentence form. Although I agree with Récanati that ISAs and nonliteral utterances are both secondary in character, I also think that it is helpful to distinguish ISAs from nonliteral utterances in the same way as Bach and Tsohatzidis. Thus, nonliteral expressions include metaphors, irony and other figurative utterances while ISAs are a type of speech act often expressing an action. That said, as both the latter two theorists have demonstrated, some utterances include both indirection and nonliteralness simultaneously.

Second, what arises from the above research is a *gradation of indirectness of force* expressed by various types of utterances. Morgan points to this phenomenon with his short-circuited, convention of usage descriptions. Morgan demonstrates how conventions of usage do not constitute idioms in the Sadockian sense with the expression *Break a leg!* uttered to wish someone good luck in a performance. It is not an idiom as the sentence "John really broke a leg last night" cannot mean "John really had good luck/did well in his performance last night." Yet, Morgan concedes that certain types of expressions can go from usage convention to the eventual status of meaning convention. For Morgan, this occurs when the connection between an addresser's purpose and means becomes obscured.

Following along this line of thought, William G. Lycan also recognizes this phenomenon from his own analysis and proposes a tripartite stage description of ISAs.³⁶⁸ Type 1 utterances *can* be used with indirect force; Type 2 *normally* express indirect force and; Type 3 *only* express indirect force. Type 1 sentences are like *It's cold in here*. The indirect intention directly depends upon the literal semantic content of the sentence and is calculable while not involving conventional use. Type 2 utterances like (2a) fall in line with the Searle's and Morgan's notion of convention of usage or "semiconvention" as Lycan defines these types. However, the implicature still derives from the semantic content and is calculable in principle. The issue raised by these types of utterances is not how such utterances express indirectness, but why they normally do. For Lycan, the reason is because conventions of usage have arisen to that effect.³⁶⁹ Type 3 utterances are such as *Why paint your house purple?* (initially discussed by Gordon/Lakoff³⁷⁰) which are used *exclusively* with indirect force with no necessity of calculation. With such an utterance, Lycan claims with Gordon/Lakoff that it "cannot be understood as an ingenuous *or* disingenuous request for information about the hearer's state of mind."³⁷¹ It is never understood as a straightforward question.³⁷² With this type, the syntax of a sentence is "affected by diffuse and obscure pragmatic factors."³⁷³ To identify this final categorical type Lycan applies Morgan's short-circuit shift from Type 1 to Type 2 and proposes a similar scenario occurring with Type 3 utterances in connection to Type 2. Thus, through an utterance's historical association with its conventional use it ultimately became established among language users to first assume its indirect force with its literal meaning understood in only unusual discourse settings.³⁷⁴ Lycan's proposal also fits Morgan's additional observation that utterances could quite plausibly go from usage to meaning convention as in a Sadockian sense. A good example of this is the utterance *May God be with you* to express the parting convention *Goodbye*.³⁷⁵ The shift from convention of usage to meaning becomes complete when uttering the latter. As Laurence Horn and Samuel Bayer point out, *Goodbye* becomes fully conventionalized in meaning the first time an atheist could utter

---

368. See Lycan, *Logical Form*, 174–86; see also Geis, *Conversational Interaction*, 129–30.
369. Lycan, *Logical Form*, 180.
370. See Gordon/Lakoff, "Conversational Postulates," 96.
371. Lycan, *Logical Form*, 164.
372. Gordon/Lakoff, "Conversational Postulates," 96.
373. Lycan, *Logical Form*, 182.
374. Ibid., 183.
375. See Morgan, "Two Types of Convention," 271–72; see also Geis, *Conversational Interaction*, 128–29.

it sincerely.[376] Even Grice confessed that "it may not be impossible for what starts life, so to speak, as a conversational implicature to become conventionalized."[377] For Horn/Bayer, short-circuit implicature "is a natural halfway house along this route" of implicature to convention, from usage to meaning.[378] Along similar lines, Green also observes that certain expressions convey indirection more readily than others. Thus, the sentence *The rain that's coming in the window will ruin the rug* in most languages invariably *hints* at the desire of an addresser for an addressee to shut the window.[379] According to Horn/Bayer, this phenomenon should "be expected if, as is plausible, hints involve *non*-short-circuited, and hence non-detachable, implicatures."[380] Yet, as Lycan and others have observed, very few sentence types have reached this Stage 3 status and perhaps because only a few utterances exist, at least in English, that express simple messages in very specific contexts such as *Kick the bucket* and *Goodbye*.[381] Along similar lines and also quite helpful is van Eemeren/Grootendorst proposal of a continuum of conventionalization which recognizes certain, special fixed modes of expressions (*Can you? Will you?*) do not require well-defined contexts (strongly conventionalized) while others do (weakly conventionalized). This contextual strength continuum provides a complimentary framework alongside the notion of IAs operating along a spectrum of strengths. With all this in place I am now in a position to draw conclusions concerning my three guiding questions.

---

376. Horn/Bayer, "Short-Circuited Implicature," 405.
377. Grice, *Way of Words*, 39.
378. Horn/Bayer, "Short-Circuited Implicature," 405.
379. Green, "Get People to Do Things," 138–39.
380. Horn/Bayer, "Short-Circuited Implicature," 405. Asher/Lascarides claim that the hallmark of all ISAs "seems to be that Gricean reasoning provides a connection between one kind of speech act and an incompatible kind of speech act" ("Indirect Speech Acts," 194). These two theorists, though, distinguish between *unconventionalized* ISAs that are calculable through Gricean principles (following Gordon/Lakoff) and *conventionalized* ISAs that involve general pragmatic processes for interpretation (following Searle and Morgan). With the latter ISAs, Asher/Lascarides employ a blocking principle (following Horn/Bayer) and thus with utterances like (2a) they normally block its paraphrases from having an ISA interpretation, even if this interpretation is calculable.
381. So Geis, *Conversational Implicature*, 128–29. For a different description of the stages of implicatures see Peter Cole, "The Synchronic and Diachronic Status of Conversational Implicature," in Cole and Morgan, eds., *Syntax and Semantics 3*, 257–88.

What Is the Relationship Between Implicatures and Speech Acts?

Bertolet raises an important point concerning the illocutionary nature of an indirect type utterance. To recall, Bertolet demonstrates that (2a) has the force of a request, but one cannot claim that it constitutes a request; it is *as if* it has, *counts as* having the force of a request, but certainly does not possess the semantic property of a request. Bertolet bases this conclusion on Grice's descriptions of implicatures as inferred data, not actual, literal assertions. As described above, Grice views implicatures as something *implied*, *suggested*, or *meant* from a literal utterance. In contrast, Searle identifies the indirect meaning of certain utterances as an actual IA. This makes sense within the Searlian paradigm as all utterances are considered speech acts, even indirect ones. Yet, Searle does recognize an ISA as *nonliteral* and derived from a *literal* utterance. Moreover, Searle clearly distinguishes between his classic performative/directive illocution and an ISA. The problem raised by Bertolet remains, however, *how can one consider an implicature an actual assertion or IA?*

Scott Soames confirms Bertolet's basic conclusions on Grice's view of the nature of implicatures, but he also observes a tension in Grice's own descriptions. Soames claims that "the official story" Grice "tells of what conversational implicatures are makes no room for implicatures that are said or asserted"; however, some of his examples "involve cases in which what he claims to be implicated *is* asserted by the speaker."[382] Soames follows this lead and claims that Grice's conversational maxims contribute to what is asserted indirectly. For Soames, *classical implicatures* occur in cases when a person utters or asserts one thing and, as a consequence, implicates something else that is not asserted.[383] Yet there are other types of implicatures that could be categorized as assertions. To demonstrate his conclusions Soames finds a number of affinities with Bach, Récanati, as well as Relevance Theorists (see below), especially with the notions of *completion*, *expansion*, and *enrichment*, but differs from the latter by appealing to a rational reconstruction of meaning rather than a psychological causal explanation.[384] For Soames, Grice's

---

382. Soames, *Philosophical Essays, Volume 1. Natural Language: What it Means and How We Use It* (Princeton: Princeton University Press, 2009), 303 n. 4.

383. Soames, *Natural Language*, 320. Bach agrees with this basic view as well (see, e.g., "Conversational Implicatures," 124–62 (cf. 140–41).

384. See Soames, *Natural Language*, 320 n. 22, 323.

maxims help determine what an utterance asserts by narrowing the class of possible enrichments to those that most effectively advance the conversation. When several enrichments are otherwise feasible, the maxims dictate that one select the strongest, most informative, and relevant propositions among them for which one has adequate evidence.[385]

Soames illustrates his claim in one instance through the basic utterance: *I have two Fs* which contextually isolated conveys several possible implicatures. The questions *How many children do you have?* and *Do you have two beers in the fridge?* typically prompt the same response: *I have two Fs*, but the former question requires a precise number whereas the latter precision is unnecessary. With the first question, the response *I have at **least** two children* would violate the first maxim of Quantity (*Don't say too little*) and thus the addressee selects a stronger enrichment that asserts a precise answer, *I have **exactly** two children*. With the second question, the answer *I have **exactly** two beers* is rejected due to violation of the same maxim (in this case *Don't say too much*) along with the issue here being whether one has two or more Fs. Consequently, the addressee selects a weaker enrichment with the resulting assertion *I have **at least** two beers*.[386] For Soames, then, what is asserted derives jointly from conversational maxims plus the semantic content of the sentence uttered. With all this, Grice's descriptions of typical or classic implicates are, as Bertolet emphasizes, not actual assertions, but derived information from assertions. Yet, although Soames is not dealing directly with ISAs he does demonstrate through Grice's own maxims that certain implicatures for all intents and purposes are assertions or at the very minimum *count as* assertions.

As for most theorists who employ Gricean principles, ISAs *rely on* conversational implicatures to express the intended force rather than differentiate from one another. As I described above, Récanati considers both implicatures and ISAs as secondarily derived from a literal utterance while he also distinguishes them. Both involve inference from an utterance's literal speech act meaning to its derived meaning, yet one secondary inference is considered an implicature and the other an ISA. Récanati also tends to use the terms "inference" and "derive" for what others would call "implicature." For Grice, an implicature is a derived, inferred meaning. Bach, though, observes some complications in Grice's own description of

---

385. Ibid., 317.
386. Ibid., 306–309, 316–19.

what is said. On the one hand, *what is said* corresponds with propositional content while *implicature* represents anything else communicated. On the other hand, he distinguishes "saying" from "making as if to say" as with irony and metaphor.[387] For Grice, implicatures constitute something meant *in addition to*, not meaning something else instead or "contradictory" as with irony and metaphor.[388] Bach suggests two ways to improve on Grice's taxonomic scheme while retaining his criterion of *close syntactic correlation*. First, replace his distinction between *what is said* or *saying* and *making as if to say* with the distinction between explicitly saying as in Austin's IA (*what is said*) and saying as in Austin's locutionary sense (making as if to say) respectively. Second, distinguish nonliterality from implicature. As a result, implicature is a kind of ISA as also claimed by Récanati[389] whereas irony and metaphor are species of nonliteral and are direct speech acts, not implicatures.[390]

I consider these distinctions quite helpful, but still need further refining. For Bach, nonliterality and indirection are "two well-known ways in which the semantic content of a sentence can fail to determine the full force and content of the illocutionary act being performed in using the sentence" and both rely on the processes expressed by Grice's conversational implicatures.[391] As evidenced throughout this chapter with the use of terminology among theorists, Bach's use of terms and concepts can also be quite confusing. In the end, what Bach seems to present is that ISAs are kinds of implicatures whereas nonliteral utterances are not, but both rely on the same Gricean principles to express illocutionary meaning beyond *what is said*. The fundamental difference appears to be that when one speaks indirectly one means one thing as well as something else whereas when one speaks nonliterally she/he says something else entirely different. In doing this, Bach suggests seeing implicatures as indirect IAs or ISAs in distinction from locutionary acts. As described above, Récanati's initial thoughts on ISAs have some parallels with Bach here as he sees with (2a) the interrogative of asking as a locutionary act while

---

387. Grice, *Way of Words*, 30, 34.
388. Ibid., 34.
389. Bach, "Semantic Slack," 272; idem, "Conversational Impliciture," 144. So also Manuel Garcìa-Carpintero, "Explicit Performatives, What Is Said, and the Social Character of Assertion," in Penco and Domaneschi, eds., *What Is Said and What Is Not*, 111.
390. See Bach, "Conversational Impliciture," 140–44; Bach, "Semantic Slack," 271–72.
391. Bach, "Philosophy of Language," 468.

performing an IA of requesting.[392] It is significant that although Bach the Minimalist and Récanati the Maximalist fundamentally disagree on a number of ideas concerning how meaning transpires, they essentially agree that ISAs secondarily derive from a literal linguistic form and are a type of implicature. They also agree in their distinctions of implicature and specifically irony. For Récanati, in contrast to conversational implicatures irony lacks "the force of a serious assertion" in line with Grice's description of "make as if to say."[393]

Thus, inferentially (no pun intended) Récanati sees implicatures expressing some type of assertion whereas irony does not. Vanderveken, on the other hand, sees every utterance as an IA, in line with Searle, which also includes ironic utterances. That said, what all three of these theorists agree on is how inferential processes, notably those suggested by Grice, inform the interpretation of both indirect and nonliteral type utterances. Further, they all agree that determining the indirect meaning is a two-step calculative process beginning with the linguistic form in line with Searle and Morgan. The gradation of indirectness is helpful towards determining the various degrees of inference involved with utterances; however, establishing with indirect utterances where the semantic meaning ends and the implicature begins remains for me ultimately indeterminable.

Correlated with this gradation of indirection notion is the spectrum of strengths I presented above as initially observed by Briggs and Thiselton. To rehearse, a way through the constantive/performative blurring/distinction problem is to view all utterances as speech acts but differing in strength with constatives and performatives lying at each end of this weak–strong scale. Bach's, as well as Récanati's, distinction between locutionary acts and IAs finds implicit correspondence with this type of strength differentiation, especially as Austin himself identified his locution category with constatives. I prefer to identify weak speech acts with constative or locutionary type implicatures and strong speech acts with illocutionary or performative type implicatures. Strong illocutionary implicatures are *not* actual IAs, but they *count as* IAs based on conversational principles as proposed by Grice and others. Thus, the ISA of a sentence like (2a) is an inferred implicature derived from a linguistic form and in this instance includes the performance of some type of action. In addition, certain ISAs can simultaneously express nonliteral dimensions (metaphor and/or irony) as Bach and Tsohoatzidis have demonstrated.

---

392. Récanati, "Explicit Performatives," 210.
393. Recanti, *Literal Meaning*, 71.

Implicature, Explicature, Impliciture

Dierdre Wilson and Dan Sperber, as well as Robyn Carston, build their Relevance Theory from Grice's pragmatic proposals, but suggest a completely alternative theory. According to Wilson, the consistent central claim of Relevance theorists is that "the very act of communicating creates precise and predictable expectations of relevance, which are enough on their own to guide the hearer towards the speaker's meaning."[394] One of the main divergences of this theory from Grice's is the shift from a semantic or philosophical theory of meaning to a psychological theory of communication or from the perspective of usage principles to cognitive principles.[395] For Wilson/Sperber, the "central problem for pragmatics is that the linguistic meaning recovered by decoding vastly underdetermines the speaker's meaning."[396] Wilson/Sperber agree with Grice's notion of sentence meaning as *what is said* and that intended speaker-meaning is inferred while also recognizing a clear distinction between these two. However, they find Grice's pragmatic description of explicit communication inadequate as he sees it "largely a matter of linguistic and contextual decoding, and only implicit communication as properly inferential."[397] The semantics–pragmatics distinction cannot simply be reduced to a distinction between *what is said* and *what is implicated*. In fact, an addressee "uses Grice's maxims as much in determining what proposition has been expressed as in determining its conversational implicatures."[398] Further, the Gricean maxims do not independently generate implicatures, but rather should be reduced to solely his maxim of Relation which Wilson/Sperber identify as the maxim of *Relevance*. Within this maxim there are two principles of relevance: Cognitive and Communicative. Communicative inference is intuitively relevant to addressees that they unconsciously process. "Communicators do not 'follow' the principle of relevance; and they could not violate it even if they wanted to. The principle of relevance applies without exception: Every act of ostensive communication communicates a presumption of relevance."[399]

---

394. Deirdre Wilson, "Relevance Theory," in Cummings, ed., *The Routledge Pragmatics Encyclopedia*, 396; see also Deirdre Wilson and Dan Sperber, "Relevance Theory," in Horn and Ward, eds., *The Handbook of Pragmatics*, 607.

395. Huang, *Pragmatics*, 201.

396. Dan Sperber and Deirdre Wilson, "Pragmatics, Modularity, and Mind-Reading," *Mind & Language* 17 (2002): 3.

397. Ibid., 6; see Grice, *Way of Words*, 25.

398. Wilson/Sperber, "On Grice's Theory of Conversation," 348.

399. Dan Sperber and Deirdre Wilson, "Précis of Relevance: Communication and Cognition," *Behavioral and Brain Sciences* 10 (1987): 704.

Another key element within Relevance Theory is the pragmatic dimension identified as *explicature* which supplements Grice's implicature notion. Grice's view of the pragmatic dimension of interpretation as implicature is far too narrow as the role of pragmatics should center on the *explicit* content of an utterance. *Explicature* "(as a counterpart to implicature)" refers to the "primary component of speaker meaning, which is a pragmatic development of the linguistically decoded content."[400] Explicatures "are derived by pragmatically enriching the linguistically encoded logical form."[401] More elaborately, the first task of inferential comprehension is to complete or pragmatically enrich the linguistically encoded logical form recovered by decoding and identifying the explicit content or explicature of an utterance. Thus, pragmatic expansions and completions constitute explicit contents of an utterance.

For Relevance theorists, there are two types of implicatures: *implicated premises* and *implicated conclusions*. The latter are deduced from the explicit content of a sentence in its context whereas the former are added to the context by addressees either by retrieval from memory or constructed ad hoc.[402] Both explicatures and implicatures constitute pragmatic inferences independently derived from the same cognitive processes and communicative principles.[403] For meaning to transpire, Relevance theorists identify the phenomenon of *parallel* or *mutual adjustment* lying between explicatures and implicatures. To illustrate this, Sperber/Wilson use the following:

Peter: *Do you want to go to the cinema?*

Mary: *I'm tired.*

Mary's response does not answer Peter's question, but he draws two initial inferences:

Mary's being tired is a sufficient reason for her not to want to go to the cinema.

Mary doesn't want to go to the cinema because she is tired.

---

400. Robyn Carston, "Word Meaning, What Is Said and Explicature," in Penco and Domaneschi, eds., *What Is Said and What Is Not*, 177.
401. Robyn Carston, "Relevance Theory and the Saying/Implicating Distinction," in Horn and Ward, eds., *The Handbook of Pragmatics*, 645.
402. See Sperber/Wilson, "Précis of Relevance," 705–706.
403. See Robyn Carston, "Implicature, Explicature, and Truth-Theoretic Semantics," in *Mental Representations: The Interface Between Language and Reality*, ed. R. M. Kempson (Cambridge: Cambridge University Press, 1988), 157–58.

For these two implicatures "to be soundly derived, Mary must be understood as saying something stronger than that she is tired *tout court*: her meaning must be enriched to the point where it warrants the intended inferences. The process is one of *parallel adjustment*: expectations of relevance warrant the derivation of specific implicatures, for which the explicit content must be adequately enriched."[404] Quite complexly, Relevance theorists view implicatures and explicatures pragmatically independent while at the same time explicatures are *logically prior* to implicatures and thus explicatures function as premises for implicature inferences; specifically implicated conclusion types.[405] Yet, explicatures are not necessarily *temporally prior* to implicatures. Carston claims that "there is no generalization to be made about which of the two kinds of communicated assumption is recovered first and functions as input to the recovery of the other; the *parallel adjustment* process entails that neither is wholly temporally prior to the other."[406]

Carston here defends the position of Relevance theory over against a *sequential model* that she accuses Récanati of employing with explicatures and implicatures which he ironically criticizes similarly with the hierarchal implicature scheme he sees with Grice. Récanati, though, claims that he actually agrees with Sperber/Wilson's "mutual adjustment" process[407] and thus denies that his view commits him to any such sequential process.[408] Yet, Récanati goes on to assert: "What matters from my point of view is only this: there is an *asymmetry* between implicature and explicature, in that the implicature must be grounded in, or warranted by, the explicature. Both Carston and Sperber/Wilson grant this point, at least as far as 'implicated conclusions' are concerned."[409] In the end, it appears that Relevance theorists view explicatures and implicatures functioning pragmatically independently with explicitly implicated conclusions deriving from explicatures while Récanati sees all implicatures prompted by explicatures.

---

404. Dan Sperber and Deirdre Wilson, "The Mapping Between the Mental and the Public Lexicon," in *Pragmatics II: Critical Concepts in Linguistics, Volume 2*, ed. A. Kasher (London: Routledge, 2012), 61, 62 (italics mine).

405. Robyn Carston, "Linguistic Meaning, Communicated Meaning and Cognitive Pragmatics," *Mind & Language* 17 (2002): 143; see further Sperber/Wilson, "Précis of Relevance," 705; idem, *Relevance*, 182–83; Carston, "Relevance Theory," 633–56, cf. 635–36.

406. Carston, "Linguistic Meaning," 143.

407. Récanati specifically quotes Sperber/Wilson, "Public Lexicon," 65.

408. See Récanati, *Literal Meaning*, 21–22, 49.

409. Ibid., 47, see further pp. 49–50.

For Bach, the term *explicature* is not entirely clear in referring to the explicit content of an utterance when it is a cognate of *explicate*, not *explicit*.[410] Regarding the notion of explicature, Bach suggests an alternative with *impliciture* (replacing "a" of implic*a*ture with "i" to associate the category with *implicit*).[411] This term more appropriately addresses the "middle ground" between *what is said* and *what is implicated* as "part of what is meant is communicated not explicitly but implicitly, by way of expansion and completion."[412] Bach identifies Grice's claim that *what is said* closely relates to the conventional meaning of the words and their syntactical order[413] as the "Syntactic Correlation Constraint" which for Bach represents this in-between area of *what is said*.[414] Similar to implicatures, "implicitures go beyond *what is said*, but unlike implicatures, which are additional propositions external to *what is said*, implicitures are built out of *what is said*."[415] Implicatures are completely separate from *what is said* and is implied *by* it whereas implicitures are implicit *in what is said*. Implicitures are built up from the explicit content of an utterance by conceptual strengthening or what Sperber/Wilson would identify as "enrichment."[416] Grice's conversational implicatures are completely separated from, inferred from, and additional propositions external from *what is said*.[417] Bach, though, sees implicitly in Grice's own articulations that "saying" (in his favored sense) virtually equates to *explicitly state* which correlates with *what is said* in distinction to "as if to say" with instances of irony, metaphor, etc. For Bach, to implicate something

---

410. Bach, "Semantic Slack," 270.

411. On the similarities and differences of explicature and impliciture according to Bach, see his "Impliciture vs Explicature: What's the Difference?" in *Explicit Communication: Robyn Carston's Pragmatics*, ed. B. Soria and E. Romero (Basingstoke: Palgrave Macmillan, 2010), 126–37.

412. Bach, "Pragmatics," 469.

413. See Grice, *Way of Words*, 25, 87.

414. See Kent Bach, "You Don't Say," *Synthese* 128 (2001): 15–44.

415. Bach, "Semantic Slack," 273 (italics mine).

416. See Bach, "Conversational Impliciture," 140. For a summary of the main proposals on the nature of *what is said*, see Huang, *Pragmatics*, 216–42.

417. Bach, "Conversational Impliciture," 140–41. Bach finds parallels with impliciture and Grice's remarks that in a number of instances it is "unnecessary to put in...qualificatory words," but in other occasions it is "feasible to strengthen one's meaning by achieving a superimposed implicature" (*Way of Words*, 44, 48). Bach understands Grice to mean by "strengthening" as "increasing the information content of what is said, not adding a whole separate proposition to what was said" ("Semantic Slack," 273).

is to state or mean one thing (Grice's saying in his favored sense) and meaning something else *as well*, not as meaning something else instead as with nonliteral utterances. Bach, then, suggests two ways to improve on Grice's taxonomic scheme:

1. Replace Grice's *saying* (in indicative cases) with explicitly saying and *as if to say* with Austin's locutionary act.
2. Do not classify nonliterality as implicature (as implicature is a kind of ISA).[418]

With this established, Bach further suggests that we can have the notion of *what is said* (correlated with Grice's saying) applying uniformly to three situations: (a) where addressers mean what they say and something else as well as in the cases of implicature and ISAs; (b) where addressers say one thing and mean something else instead as with nonliteral utterances; and (c) where addressers say something and do not mean anything[419] as when someone reads another person's poem.[420] Where Bach differs from Grice's dichotomy of meaning is with a neo-classic Gricean paradigm proposing a trichotomy with *what is said* related to semantics and implicature and implicature related to pragmatics. Similarly to the relevance notion of explicature, implicatures are prompted by implicitures.[421] Thus, there is no significant pragmatic intrusion on *what is said*.[422] Interestingly, in one is his latest essays Bach confirms and even strengthens Searle's Principle of Expressibility by claiming that "it is arguable that all of our thoughts are explicitly expressible, in which case for every thought there is at least one sentence that would express it explicitly."[423]

What the above descriptions of explicature and impliciture highlight is what is known as Grice's Circle. Huang defines this as follows: "how what is conversationally implicated can be defined in contrast to and calculated on the basis of what is said, given that what is said seems to both determine and to be determined by what is conversationally implicated."[424] Levinson acknowledges that Grice's Circle equally afflicts

---

418. Bach, "Semantic Slack," 272.
419. Ibid.; see also Bach, "Philosophy of Language," 472.
420. This example for Bach's third type of use of Grice was personally communicated to Huang (*Pragmatics*, 218).
421. See further Horn, "Implicature," 21–24; Huang, *Pragmatics*, 238–39.
422. For a similar view see Nathan Salmon, "The Pragmatic Fallacy," *Philosophical Studies* 63 (1991): 83–97.
423. Bach, "Impliciture vs Explicature," 129.
424. Huang, *Pragmatics*, 203.

any theory seeking to make a semantic/pragmatic distinction[425] which is presented in Salmon's above observations. In the end, both explicatures and implicitures similarly constitute pragmatic principles based on the same basic inference processes derived from some linguistic/semantic content. Thus, I agree with Levinson, especially in regards to my purposes here, as he concludes that "all such terminological efforts are fruitless: Grice's circle ensures that there is no consistent way of cutting up the semiotic pie such that 'what is said' excludes 'what is implicated.'" Neither Sperber/Wilson and Carston, Récanati, or Bach "consider that the processes involved in deriving explicatures or implicitures and so on are essentially different in kind from those used in deriving implicatures. Merely relabeling pragmatic inferences that play a role in fixing the intended proposition something other than 'implicature' hardly alters the nature of the problem."[426]

While maintaining much of a Gricean picture of meaning, Green acknowledges that the majority of implicatures addressers most commonly involve violations of Grice's maxim of Relation as Relevance theorists have isolated. She illustrates this with a comic strip where Arlene asks Garfield a question and he responds with an apparent irrelevant question:

Arlene: *Do you love me more than you love food, Garfield?*

Garfield: *Do chickens have lips?*

As intended, Arlene infers the obvious, negative polarity of this "cliché" RQ that the relevance of Garfield's response is "that the true answer to her question is likewise obviously negative." Further, what is implicated is *No* and at the same time *as you ought to know*.[427] Yet, Green also recognizes that one "can simultaneously openly violate Relation and the first maxim of Quality for effects similar to Garfield's." For example, a communicative exchange between addresser A and addressee B:

A: *You know, I can crush rocks with my bare hands.*

B: *Yeah, and the sun rises in the west.*

Respondent B utters an obviously and outrageously false statement with no apparent relation to A's remark. "But if A assumes that B means to be conveying something not false that is relevant, B may be successful

425. Levinson, *Presumptive Meanings*, 186.
426. Ibid., 198; see further Horn, "Implicature," 17–24.
427. Green, *Pragmatics*, 101–102.

in implicating that A's assertion is equally false."[428] Grice additionally included understatement, hyperbole, and sarcasm as instances of the violation of his Quality maxim that implicate something true and for Green also relevant.[429] For example, an addresser utters sarcastically *That was smart!* to implicate "That was stupid!" with the literal proposition remaining relevant within the respective communicative context, but expressing something false. What is interpretively important here for me is that the purposeful irrelevancy displayed with the above responses is more readily recognized whereas other instances of violations of Relevancy may prove more difficult to identify.

To draw this altogether, language specialists continue to use implicature in one way or another when referencing inferential aspects of linguistic forms. Specifically, Récanati, Bach, and many others agree that implicatures are types of ISAs. Thus, I will use the term implicature to refer to an intended meaning derived indirectly to one degree or another from a literal linguistic form recognized through pragmatic processes within a particular communicative context. As I described above, Grice sees both *what is said* and *what is implicated* as providing the data for *what is meant*, thus creating a distinction between *what is implicated* and *what is meant*. Yet, at the same time *what is implicated* refers to specific inferential data which produces a blending between *what is implicated* and *what is meant*. Thus, the term implicature appears to include both the *implicated* inferential processes as well as the derived data which informs *what is meant* (along the lines of Levinson's above observations as well as Horn's definition of implicature). The *middle phenomena* or *ground* that Relevance theorists and Récanati identify as *explicature* and what Bach identifies as *impliciture* for my purposes here designates the pragmatic processes and inferential data triggered by *what is said*. Addressees employ such inferential mechanisms and implicated information to recognize and understand *what is implicated* (implicature) and ultimately *what is meant*. To clarify further, (2a) is classically identified as an ISA, but such an expression clearly contains both a literal meaning and non-literal intended meaning. The non-literal intended meaning derives through pragmatic processes and constitutes *what is implicated*. With (2a), what actually constitutes as the implicature is the inferred intended IA which is the actual ISA of a request in contrast to the literal interrogative IA. What Relevance theorists, Récanati, Bach and many others have shown, though, is that because propositional content most

---

428. Ibid., 102.
429. See Grice, *Way of Words*, 34–35.

often underdetermines what addressers explicitly express, an aspect of *what is said* is not linguistically derived. Thus, most all contemporary theorists agree that more pragmatic intrusion enters into the conventional, truth-conditioned linguistic content of *what is said* than Grice explicitly described and even overlooked.[430]

How Many Illocutionary Forces Are Expressed with a Single Indirect Utterance?

Following along the line of my above conclusions, two IAs are expressed with a typical indirect type of utterance: an intended IA is conveyed through the performance of a literal IA. The intended inferred IA is not an actual IA, but interpretively expresses the force of an IA; it *counts as* an IA. Expanding upon this and applying Alston's notion of IAP, certain literal sentences express particular implicatures or indirect IAPs with addressers intending a single, particular force. This intended IA is expressed through a literal linguistic sentence due to the fact that the inferred meaning goes beyond *what is said* as typified by (2a).

This leads to another question, *what happens to the literal linguistic meaning of an indirect utterance?* From the above analysis, in instances of nonconventional indirect utterances (Lycan's Type 1 and Type 2), the literal IA of most indirect type utterances does not simply disappear from addressees' calculable data as a possible interpretation. Both IAs, the literal meaning and the intended implicature, remain possible meanings with one being the most plausible and natural determined by both its linguistic form and cooperative communicative context. Although Récanati does not explicitly apply his parallel process model to ISAs,[431] such an understanding has affinities with this depiction on how addressees go about interpreting such expressions. With this model, the intended indirect meaning derives from the linguistic form of an utterance, but at the same time the literal semantic meaning and the derived meaning are processed in parallel, and compete with no privileged status for either. The literal meaning *triggers* possible associatively derived meanings and based on the immediate communicative context one derived meaning is chosen with the others as well as the literal meaning suppressed.[432]

---

430. See Huang, *Pragmatics*, 189.

431. Récanati classifies meanings conveyed by an utterance in a secondary sense and derived from some antecedent meaning expressed by the utterance as nonliteral (*Literal Meaning*, 71). In his description of his parallel model, he uses similar terminology as with ISAs while using nonliteral examples (see ibid., 28–29).

432. See above and ibid., 28–29.

Récanati's triggering notion, though, should not be confused with Gu's *transactional* or van Eemeren/Grootendorst's *interactional* views which conceive PEs being additionally *triggered* by the intended meanings of speech acts. Brought together, certain indirect type utterances *trigger* intended IAs which in turn *trigger* intended PEs. Yet, as described above a few sentence types eventually become fully conventionalized through usage and time that necessitate little to no calculable pragmatic processes or parallel processing. In these specific instances, the literal linguistic meaning dissipates and thus the sentence *only* expresses an indirect force; the meaning of a particular sentence transcends its linguistic content. The above description also highlights the degree of addressee involvement with determining the inferential intention of ISAs. With Lycan's Type 1 ISAs the addressee is left with much more inferential calculation needed to determine its intended meaning than with a Type 3 type sentence.

How Does a Literal Linguistic Form Express an Indirect Illocutionary Force and How Do Addressees Recognize That Force?

This question relates to Vanderveken's two questions presented above which essentially concern determining how addressees successfully recognize addressers' illocutionary intention. As noted above, related questions raised by theorists include: *how do addressees distinguish a conversational implicature from linguistic meaning* and *how much information is determined by semantic meaning and how much is due to pragmatic principles?* I am not about to presume that I can produce a systematic way of determining how addressers convey more than their linguistic form semantically allows and thus solve Grice's paradox and the mystery of indirect utterances; rather, my descriptions here are far more modest. My primary goal here is to provide ways to interpret and understand the basic function of nonliteral utterances and ultimately RQs and thus my descriptions will present various ways addressees can calculate speaker-meaning from a linguistic form.

When it comes to conversations, it is assumed that addressers and addressees both have the ability to use and process linguistic information. Further and as the above language specialists highlight, when people verbally interact with one another they cooperate conversationally and abide by certain unspoken and assumed conversational principles. Regarding addressers, they normally provide an appropriate amount of information, tell the truth, are relevant, and attempt to be as clear as possible. Within a conversation addressers' goal is for addressees to recognize and understand their intended meaning. Further, addressers invite addressees to respond to utterances in one way or another. Addressees recognition and understanding occurs through various and specific means. These interpretive processes will include the semantic content of the utterance along with pragmatic processes such as the conversational rules and/or maxims, the context of the utterance, sincerity conditions, direction of fit, mutual background information, and reciprocity. Addressees assume that addressers are conversationally cooperating, even when addressers appear to flout or violate (a) communicative rule(s) or maxim(s) while addressees use various inferential triggers throughout the conversation to recognize addressers' intention of meaning.

To illustrate, when an addresser utters (2a) at the dinner table with salt and pepper containers located on the table the addressee is faced with the semantic content of an interrogative asking about one's ability to pass the salt. The addressee initially uses that linguistic form to interpret the addresser's intended meaning. The mutual understanding between addresser and addressee in this specific context would normally assume that the addressee currently possesses the ability to pass the salt and thereby the addressee knows the utterance is not functioning in an interrogative sense; something more is being expressed. From the mutual background information the addressee recognizes the incompatibleness of the felicity/sincerity/responsibility conditions of the literal interrogative. The addressee assumes the addresser maintains cooperative communication despite this semantic violation while at the same time the addressee knows the addresser continues the exchange due to the assumed sincerity/responsibility condition which the addresser fulfills with the intended use of the sentence.

In relation to the above and specifically applying Gricean principles, the linguistic form of (2a) does not convey a sincere request by the addresser with the closest maxim applicable being that of Quality (*Don't say something false*). Now the sentence *It is cold in here!* most readily exploits this maxim as an addresser experiencing a particularly cold room is not making a false claim while at the same time requests to make the room warmer. However, Grice's Quality maxim with (2a) does not exactly apply while it also needs a sincerity/responsibility component. Vanderveken's generalized version of this maxim (*Let your IA be felicitous*) with its multiple possible sub-maxim IAs as well as van Eemeren/Grootendorst's responsibility condition (*Don't be insincere; be honest, correct*) provide necessary broadening of Grice's initial conception. Also and in a general sense, one could see how all implicatures derive from a violation of the maxim of Relevance. However, as Green has observed, the violation of other Gricean maxims can simultaneously occur which provide supplemental and complimentary angles for interpreting nonliteral sentences.

With the interrogative of (2a) an addresser abides by the communicative principles if she/he literally asks a genuine question. However, in the context of eating at a table (2a) does not intentionally function as such. Thus, the literal speech act violates the generalized maxim of Quality including the sincerity/responsibility condition as well as the maxim of Relevance. As such, the addressee rejects the interrogative dimension of the utterance. Cooperative communication ensues and the violation of any communicative rules remains only apparent when the addressee recognizes the addresser is doing something else with (2a). In other words, the utterance remains felicitous if the addressee recognizes that the addresser intends to express an additional inferred meaning with (2a). From the possible IAP implicatures the addressee selects the most felicitous and non-defective. The inferred IA complies with the communicative principles in this particular context. Thus, the addresser remains conversationally cooperative with (2a) understood as a request.

Another, but related, angle at this is the felicity condition of directional fit. Utterances like (2a) have obviously two dimensions: Interrogative and Directive. Interrogatives in general fall within the illocutionary category of a Directive; however, different types of questions express other types of speech acts while also degrees of strength.[433] Directives have a world-to-words fit and uttering this IA an addresser wants the addressee to match the world to her/his request; accomplish the request so that the world is transformed to fit the propositional content of that request. To my knowledge, speech act theorists have not discussed in any detail the direction of fit with interrogatives requesting information or with simple *Yes* or *No* answers. With these types of questions the addresser does not want the addressee to *do* anything as in the sense of Searle's genuine Directive. Interrogatives of this former type do not readily find a place within the directional fit paradigm. Yet, certain interrogatives like (2a) can operate along similar lines as assertions in relation to directional fit. Assertions have words-to-worlds fit as a felicitous utterance must match the current state of affairs. When an addresser utters (2a) in the above scenario the question of ability violates in a similar way the direction of fit of an assertion. In other words, the addresser's question of ability is incompatible with and does not satisfactorily match the mutually assumed reality that she/he obviously does possess that questioned ability. The only satisfactory function of such an utterance is that of a request with the

---

433. SAT theorists have not engaged much in discussing degrees of strength with questions. For a brief description see Daniel Vanderveken, *Meaning and Speech Acts, Volume 1: Principles of Language Use* (Cambridge: Cambridge University Press, 1990), 127–28, 149.

world-to-language fit. Following Vanderveken and especially Holdcroft's proposals, utterance (2a) is either a question inquiring about an addressee's ability or a request to pass the salt. As the utterance *You will be there* allows for either direction of fit, (2a) expresses both an interrogative and a request with the intended meaning of the sentence dependent upon its communicative context with the latter the more natural meaning due to the criteria of fit. Directional fit, then, can provide an additional angle at determining the intended meaning of certain ISAs.

In this chapter I have presented the primary conceptualizations of the nature of ISAs and the various ways theorists envision how addressers imply meaning while addressees interpretively infer that intended meaning. This chapter essentially concerns ISAs with a few references to RQs. As I discussed earlier, my hope is that this analysis will provide research for examining ISAs in the biblical text. In the following chapter, I will build upon my ISA research here as well as apply it to describe the performative nature and function of RQs.

Chapter 2

ANALYSIS OF RHETORICAL QUESTIONS
AND OTHER SIMILAR TYPES OF INTERROGATIVES

In this chapter I build on my introductory thoughts as well as incorporate my analysis of ISAs to describe and define the performative nature and function of RQs along with describing the characteristics of other similar types of interrogatives. I go about accomplishing this here by initially using Ilie's descriptions with which I critically interact while supplementing with additional research. The reason for utilizing Ilie's work is that it remains prominent among the literature because of her detailed and insightful analysis of RQs as well as interrogatives in general. Although not exhaustive,[1] her work is particularly appealing for my study as she also views RQs as types of ISAs while focusing on the pragmatic function of such interrogatives. Further, numerous Hebrew Bible scholars discussing RQs frequently appeal to her work, but do not typically engage in the speech act potential of her analysis.

To begin, contemporary language specialists have proposed various unique features of RQs to distinguish them from other types of interrogative utterances. For instance:[2]

- RQs are syntactically interrogatives, but function semantically as strong assertions that express implied, understood, obvious, and biased claims.[3]

---

1. See, e.g., Pauline Slot, review of Cornelia Ilie, *What Else Can I Tell You? A Pragmatic Study of English Rhetorical Questions as Discursive and Argumentative Acts*, *Argumentation* 11 (1997): 383–86.

2. The following list is based on Ilie's summary of the characteristics she found primarily in reference books which I have slightly revised with regards to description while also supplementing representative language specialists (*What Else Can I Tell You?*, 42).

3. E.g., John Beekman and John Callow, *Word of God* (Grand Rapids: Zondervan, 1974), 229–48 (cf. 229, 231, 238–45); Randolf Quirk et al., *A Comprehensive Grammar of the English Language* (London/New York: Longman, 1985), §11.23.

- RQs are restricted information-seeking interrogatives.[4]
- RQs are interrogatives asked without the intention of receiving any type of reply (verbal or nonverbal).[5]
- RQs as interrogatives to which answers are immediately supplied[6] or expecting specific answers[7] or inviting addressees to supply assumed, obvious answers.[8]
- RQs assert something known to addressees which cannot be denied.[9]
- RQs do not elicit information but produce a stylistic effect[10] or express intense conviction of a certain view[11] or are asked for emphasis, especially in a series of RQs.[12]
- RQs express a strong assertion of the opposite polarity from what is asked: usually a positive RQ expresses a negative assertion whereas a negative RQ expresses a positive assertion.[13]
- Questions that present the argument in an interrogative form.[14]

---

4. E.g., van Rooy, "Negative Polarity," 240, 250–60.

5. E.g., Anzilotti, "Rhetorical Question," 290–91; J. A. Cuddon, *The Penguin Dictionary of Literary Terms and Literary Theory*, rev. C. E. Preston (Oxford: Blackwell, 1998), 748–49; Fiengo, *Asking Questions*, 62; Ferenc Kiefer, "Yes–No Questions as Wh-Questions," in Searle, Kiefer, and Bierwisch, eds., *Speech Act Theory and Pragmatics*, 98; Geoffrey N. Leech, *A Linguistic Guide to English Poetry* (London: Longman, 1973); Brown/Levinson, *Politeness*, 223; Emily N. Pope, *Questions and Answers in English* (The Hague/Paris: Mouton, 1976), 36.

6. E.g., Cuddon, *Literary Terms and Literary Theory*, 749.

7. E.g., Joseph T. Shipley, *Dictionary of World Literary Terms* (London: George Allen & Unwin, 1955).

8. M. H. Abrams, *A Glossary of Literary Terms* (New York: Holt, Rinehart & Winston, 1985).

9. Katie Wales, *A Dictionary of Stylistics* (London: Longman, 1989).

10. Karl Beckson and Arthur Ganz, *Literary Terms: A Dictionary* (London: André Deutsch, 1990); Kiefer, "Yes–No Questions," 98.

11. Leech, *Linguistic Guide*.

12. E.g., Cuddon, *Literary Terms and Literary Theory*, 748–49.

13. E.g., Chung-Hye Han, "Deriving the Interpretation of Rhetorical Questions," in *Proceedings of the 16th West Coast Conference on Formal Linguistics* 16 (1978): 1–17; idem, "Interpreting Interrogatives"; Sadock, "Queclaratives"; idem, *Toward a Linguistic Theory of Speech Acts*, 79–88; R. Quirk S. Greenbaum, G. Leech, and J. Svartyik, *A Grammar of Contemporary English* (London: Longman, 1974), §11.23.

14. Olivier Reboul, *Introduction à la rhétorique* (Paris: Presses Universitaires de France, 1991).

Ilie observes that what each of most of these descriptions "have in common is an attempt to account for the particular force of rhetorical questions in terms of the discrepancy between their interrogative form and their assertive function and of the polarity shift between the question itself and the implied answer." Where they differ centers on the perception and interpretation of the answer to RQs.[15] She also observes that most definitions for RQs are based in more syntactic and/or semantic addresser-oriented aspects over and against pragmatic addressee-oriented factors.[16] According to Ilie, the former approaches have not successfully described the nature of RQs as primarily evidenced by most of the recent research on these interrogatives being based on pragmatic and cognitive approaches. Earlier approaches viewed RQs strictly in linguistic terms that understood and labelled them as interrogatives that do not ask for answers or responses of any kind from addressees.[17] Quite to the contrary, RQs expect a type of response while such a restricted syntactic and/or semantic analysis cannot account for the complexity and multifunctionality of these expressions. Ilie's pragmatic approach recognizes that RQs "emphatically focus on the interaction between the addresser and the addressee."[18] More specifically, pragmatic approaches concentrate on the answer to RQs which is the less obvious and the more difficult to ascertain inferential characteristic directly related to addressee-reception, answer-expectation and to the nature and function of the answer.[19] Further, pragmatic approaches typically identify the intentionality of RQs in their persuasive effect on addressees (theorists vary on how this persuasive element works out) and thus have an expected answer.[20]

Ilie employs an Integrative Pragmatic approach for understanding the varieties and functions of RQs as well as to distinguish these expressions from genuine and other special types of questions.[21] For Ilie, RQs display a dual nature consisting of a *question* and a *statement* which corresponds to her understanding that RQs are types of ISAs. As such, Ilie's pragmatic angle does not ignore the linguistic dimension of RQs.

---

15. Ilie, *What Else Can I Tell You?*, 43.
16. For Ilie's descriptions and critiques of the various approaches to RQs see ibid., 10–34.
17. See ibid., 12–24.
18. Ibid., 98.
19. Ibid., 24, 216.
20. Ibid., 25.
21. Ilie, "Rhetorical Questions," 405.

Thus, with RQs both the interrogative and assertive dimensions are encountered by addressees and consequently both come into play when deciphering this intended function. So, as I described above with ISAs, the semantic content provides an interpretive element for understanding RQs pragmatic intention.

With these basic ideas in place, Ilie defines these types of interrogatives as follows:

> A rhetorical question is a question used as a challenging statement to convey the addresser's commitment to its implicit answer, in order to induce the addressee's mental recognition of its obviousness and the acceptance, verbalized or non-verbalized, of its validity.[22]

Along with her definition, Ilie presents five distinctive features that characterize and define RQs while also function as the essence of her understanding of the nature of these expressions.[23] The initial two characteristics are syntactico-semantic in nature and are essentially agreed upon by all theorists whereas the final three are pragmatic characteristics which such linguistic approaches cannot account for.

Ilie's Five Characteristics of Rhetorical Questions

The Discrepancy Between the Interrogative Form of the Rhetorical Question and its Communicative Function as a Statement

This characteristic is generally recognized as what marks RQs, and for Ilie the divergence between *form* and *function* manifests itself in "the lack of correspondence between the sentence type and the speech act type."[24] For example, the interrogative *Is there a better place than home?* implicates the assertion *There is no better place than home!* Thus and in contrast to genuine questions eliciting information, RQs "normally *provide information* about the speaker's state of mind, opinion, and/or emotions."[25] Such divergence between form and function, though, is not solely reserved for RQs as speech act theorists have demonstrated. As displayed with ISAs, not all linguistic interrogatives intentionally function as information-eliciting questions. As the interrogative (2a) *Can you pass*

---

22. Ilie, *What Else Can I Tell You?*, 128.
23. Ilie initially introduces these distinctive features in ibid., 45–46.
24. Ibid., 46; for her full discussion see 46–51.
25. Ilie, "Rhetorical Questions," 405 (italics mine).

the salt? most often indirectly implies a request, so RQs often indirectly convey an assertive type answer. Further, not every assertion simply constitutes a statement about the state of affairs; certain assertive illocutions, for example, can express a confession. Yet, some RQs infer answers that are not statements along the lines of (2a) which I will explore below.

According to Ilie, because of their hybrid nature RQs share certain features with genuine questions and other features with statements while at the same time display their uniqueness from other interrogatives. As to their uniqueness and first, RQs can only be quoted, not reported or represented. The interrogative form of RQs displays that they can be answered like genuine questions. Yet, due to their challenging and assertive function RQs cannot be reported indirectly or represented; their rhetorical nature is only retained when quoted. Second, RQs can be followed by responses of agreement or disagreement which confirms their status as indirect statements. Third, RQs can function as valid answers to genuine questions which also corroborates with their indirect statement nature. Finally, RQs functioning as answers can often be interpreted as argumentative wherein addressers convey particular points of view or attitudes as well as their reason for it.[26]

Before moving forward, and as I introduced above, Ilie consistently adopts Searle's dual illocutionary description of ISAs and views RQs as this type of speech act.[27] However, Ilie does not discuss in any significant detail how RQs constitute two IAs simultaneously, one literal and the other inferred. More specifically, she does not address the problem raised by other theorists on how an inferred idea or implicature possesses the semantic property of a statement/assertion. To recall from Chapter 1, for Grice implicatures constitute inferred or implied data while Searle identifies the indirect meaning of a sentence as an IA. This raises up the serious problem for many theorists as to how it is possible for an implicature or indirect derived meaning to constitute an assertion or another IA? As I addressed in my previous chapter and following along the lines of Bertolet, Hornsby, and Soames, within a particular communicative context an inferred implicature can *count as* a particular illocutionary force, yet does not constitute an IA. Thus, RQs contain the semantic property of an interrogative while pragmatically implicate an answer that *counts as* an IA.

---

26. Ilie, *What Else Can I Tell You?*, 49–51, 64.
27. Ene (Ilie), "Theory of Speech Acts," 38–45; Ilie, *What Else Can I Tell You?*, 30–31, 35–36.

The Polarity Shift Between the Rhetorical Question and Its Implied Answer

In connection with the above characteristic, the reverse polarity shift provides another key distinguishing criterion for identifying RQs. Typically, an affirmative or positive interrogative form implies a negative response such as *Is it necessary to shout like that?* with the answer of *No, of course not!* Conversely, a negative interrogative form implies an affirming answer as with *Isn't the answer obvious?* with the answer of *Yes, the answer is clearly obvious!*[28] Combining the first two definitions and following Sadock, Chung-hye Han argues that the general nature of RQs have "the illocutionary force of an assertion of the opposite polarity from what is apparently asked."[29] Ilie, though, does observe how both affirmative and negative rhetorical *wh*-questions (i.e., *who, what, where, when, why*) display a negative polarity shift.[30]

While agreeing with much of Ilie's research, Deborah Schaffer highlights a unique type of RQ that she identifies as "RQ-as-retort" typified by *Is the Pope Catholic?* Schaffer observes from a large number of English examples that this type of RQ is "offered as a response to a prior question which is a true information—or action-eliciting question."[31] She specifically identifies a RQ-as-retort pattern where the second question (the RQ) intends to provide an answer to the first question (the true, genuine question) "as well as emphasize that answer's obviousness through a specific chain of *conversational implicature*: the answer to question #2, which must be easily inferred by the hearer, will also be unavoidably understood to function as the answer to question #1."[32] For example,

How do you like school?
How do you like prison?

---

28. Ilie, *What Else Can I Tell You?*, 51–52.
29. Han, "Rhetorical Questions," 1; idem, "Interpreting Interrogatives," 202.
30. Ilie shows this with the example: *What family doesn't have its ups and downs?* With this particular type of rhetorical wh-question Ilie observes a two-step interpretive process. The first step involves a negative polarity shift resulting in: <u>No</u> *family surely doesn't have its ups and downs*. Since a double negation results from the first step a second step becomes necessary to turn the double negative into an affirmation: *Surely every family has its ups and downs* (*What Else Can I Tell You?*, 52).
31. Deborah Schaffer, "Can Rhetorical Questions Function as Retorts? Is the Pope Catholic?" *JP* 37 (2005): 435.
32. Ibid., 436 (italics mine).

Schaffer identifies Green's cliché type RQs as retorts and Garfield's response to Arlene *Do chickens have lips?* as a prime example. Shaffer also points out how Green sees this RQ violating Grice's maxim of Relation which Relevance theorists have isolated. In this instance, the addressee infers that the answer to the second question, to be relevant, must be the same as the answer to the first question (see Chapter 1).[33] As this comic strip displays, RQs-as-retorts are also typically formulated to express humor to provoke laughter as well as to convey sarcasm. What is truly unique about these types of expressions is "the positive or negative value of the answers does not usually correlate with the positive or negative value of the RQs themselves, unlike the polarity relationships of other RQs and their answers."[34] Schaffer suggests that a possible reason for this phenomenon is that this type of RQ's

> role as an obvious analogy or mirror to the prompting question requires them to match that question's polarity in both question structure and expected answer. Since the prompting questions are not rhetorical, but informational or action eliciting, a match in polarity between them and their answers creates no problem, and the RQs-as-retorts will then necessarily parallel the pattern of their prompts, regardless of polarity requirements for other types of RQs.[35]

This does not mean, though, that some RQs-as-retorts do not reverse in polarity, but such instances are typically used in correlation with the polarity of the prompt as exemplified above and with similar type RQs, such as *Do Elephants hate peanuts?* and *Do alligators grow geraniums?*[36]

---

33. See ibid., 437. Morgan also briefly addresses these types of RQs ("Two Types of Convention," 278).

34. Schaffer, "Is the Pope Catholic?" 453.

35. Ibid., 443; see also Fiengo, *Asking Questions*, 63. Pope excluded these types of expressions from her analysis of RQs because they "break some otherwise valid rules" (*Questions and Answers*, 36).

36. Moshavi misses this point as she claims that the answer to the RQ-as-retort "does not have reversed polarity" ("Can a Positive Rhetorical Question Have a Positive Answer in the Bible," *JSS* 56 [2011]: 254 n. 5; "Two Types of Argumentation Involving Rhetorical Questions in Biblical Hebrew Dialogue," *Bib* 90 [2009]: 33 n. 6; "'Is that Your Voice, My Son David?' Conducive Questions in Biblical Hebrew," *JNWSL* 36 [2010]: 67 n. 5).

The Implicitness and the Exclusiveness of the Answer to the Rhetorical Question

As with ISAs, RQs convey their message inferentially. Addressers imply a solitary, obvious answer that at the same time excludes all other possible answers. Further, the "addresser intends to instill to the audience a *sense of mutual understanding and trust*, by pointing to *commonly shared values and beliefs* and by excluding other values and beliefs."[37] Importantly, this exclusion of all other possible answers but one constitutes "a major criterion for distinguishing rhetorical questions from other types of questions."[38] For Ilie, this fact also distinguishes RQs from Sadock's *Queclaratives* category (the combination of a question and Declarative) which also display an assertive IA of reversed polarity, e.g., *Isn't syntax easy?*[39] Where these two interrogatives essentially differ is that RQs do not convey ignorance (non-information eliciting) while at the same time imply an exclusive, self-assured answer.[40] Before moving forward, I want to highlight here how Ilie's claims above concerning mutually shared values and beliefs does not appear to correspond with her thesis that RQs challenge addressees as well as her conclusion that they "normally *provide information*."

The Addresser's Firm Commitment to the Implicit Answer of the Rhetorical Question

In contrast to genuine questions, addressers employing RQs are unswervingly committed to a single implied answer which most language specialists see also as a distinctive characteristic of such expressions. With this in mind, there are certain parallels between RQs and Conducive and Leading questions and primarily because each expects and pragmatically implies a specific, intended answer already known by addressers and thus exhibit a low degree of elicitative force.[41] It is important to note that language specialists do not provide a clear, definitive semantic or linguistic distinction between Leading and Conducive questions other than the respective characteristic contextual uses and/or settings. Essentially Leading questions are Conducive questions, but become distinguished from the latter

---

37. Ilie, *What Else Can I Tell You?*, 53 (italics mine); see further 53–55.
38. Ibid., 93.
39. Sadock, "Queclaratives," 223–31.
40. See Ene (Ilie), "Rhetorical Questions," 41–42.
41. See Ilie, *What Else Can I Tell You?*, 80–81; see Stenström's degree of elicitative force graph in *Questions and Responses*, 56.

type when used in legal contexts and specifically for cross-examinations.[42] In these situational instances, addressers elicit an answer expected to confirm their assumptions about certain facts and/or data assumed to be known by both questioners and respondents. For example, the question *How fast was each car going when they contacted?* conveys a fairly neutral position whereas the Leading question *How fast was the red car going when it smashed into the blue car?* implies that the red car was at fault as well as traveling at a high speed.[43]

Conducive questions are also identified as Biased, Presumptive, and/or Declarative questions and fall within the larger category of Closed interrogatives.[44] Because of their close similarities, some language specialists consider RQs and Conducive questions as essentially the same type of interrogative. For instance, Stenström views RQs as a sub-type of Conducive questions.[45] Further, she claims that RQs

> behave very much like conducive Q[uestion]s in general in that they are very often responded to, and the statement that R[esponse] is not expected is not correct in actual discourse where I have found that rhetorical Qs, exclamatory Qs, and suggestions generally receive an R. The reason is that, in conversation, A utters something for B to respond to.[46]

---

42. According to Ilie, when "used in cross-examinations, *conducive questions* are usually referred to as *leading questions* and they are indeed intended to lead the cross-examined to supply the answer implied by the cross-examining counsel, by not leaving him/her any other alternative" (*What Else Can I Tell You?*, 91). Thus, Leading questions are a type of Conducive question. Language specialists, though, typically remain a bit inconsistent with the identification of these two interrogatives. For instance, Pope identifies the question *Weren't you at the scene of the crime at 10:00 on the night of the murder?* as a Leading question while also claiming that this same question "is definitely *biased* toward the positive answer" (*Questions and Answers*, 68 [italics mine]). Wolfram Bublitz, though, identifies this question from Pope's own analysis as a Conducive question ("Conducive Yes–No Questions in English," *Linguistics* 19 [1981]: 857–58).

43. See Pope, *Questions and Answers*, 68–69; Howard I. Weinberg, John Wadsworth, and Robert S. Baron, "Demand and the Impact of Leading Questions on Eyewitness Testimony," *Memory & Cognition* 11 (1983): 101–104.

44. On Conducive questions in general see Hudson, "Questions," 13–18; Huddleston, "Clause Type," 879–86; Robert Piazza, "The Pragmatic of Conducive Questions in Academic Discourse," *JP* 34 (2002): 509–27; Quirk et al., *Comprehensive Grammar*, §§11.6–13; Stenström, *Questions and Responses*, 47–56.

45. Stenström, *Questions and Responses*, 48.

46. Ibid., 55–56.

Ilie acknowledges parallels between these two types of interrogatives, but also sees clear distinctions. For Ilie, RQs "are conducive inasmuch as they imply a specifically intended answer." As such, these two types of interrogatives primarily infer their intended answers pragmatically;[47] however, RQs differ from Conducive questions in significant ways. For instance, particular devices and lexical markers can provide clues for conduciveness.[48] Further, Conducive questions *elicit* (i.e., suggest and require) the verbalization of the implied answer whereas RQs direct addressees to *infer* the implied answer.[49] Put another way, with Conducive and Leading questions addressers *explore* addressees' minds while expecting a verbal response; conversely, addressers use RQs to *influence* addressees' minds, but do not expect a verbal response.[50] Importantly, Conducive questions remain interrogatives whereas RQs often inferentially and intentionally transform into statements. What truly distinguishes these two types of interrogatives, as well as all other types, is that Conducive questions *elicit*, i.e., *suggest* and *require* the *verbalization* of an intended answer by addressees and in contrast RQs *elicit* the *inference* of the implicit answer, to which addressers are *committed*, by excluding all other possible alternatives.[51] Moshavi also sees clear differences between RQs and Conducive questions, firstly because the latter "do not serve as implicit assertions," unlike RQs. "Replacing a conducive question with an assertion changes the meaning of the utterance." Second, Moshavi claims that Conducive questions "do not relate to obvious information, as RQs do, but usually to situations involving uncertainty or surprise."[52] This latter point needs sharpening, which I will undertake in more detail below. For starters, although all types of Conducive questions retain their interrogativity, the primary type does not involve uncertainty or surprise; rather, it elicits information addressers assume to be true and expect addressees to confirm.[53]

47. Ilie, *What Else Can I Tell You?*, 92; so also Bublitz, "Conducive Yes–No Questions," 863. Hudson emphasizes the pragmatic aspect of Conducive questions and claims that the "conducive aspect of questions is always read into them by the hearer" ("Questions," 16).
48. See Huddleston, "Clause Type," 882; Quirk et al., *Comprehensive Grammar*, §11.6; Stenström, *Questions and Responses*, 48–53.
49. Ilie, *What Else Can I Tell You?*, 90, 93.
50. Ibid., 56; here Ilie specifically contrasts RQs with Leading and examination questions.
51. Ibid., 93, 220.
52. Moshavi, "Positive Rhetorical Question," 267.
53. Moshavi essentially knows this dimension of Conducive questions (see ibid., 257, 263, 264; idem, "Conducive Questions," 65, 67).

In Hebrew Bible studies, some interpreters have identified certain interrogatives with matched polarity as RQs. Most recently, de Regt claims that certain positive RQs in Job prefixed with ה imply an affirmative answer (6:26; 13:25; 15:11), but does not offer any justifiable explanation for such instances.[54] Quite a bit earlier and most notably, Robert Gordis argues that certain "*questions seeking an affirmative reply occur without a negative.*"[55] To substantiate his claim, Gordis proposes a psychological argument illustrated with the scenario of a person who desires for an addressee to agree that her/his house is beautiful. The addresser would not use the question *Is the house beautiful?* Rather, she/he would insert a negative particle in order to permit the addressee "the pleasurable function of contradicting her/his superficial statement by replying, in effect: 'You imply that the house is not beautiful. On the contrary, it *is* beautiful.'"[56] Following this line of thought, Gordis examines specific interrogatives in the Hebrew Bible such as 1 Sam. 10:24:

Do you see whom Yahweh has chosen?	הראיתם אשר בחר־בו יהוה:
Certainly there is none like him among all the people!	כי אין כמהו בכל־העם:

According to Gordis, English demands the insertion of the negative particle. The reason for this omission in Hebrew is because "under very special circumstances" when the addresser "is animated by an all-powerful certainty of the truth of her/his contentions, so that she/he feels it inconceivable for anyone to differ, she/he can neglect this sop to the ego of her/his audience."[57] Consequently, Gordis views certain RQs functioning with matched polarity, but this conclusion obviously does not correspond to how these types of interrogatives characteristically function. I agree with Moshavi that the question *Is not the house beautiful?* does not convey a self-evident assertion *Clearly the house is beautiful!* Rather, this is a classic Conducive question seeking agreement which pragmatically conveys *I think the house is beautiful, don't you agree?*[58]

---

54. Lénart J. de Regt, "Implications of Rhetorical Questions in Strophes in Job 11 and 15," in *The Book of Job*, ed. W. A. M. Beuken, BETL 114 (Leuven: Leuven University Press, 1994), 60. De Regt does acknowledge that the RQ in 6:26 can also express a negative answer (62).

55. Robert Gordis, "A Rhetorical Use of Interrogative Sentences in Biblical Hebrew," *AJSL* 49 (1932/33): 212 (italics original).

56. Ibid., 213 (pronouns revised).

57. Ibid., 214 (pronouns revised).

58. Moshavi, "Positive Rhetorical Question," 259. Moshavi also observes in GKC an "Asseverative Hypothesis" of the interrogative (ibid., 259–60). Among

Conducive questions elicit a specific, intended answer with certain types displaying matched polarity with one type functioning similarly to RQs with reversed polarity. According to Sadock/Zwicky, these types of questions as found in most languages[59] are used "to express his or her belief that a particular answer is likely to be correct and to request assurance that this belief is true."[60] Perhaps one of the earliest instances of the term "conducive" is found in the work of Dwight Bolinger who uses it primarily in relation to affirmative and negative polarity. He classified a particular question in English that "'conduces' a certain type of answer" while the "given answer is expected or desired."[61] Bolinger sees a distinctive instance of conduciveness with negation and particularly

different hypotheses for apparent RQs with matched polarity, she addresses within GKC that "apparently rhetorical questions express strong affirmations" (ibid., 257). How Moshavi defines the issue here and then addresses it later in this particular essay ends up a bit confusing to me. Immediately following a discussion on RQs (§150d), GKC describes a certain type of interrogative that "is altogether different from our idiom, since it serves merely to express the conviction that the contents of the statement are well known to the hearer, and are unconditionally admitted by her/him" evidenced in Gen 3:11; 27:36; 29:15; Deut 11:30; Judg 4:6; 1 Sam 2:27; 20:37; 1 Kgs 22:3; Mic 3:1; Job 20:4 (§150e; pronouns revised). Moshavi views GKC presenting instances of "rhetorical matched-polarity questions, as well as other questions not of this type" (259), which express certainty. Moshavi then admits that the divergence between the rhetorical and asseverative hypothesis is quite subtle, "since RQs also typically express strong assertions." Still, she sees in GKC a "functional distinction is apparently intended between RQs, which express obviousness, and matched-polarity questions, which have an asseverative function" (ibid., 260). Instead of RQs with matched polarity expressing strong affirmation, it appears to me that the primary problem Moshavi addresses with GKC is its identification of certain interrogatives expressing asseveration rather than properly conduciveness (cf. Gen 27:36; 1 Sam 2:27; 1 Kgs 22:3). If I understand her correctly and with the examples she highlights, I agree that certain interrogatives that GKC proposes as instances of asseveration are best identified as Conducive questions. That said, although GKC translates certain interrogatives in an asseverative sense (e.g., "surely," "verily"), the above description closely resembles how certain Conducive questions are generally defined in the literature as I discuss in this section.

59. See, e.g., W. S. Chisholm Jr., ed., *Interrogativity: A Colloquium on the Grammar, Typology and Pragmatics of Questions in Seven Diverse Languages*, Typological Studies in Language 4 (Amsterdam/Philadelphia: John Benjamins Publishing, 1984), 33–35, 86–92; Rakić, "Serbo-Croatian," 696–98, 703–704, 707–708.

60. Sadock/Zwicky, "Speech Act Distinctions," 180; see also Bublitz, "Conducive Yes–No Questions," 855.

61. Dwight L. Bolinger, *Interrogative Structures of American English (The Direct Question)*, Publication of the American Dialect Society 28 (Alabama: University of Alabama Press, 1957), 10, 97.

on occasions of argumentation that conveys an "'expectation of a given answer on the basis of assumed absence of any reason for disagreement on the part of the hearer (often on the basis of known prior agreement).' Witness its use in argumentation: 'He accepted the money didn't he?' (a fact that the hearer is known to accept)—'Yes'—'Well, then, why dispute the obvious conclusion?'"[62]

Wolfram Bublitz analyzes the nature of Yes–No Conducive questions while focusing on the specific instances of such questions and their similarities with negative Yes–No RQs. Bolinger's definition of conduciveness is too imprecise for Bublitz. In addition, he takes issue with Emily N. Pope's apparent difference between her concept of bias and the expectation of an answer with Conducive/Leading questions.[63] For Bublitz, one must distinguish between more than the desired and the expected answer. Bublitz sees a main distinction between two types of answers to Yes–No questions: (1) the *expected answer* which addressers *expect* addressees to provide which may or may not be desired by addressers and is difficult, if not impossible, for addressees to recognize and (2) the *expectable answer* which the linguistic form of a Conducive question itself points to which addressees can inferentially recognize, but likewise may or may not be desired by addressers.[64] Towards demonstrating this, Bublitz looks at four types of Yes–No Conducive questions with a main concern of examining "the polarities of the speaker's assumptions and of the sentence form."[65] According to Bublitz, polarity is not the sole criterion for conduciveness, but involves "more complex interrelationships between answer, speaker's assumptions and expectations, and the form of the question." For all Conducive Yes–No questions there underlies "a specific positive or negative assumption concerning

---

62. Ibid., 99; see further Dwight Bolinger, "Yes–No Questions Are Not Alternative Questions," in *Question*s, ed. H. Hiz (Dordrecht/Boston: D. Reidel, 1978), 103–104. For critiques of Bolinger and his notion of conduciveness see Bublitz, "Conducive Yes–No Questions," 858; Ilie, *What Else Can I Tell You?*, 90, 93.

63. See Bublitz, "Conducive Yes–No Questions," 857–58; see Pope, *Questions and Answers*, 68–69.

64. Bublitz, "Conducive Yes–No Questions," 858. Stenström states that she agrees with Bolinger's definition of a Conducive question as the given answer "is 'expected' but also that it might be 'desired.'" Yet, she also appears to endorse Bublitz's notion of the expectable answer with such questions which Bublitz argues as different from Bolinger (*Questions and Responses*, 48, 56).

65. For Bublitz, analyzing an addresser's assumptions is a necessary prerequisite for understanding Conducive questions which includes Gricean type mechanics ("Conducive Yes–No Questions," 859).

the existence and nature of the particular event or state which has been called into question."⁶⁶ Further, two underlying assumptions, *old* and *new*, produce different types of Conducive questions. In actuality, though, old or original and new assumptions are essentially two opposing polarities of a single assumption. With some Conducive questions a change occurs from the affirmative old assumption to the negative new assumption while with others a movement from the negative original to the affirmative new one can be observed.⁶⁷ With specific negative Conducive Yes–No questions (Bublitz's type IV) no such change occurs as the addresser's original assumption remains. In fact, there is only one underlying addresser-assumption with this type. These types are also "only *seemingly* based on a discrepancy between an affirmative original and an affirmative new assumption."⁶⁸ According to Bublitz, these particular negative Conducive Yes–No questions are similar to negative Yes–No RQs. These types of RQs differ in that addressers do not expect an answer nor *pretend* that a discrepancy with their underlying assumptions exists.⁶⁹ Ilie agrees with Bublitz's basic parallel analysis, but correctly argues that affirmative or positive RQs also function similarly to Conducive questions in the sense of addresser assumptions and polarity, not solely negative Yes–No RQs.⁷⁰ Ilie, though, observes from Bublitz's work how RQs and Conducive questions are not the same type of interrogative. For instance and first, the distinctions between the expected and expectable answer does not apply to the implicit answer of RQs since this type of interrogative only implies one answer which could be regarded as both expected and expectable. Second, Bublitz's notion of old and new assumptions does not apply either to RQs since this type only allows for one well-defined assumption to which addressers are committed.⁷¹

From the literature, three main types of Conducive questions arise.⁷² The most prominent seeks to confirm a proposition that addressers believe

66. Ibid., 853.
67. See ibid., 853–56.
68. Ibid., 861.
69. Ibid., 863.
70. Ilie, *What Else Can I Tell You?*, 92.
71. Ibid., 93.
72. Ferenc Kiefer identifies three types of Conducive questions: (1) negative inverted Yes–No questions; (2) assertive Yes–No questions; and (3) tag questions ("Yes–No Questions," 98). Kiefer's first category consist of questions, though, that Pope identifies as Leading questions such as *Weren't you at the scene of the crime at 10:00 on the night of the murder?* which Kiefer uses as an example while referencing Pope.

is true, such as *She was pushed, wasn't she?*[73] Such Conducive questions intend to confirm the proposition in order to establish a state of agreement between addressers and addressees.[74] Another type of Conducive question expresses an aspect of surprise, such as *Did your children really go to school today?* This type of conduciveness displays a discrepancy between addressers' anticipated or assumed disagreement and the actual affirmative answer.[75] Quirk et al. also include negative oriented Conducive questions in this category that often include critique, disappointment, disapproval, and/or annoyance such as with *Can't you drive straight?* or *Aren't you ashamed of yourself?*;[76] while the initial interrogative in this category additionally conveys such negative connotations as well. A third type seeks explicit agreement with the proposition such as *Don't you like those new pink ties I gave you for Christmas?*[77] According to Bublitz, these types in English typically occur as Conducive negative Yes–No questions with a reversed polarity of affirmation with the addressee not agreeing with the negative proposition, but agreeing with the affirmative assumption expressed by the addresser.[78] Addressers do not employ this type of Conducive question to confirm their knowledge, but rather to ascertain addressees' explicit agreement to the truth of the assumption expressed.[79] Bolinger also briefly identifies a type of interrogative that "embody information that the speaker is passing on to the hearer."[80] Moshavi categorizes this as an Information-Conveying use of the Conducive question with reversed polarity. Addressers use interrogatives like *Do you know that this has been a record month for snow?* not to elicit information, but provide information specified in the propositional content of the interrogative.[81] In sum, based on the intended pragmatic function of Conducive questions in English, certain types seeking confirmation and expressing surprise match

---

73. See Huddleston, "Clause Type," 881–82.

74. Bublitz, "Conducive Yes–No Questions," 865.

75. See Quirk et al., *Comprehensive Grammar*, §§11.6; see also Hudson, "Questions," 17–18; Rakić, "Serbo-Croatian," 703–704.

76. Quirk et al., *Comprehensive Grammar*, §§11.7.

77. Bublitz does not include this particular question in his type IV list, but he does identify it as belonging to the category of "negative conducive yes-no questions" while displaying "a discrepancy between an affirmative old and a negative new assumption" ("Conducive Yes–No Questions," 857).

78. Ibid.

79. Ibid., 862.

80. Ibid., 88.

81. Moshavi, "Conducive Questions," 76. Moshavi identifies 2 Kgs 2:3 as an example of this type of Conducive question and possibly Judg 18:14 (77).

in polarity whereas those seeking agreement or providing information display a reversed polarity.

Rakić observes that Conducive questions, especially confirming types, violate Searle's first Preparatory condition for questions to which addressers do not know the answer (see Chapter 1).[82] I agree with Rakić here, but specifically in the sense that Conducive questions violate this condition on an information-elicitation level. In contrast to the intended polarity reversal of RQs, with Conducive questions a distinct aspect of interrogativity remains. Thus, Conducive questions retain their interrogative function while conveying a low level of information-elicitative force. That said, and in light of my previous chapter, like RQs these types of interrogatives also violate the Sincerity condition and broadly Grice's maxim of Quality by using a linguistic form to ask such a type of question. Along with this and towards differentiating Conducive from genuine questions, Stenström bases such a distinction on the degree of addresser assumptions and strength of belief (especially with Yes–No questions):

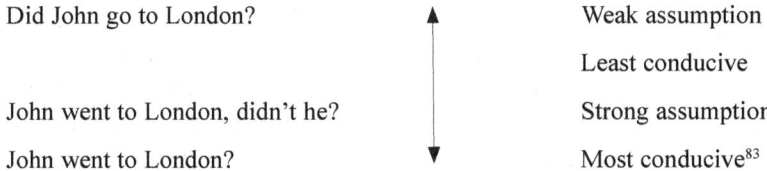

Did John go to London?		Weak assumption
		Least conducive
John went to London, didn't he?		Strong assumption
John went to London?		Most conducive[83]

Figure 2.1. Stenström's Degrees of Addresser Assumptions
and Strength of Belief

Returning to 1 Sam 10:24, with Samuel's interrogative interpreted as a RQ the obvious answer would be *No!* which would be a contextually unanticipated response, especially followed by the likely asseverative or emphatic כי clause.[84] Gordis suggests, though, an assumed negative particle which as a RQ would then convey an affirmative reversed polarity *Yes!* Thus, Gordis correctly interprets the intention of this interrogative, but incorrectly categorizes it as an RQ. Rather, this interrogative and similar types should be understood as a Conducive question.[85]

---

82. Rakić, "Serbo-Croatian," 710, see also 696–98.
83. Stenström, *Questions and Responses*, 49.
84. On this use of כי see Joüon-Muraoka §164b; *IBHS* §39.3.4e.
85. See further Moshavi, "Positive Rhetorical Question," 253–73; idem, "Conducive Questions," 65–81.

Tryggve N. D. Mettinger incorporates Austin's SAT notions in his understanding of the monarchical development in Israel and in this particular instance he views Israel's response יחי המלך "Long live the king!" to Samuel's interrogative as performative. For Mettinger, the "acclamation comes as the answer to this question. This shows that the acclamation had the character of a *performative* utterance. It was through the acclamation that Saul was here made king by the people." Mettinger also sees evidence from Samuel's writing of the regulations defining the relationship between the king and the people (v. 25) that the "acclamation of the people forms a declaration, a solemn oath, that the people are willing to enter into this relationship."[86] I agree that this acclamation functions in a Declarative illocutionary sense, but Mettinger does not discuss the type of question asked by Samuel which interpretively impacts the nature of the acclamation. Clearly the form of Samuel's initial utterance is linguistically an interrogative that elicits a verbal response, but pragmatically does not function as a question seeking information. As such, Samuel's interrogative conveys a low degree of information-elicitation while violates Seale's Preparatory condition and also the Sincerity/Responsibility condition and therefore most naturally functions as a Conducive confirmation-eliciting question with matched polarity. This is further evidenced by the fact that Israel provides a confirming verbal response *Long live the king!* and not an answer informing Samuel whether or not the nation actually sees Saul.[87] Samuel uses this interrogative speech act to implicate the intent of establishing agreement between Israel with himself and Yahweh.[88]

86. T. N. D. Mettinger, *King and Messiah: The Civil and Sacral Legitimation of the Israelite Kings*, ConBOT 8 (Lund: Gleerup, 1976), 135–36.

87. Moshavi identifies Samuel's Conducive question as a "subtype of the confirmatory question" which "is used to draw the addressee's attention to an object in his or her vicinity to a fact the addressee is already aware of. Such questions are often used as a preface for what the speaker intends to say next. The question often involves the 'Do you see' formula. The speaker does not wait for an answer, which is expected to be positive" (see also 1 Sam 17:25; 1 Kgs 20:13; 22:3–4) ("Positive Rhetorical Question," 266, see also 271; see also idem, "Conducive Questions," 73–74).

88. Bublitz briefly proposes that negative Conducive Yes–No questions are types of ISAs ("Conducive Yes–No Questions," 867–68). I can understand this correlation to a point as clearly Conducive questions inferentially imply an intended obvious answer. Yet as I describe above, these types of questions remain interrogatives. They do not express two IAs simultaneously: one literal and one indirectly intended. Nor do they indirectly make a request to do something like with a classic ISA (2a) or intentionally transform into exclusive answers as with RQs.

Samuel's Conducive question intentionally implicates an affirmative response for Israel to confirm Saul as its king. Still, rather than Israel on its own performatively instituting Saul as king which Mettinger appears to suggest, more precisely the nation confirms Yahweh's choice in Saul and ultimately the establishment of the monarchy. Thus, the acclamation is more of some type of confirming Declarative (an extralinguistic performative that confirms Yahweh's choice that then transforms the states of affairs in the nation Israel). Israel's confirming compliance with the implicated intention of Samuel's Conducive question leads the nation to inaugurate the reign of Saul with its affirmative Declarative. This verbal response is also a multidimensional self-involved speech act that includes the Expressive and Commissive IAs as well (see the Introduction and below). With the Expressive dimension Israel takes the stance that Saul and those who follow will be its king and with the Commissive Israel commits itself to serving its king with both these IAs including interrelated behavioral entailments. Thus, Yahweh gives Israel what it requests and with this Conducive question intentionally leads Israel to confirm his choice of its new king.

The Multifunctionality of the Rhetorical Question

For Ilie, what all RQs have in common is their *challenging force* primarily conveyed by their questioning form. When encountered by RQs addressees are challenged to think of an alternative answer which is ultimately rejected by addressers from the very beginning with an implied specific and exclusive answer. As evidenced with Quintilian, language specialists have recognized the diverse use of RQs (e.g., express strong beliefs, attitudes, judgement, disagreement, standpoints, accusations, complaint, exacerbation, humor, ironical and sarcastic remarks and/or stances, retorts, etc.). Yet, Ilie also highlights how addressers use RQs to fulfill one or more different functions simultaneously. She offers the example of a person uttering the challenging RQ *How could they have used the word "celebration" instead of "commemoration"?* while reflecting upon a created ghetto scene of Auschwitz with Jewish cantorial music in the background. The reporter perceives and refers to the RQ as a complaint while at the same time it conveys a strong reproach and indignation.[89] Another example is *What will become of these kids when they grow up?*, which also expresses a complaint and simultaneously serious concern and even despair. With each of these RQs, the addresser responds to the current state of affairs while also indirectly justifying that response.

---

89. See Ilie, *What Else Can I Tell You?*, 59.

Ilie's observations here have parallels with Tsohatzidis' conclusions that addressers can say something figuratively and indirectly simultaneously, e.g., *Your baby has become a piglet* (see Chapter 1). In addition, Ilie observes how others can interpret a RQ quite differently from the specific intended addressee.[90]

Ilie's Three Misconceptions of Rhetorical Questions

These five distinctive features mark RQs for Ilie as well as her pragmatic approach which also dispels three misconceptions about RQs that additionally help to identify the three pragmatic characteristics of RQs supplemented to the two syntactico-semantic features.

The Misconception That Rhetorical Questions Are Non-Answer Eliciting Questions

Clearly RQs do not elicit information like genuine questions, but they do intentionally elicit a mental assent ("mental answer-eliciting") to the intended answer which addressees are expected to infer.[91] Conversely, Ferenc Kiefer asserts that "'genuine' rhetorical questions...should not be treated as indirect speech acts." Kiefer bases his claim on the assumption that an interrogative "is rhetorical if the speaker doesn't want the addressee to answer this question: she/he knows the answer perfectly well, in fact, she/he answers the question her/himself." RQs "do not require an answer (and they *do not require a non-verbal response* either) because they are uttered in soliloquy or because the answer is given by the speaker her/himself."[92] Kiefer's conclusions here concerning elicitation are incorrect and at the same time he ironically highlights how RQs are in fact ISAs as addressers violate communicative principles by using interrogatives ingenuously to indirectly convey something else.

The Misconception That Answers to Rhetorical Questions Are "Known" to Both the Addresser and the Addressee

The answer to a RQ is "inferable" rather than known. This is evidenced by several reasons. First, the exact answer can be either known (partially or completely) or unknown by addressees (also displayed by intentional and unintentional misunderstandings of RQs). Second, the answer to a

---

90. Ilie draws this conclusion from a multiple-choice questionnaire she developed on how interpreters understand how a particular RQ functions (ibid., 59–60).
91. See Ilie, *What Else Can I Tell You?*, 84–85.
92. Kiefer, "Yes–No Questions," 98 (italics mine; pronouns revised). For similar conclusions see Davison, "Indirect Speech Acts," 151.

RQ can never be truly known unless the addresser and/or the addressee verbalizes it, which is atypical with RQs. Consequently, a comparison of answers is not characteristically possible as addressers imply while addressees infer the answer.[93] Yet, as I discussed in Chapter 1 with Lycan's three levels of degree of indirect force and will describe further below, some RQs have reached a level of conventional meaning or the answer is so unquestionably transparent that they do not require much inferential calculation, if any. Thus, in certain instances like the RQ-as-retort addressers assume that addressees know the answer and also that they know that everyone relevant knows the answer, including addressers.[94]

The Misconception That Verbalized Answers to Rhetorical Questions Are Supplied Exclusively by the Addresser

Here Ilie explicitly responds to John Beekman's addresser and addressee answer criterion for distinguishing between genuine questions and RQs. Beekman concludes that in "the New Testament, we can expect then that real questions when answered will always be answered by someone other than the questioner, and that rhetorical questions when answered will always be answered by the questioner her/himself, never by someone else."[95] For Ilie, that only addressers supply answers to RQs excludes the evidence that RQs can be answered by addressees or by both addressers and addressees.[96] But again, verbalized answers are not elicited or expected with RQs while in some instances Ilie has observed in various scenarios both addressers and addressees supplying answers.[97] Relatedly, the non-verbalized response to a RQ does not solely indicate an addressee's assent to the exclusive answer. A verbalized answer can indicate an addressee's reception of the RQ's message, but this may be an appropriate or inappropriate answer while addressees can also express agreement or disagreement.

Rhetorical Questions as Indirect Speech Acts

For Ilie, the hybrid nature forces RQs to comply with the constraints of both interrogatives and assertions. She goes on to say that the

---

93. See Ilie, *What Else Can I Tell You?*, 85–88; see also 98–133.
94. Green, *Pragmatics*, 160.
95. John Beekman, "Analyzing and Translating the Questions in the New Testament," *Notes on Translation* 44 (1972): 4 (pronouns revised).
96. See Ilie, *What Else Can I Tell You?*, 90–93.
97. See ibid., 88–89.

fact that rhetorical questions can get *explicit answers* can be regarded as evidence that they function partly as questions, i.e., as challenges directed at the addresser. However, the fact that they can be responded to by replies expressing agreement, such as *You are right*, or disagreement, such as *You are wrong*, can be regarded as evidence that rhetorical questions function partly as indirect statements.

The force of a RQ consists in the *challenging double effect* of a question and an indirect statement. For Ilie, this explains why RQs "can act as *amplifiers* or as *mitigators*, by emphasizing or by toning down the addresser's opinions, beliefs, assumptions. By means of amplification or mitigation, rhetorical questions can *induce, reinforce, or alter assumptions, beliefs or ideas in the addressee's mind*, and therefore may be used to exert manipulation, as well as counter manipulation." With this, Ilie sees the main discursive function of RQs as follows:

- *to induce* assumptions, beliefs, ideas, in addressees' minds
- *to reinforce* addressees' assumptions, beliefs, ideas
- *to alter* addressees' assumptions, beliefs, ideas

Responses to RQs "add further emphasis to the implicit rhetorical answer, either by *reinforcing* the implied message or by *recontextualizing* it through *qualifications* or *cancellations*, i.e., alterations of the initially implied/inferred answer." Ilie also sees three main functions fulfilled by verbalized responses to RQs:

- *to reinforce* the implication of the RQ
- *to qualify* the implication of the RQ
- *to cancel* the implication of the RQ[98]

Based on her thesis and in one of her latest essays, Ilie asserts that in pragmatic terms a RQ "can be described as having the literal *illocutionary force* of a question and the *perlocutionary effect* of a statement."[99] Her conclusion here is obviously succinct and basic, but has far-reaching implications while needing further explanation in light of her more comprehensive view of RQs as ISAs. To begin, in one of her earliest essays, Ilie claims that RQs "are rooted in an indirect speech act, since they question whether the intrinsic conditions hold or not, while the answer is conveyed indirectly, in the deep structure of the question."[100] RQs

---

98. Ibid., 128.
99. Ilie, "Rhetorical Questions," 406 (italics mine).
100. Ene (Ilie), "Theory of Speech Acts," 41 (on this page Ilie presents a list of some of the intrinsic conditions for RQs).

display in their deep structure a performative utterance introduced by the performative verb *to doubt* or *to wonder* which replaces the verb *to ask*, the indicator of a genuine question. Further, these performative verbs mark an ISA and account for the polarity shift occurring in the biased answer of RQs. For example, the interrogative *Who wishes to grow old?* understood as a RQ questions and eventually denies its apparent presupposition *Someone wishes to grow old* and cancels the direct speech act of asking a question and introduces an indirect performative sentence which challenges or questions the very existence of the referent in the surface grammar *I doubt whether there is anyone who wishes to grow old* while implicating an indirect negative assertion *No one wishes to grow old.*[101] What is missing in this analysis is the aspect of PEs which she does include in her later descriptions.

Although Ilie views RQs as ISAs in a Searlean sense, she also recognizes Searle's reductionist view of questions to real and exam types while additionally showing how his rules for questions, except for the first one, do not adequately apply to RQs. Using Searle's Rules/Conditions (see Chapter 1) and in contrast to genuine questions (see Table 1.2), Ilie presents her understanding of the IAs conveyed by RQs:

Table 2.1. Ilie's Illocutionary acts conveyed by Rhetorical Questions

Rules/Conditions	*RQs*
Propositional Content	Any proposition or propositional content
Preparatory	1. *S* knows and implies "the answer," expected to be inferred by *H*
	2. It is obvious to both *S* and *H* that they have the information referred to in the implicit answer and that no information is required from *H*; it is not obvious that *H* realizes without being told that *S* is committed to the implicit answer
Sincerity	*S* wants her/his commitment to be recognized and accepted by *H*
Essential	Counts as an attempt to get *H's* recognition and acceptance of *S's* commitment to the implicit answer[102]

Ilie's grid here provides an important supplement to Searle's rules/conditions framework for genuine questions as RQs obviously function quite differently from such interrogatives. However, because RQs are in fact interrogatives Searle's scheme remains interpretively helpful. Specifically, as I presented above, his framework provides criteria for recognizing how

---

101. Ibid., 39, 41; see also Ilie, *What Else Can I Tell You?*, 30–31.
102. Ilie, *What Else Can I Tell You?*, 37.

the interrogative dimension of RQs violate Searle's first Preparatory and Sincerity conditions, thus triggering for addressees that addressers are implicating something else with the respective literal interrogative. Searle, though, does observe that in general the literal interrogative of sentences like (2a) becomes defective in certain contexts when the addresser already knows the answer while operating successfully as an ISA.[103]

Ilie acknowledges how SAT cannot solve the correlation between a RQ and its answer as well as addressers' intended response and addressees' supplied response.[104] As I have described, addressees of RQs can disagree with the intended answer. According to Ilie, the discrepancy between the intended and actually achieved PE of an IA is typically explained away by speech act theorists as either *insincere* or *infelicitous*. Consequently, a more in-depth analysis is necessary to deal with this deviation and specifically regarding "the correlation between illocutionary and perlocutionary acts in terms of the addresser's and the addressee's respective roles and goals, namely the addresser's intentions and commitments, the addressee's expectations, commitments, and perception of the message."[105] With this aim, Ilie proposes the perlocutionary impact of RQs on addressees with two goals: the *Primary Goal* and the *Ultimate Goal*. According to Ilie:

- Addressers *Primary goal* aims at making addressees becoming aware of the rhetorical use of the question, namely to recognize the implied message intended by addressers. When the primary goal is achieved, it is manifested by addressees' *acknowledgement* of the question as being rhetorical, i.e., by understanding its message appropriately.
- Addressers *Ultimate goal* is to make addressees become committed to the message implied by the RQ, namely to agree with its implication. When the Ultimate goal is achieved, it is manifested by addressees' *agreement* with the reasonableness and/or usefulness of addressers' implied message. Despite the possibility of disagreement by addressees, addressers intend to induce in addressees the disposition and willingness to act on this assumed shared commitment.[106]

Ilie also adapts Stenström's elicitation ideas (see the Introduction) and identifies these two goals as two types of elicitation respectively.

103. Searle, *Expression and Meaning*, 43.
104. Ilie, *What Else Can I Tell You?*, 35.
105. Ibid., 38.
106. Ibid., 40–41.

Addressers use RQs to elicit the *mental response* of addressees involving (1) the inference of the implicit, obvious answer of RQs and (2) the agreement and commitment to the statement derived from the implicit answer.[107] Because of van Eemeren/Grootendorst's argumentative view of speech acts as a bilateral process, Ilie additionally sees her two perlocutionary goals roughly corresponding to their *Inherent* or *Minimal perlocutionary effects* and *Consecutive* or *Optimal perlocutionary consequences* respectively.[108] To recall from Chapter 1, the *Minimal* goal consists in the *acceptance* of the speech act by addressees while the *Optimal* goal is the complete intended satisfaction of the entailed consequences of the acceptance of the speech act.[109] Addressees obviously can also disagree with the Ultimate goal whereby they commit themselves to particular stances in reference to the intended answer. In these instances, addressees understand the interrogative as a RQ, but do not accept its intended force.[110]

For Ilie, the addresser uses a RQ with the intention "to persuade the addressee to *reconsider* his/her own beliefs, assumptions or opinions. It is by reinforcing, qualifying or cancelling these beliefs, assumptions or ideas, that the addresser expects to get the addressee to accept them." With all this, Ilie proposes two interdependent stages for analyzing interrogatives functioning as RQs with the second stage containing two substages.

Table 2.2. Ilie's Theoretical Frame for the Analysis of Rhetorical Questions

- The *Interactional* stage (*what is said*): where the RQ is perceived as an interrogative sentence and consequently, addressees react to its questioning challenge by looking for a contextually appropriate answer.
- The *Implicational* stage (*what is meant*): where the RQ is seen to imply an answer to which addressers are committed and which addressees are expected to infer.
  1. The *Obligatory* substage of *conventional implication* (*what is conventionally meant*): where addressees are led to derive from the implicit answer the statement implied by addressers.
  2. The *Optional* substage of *contextual implication* (*what is contextually meant*): which is resorted to whenever the conventional implication does not yield a plausible message; addressers' messages are understood by inferring a further implication.[111]

---

107. See ibid., 81, 130.
108. See ibid., 39–41.
109. See van Eemeren/Grootendorst, *Argumentative Discussions*, 24; see further my discussion in Chapter 1.
110. See Ilie, *What Else Can I Tell You?*, 110–11.
111. Ibid., 60–61 (italics mine).

According to Ilie, the contextual implicational aspect occurs when "the conventional implication does not yield a plausible message" and thus further inferencing becomes necessary.[112]

In connection to the hybrid nature of RQs as well as with the above two substages, Ilie identifies two types of responses to RQs: *Implicit Rhetorical Answer* and *Explicit Answer*. The former is a *covert, obligatory mental response* implied by addressers and elicited from addressees and the latter is an *overt, optional verbal response* either self-supplied by addressers or an unelicited optional response offered by addressees. As presented above, the *mental* or *non-verbal response* consists in both the *Primary* and *Ultimate Goals* and related to the *Obligatory* substage. Ilie distinguishes two types of verbalized responses with *Explicit Answers* and *Replies* which comply with as well as support the double nature of RQs view. The former responds to the interrogative dimension of the RQ whereas the latter responds to the derived indirect statement. Ilie also identifies addressees' *Acknowledgement* or *Non-Acknowledgement* of the rhetorical force of an interrogative. *Acknowledgement* is the initial step of addressees recognizing an interrogative intentionally functioning as a RQ (as with the *primary goal*) while the second step concerns addressees' commitment to the implied statement by either agreeing (as with the *ultimate goal*) or disagreeing with it. Through verbalized responses addressees can either express *Agreement* or *Disagreement* while *Non-Acknowledgement* of the rhetorical force of an interrogative can either be *Intentional* or *Unintentional*. The latter is typically due to a misunderstanding or misinterpretation of RQs whereas the former normally occurs when addressees disagree with the inferred statement. According to Ilie, these two related distinctions between *Acknowledgement* versus *Non-Acknowledgement* of the rhetorical force and *Agreement* versus *Disagreement* of its inferred message relate to van Eemeren/Grootendorst's perlocutionary distinctions.[113] Ilie adds a third idea of Qualification where addressees can qualify the implied message of a RQ.[114] As I also presented above, she succinctly concludes that the "*discursive functions of rhetorical questions* consist in inducing, reinforcing or altering assumptions, beliefs, ideas, in the addressee's mind. The *discursive functions of verbalized responses* to rhetorical questions consist in reinforcing, qualifying or cancelling the implications of the rhetorical answer."[115]

---

112. Ibid., 64.
113. See ibid., 98–133; cf. 101–102, 110–11, 130–31.
114. Ibid., 110.
115. Ibid., 131.

As I depicted in my Introduction, ISAs and RQs likewise express two IAs simultaneously:

ISAs
1. Literal interrogative
2. Indirect assertion, request, etc.

RQs
1. Literal interrogative
2. Indirect answer

Ilie's basic view of RQs is as follows:

1. Literal force of a question
2. Perlocutionary effect of a statement

Slightly different from this basic view, Ilie's above framework contains an Interactional stage (*what is said*) and Implicational stage (*what is meant*). Although Ilie does not include her two-fold elicited goals within her scheme, with her basic view she implicitly equates her Implicational stage with the PE of a statement. Also within her framework, the *Implicational* stage closely resembles Grice's notion of *implicature*, which focuses on the implicated answer of RQs (*what is meant*). This corresponds to her notion that in contrast to genuine questions "the performative *I doubt/ wonder* are supposed to mark the illocutionary force of a rhetorical question as a persuasive act."[116] In her conclusion, Ilie summarizes how her two theoretical stages (see Table 2.2) correlate with her two perlocutionary goals,[117] but this also makes clearer her blending of these dimensions which in the end displays parallels with her basic view:

> The two stages, i.e., the interactional and the implicational stage, are correlated with the two goals pursued by the addresser of the rhetorical question. At the first stage, the addresser's *primary goal* is *to elicit the addressee's recognition of the rhetorical force of the question*, i.e., the addressee's inference of the implicit rhetorical answer. Thus, the addressee is expected to understand the message of the rhetorical question. At the second stage, the addresser's *ultimate goal* is *to elicit the addressee's agreement with the message implied by the rhetorical question*, i.e., the addressee's agreement

---

116. Ibid., 31.
117. Although Ilie calls her two Primary and Ultimate stages as "goals," she explicitly identifies these as perlocutionary in nature as I describe above (see also ibid., 40–41).

with, and preferably, commitment to the implication of the rhetorical question. By pursuing the ultimate goal, the addresser of a rhetorical question intends to induce in the addressee the disposition and the willingness to act on this shared commitment.[118]

I find Ilie's framework generally helpful as well as I concur with the proper inclusion of PEs with RQs. I also find Ilie's use of van Eemeren/Grootendorst's perlocutionary notions and her own descriptions of her two perlocutionary goals insightful. Further, I agree somewhat with her observation that while "it is theoretically possible, as well as necessary, to discuss the distinction between locutionary, illocutionary, and perlocutionary acts, it is nevertheless impossible to separate them in reality, since all speech act events consist of varying sorts of combinations of these three categories. In theory, an illocutionary act becomes felicitous when it succeeds in triggering (in the hearer) the perlocutionary effect intended by the speaker."[119] It is also important to rehearse that Ilie appeals to van Eemeren/Grootendorst's perlocutionary notions to better address the discrepancy between intended PEs and actual achieved PEs and to provide a more in depth analysis of the correlation between illocutionary and perlocutionary acts.[120] How she conceives her perlocutionary goals functioning, though, becomes theoretically problematic within a speech act account. First and as I described in Chapter 1, Ilie's conclusion about the felicitousness of IAs needs sharpening from a speech act account perspective. Illocutions do not become successful when accompanied PEs have triggered the intended effect with addressees as PEs are ultimately caused by addressees. Searle obviously displays an unfounded confidence in semantics for determining meaning as well as in his Principle of Expressibility ("whatever can be meant can be said"), but still PEs transpire outside of language and concern the nonlinguistic psychological effects of IAs occurring within addressees. As Bach claims, IAs are felicitous when addressees recognize addresser's intention (as with Ilie's Primary perlocutionary goal) while PEs succeed when addressees comply with or act on that intention.[121] This *recognition* occurs through Hornsby's *reciprocity* (see Chapter 1) notion (addressees recognizing intended meaning through normal linguistic exchange) as well as pragmatic processes, not PEs. Van Eemeren/Grootendorst essentially concur with Bach with their view

118. Ibid., 219.
119. Ilie, "Speech Acts and Rhetorical Practices," 339.
120. Ilie, *What Else Can I Tell You?*, 37–38; see also Ilie, "Speech Acts and Rhetorical Practices," 339–42.
121. Bach, "Pragmatics," 151.

of two distinct aspects of the complete speech act: the IA relates to the communicative aspect expressed in the attempt to achieve understanding while the perlocutionary act relates to the interactional aspect expressed in the attempt to achieve acceptance.[122] Concerning Ilie's Primary goal, she correlates this aspect with the literal interrogative, with *what is said*. In contrast, speech act theorists typically conceive PEs deriving from IAs (cf. Austin; Searle; Alston), not equated with nor producing IAs. Ilie's basic view suggests that the PE of a statement derives from the interrogative of the RQ. This makes some sense from a speech act account as IAs trigger PEs. Further, multiple PEs can occur with any expression, both intentional and unintentional. Still, I find her correlation of PEs with *what is said* conceptually problematic. What truly becomes confusing is the way she describes her Primary goal and her first Implicational Obligatory sub-stage in very similar terms. For Ilie, the former consists in "the addressee's inference of the implicit rhetorical answer," thus understanding "the message of the rhetorical question" and the latter "where the addressee is led to derive from the implicit answer the statement implied by the addresser." Even more confusing, Ilie correlates her Ultimate goal with her second stage, but her descriptions of her Primary goal and her second sub-stage closely correspond. With RQs, although the derived answer and statement essentially operate along the same lines as the intentional meaning or message of the RQ, there can be a semantic difference between the answer and the derived statement. Further, as Pauline Slot demonstrates (see below), the general principle for most RQs entails that the reconstructed presupposed answer to the literal question equals the intended propositional content.[123]

Within the speech act descriptions of perlocutions as conceived by Searle and others, Ilie's inclusion of PEs with RQs do not schematically correspond and perhaps intentionally so. As I presented in Chapter 1, it is important to make clear that Searle does not explicitly factor PEs into his descriptions of ISAs. He understands ISAs expressing two IAs, not an IA and a PE; or more specifically not an intended IA with an accompanied PE by way of a literal IA. Perhaps Searle assumes an inclusion of this perlocutionary dimension from his direct speech act descriptions? Searle, though, does incorporate inferential processes similar to Grice's principles that trigger intended IAs. To recall, Searle views ISAs expressing an intended IA by way of a literal IA. Bach/Harnish and Vanderveken view ISAs operating in this same sense, but explicitly incorporate Gricean notions

---

122. Van Eemeren/Grootendorst, *Argumentative Discussions*, 51.
123. Slot, *How Can You Say That?*, 98, 195.

while correspondingly not factoring in a perlocutionary dimension. Gu and van Eemeren/Grootendorst both correctly emphasize the necessity to clarify as well as further define the proper role of PEs within SAT (see Chapter 1). Further, van Eemeren/Grootendorst, in line with Gu while in contrast to Searle and others, correctly explain how PEs are *interactional* with the addressees determining whether or not the intended PE is embraced, but still PEs derive from the speech act for these two theorists. At the same time, for van Eemeren/Grootendorst direct IAs and ISAs remain distinct because ISAs are performed by means of *two illocutions* whereas direct illocutionary perlocutions are performed by means of *one illocution* and *one perlocution*. In contrast to their illocutionary perlocutions category, successful ISAs only require that addressees "recognize *both* of the *two illocutionary forces* (and the propositional content) and thus *understand* the illocutions."[124] With ISAs, van Eemeren/Grootendorst also follow Searle by not including PEs while explicitly incorporating Grice's principles for conceiving how addressees recognize intended meaning.

It appears that the reason for each of the above specialists' descriptions, despite their slight differences, is that they all conceive ISAs expressing two IAs in a Searlean sense. Ilie's adoption of Searle's ISA scheme for understanding RQs is also implicitly reflected in her two stages of *what is said* and *what is meant*, but she does not identify the intended message as an IA in this instance while in her basic view she identifies the intended message as a PE of a statement. Further, how Ilie describes her two-fold perlocutionary goals essentially corresponds to the pragmatic processes for *recognizing* intended meaning, but, as I touch on above, not how PEs are typically understood which focuses on the actual intended consequences or effects complied with or acted upon by addressees beyond recognizing and understanding addressers' intent.[125] With ISAs the intended PEs lead to a specific response and/or action; specifically with (2a) the implicated illocutionary request has the intended PE of actually passing the salt (see Chapter 1).

Along with numerous speech act theorists and as I described in detail in Chapter 1, I also find Searle's dual illocutionary understanding of ISAs to be *pragmatically* sound, but with certain qualifications and mainly that the inferred speech act *counts as* an IA; it does not constitute the semantic property of an IA. Thus, I consider Ilie's second stage of *what*

---

124. Van Eemeren/Grootendorst, *Argumentative Discussions*, 53 (italics mine with the first clause).

125. See further Huang, *Pragmatics*, 282; Sadock, "Speech Acts," 55–56; Wharton, "Speech Act Theory," 455.

is meant better categorized to represent the intended IA of the RQ which is essentially how she describes this stage, but should not be additionally correlated with a PE. In the final analysis, Ilie's two-fold perlocutionary goals for RQs has interpretive merit, but I am convinced more so when conceived within a typical speech act account. Thus, despite the clear existence of intended and actually achieved PEs, I find it more sound to maintain the usual speech act sequence of PEs deriving from intended IAs. Within a speech act account, then, I understand intended PEs triggered from the implicated data of a RQ that *counts as* an IA (*what is meant*) and thus I identify this stage as Perlocutionary.

Apart from the triggers accompanied with the pragmatic characteristics of RQs (e.g., elicitative force), Ilie does not expand in much detail on exactly *how* addressees infer from the linguistic interrogative (*what is said*) the intended meaning; more specifically how addressees *recognize* her Primary goal. As I discussed with ISAs, this inferred area of meaning is what Grice and numerous language specialists have focused on with the concept of pragmatic processes and specifically the notion of *implicature*. Interestingly, although Ilie identifies her second stage as *Implicational*, she does not explicitly discuss or incorporate Grice's inferential notions nor van Eemeren/Grootendorst's inferential scheme into her own two-stage RQ framework.[126] Thus, I find Ilie's framework mistakenly bypassing the Gricean implicature dimension or pragmatic principles that van Eemeren/Grootendorst include in their inferential scheme for ISAs which, as I will describe below, Slot does employ for analyzing RQs.

Some time ago, Robert Koops examined RQs in the book of Job while utilizing the notion of implicature as conceived by Levinson and specifically his revision of Grice's maxim of Quality.[127] For Koops, "RQs represent an example of implicature generated by the flouting of one of the 'maxims' of human verbal interaction, namely the maxim of 'sincerity' or 'quality.'" He goes on and says that during an ordinary conversation "a question is assumed to be a request for information. When it becomes evident to the hearer that the 'information' in question is already well known to both of them, she/he understands that the speaker must be deliberately flouting the expected pattern, and thereby doing something else, namely emphasizing a point."[128] In particular, Koops examines a section of interrogatives in Eliphaz's second speech found in Job 15:

126. Ilie briefly refers to Pauline Slot's observation of the narrowness of Grice's maxims for analyzing RQs (see *What Else Can I Tell You?*, 33).
127. Levinson, *Pragmatics*, 110.
128. Roberts Koops, "Rhetorical Questions and Implied Meaning in the Book of Job," *BT* 39 (1988): 418 (pronouns revised).

⁷Are you the First Human born
    and were you brought forth before the hills?
⁸Do you listen in the council of God?
    And do you limit wisdom to yourself?
⁹What have you known that we do not know,
    you understand that which is not within us?

הראישון אדם תולד
ולפני גבעות הוללת:
הבסוד אלוה תשמע
ותגרע אליך חכמה:
מה־ידעת ולא נדע
תבין ולא־עמנו הוא:

With these RQs, Koops identifies three "different levels, or stages, of implied meaning":

(1) the *rhetorical*, in which the negative–positive polarity is reversed.
(2) the *conventional*, in which a connection is made between a physical state (old or young), or an attitude (you limit wisdom to yourself) and a mental state (wise, foolish, or proud)
(3) the *pragmatic*, in which the conclusion is drawn that certain behavior should follow from certain conditions.[129]

De Regt implements Koops' three stages throughout his more recent analysis of the RQs in Job and explicitly views them as more precise than simply attempting to look at the function of RQs.[130] He also applies these three stages to Job 15:7–8: "At the *rhetorical* level, it is implied that Job is not the first man that was born, and the he has not listened in the council of God. At the *conventional* level, it is implied that wisdom is in the council of God only. At the *pragmatic* level, Eliphaz makes clear that Job should not be so presumptuous."[131]

Koops displays some interpretive insight from Levinson's use of Grice, especially for determining when an interrogative functions as a RQ based on the violation of Levinson's broadened Quality maxim that includes a sincerity component. Also, his different levels of implied meaning exhibit some correspondence with more current research, but at the same time his definitions of particular terms are unclear while he puzzlingly blurs certain concepts. To begin, *implied meaning* essentially constitutes the intended *pragmatic* intention of *rhetorical* questions. Specifically addressers use RQs to imply intended meanings while addressees infer

---

129. Ibid., 420.
130. de Regt, "Implications," 322.
131. Ibid. (italics mine); see also pp. 324–25; idem, "Discourse Implications," 56–57, 66.

those implied meanings through pragmatic processes. Regarding his stages in particular, his association of *rhetorical* with "reversed polarity" points to one of the chief defining characteristics of RQs, but I understand the *rhetorical* dimension relating to the entirety of its rhetorical goal to prompt, challenge or reinforce the beliefs and commitments of addressees. How Koops defines *convention* is not exactly clear to me, nor is how de Regt applies it. For specialists, *convention* as applied to language usually refers to the relationship between a linguistic form and its agreed-upon meaning established by the conversational participants during a specific time and space.[132] With this in mind, and as I discussed with ISAs, certain RQs imply a conventional meaning that does not vary from one communicative context to another while others have a wider range of meaning and thereby need more well-defined contexts as van Eemeren/Grootendorst describe (see Chapter 1). Finally, what Koops defines as *pragmatic* would include Ilie's final three characteristics of RQs, but in broad terms refers to how addressers use a linguistic interrogative to indirectly imply an obvious answer which addressees infer through pragmatic processes. That said, what he identifies as pragmatic, as well as de Regt's application of it, points in the direction of self-involvement and in particular the stance and entailments of the intended IAs of RQs.

Slot explicitly addresses this pragmatic area of meaning with RQs while also incorporating van Eemeren/Grootendorst's work. She identifies her method as a Pragma-Dialectical Ideal model "which is specifically designed for the monologually structured discussion" and in particular for interpreting RQs in argumentative texts.[133] In her analysis, Slot focuses on RQs that function as assertions and as argumentation while also recognizing they can function as Assertive, Directive, Expressive, and Commissive speech acts;[134] unfortunately, she does not explore how RQs convey these forces. In line with van Eemeren/Grootendorst, she finds both Searle and Grice providing insights for ISAs and RQs. Slot also agrees with Searle's dual IA nature of ISAs as well as what she identifies as his suggested conditional connections between *what is said* and *what is meant* for these types of speech acts.[135] As discussed above, Searle restricts ISAs to illocutionary indirectness and, as earlier theorists have highlighted, does not provide an adequate instrument for interpreting

---

132. See, e.g., Marina Terkourafi, "Conventionality," in Cummings, ed., *The Routledge Pragmatics Encyclopedia*, 79–81.
133. Slot, *How Can You Say That?*, 193; see further 7–9, 17–34.
134. Ibid., 7.
135. See ibid., 63–69.

indirect expressions like RQs, irony, and metaphors which are not connected to and established through a felicity condition. Also, as I introduced in the previous chapter, with Searle's indirect request RQ examples Slot confirms how his reconstruction for interpreting ISAs in this instance and similar ones cannot "be carried out with one of the felicity conditions for the intended speech act as a guiding principle, and they do therefore not fit in his characterization of an indirect speech act."[136] Slot also finds Grice's CP and maxims needing adjustments, especially for interpreting RQs. Specifically, Grice's CP needs broadening in its scope while his maxims require more precision. In particular, Grice regrettably limits this maxim of Quality to only true and false expressions. Slot, without referencing Levinson, also sees this maxim necessarily requiring a Sincerity component. For example, sentences like *Thanks for slamming the door in my face!* express something sincere or insincere, not something true or false.[137]

Slot slightly revises van Eemeren/Grootendorst's synthesized inference framework (see Table 1.4) for interpreting ISAs and RQs. Slot agrees with their first two inference aspects, but then presents a number of different rules for various indirect expressions. Slot's basic inference scheme for RQs (which only slightly differs from her rules for ISAs[138]) is as follows:

Table 2.3. Slot's General Inference Scheme for Rhetorical Questions

1.
The addresser A has uttered U

2.
If U is taken literally,
A has performed speech act 1,
with communicative function 1
and propositional content 1.

---

136. Ibid., 64–65.
137. Ibid., 60; Ilie concurs with this critique (*What Else Can I Tell You?*, 33).
138. To provide clarifying correspondence, with Table 2.3 I have incorporated Slot's basic inference scheme for RQs (see ibid., 75–82, cf. 75–77) into van Eemeren/Grootendorst's General Inference Scheme (see Table 1.4). Slot uses the term "rule" to refer to several different aspects to her inferential scheme resulting in a blurring effect with her rules. I will identify each element of van Eemeren/Grootendorst's inference scheme table as "inference rules" coupled with the respective numeral. Here, I have also slightly adjusted Slot's numbers in Table 2.3: 3b is Slot's 3 and 4b is Slot's 4.

Direct Speech Acts	RQs
3a. In Context C, speech act 1 observes the rules of communication.	3b. In context C, speech act 1 is a violation of one or more rules of communication.
4a. *Therefore*: Speech act 1 is a correct interpretation of *U*.	4b. In context C, speech act 2 rectifies the violation of rules of communication 2 and 3.
	5. Speech act 1, speech act 2 and the context *C* can be linked by means of rule *i* (1, 2, 3, 4 or 5) via […],[139] in the case of ironic utterances via […], and in the case of […] via […]
	6. Therefore: Speech act 2 is a correct interpretation of U.

For Slot, in order to determine indirectness the violation of at least one of the communicative rules must occur while assuming the observance of van Eemeren/Grootendorst's Principle of Communication. Specifically, she examines which of her communicative rules are violated with RQs that closely correspond with van Eemeren/Grootendorst's inference framework while also interacting with Searle's felicity conditions for Questions (see Chapter 1). First, the *Efficiency* rule is the violation of inference scheme 3b (Searle's first Preparatory condition) as the literal interrogative is *superfluous* because addressers already know the answer. Pope argues that the answer to a RQ is obvious to both addressers and addressees,[140] but this only occurs through inferential means and for Slot the possibility of addressees knowing the answer cannot function as a criterion for indirectness. Rather, only when addressees understand that addressers already know the answer can this provide a possible clue that the interrogative is intended to function as a RQ.[141] Second, the *Sincerity* rule is a violation of the inference scheme 2 and is a direct consequence

---

139. Within this rule, Slot presents quite complex derivational patterns for rhetorical yes/no questions, wh-questions, and alternative questions (see *How Can You Say That?*, 95–125, cf. 122–25).
140. Pope, *Questions and Answers*, 36.
141. Slot, *How Can You Say That?*, 87–89.

of the *Efficiency* rule. If addressers already know the answer and have no interest in an answer then addressers are insincerely eliciting information from addressees (Searle's Sincerity condition).[142] According to Slot, only the violation of both of these two inference scheme components properly allows for the identification of a RQ from an interrogative. The third is the *Comprehensibility* rule which directly depends upon the previous two violations. This rule violates inference scheme 1 as the interrogative is not intending to elicit information. Finally, the *Relevancy* rule directly relates to van Eemeren/Grootendorst's rule/maxim 5 and is violated when an inappropriate speech act occurs in a communicative sequence. This rule functions as a contextual clue for highlighting other communicative violations inherent with RQs; however, this rule does not operate as a criterion for identifying indirectness.[143] Nor is this rule related to how Relevance theorists envision the maxim of Relevancy.

As I presented above, Slot observes one basic and consistent step involved for reconstructing the intended propositional content for all types of RQs: formulating the presupposed answer to the literal question. The general principle, then, is that the reconstructed presupposed answer to the literal question equals the intended propositional content.[144] This principle plays out with Yes–No RQs and the typical characteristic of polarity reversal. However, in some rare instances the proposition remains the same, as with RQs-as-retort.[145] In the majority of instances of wh-questions a complete proposition is not expressed which the addressee completes with the answer. "Completing the propositional function is the pattern that can be used in the reconstruction of the propositional content of wh-questions."[146] Two possible reconstructions are involved: either by adding a *null set* (adding a missing element) or by adding the *most obvious answer*.[147] In rarer instances a positive element requires insertion.[148] Alternative RQs always consist of two propositions that are mutually exclusive while only one of the propositions represents the presupposed answer. In reconstruction, the other proposition can therefore be deleted if it directly contradicts the preferred proposition or a negation can be added

---

142. Rakić agrees that RQs violate Searle's Sincerity condition for questions, but does not go beyond this ("Serbo-Croatian," 706, 710).

143. Slot, *How Can You Say That?*, 90–93.

144. Ibid., 98, 195.

145. Slot does not explicitly discuss RQs-as-retorts. For Slot's discussion on RQs not displaying reversal of polarity see ibid., 100–113.

146. Ibid., 114.

147. Ibid., 114–16; see also Pope, *Questions and Answers*, 42–51.

148. See Slot, *How Can You Say That?*, 116.

if the propositions are mutually exclusive. In certain instances, the type of proposition requires changing.[149]

For Slot, the three main rules of Efficiency, Sincerity, and Comprehensibility also provide significant criteria whereby to identify indirectness in general and indirectness with RQs as well as to distinguish RQs from genuine questions. That said, the violations of these rules for Slot merely signal that an interrogative has a different pragmatic function than a question; they alert addressees of indirectness, but are not always sufficient enough to definitively identify a RQ.[150] Consequently, it is necessary to reconstruct the intended speech act. For Slot, then, only when one determines what the intended speech act is and exactly how it derives from the literal speech act can one distinguish between our (2a) and the RQ like *Can you blame her?*[151] This centers on determining the connection between *what is said* and *what is meant*. To accomplish this, first one must establish different connections between the intended function of the expression and its literal propositional content. Slot highlights how ISAs in general can be illocutionarily indirect, propositionally indirect or both simultaneously. Whereas with RQs, only two possibilities can occur: the expression is either indirect on the level of communicative function or indirect on both the levels of communicative function and propositional content. It is impossible for RQs to express a propositional indirectness alone since it is essential with RQs that the literal interrogative transform into a different communicative function. Thus, Slot proposes separate reconstruction patterns for the communicative function and propositional content of different types of RQs. One must also address the various types of RQs. Since Yes–No questions, wh-questions, and alternative questions presuppose different types of answers, so RQ versions of these types of questions would expect to operate the same way.

Slot's proposals correspond as well as refine other language specialists use of Searlean and Gricean insights for interpreting ISAs and RQs. As I presented in Chapter 1 and above, both Levinson and Vanderveken broaden and generalize Grice's Quality maxim. However, van Eemeren/Grootendorst's notions and Slot's use of their work more specifically address RQs in line with Levinson. Further, Slot confirms the link between the inferred, intended assertion and the literal interrogative. Along with van Eemeren/Grootendorst, Slot also adopts a Searlean view of ISAs, however, she does not explicitly concern herself with how the

---

149. See ibid., 117–21.
150. Here Slot claims that she contrasts Pope's understanding of RQs (ibid., 98); see Pope, *Questions and Answers*, 36–67.
151. Slot, *How Can You Say That?*, 94.

inferred aspect of an ISA *counts as* an IA nor does she discuss PEs with ISAs or RQs. It is quite interesting that Ilie closely adapts van Eemeren/Grootendorst's two-fold PE scheme into her understanding of RQs, but does not include their combining of Searlean and Gricean insights while Slot does the exact opposite.[152]

Rhetorical Questions Conveying Various and Multiple Illocutionary Forces

In contrast to Stenström[153] and numerous other specialists as well as biblical scholars who view RQs solely inferring assertions, I agree with Slot that particular RQs can convey other illocutionary forces. Slot notes that whereas others "who restrict the term 'rhetorical question' to questions which function as assertions, I use the term in a broader way to refer to questions which function as an assertive, directive, expressive, or commissive speech act."[154] Evidenced here, Slot also seems to restrict the classifications of forces to Searle's types (minus Declaratives), but as I described in Chapter 1 it is best to maintain both Austin and Searle's taxonomies while considering them both as functional and neither as definitive. Speech act theorists have not described in much detail the different types of forces ISAs can possibly convey and certainly not with RQs. As I presented in Chapter 1, Searle primarily recognizes two forces with ISAs: indirect Directives and indirect Commissives (see also Table 1.3). With the former, addressers make a request as with (2a) and with the latter make an offer or in some instances a promise. To my knowledge, speech act theorists, though, have not explored the possibility of additional forces with ISAs expressed beyond an intended IA. Ilie consistently identifies the inferred answer as a statement or an assertion, but she does describe RQs expressing other feelings and/or attitudes (e.g., reproach, complaint, indignation) simultaneously with her *multifunctional* characteristic notion without appealing specifically to any speech act taxonomies. As I only touched on in Chapter 1 concerning speech acts, Sadock has demonstrated that various illocutionary forces are not independent or disassociated one from another, but rather the various dimensions or other forces are often incorporated into a single expression, with one force typically being primary.[155] Searle also observes that we often combine more than one of

---

152. Without any critique, Ilie briefly describes Slot's use of van Eemeren/Grootendorst's inference scheme, with its integration of Gricean and Searlean insights (*What Else Can I Tell You?*, 33).
    153. Stenström, *Questions and Responses*, 54–55.
    154. Slot, *How Can You Say That?*, 7 n. 6.
    155. Sadock, "Typology of Speech Acts," 395–402.

his five illocutionary forces "at once in the same utterance"[156] while his own hybrid assertive-declarative category exemplifies this phenomenon.[157] Further, the performative *I promise to*... combines at least the Declarative and Commissive forces. Thus, speech acts are often, if not always, *multidimensional* IAs. Briggs recognizes this in Searle's earliest writings which "should lead us to *expect* hybrids as the normal occurrence."[158] Briggs concludes that a "performative utterance is a certain kind of 'multiple' illocutionary act" with one force being primary.[159] Applying these observations to RQs, it appears clear that all RQs convey the Assertive force to one degree or another with numerous RQs expressing it in a primary sense while additional forces may simultaneously occur. Yet, certain RQs can express a different primary force from the Assertive, as Slot appears to claim, but typically include the Assertive force.

Regarding the Directive force, all RQs naturally include this force. Austin placed questions under the category of Expositives while for Searle questions are a subclass of his Directives category as addressers attempt to get addressees to verbally provide an answer whereas with proper Directives addressers attempt to get addressers to do something (see Chapter 1). Following along these lines, RQs elicit mental responses and thus inherently convey this force. Thus, the Directive essentially corresponds with the fundamental pragmatic intent of RQs with the illocutionary point of the force attempting to get addressees to agree with, assent to, or confirm the answer. This force with RQs, though, does not operate the same way as with genuine questions. If an addressee rejects the inferred answer and offers a contrary answer to the interrogative dimension, this answer does not match the intended Directive force of the respective RQ as with genuine questions because the addresser is not eliciting for a verbal response and/or for unknown information.[160] Yet, some RQs may function as genuine Directives as Searle conceives them and in line with Slot's suggestion. Ilie contends that a RQ "can *never be* information- or *action*-eliciting, although it may eventually lead to an act of decision-making aimed at a certain course of action as a desirable ulterior goal."[161] For Ilie, a prime example of an action-eliciting question

---

156. Searle, *Expression and Meaning*, 29; see also Searle/Vanderveken, *Foundations of Illocutionary Logic*, 52.

157. See Searle, *Expression and Meaning*, 19–20.

158. Briggs, *Words in Action*, 52.

159. Ibid., 68.

160. In my earlier work, I imprecisely claimed that based on the hybrid nature of RQs the interrogative dimension conveys the Directive force requiring "a response from the listener" (*Performative Nature*, 138).

161. *What Else Can I Tell You?*, 77 (italics mine).

is *Would you mind closing the door, please?* which requires an action to be performed by the addressee for the benefit of the addresser.[162] One of Searle's example Directive RQs *How many times have I told you (must I tell you) not to eat with your fingers?* infers the Directive *Stop eating with your fingers!* which obviously elicits an action. Further, this RQ does not convey much of an Assertive force, but the addresser does additionally express frustration and disgust. Other English examples of RQs inferring a primary Directive force include: *Do you want to teach the class today? Why not stop here? Do you want to get fired? Do you want to live at home in the basement for the rest of your life? When will you be satisfied? Have you lost your tongue?* With most of these RQs there is a dominant verbal dimension that impacts the reconstruction of the inferred answer to reflect the action expressed in the literal interrogative. For Ilie, the difference between information- and action-eliciting questions and RQs is that the latter do not require the compliance of addressees to fulfill the request for the benefit or relevance of addressers. In addition to this, the former types of interrogatives do not pragmatically transform into obvious and exclusive answers.[163] Characteristic to all RQs, types that infer a primary Directive force likewise pragmatically infer obvious and exclusive answers, but these answers convey an action-eliciting dimension. As I discussed above with perlocutionary effects and will describe in more detail below, with RQs inferring a primary Directive force addressees retain the option whether or not to mentally agree with and assent to the inferred answer and thereby respond accordingly. So in agreement with Ilie, RQs *are not* and thus *do not operate* the same way as action-eliciting questions in parallel with genuine information-eliciting questions; however, and in a stronger sense than Ilie describes, as certain ISAs pragmatically infer an indirect Directive request like (2a) certain RQs infer a Directive illocution that initially elicits a mental response as well as an accompanied responsive action.

The Expressive force typically accompanies a primary Assertive force as the addresser infers an assertion about the world while at the same time takes a stance in relation to that assertion. More technically, with the Expressive force addressers express committed psychological attitudes or feelings specified in the sincerity condition about a state of affairs specified in the propositional content. With this force there is no direction of fit, rather the truth of the expressed proposition is presupposed. For example, when someone apologizes for the state of affairs corresponding to the linguistic content she/he sincerely expresses sorrow or remorse

---

162. Ibid., 74.
163. See ibid., 72–77 and especially 129.

for that state of affairs.¹⁶⁴ To attempt to propose how RQs convey the Expressive force, it seems best to relate this force to both what prompts the interrogative as well as the inferred IA. Regarding the former and similar to Ilie's descriptions with her multifunctional notion as well as Schmidt-Radefeldt's self-involving ideas (see the Introduction), addressers express their attitude or feelings about a certain state of affairs that prompt and justify the response, while the force is related to the pragmatic function of the interrogative. Concerning the latter and as I stated earlier, most often RQs express a primary Assertive force as they typically transform indirectly into statements. The Expressive force, then, directly relates to this inferred Assertive force, the exclusive answer addressers are utterly committed to. The addresser's attitude or feeling is specified in the sincerity condition about the state of affairs represented by the inferred propositional content. Further, Searle's Expressive force closely corresponds to Austin's Behabitive which Evans directly identifies as one of the primary forces expressing self-involvement (see the Introduction and Chapter 1). Evans claims that "Behabitives are utterances in which the speaker implies various mental states (intentions, attitudes) other than, or in addition to, belief."¹⁶⁵ For Austin, Behabitives concern "attitudes and *social behavior*."¹⁶⁶ This force then is what Briggs associates with the *stance* of addressers entailed in the propositional content.¹⁶⁷ However and applying Thiselton and Brigg's spectrum of strengths scheme here (see Chapter 1),¹⁶⁸ depending upon the type of RQ this force can either express a weak or strong stance in direct relation to the inferred answer. To recall from my Introduction, the expression *It is raining* constitutes a weak assertion that does not contain any consequential entailments of the stance taken whereas *God is creator* is a strong assertion that logically entails behavioral implications. So, all RQs naturally include the Directive force while including the Assertive force and in many instances this force is primary and that usually includes an accompanied Expressive force and in these instances the RQs infer strong assertions as well as Expressives whereas others infer weak assertions and Expressives.

RQs that infer a strong Assertive and accompanied Expressive then also often include the Commissive force. For Evans, the Commissive is the companion force to the Behabitive with both comprising the two essential

---

164. See Searle, *Expression and Meaning*, 15–16; Searle/Vanderveken, *Foundations of Illocutionary Logic*, 38–40, 58–59.
165. Evans, *Self-Involvement*, 57.
166. Austin, *Things with Words*, 152.
167. See Briggs, *Words in Action*, 148–52.
168. See ibid., 63–65; Adams, *Performative Nature*, 3–37.

aspects of self-involvement. "Commissives are utterances in which the speaker commits her/himself to future patterns of more-than-verbal behavior."[169] For both Austin and Searle, Commissives commit addressers to a particular future course of action.[170] Briggs relates this force to the notion of *entailment* which directly derives from the *stance* expressed in the propositional content reflecting the state of affairs. These two dimensions represent the dual focus of a hermeneutic of self-involvement: *stance* and *entailment*.[171] With the Commissive force addressers commit themselves to particular behavioral actions entailed from the public stance taken (Austin and Evans' Behabitive or Searle's Expressive) specified in the propositional content.

Proposed Theoretical Framework for the Analysis of Rhetorical Questions

As language specialists highlight, the interpretive processes for deciphering any type of expression, in particular indirect types, do not transpire in a nice neat compartmentalized succession. That said, it remains interpretively helpful to present a theoretical sequential process for conceptualizing the function of RQs; however, a certain amount of interdependence may occur between the interpretive stages of my framework similar to how Ilie conceives her own and as van Eemeren/Grootendorst envision communication where addressees interactionally engage in determining addressers' intended meaning. In conjunction with this and along with Schmidt-Radafeldt's hybrid description of RQs, addressees engage with both the interrogative and inferred, intended answer in a parallel way somewhat along the lines of Récanati's more recent interpretive view (see Chapter 1). I am convinced that addressees use the literal interrogative to one degree or another to inferentially derive the intended IA. Yet and without adopting Récanati's entire interpretive program, aspects of his alternative parallel processing notions appear to most naturally work with RQs. This parallel interpretive process highlights how addressees engage with RQs with the literal and derived IAs competing in the computation process with addressees determining which IA to engage with and/or assent to. Also, as I described in my Introduction, it is this very hybrid characteristic that initiates and implores the self-involvement of addressees as the interrogative prompts interactive contemplation while the inferred aspect implies

---

169. Evans, *Self-Involvement*, 57 (pronouns revised).
170. Austin, *Things with Words*, 157; Searle, *Expression and Meaning*, 14.
171. See Briggs, *Words in Action*, 148–52.

for addressees to agree with, assent to, or confirm the intended answer which addressers are committed to. My framework below attempts to reflect the ISA nature of RQs and specifically their hybrid features along with the typical interpretive process involved. I additionally include both dimensions of *what is implicated* and *what is meant* in my second stage. As I discussed in Chapter 1, this reflects how Grice and others broadly see both *what is said* and *what is implicated* as providing the data for *what is meant*, thus creating a distinction between *what is implicated* and *what is meant*. Yet, at the same time for specialists *what is implicated* refers to the specific inferential data which ends up blending *what is implicated* and *what is meant* (this blending also appears to be reflected in Ilie's second stage). Thus, the term implicature appears to refer to both the implicated derived data as well as the pragmatic processes which informs *what is meant*. This area between *what is said* and *what is implicated* for me best refers to the pragmatic processes triggered by *what is said* to one degree or another that addressees employ to recognize and understand *what is implicated* and ultimately *what is meant*. With the dual hybrid nature of RQs, I include a perlocutionary dimension triggered by the inferred, intended IA (*what is meant*). Thus, I identify the inference aspect of the intended IA with the notion of implicature rather than perlocutionary as Ilie proposes. With all this, my framework is as follows:

Table 2.4. Proposed Theoretical Framework for the
Analysis of Rhetorical Questions

1. Literal Illocutionary Interrogative (*what is said*): Addressers use a literal force of an interrogative that prompts addressees to provide a contextually appropriate answer.
2. Inferred Illocutionary Answer: Addressers imply an intended, exclusive answer which addressees infer from the literal interrogative, pragmatic processes, and contextual factors.
    - Implicature aspect (*what is implicated*): Addressees recognize that the interrogative violates the immediate contextual communicative principles and rules which prompts inferential, pragmatic processes.
    - Intentional Meaning aspect (*what is meant*): Addressees infer the intended, exclusive answer which *counts as* an IA and communicatively cooperates within the immediate conversation.
3. Perlocutionary Effects
    - Initial Perlocutionary goal: Addressees acknowledgement and understanding of what the inferred IA means and specifically the intended implications of agreeing with the obvious answer.
    - Intended Perlocutionary goal: Addressees agreement and commitment to the inferred IA with its accompanied stances and entailments.

Generally speaking, the nature as well as the interpretive process of the majority of all RQs reflect the above framework. Yet, due to the complexity of language, how discourse participants use language in varying communicative contexts and for specific purposes, RQs may deviate from particular aspects of my framework.

Literal Illocutionary Interrogative

An addresser utters a literal interrogative and abides by the communicative principles if she/he literally asks a genuine question. The addressee understands the literal interrogative, but in a particular communicative context it does not appear that the addresser is eliciting her/him for some unknown information. Consequently, the literal speech act violates the communicative principles of rational conversational engagement. The addressee, though, assumes the addresser is conversationally cooperating and is thus doing something different with the interrogative.

Inferred Illocutionary Answer

Implicature Aspect

The addressee recognizes that the addresser is using an interrogative differently from its literal meaning. In a particular communicative context, the interrogative understood literally would be incomprehensible to an addressee (van Eemeren/Grootendorst's rule 1; Slot's Comprehensibility rule). Also, various communicative rules and felicity conditions along with the violation of some of these conditions trigger the addressee's recognition that the addresser is doing something beyond the literal interrogative.

Levinson in his earlier work and later with Penelope Brown regarding politeness, observes with RQs that "an implicature is generated by flouting the maxim of Quality." However, as shown above with Koops' use of his earlier work, he does not restrict this maxim to truthfulness as in a Gricean sense, but includes a sincerity condition in this instance[172] which similarly Vanderveken proposes with his sub-maxim of Quality for assertions (see Chapter 1). To recall from my conclusion of Chapter 1 and above with Slot, Grice's maxim of Quality (*Don't say something false*) is too narrow and specific. For example, the sentence *It is cold in here!* most appropriately falls within the category of exploiting this maxim as an addresser experiencing a particularly cold room is not making a false claim while at the same time requests to make the room warmer. However, with (2a) this maxim does not exactly apply, it also needs a Sincerity

---

172. Levinson, *Pragmatics*, 109–10; Brown/Levinson, *Politeness*, 223.

component. This is also true for RQs as Slot claims.[173] Vanderveken's generalized version of this maxim (*Let your IA be felicitous in the context of your utterance*) with its multiple possible sub-maxim IAs as well as van Eemeren/Grootendorst's Responsibility condition (*Don't be insincere; be honest, correct*) provide a necessary expansion of this maxim.

David Braun similarly modifies Gricean conversational implicature theory to accommodate how asking questions can implicate in certain instances propositions and in others questions as well as how asserting propositions can implicate questions. In particular, Braun adds a Maxim of Literalness and revises the maxim of Quality. The former maxim entails *Be literal* and specifically with questions addressees assume that addressers locuting semantic questions with interrogatives are in fact asking questions.[174] Regarding the Quality maxim and following Levinson, Braun completely reformulates it as a Maxim of Sincerity while including Grice's ideas of true and false aspects. Both these maxims come into play for instance when a professor says to another professor *Did you grade a million exams last night?* With this nonliteral question, both maxims are violated as the addressee knows that the interrogative is not literal (flouting the Maxim of Literalness) and the addresser already knows that the addressee did not actually grade a million exams as well as does not want to be told so (flouting the Maxim of Sincerity). Maintaining Grice's CP, the addressee recognizes that the addresser implicates a question from which the addressee infers that the addresser is asking (roughly) whether she/he graded a lot of exams the previous night.[175] Similar to Récanati, Bach, and others who observe that ISAs are types of implicatures (see Chapter 1), Braun concludes that "acts of indirect asking counts as acts of implicating" and specifically propositional or interrogative implicatures,[176] which comparably relates to how RQs function. Also, as I discussed in Chapter 1, Green concurs with Relevance theorists that the majority of implicatures conveyed involve apparent violations of Grice's maxim

---

173. Manuel Garcìa-Carpintero associates RQs with ISAs as well as recognizes the necessity to revise Grice's maxim of Quality with these types of expressions, but does not go into any specific detail on what exactly such a revision entails (see "Explicit Performatives," 111–12).

174. David Braun, "Implicating Questions," *Mind & Language* 26 (2011): 587–88.

175. Ibid., 591–92.

176. Ibid., 592. Braun also shows how questions like *Is this lipstick?* is a semantic question uttered by a wife to her husband which indirectly implicates additional questions such as *why is there lipstick on his shirt collar?* and *is he having an affair?* as well as she expects her husband to realize she has such expectations (ibid., 584).

of Relation. In instances where the maxim of "Be relevant" appears to be disregarded, but where *what is said* is correctly understood only by assuming that what is apparently irrelevant is, in fact, relevant.[177] Yet, as Green has also demonstrated, the violation of other maxims can simultaneously occur; still, Grice's maxims need revision and expansion as just described above.

Hannah Rohde proposes a new condition for the felicitous use of RQs: the addresser and addressee "must share *prior* commitments to similar and obvious answers."[178] RQs are biased and at the same time *uninformative* and their "effect is to synchronize discourse participants' commitments, *confirming* their shared beliefs about the world." Thus, RQs reiterate information, the answer is predictable to both addresser and addressee. As such RQs are neither *information-seeking* as with genuine interrogatives nor *information-providing* like statements and thus Rohde classifies them as "redundant interrogatives." Specifically Rohde identifies three felicity conditions: (1) the presence of an obvious answer; (2) the uninformativity of the answer; and (3) the sufficient similarity of the addresser and addressee's answer.[179] Interrogatives, then, function as RQs when addresser and addressee share sufficiently obvious and similar answers. Further, RQs are uninformative "not because they *commit* neither participant, but because they require that both participants *already be committed* to a *joint mutual belief.*"[180] A prime example for Rohde is when an addresser utters an information-eliciting question:

So, who is your favorite basketball team?

The addressee wearing a purple and gold sport's jacket responds:

Who do you think? The Los Angeles Lakers!

The addressee's interrogative succeeds as a RQ when both discourse participants know or deduce the obvious answer to the addresser's question. Even though the addressee provides an obvious answer, it informs neither of the participants because they already know or can readily derive the answer from their knowledge about the addressee's public commitments displayed by her/his Laker's jacket. Rohde's provides another example with:

177. Green, *Pragmatics*, 101.
178. Rohde, "Redundant Interrogatives," 134 (italics mine).
179. Ibid., 135 (italics mine).
180. Ibid., 145 (italics mine).

Who was the only heavy weight champion to retire undefeated?

This interrogative is felicitous as a RQ when both participants know about famous boxers. If the addressee cannot identify Rocky Marciano as the obvious answer, the question serves to indicate a misalignment in the addresser and addressee perceptions of each other's knowledge.

For Rohde, the felicitous use of a RQ "depends on shared commitment in the Common Ground." Rohde follows Christine Gunlogson's formulation of Common Ground[181] which separates "out participants' commitments into independent commitment sets composed of worlds that are consistent with that participant's public beliefs." The Common Ground, then, consists of the union of worlds from all commitment sets.[182] The failure of the above RQ demonstrates the importance of separating the Common Ground of (1) the commitment sets of both the addresser and addressee and (2) the perceptions of the other conversational participant's commitment sets.[183] Although RQs operate as interrogatives invoking an answer set, "they are *redundant* interrogatives because they serve only to reiterate information already in the Common Ground." Answers to RQs do not update any participant's commitment sets.[184] For Rohde, this Common Ground is a second condition related to RQs uninformativity. Her first condition establishes a metric for evaluating the presence of an obvious answer based on *entropy* as utilized by van Rooy.[185] This condition concerns the aspect of surprise or uncertainty. With information-seeking questions a high degree of entropy occurs whereas with RQs there is a clear lack of surprise which is further evidence of their uninformativity. Entropy provides a mathematical way for measuring the surprise associated with an answer to a question. Thus, with RQs there is a complete lack of surprise because of the predictability of the answer and thus they are not genuine questions.[186]

I find much of Rohde's work insightful, but where I have problems is with her claim that *all* RQs are redundant interrogatives. I agree that the intended answer of a RQ is obvious, known and/or inferable, but it appears to me that Rohde's synchronization and confirmation of the

---

181. Christine Gunlogson, "True to Form: Rising and Falling Declaratives as Questions in English" (PhD diss., University of California, 2001).
182. Rohde, "Redundant Interrogatives," 143.
183. Ibid., 162.
184. Ibid., 152.
185. See van Rooy, "Negative Polarity Items," 15–21.
186. Here is where Rohde differs from van Rooy who argues that RQs are information-seeking interrogatives based on the same metric of Entropy.

discourse participants' shared mutual joint beliefs condition does not apply to each and every RQ and thus cannot be considered as the sole criterion for identifying such expressions. As I quoted above, Ilie correspondingly agrees with Rohde as she asserts that addressers intentionally use RQs to instill in addressees a sense of *mutual understanding* and *trust* by pointing to commonly shared *values* and *beliefs* while excluding other *values* and *beliefs*.[187] Yet, as I also touched on above, this understanding of RQs appears to counter Ilie's overarching persuasive and challenging function of RQs. To specifically recall Ilie's definition of RQs, she describes them as *challenging* statements that convey the *addresser's commitment* to the implicit answer in order for the addressee to ultimately *accept its validity*. Further, and as I quoted above, addressers use RQs to persuade addressees to *reconsider* their own beliefs, assumptions, or opinions[188] and also that RQs "normally *provide information*."[189] Yet, all RQs for Rohde are *uninformative*, "because they require that both participants *already be committed* to a joint mutual belief." Importantly, though, Rhode qualifies her description here with a subsequent claim that shared "knowledge about others' beliefs and about the real world is *precisely* what licenses rhetorical questions."[190]

Combining the descriptions of both these specialists, I suggest viewing RQs expressing *degrees of informativity*. Ilie actually points to this conclusion in her work when she describes that the main discursive functions of RQs is to *induce, reinforce,* or *alter* addressees' assumptions, beliefs, and ideas. Along these same lines, when Ilie describes her Ultimate perlocutionary goal she claims that it "is not reached unless the message implied by the rhetorical question has succeeded in making the addressee's assumptions, beliefs or opinions compatible with the addresser's, i.e., by *altering* them if they were different, or by *reinforcing* them if they were already similar."[191] Ilie comes very close to Rhode's above qualified statement while including her challenging aspect of RQs as she concludes:

> Because rhetorical questions rely on the addresser's and addressee's *mutually shared knowledge* about facts, ideas, events, etc., *the addresser* can express a certain *commitment* about them, which is assumed to be *inferable*

---

187. Ilie, *What Else Can I Tell You?*, 53; see also idem, "Rhetorical Questions," 406.
188. Ilie, *What Else Can I Tell You?*, 61.
189. Ilie, "Rhetorical Questions," 405 (italics mine).
190. Rohde, "Redundant Interrogatives," 144–45 (italics mine).
191. Ilie, *What Else Can I Tell You?*, 40 (italics mine).

by the addressee. A number of rhetorical questions can function argumentatively, because they are cognition-oriented, i.e., elicit the addressee's mental *reconsideration* of beliefs, ideas or assumptions, due to the addresser's *challenging* message.[192]

It is quite curious how in one of her most recent essays, Ilie both claims that RQs characteristically *provide information* and at the same time endorse Rohde's synchronization thesis as "a major condition for the felicitous use of rhetorical questions" without any qualifications.[193] That said, Ilie does not include Rohde's conclusion that RQs are *redundant interrogatives*. While sharpening Rhode's descriptions and in light of Ilie's various descriptions and towards defining my degrees of informativity suggestion, I propose that

> what licenses interrogatives to operate as felicitous RQs is that both communicative participants share a specific knowledge about the other's beliefs and values regarding the real world. Addressees may or may not be committed to the same beliefs and values held by addressers. Addressees already know and/or can readily infer the obvious and exclusive answers that addressers imply and are utterly committed to.

Before drawing any further conclusions, I will return to Job 15, beginning with v. 7:

⁷Are you the First Human born	הראישון אדם תולד
and were you brought forth before the hills?	ולפני גבעות הוללת:

These parallel interrogatives are located in Eliphaz's second speech where in the first section (vv. 2–16) he directly responds to Job and in particular with vv. 7–10 he confronts Job's assertions that his wisdom is at least on par with that of his friends (12:2–3; 13:1–2; see also 12:7–12). With v. 7 Eliphaz sarcastically addresses Job's *apparent* claim that he possesses superior wisdom by questioning whether or not he is the first person created before all else.[194] More specifically and similar to Lady Wisdom

---

192. Ibid., 77 (italics mine).
193. Ilie, "Rhetorical Questions," 406.
194. Robert Alter identifies Eliphaz's expressions in vv. 7–8 as "sarcastic hyperbole" (*The Art of Biblical Poetry*, rev. ed. [New York: Basic, 2011], 109). Interestingly, Norman C. Habel observes in Eliphaz's first section that "Job is addressed directly in the second person and *indirectly* through third-person rhetorical questions" (*The Book of Job*, OTL [Philadelphia: Westminster, 1985], 248 [italics mine]).

in Prov 8:22–31 (cf. v. 25b and Lady Wisdom's claim: לפני גבעות חוללתי "I was brought forth before the hills"), he questions if Job is the primordial First Human, commonly known within the ANE, who was considered born directly from God endowed with supernatural wisdom.[195] Based on the shared knowledge of both discourse participants, Eliphaz and Job unreservedly know the obvious answer that Job is not this mythical figure and thus the interrogative appears to function as a RQ. With this RQ Eliphaz and Job share identical beliefs regarding the inferred answer which also does not arouse any uncertainty and/or surprise; the implied answer is completely predictable. In fact, such a claim would be absurd![196] Thus, this RQ is uninformative in the terms of how Rhode narrowly defines all RQs. Eliphaz's RQ confirms and synchronizes the joint mutual belief of both him and Job. As such, in reference to the spectrum of strengths scheme the inferred Assertive force here is weak and consequently also the Expressive force in relation to the assertion. Yet, still with this RQ Eliphaz expresses sarcasm. Also as I will explore further below, Eliphaz in this speech employs a string of RQs and assertions to challenge and persuade his friend to change Job's thinking towards his own, but this parallel RQ and others are uninformative and not persuasive in-and-of themselves.

Before summarizing my conclusions concerning the degrees of informativity notion, another felicity condition for identifying a RQ is directional fit as assumed by Vanderveken and specifically proposed by Holdcroft with ISAs. To recall from Chapter 1, an interrogative functioning as a speech act Directive have a world-to-words fit and uttering such an IA addressers want addressees to match the world to their request. Assertions have words-to-world directional fit as a felicitous utterance must match the current state of affairs. When an addresser utters (2a) at a dinner table the question of ability violates in a similar way the direction of fit of an assertion. In other words, the addresser's question of ability is

---

195. See cf. Leo G. Perdue, *Wisdom in Revolt: Metaphorical Theology in the Book of Job*, JSOTSup 112 (Sheffield: JSOT Press, 1991), 166–68; idem, *Wisdom and Creation: The Theology of Wisdom Literature* (Nashville: Abingdon, 1994), 156–57; idem, *Wisdom Literature: A Theological History* (Louisville: Westminster John Knox, 2007), 113–14; see also David J. A. Clines, *Job 1–20*, WBC 17 (Dallas: Word, 1989), 349–50; Habel, *Book of Job*, 250, 253–54, 537, 541; John E. Hartley, *The Book of Job*, NICOT (Grand Rapids: Eerdmans, 1988), 245–46; Marvin H. Pope, *Job*, AB 15 (New York: Doubleday, 1973), 115. See further R. N. Whybray, *The Heavenly Counsellor in Isaiah 13–14: A Study of the Sources of the Theology of Deutero-Isaiah* (Cambridge: Cambridge University Press, 1971), 54–56.

196. Hartley, *Book of Job*, 246.

incompatible with and does not satisfactorily match the mutually assumed reality that she/he obviously does possess that questioned ability. The only satisfactory directional fit of such an utterance is that of a request. Applying this condition to RQs and specifically with Job 15, Eliphaz continues his confrontation of Job:

⁸Do you listen in the council of God?   הבסוד אלוה תשמע
    And do you limit wisdom to yourself?   ותגרע אליך חכמה:

Eliphaz continues with common ANE ideas and specifically that of the council of the gods primarily described in Mesopotamian and Canaanite literature[197] which is also similarly depicted in the Prologue (1:6–12; 2:1–6; see also 1 Kgs 22:19–23). As with a number of interpreters, it makes logical sense that the primeval Human also has immediate access to such a council.[198] However, due to the lack of a detailed ANE description of this figure and his activities, any direct connection with the council of the gods ultimately remains allusive.[199] Thus, v. 8a could be understood as an information-providing RQ[200] or even a genuine question. There is no evidence, though, within the literary world of Job that he has participated in the council of God (the Prologue does not show Job engaging in any of the depicted council sessions). All of these interrogatives taken as genuine questions do not satisfactorily match the shared knowledge and mutually assumed reality of both conversational participants. In other

---

197. Cf. E. Theodore Mullen Jr., *The Divine Council in Canaanite and Early Hebrew Literature*, HSM 24 (Chico: Scholars Press, 1980).

198. So, e.g., Clines, *Job 1–20*, 350; Habel, *Book of Job*, 253–54; Hartley, *Book of Job*, 245–46; see also Pope, *Job*, 115.

199. Perdue does not directly associate the mythology of First Human with the council of the gods. Tryggve N. D. Mettinger suggests that contrary to the idea that divine wisdom is a direct result of access to the divine council, what is presented in this Job passage "is the development of the notion of the god-granted wisdom of the first man into the notion that this wisdom was attained without divine authorization" (*The Eden Narrative: A Literary and Religio-historical Study of Genesis 2–3* [Winona Lake: Eisenbrauns, 2007], 92).

200. It appears that J. Gerald Janzen understands the interrogatives in v. 8 as information-providing RQs or genuine questions. Janzen states that the "rhetorical assurance of verse 7 seems thoroughly warranted; but the phraseology of verse 8 signals to the reader that what Eliphaz is denying is not so quickly to be ruled out." Janzen bases this claim on the fact that certain prophets claim to listen in on the council of God (e.g., 1 Kgs 22:19–23; Jer 23:18, 21–22; Isa 40:1–8) as well as prophets like Hosea and Isaiah contrasted their message as true wisdom against the so-called wisdom of others (*Job*, Int [Atlanta: John Knox, 1985], 116).

words, Eliphaz's question of Job as the First Human as well as having special access to the council of God is incompatible with and does not satisfactorily match the mutually assumed reality wherein Job would fit such categorical descriptions. It would be utterly incomprehensible for Job to consider himself as such. As with the previous RQs, the inferred Assertive force here is thereby weak and consequently also the Expressive force while Eliphaz continues to express his sarcastic tone.

Verses 7-8a function as premises for Eliphaz's subsequent interrogative in v. 8b. Job considering himself as the First Human endowed with wisdom from God as well as benefiting from special access to God's council would naturally lead him to the conclusion that he does in fact have a monopoly on wisdom. Yet operating as the conclusion to the previous uninformative RQs, v. 8b would also function as another uninformative RQ for Eliphaz. Additional support for this is that Job has never made the claim that he is the sole bastion of wisdom. With all this, Eliphaz's interrogatives do not function sincerely as genuine questions and thus the interrogative dimension disappears; nor are the RQs information-providing. Both Job and Eliphaz know the obvious answer to these positive, sarcastic RQs and Job would unhesitatingly observe the characteristic reversal of polarity and thereby mentally transforms them into negative assertions: *Of course I am not the First Human, I have not participated in the council of God, nor do I monopolize wisdom!* In contrast to the interrogative dimension, the answer/assertion matches a words-to-world directional fit within the mutually shared knowledge of both Eliphaz and Job as well as the reader.

For de Regt, the conventional level of vv. 7–8 implies that wisdom is only found in the council of God while at the pragmatic stage Eliphaz confronts Job's presumptuousness.[201] However, these RQs are uninformative and both discourse participants share the same mutual belief that the inferred assertions claim. Thus, they are not individually providing any information nor challenging Job in any way. Eliphaz, though, employs these RQs to set up his following claims for Job to draw specific conclusions about his level of acquired wisdom:

⁹What have you known that we do not know,	מה־ידעת ולא נדע
you understand that which is not within us?	תבין ולא־עמנו הוא:

---

201. Habel similarly claims that Eliphaz "accuses Job of being as presumptuous as First Man (vv. 7–8), pretending to know wisdom hidden from his friends" (*Book of Job*, 254). For Perdue, Eliphaz's question in v. 7 addresses "what he perceives to be a Job filled with arrogance" (*Wisdom and Creation*, 156).

¹⁰Both the gray-headed and the aged are among us	גם־שב גם־ישיש בנו
older in days than your father!	כביר מאביך ימים

Eliphaz could also intend the two interrogatives to function as genuine questions.²⁰² Yet Job has already been challenging the comprehensiveness of his friends' wisdom (12:1–14:22) while Eliphaz has made his counter position quite clear (4:2–5:27). To ensure, though, that these two interrogatives are understood as RQs Eliphaz follows them with two supporting assertions that function indirectly²⁰³ and in this instance violate Grice's maxim of Quantity. To recall from Chapter 1, Grice presented two dimensions for this maxim:

- Make your contribution as informative as is required (for the current purposes of the exchange), i.e., don't say too little.
- Do not make your contribution more informative than is required, i.e., don't say too much.

Grice illustrates the violation of this maxim with an instructor writing a recommendation for a student applying for a philosophy job which reads:

> Dear Sir, Mr. Smith's command of English is excellent and his attendance in class sessions has been consistent. Yours truly.

With this, the instructor implicates that the student does not have any skill in philosophy whatsoever. How is this so? The instructor is cooperating conversationally by writing a letter of recommendation while the reader naturally infers that if the recommender had more positive things to say she/he would have included such details. By not providing additional information, the instructor expects the reader to implicate that Smith does not possess the adequate professional qualifications for the position in question. Therefore, the recommendation is a negative one; not explicitly stated, but implicated indirectly.

Vanderveken revises this maxim as follows: *Let the illocutionary act that you mean to perform be as strong as required (neither too strong nor too weak)!* This revision is very similar to Grice, but intentionally generalized to apply to expressions beyond simply providing information. For Vanderveken, an ISA is a premier instance of exploiting this maxim. For

---

202. Clines comments that Eliphaz seriously asks Job here in v. 9 (*Job 1–20*, 350).
203. Clines observes here that "Eliphaz does not say *directly* what he means" (ibid., 351, italics mine).

example, with the understatement in a particular conversational context *That painting is not bad!* an addresser exploits the maxim of Quantity. Another example offered by Green is the familiar expression, *It was interesting* in response to a scholarly paper or artistic performance.[204] In the former instance, the felicity conditions are met as the addresser indirectly means to convey a stronger assertion than the literal one that she/he intends the addressee to recognize that she/he is obviously quite impressed by the painting. With the latter, the addresser indirectly means to convey a weaker assertion for the addressee to recognize that she/he is obviously quite unimpressed.

Eliphaz in v. 10 asserts that his community consists of aged individuals who are older than Job himself.[205] Within this intellectual society true wisdom lies solely with the aged (Job 12:12) while the collective ancient tradition is tried and true (8:8–9),[206] specifically in regards to the doctrine of retribution: a direct correspondence between one's behavior and experience of blessing or suffering. Thus, with these parallel assertions Eliphaz violates the first dimension of Grice's Quantity maxim or, in Vanderveken's terms, he does not make his parallel assertions strong enough. Directly related to the previous RQs, Eliphaz indirectly intends the stronger assertion that because Job's friends are obviously older they are consequently wiser than Job which Eliphaz intends for Job to inferentially implicate through the mutually accepted background of their common sapiential community. Job, then, is to thereby adopt the appropriate position and posture among his wise counselors. Another angle at this assertion is along somewhat similar lines as to what I presented in my Introduction, when a person utters *I love the sound of your voice* to say in an ironic, sarcastic, and nonliteral way that she/he cannot stand the sound of his voice while simultaneously asking him indirectly to stop singing. This also has affinities with Tsohatzidis' observations of sentences functioning indirectly and figuratively at the same time (see Chapter 1) and Ilie's multifunctional observations of RQs. Thus, the two interrelated implicatures derive from the assertions in v. 10: Job is younger and therefore not as wise. Returning to v. 9, then, with these interrogatives Eliphaz does not pose sincere questions; rather, he intends Job to infer from the positive RQs the answer *Nothing!*

---

204. Green, *Pragmatics*, 103.
205. The terms שׂב and ישׁישׁ are in the singular and so some scholars conclude that the referent is Eliphaz himself (e.g., Clines, *Job 1–20*, 351).
206. See Perdue, *Wisdom in Revolt*, 168.

Frans H. van Eemeren et al. recognize RQs as ISAs and briefly analyze them in argumentation.[207] They use the example of *Let's take an umbrella, or do you want to get wet?* and understood literarily the addresser confronts the addressee with a proposal accompanied by a question. The RQ, though, demands that the addressee interpret it "as a reason to accept the implicit standpoint that the two should take an umbrella." To correctly determine, then, the addresser's commitments the addressee "must diagnose this discourse as containing an implicit (and indirect) standpoint defended by an implicit (and indirect) reason: 'We should take an umbrella, for we do not want to get wet.'" Moshavi adds that the RQ "serves as an indirect assertion, 'We do not want to get wet'; this in turn is a premise supporting the conclusion, 'We should take an umbrella.'"[208] In light of my discussion above, I would argue that the RQ here infers a Directive force in a primary way with an accompanied Assertive that elicits the action to take an umbrella which van Eemeren et al. as well as Moshavi convey in their propositional reconstruction. Setting my last thought aside, Eliphaz uses his parallel ISAs to not only ensure that the previous interrogatives in v. 9 be taken as RQs but that they also function as the premise for Job to conclude and agree with Eliphaz that he does not know more than his friends, in fact less.

With vv. 7–10, Eliphaz carefully leads Job to *unquestionably* confirm that he is not the First Human uniquely endowed with wisdom nor with special access to the council of God and therefore not monopolizing wisdom. Both would also confirm that Job is in fact younger than Eliphaz's collective intellectual community. For Eliphaz, all this should logically implicate for Job to acknowledge that he possesses less wisdom than his friends and thus undeniably has nothing to add to their collective wisdom. The implicated assertion Eliphaz intends from the positive interrogatives in v. 9 is: *Job does not possess knowledge beyond his friends!* In fact, with the two ISAs in v. 10 Eliphaz implicates that the younger Job is consequently not as wise as his older comforters.

With this RQ in v. 9 Eliphaz infers a strong primary Assertive force and also an accompanied strong Expressive force. Eliphaz continues to express sarcastic indignation prompted by Job's earlier claims while also his sincere conviction about the state of affairs specified in the inferred propositional assertion. Thus, he takes the stance that Job does not possess wisdom to add to the collective consensus and in fact his understanding

---

207. Van Eemeren et al., *Fundamentals of Argumentation*, 13–14.
208. Moshavi, "Two Types of Argumentation," 36.

of wisdom is inferior. The *question*, though, that remains is whether Job agrees or not with Eliphaz? As I will discuss below, these particular RQs appear more information-providing than uninformative as the others.

Returning to my notion that RQs express *degrees of informativity*, one angle for identifying interrogatives operating as RQs occurs through the criteria of uninformativity and information-providing in contrast to information-eliciting. Not all RQs are uninformative, as Rohde claims, while at the same time nor are all RQs information-providing, as most biblical scholars conclude following a general consensus among specialists. Rather, I suggest that RQs operate on a spectrum, with information-providing at the one end and uninformative ones at the other, with others lying between:

Information-Providing ◄─────────► Uninformative

Figure 2.2. Spectrum of Degrees of Informativity of Rhetorical Questions

As I claimed above, Thiselton and Briggs' spectrum of strengths thesis helps for understanding the performative function of RQs. These spectrums of strengths and informativity, though, do not directly correspond in the sense that information-providing RQs constitute strong IAs and uninformative RQs equate to weak IAs. Rather, all types of RQs can infer strong or weak illocutionary forces. In general terms, the more uninformative the RQ typically the weaker its illocutionary force whereas the more information-providing the stronger, as exemplified above. Yet, some uninformative RQs can infer strong illocutionary forces while some information-providing ones can infer weaker illocutions.

RQs providing degrees of information, similar to Ilie's observations as well as Schmidt-Radefeldt's (see the Introduction), typically reserve this to convey addressers' propositional attitude (e.g., reproach, indignation, protest, concern, etc.), state of mind, opinion, beliefs, commitments, and/or emotions or feelings. Dependent upon the RQ itself as well as the immediate communicative context, both information-providing and uninformative RQs indirectly convey an Assertive and oftentimes it functions as the primary force. Also, for an interrogative to operate as either an information-providing or uninformative RQ both discourse participants must possess a shared knowledge about each other's beliefs and values regarding the real world. With either type of RQ, addressees may or may not be committed to those same beliefs and values while the obvious and exclusive answer is already known and/or readily inferable which addressers are unreservedly committed to. Generally, the higher the degree of information-providing the more the particular RQ challenges addressees. Also, the more information-providing the RQ the more interrogativity involved. Both types of RQs express the Directive force and the Assertive force to one degree or another and usually operates as the primary force that includes the Expressive force. Some uninformative RQs can express a challenging or persuasive intent which Rohde does not incorporate in her view in any detailed way. However, the challenge aspect would not normally involve agreeing with and assenting to the exclusive answer, but rather solely with what that answer entails. As with the above RQs used by Eliphaz, addressers can employ a series of uninformative RQs to persuasively lead addressees to draw specific conclusions, but such RQs are not normally persuasive in isolation. Further, the communicative context of RQs additionally influences the degree of informativity. This can be illustrated with Rohde's heavy weight boxer RQ when used during a debate on who was the greatest boxer of all time. Employed in such a conversational context this would provide information concerning the addresser's opinionated belief and perhaps also factual information that Rocky Marciano retired undefeated. Along with ISAs, addressees can interpret the same RQ differently from one context to another. Applying van Eemeren/Grootendorst's observations here, strongly conventionalized RQs imply the same meaning in various communicative contexts whereas weakly conventionalized RQs require a more well-defined communicative context for addressees to infer addressers' intended meaning. Thus, the type of RQ and its immediate communicative context provide another condition for interpreting such expressions.

Rohde's use of entropy compliments Stenström's degrees of elicitation (see the Introduction), but the latter condition is obviously more linguistically and contextually derived than mathematical. To recall, the more an interrogative is information-seeking the higher the degree of elicitative force whereas the less information-seeking the lower degree of elicitative force. RQs express a close to zero degree of verbalized elicitation corresponding to their zero degree of information-seeking while Rohde sees RQs expressing a lack of uncertainty or surprise which is evidence of their uninformativity. So, the degree of elicitative force coupled with Rohde's notions of uncertainty or surprise can offer complimentary criteria for identifying the type of interrogative employed. Rohde's use of Common Ground and in particular identifying the conversational participants shared knowledge also compliments Searle's general mutual background aspect as well as other inferential mechanisms suggested by other theorists.

To summarize my degrees of informativity idea, all types of RQs express an obvious and exclusive answer that addressees infer, which *counts as* an IA. RQs naturally include the Directive force while most often infer a primary Assertive force that include the Expressive force while some may include additional forces and specifically the Commissive. Yet, particular RQs can convey other forces with one functioning as the primary force and often with an accompanied Assertive force. Also, all RQs successfully operate when both discourse participants have a mutually shared knowledge about the other's values and beliefs regarding the real world. Uninformative RQs often function to confirm (Rohde) or reinforce (Ilie) those joint mutual beliefs and values of both discourse participants whereas information-providing RQs typically challenge in various degrees addressees to agree with and assent to the inferred answer. With any type of RQ, the ultimate intention aims at synchronizing the beliefs and commitments of both conversational participants.

Characteristics and Criteria for Identifying Rhetorical Questions

In light of the above and my discussion on ISAs, the following is a list of the various and related conditions for determining if and how an interrogative is intended to function as a RQ. Ilie provides five undeniable distinct characteristics of RQs, with the latter three more pragmatic in nature; however, as I point out above, beyond the related triggers to these characteristics (e.g., elicitative force) she does not describe in much detail how addressees recognize particular interrogatives intended to function as RQs; how addressers imply for addressees to employ pragmatic processes to infer implicated answers from a literal interrogative. Following van Eemeren/Grootendorst and Slot, there is a sequential scheme of conditions that addressees interpretively engage with and follow (especially Efficiency, Quality and Sincerity/Responsibility, and Elicitative Force). Some of the following descriptions and conditions provide supplemental and complimentary criteria for identifying and interpreting RQs, which could prove helpful, especially with written and ancient RQs as found in the Hebrew Bible.

- **Maxim of Relevance**
  Addressers are relevant when using interrogatives as recognizable genuine questions within respective communicative contexts whereas addressers violate or exploit such relevance when the same interrogatives are intended as RQs. This irrelevance, though, understood as intended in turn becomes relevant. Purposeful irrelevancy, though, is more easily recognizable with particular RQs like retorts than with other types of RQs.

- **Efficiency condition (Slot's Efficiency rule; Searle's First Preparatory condition)**
  With genuine questions addressers do not know the answer whereas with RQs addressers already know the answer while they imply obvious and exclusive answers that are either known and/or readily inferable by addressees (Ilie's first Preparatory condition). In particular communicative contexts, interrogatives understood literally would be unnecessary or superfluous.

- **Maxim of Quality and Sincerity/Responsibility**
  Combining Grice's Quality maxim with the Sincerity/Responsibility condition (as with Levinson, Vanderveken, van Eemeren/Grootendorst, Slot, and Braun) and directly connected to the above Efficiency condition, to ask genuine questions addressers intentionally use interrogatives as literal speech acts (Braun's Maxim of Literalness). Intending interrogatives to function as RQs, addressers are unable to felicitously and successfully use the interrogative form in a literal sense and thus appear to not cooperate communicatively. Assuming addressers desire to continue the interaction, addressees recognize the intended violation or exploitation of the interrogative form and thereby continue to participate communicatively. Regarding the Sincerity/Responsibility dimension, addressers use interrogatives to sincerely and responsibly (honestly) ask questions concerning unknown information. Conversely, addressers use interrogatives insincerely and not literally to intentionally express RQs.

- **Elicitative Force**
  Linked to the Preparatory/Efficiency and Sincerity/Responsibility conditions, genuine questions elicit or seek information from addressees (Searle's Essential condition) and thus express higher degrees of elicitative force whereas RQs express a lower degree of information-elicitation. The intended function of interrogatives as RQs interpreted as eliciting information would be incomprehensible (van Eemeren/Grootendorst's rule 1; Slot's Comprehensibility rule) or infelicitous (Vanderveken) to addressees. The interrogative dimension of RQs is unnecessary or superfluous because addressers imply obvious and exclusive answers while also convey zero information-eliciting force. RQs also express degrees of uncertainty or surprise in relation to the predictability of the answer. With interrogatives the degree of elicitative force coupled with the aspect of uncertainty or surprise can offer complimentary criteria for identifying the type of interrogative employed.

- **Degrees on Informativity**
  Addressers imply obvious and exclusive answers with RQs that range in degree from information-providing to uninformative with others operating along the degree spectrum (see Figure 2.2). Interrogatives successfully function as RQs when the discourse participants share a knowledge about the others' beliefs and values regarding the real world. However, addressees may or may not be committed to those same beliefs and values while the obvious and exclusive answer is already known and/or readily inferable which addressers are utterly committed to. In general terms, the more information-providing the higher degree of persuasion or challenge the answer conveys which addressees are intended to infer and ultimately agree with and assent to whereas uninformative RQs typically confirm or reinforce already mutually shared beliefs and values between the communicative participants. Yet, particular uninformative RQs may express a challenging intent while certain information-providing RQs may reinforce mutually shared beliefs and values. Along similar lines of elicitative force, the more uninformative the interrogative the less inferential processes needed to determine its rhetorical function. The higher the degree of information-providing a RQ conveys, the more the interrogative dimension comes into play for addressees. Conversely, the lower the degree of uncertainty or surprise an interrogative triggers, the clearer its intended rhetorical function. Correlating with these notions, there are degrees of conventionalization with RQs (similar to Lycan's tripartite stage of ISAs). Strongly conventionalized RQs easily transfer a consistent meaning from one context to another while others are weaker, requiring more well-defined communicative contexts to imply an intended meaning (van Eemeren/Grootendorst).

- **Directional Fit**
  Addressers use interrogatives functioning as speech act Directives with a world-to-words fit intend that addressees match the world to their requests. With RQs, the interrogative dimension does not match the mutually assumed reality of the communicative participants and context while the only satisfactory directional fit occurs with the inferred assertion.

Intentional Meaning Aspect

As with ISAs, RQs express the literal illocutionary force of a question and implicates an answer. The literal interrogative is incomprehensible in the particular communicative context, but cooperative communication ensues and the violation of any communicative rules remains only apparent when the addressee recognizes the addresser is doing something else. The literal interrogative is understood by the addressee while the above communicative rules along with the violation of some or all have triggered for the addressee to recognize its intended indirectness. Through pragmatic inferential processes the addressee observes the characteristic reversal of polarity and indirectly transforms the interrogative into the intended answer implied by the addresser.

Perlocutionary Effects

I also see two PEs occurring along similar lines of van Eemeren/ Grootendorst and Ilie's use of their perlocutionary ideas, yet directly deriving from the intended, inferred answer IA (see Tables 2.2 and 2.4). Further, in line with Gu's *transactional* and van Eemeren/Grootendorst's *interactional effect* views, IAs trigger PEs which are ultimately actualized by addressees. My first PE is the Initial goal which primarily focuses on addressees inferentially recognizing implied IAs. Second, the Intended PE goal concerns addressees agreeing with and assenting to intended IAs. More specifically, the inferred IA purposefully triggers PEs with the Initial one aiming at addressees recognizing and acknowledging their understanding of the intended IA and centrally understanding the implications of agreeing with and assenting to the exclusive answer. Addressers' chief goal occurs with the Intended PE which aims at addressees agreeing with and assenting to the exclusive answer thereby synchronizing the beliefs and commitments of both discourse participants. With uninformative RQs, agreement with the obvious intended answer typically serves more for confirmation purposes than confrontational ones. It is important to also clarify that the degree of PEs corresponds directly with the degree of informativity. Thus, the higher degree of information-providing the more the RQ involves addressees in the perlocutionary dimensions whereas uninformative RQs do not require much, if anything, from the addressees to agree with and assent to the respective Intended PEs.

As I have highlighted throughout my descriptions, the hybrid nature of RQs also implores self-involvement, but here is where it directly impacts addressees whereupon they agree with the intended IA. Rakić also sees self-involvement with RQs. She correlates this notion by implicitly observing two PEs with the initial one aiming at the agreement of addressees which "may then imply further communicative acts" as with *Will your wife respect you after that?*[209] As a hybrid expression,

---

209. Rakić, "Serbo-Croatian," 706.

both the interrogative and inferred dimensions also inherently contain PEs as well as self-involved implications. To assent or dissent with the exclusive answer, RQs compel addressees to adopt particular stances and entailments in either instance, especially with inferred strong Assertive forces. Also, in correlation with the degrees of informativity, there are degrees of self-involvement with RQs. Again, in general terms, the more information-providing the RQ the higher degree of its challenging intent for addressees as well as self-involvement, whereas the more uninformative the less challenging and self-involved implications. Yet, certain uninformative RQs that intentionally challenge may also include self-involvement whereas self-involvement significantly reduces with information-providing RQs that confirm shared beliefs. All this said, Briggs has demonstrated that self-involvement constitutes a speech act category itself.[210] Thus, expressions such as confessions convey self-involvement without the explicit inclusion of PEs.[211]

Looking one last time to Job 15:7-10, Eliphaz, in van Eemeren and Grootendorst's terms, presents a constellation of statements, here primarily RQs, carefully designed to refute Job's claims. The initial goal of Eliphaz is for Job to acknowledge the implicated assertions that he has not acquired anything to add to the collective ancient wisdom and in fact his wisdom is not equal to his friends. Eliphaz's intended goal is for Job to agree with him and assent to the fact that his wisdom is actually inferior with the entailments for Job to listen to his friends' counsel and accept the consolations of God (v. 11).[212] Both discourse participants definitively agree with the uninformative RQs in vv. 7–8 as well as the implicatures derived from v. 10. Yet, the derived IA from the RQs in v. 9 does not match a words-to-world directional fit within their common shared knowledge; Job's experiential knowledge provides contrary evidence for him, as well as for the reader, to disagree with Eliphaz's implied assertion. Job innocently suffers (1:1, 8; 2:3; 6:30; 9:15; 42:7–8) and consequently for him the doctrine of retribution does not always work out mechanistically (cf. 12:2–6). Because of all this, Eliphaz's parallel RQs in v. 9 are not uninformative, but instead provide information primarily through the primary Assertive force along with the Expressive. With this RQ, Eliphaz expresses his own beliefs and commitments as well as his attitude and feelings to challenge Job's perceived maverick understanding of the way of wisdom. How can one lone younger individual know more than the

---

210. See Briggs, *Words in Action*, 148–82; see also Adams, *Performative Nature*, 45–63.
211. See Briggs, *Words in Action*, 183–215.
212. Similarly de Regt, "Implications," 324–25.

aged consensus? As a hybrid expression, though, Job would disagree with the implicated assertions while mentally answering the interrogative with a counter assertion: *I do in fact possess wisdom that you do not know!* By doing so, Job takes the self-involved stance with accompanied entailments that directly opposes his friends' collective, ancient counsel.

Conclusion

My above analysis has now provided me with specific criteria for identifying and interpreting RQs within the Hebrew Bible. As I stated earlier, I will select particular salient RQs to apply my analysis and primarily explore the performative nature and function of these unique interrogatives. Before I start my analysis, my general and succinct summary of the nature and function of RQs is as follows:

Like ISAs, RQs consist of a hybrid expression that includes a literal interrogative and an intentionally inferred answer, often an assertion that *counts as* an IA. Addressers imply an exclusive answer characteristically in the reverse polarity of the interrogative which addressees recognize through pragmatic processes. Addressers intend addressees to mentally and self-involvingly agree with, assent to, or confirm this inferred answer which sometimes elicits a particular responsive action while addressees retain the option to respond to the interrogative dimension with a counter answer and/or opinion. RQs operate along a degrees of informativity spectrum with information-providing at one end and uninformative at the other with others lying in-between. RQs are *multidimensional* that infer multiple illocutionary forces and often times with the Assertive force primary, but sometimes other forces can function in a primary way accompanied by the Assertive conveyed to one degree or another. RQs are also *multifunctional* that infer the propositional attitudes and feelings of addressers and sometimes several emotive expressions simultaneously. What licenses interrogatives to operate as felicitous RQs is that both communicative participants share a specific knowledge about the other's beliefs and values regarding the real world. Addressees may or may not be committed to the same beliefs and values held by addressers. Addressees already know and/or can readily infer the obvious and exclusive answers that addressers imply and are utterly committed to. With any type of RQ, the ultimate intention aims at synchronizing the beliefs and commitments of both addressers and addressees.

Chapter 3

THE PERFORMATIVE DIMENSIONS OF RHETORICAL QUESTIONS IN THE HEBREW BIBLE

Applying my previous research, I will now examine some particular and salient RQs in the Hebrew Bible. Before I begin, I need to preface my analysis with the obvious fact that neither I nor anyone else has access to what addressers and addressees in the Bible know and think apart from the immediate literary context and the portrayed world depicted in the text. In certain instances, through direct speech and/or dialogue literary communicators disclose their thoughts, knowledge, beliefs, values, commitments, attitudes, feelings etc. and/or the author or narrator will explicitly comment on the discourse participants thoughts etc. and at times tell us about them. As with spoken RQs, addressers using literary RQs imply their thoughts etc. along with the intended exclusive answer that the literary discourse participants and contemporary readers interpretively infer. In some instances addressers in the Hebrew Bible explicitly provide the intended answer which often occurs in poetry, but in other instances this is not the case. Consequently, when determining the function and meaning of literary RQs, as with all interpretive endeavors, the literary context and genre of the passage is of utmost importance along with the depicted literary world of the discourse participants and their historical, cultural, geopolitical worldviews. With all this in mind, I will begin my analysis with Jacob's response to Rachel in Gen 30.

Genesis 30:2

In v. 1 the narrator reports that Rachel is barren and also jealous of her sister's opposite experience (v. 1). Rachel exhorts her husband Jacob to give her children and he responds in v. 2:

Am I in the place of God who has withheld from you the fruit of the womb?	התחת אלהים אנכי אשר־מנע ממך פרי־בטן:

Because Jacob unsurprisingly would not ask Rachel if he truly is in the place of God, this interrogative functions as a fairly irrefutable RQ. Still, to prepare the way for additional and more difficult analyses I will apply my above research in specific detail here that I will then assume to a large degree with subsequent analyses. To begin and following my theoretical framework (see Table 2.4), Jacob expresses a Literal Illocutionary Interrogative (*what is said*), but he implies an Inferred Illocutionary Answer by way of this literal IA. Rachel would easily recognize that his interrogative violates the immediate contextual communicative principles (*what is implicated*) and engage in the following pragmatic processes:

Efficiency

Jacob's interrogative interpreted as a real or genuine question, he asks whether or not Rachel views him in the place of God who can supernaturally change her barrenness. Based on the shared knowledge and the joint mutual beliefs and commitments between the discourse participants, Rachel would understand Jacob's interrogative violating Searle's first Preparatory Condition (an addresser does not know the answer to a question) and Slot's Efficiency rule that Jacob already knows the answer. Understood literally, the interrogative would be unnecessary or superfluous. Conversely, Jacob's interrogative meets Ilie's corresponding condition for RQs (addressers know and imply "the answer," expected to be inferred by addressees).

Maxim of Quality and Sincerity/Responsibility

With this interrogative, Jacob is not using it truthfully (Grice's Quality maxim) or linguistically literal (Braun's maxim of Literalness); his interrogative refers to something dishonest if taken literally. Rachel knows, then, that Jacob's interrogative is blatantly false, but at the same time he does not intend to deceive her. The only way that Rachel understands Jacob as conversationally cooperating is that he intends to convey something entirely different. Regarding the Sincerity/Responsibility aspect, Jacob does not sincerely and responsibly (honestly) ask a question eliciting unknown information which indirectly generates or triggers an implicature. Jacob thus uses this interrogative insincerely. Jacob intends Rachel to recognize the incompatibility between their shared knowledge and mutual joint beliefs along with the felicity conditions of the literal interrogative. At the sentence-meaning level the interrogative is infelicitous whereas at the intended pragmatic level it succeeds. Jacob thereby conversationally implicates an indirect answer.

Elicitative Force

Linked to the Preparatory/Efficiency and Quality and Sincerity/Responsibility conditions, Jacob's interrogative understood as eliciting information would be incomprehensible (van Eemeren/Grootendorst's rule 1; Slot's Comprehensibility rule) or infelicitous (Vanderveken) to Rachel. Jacob does not appear to seek any type of information from Rachel (Searle's Essential condition) and thus expresses a very low to zero degree of information-elicitative force. The interrogative dimension of Jacob's response is unnecessary or superfluous as he implies an obvious and exclusive answer.

Degrees of Informativity

Along with general conditions of the presence of an exclusive answer with the sufficient similarity as well as the sure predictability of that answer between the discourse participants, this interrogative also meets Rohde's felicity condition of uninformativity. As I presented in my previous chapter, Rhode views RQs as *uninformative*, "not because they commit neither participant, but because they require that both participants *already be committed* to a joint mutual belief." Rhode then subsequently qualifies this claim by stating that shared "knowledge about others' beliefs and about the real world is precisely what licenses rhetorical questions."[1] Within my spectrum of degrees of informativity scheme (see Chapter 2 and Figure 2.2) while also attempting to sharpen Rhode's view, interrogatives successfully function as RQs when the discourse participants share knowledge about the other's values and beliefs regarding the real world. However, addressees may or may not be committed to those same beliefs and values while the obvious and exclusive answer is already known and/or readily inferable which addressers are unreservedly committed to. Jacob's RQ meets the two general conditions of the obvious and exclusive answer and the sufficient similarity of that answer as well as Rohde's narrow uninformative condition. Both Jacob and Rachel would unquestionably agree that Jacob is not God. This also illustrates the natural reversal polarity shift with RQs and here Jacob's positive RQ transforms into a negative answer. Through the pragmatic intention of this RQ Jacob and Rachel's commitments are synchronized, confirming their joint mutual beliefs about the states of affairs in the world.

---

1. Rohde, "Redundant Interrogatives," 144–45 (italics mine).

Jacob's response also falls within the category of a RQ-as-retort that he uses sarcastically, but Rachel's prompt is obviously not a question as with Schaffer's typical examples of these types (see Chapter 2). To recall the RQ-as-retort pattern, the obviousness of the RQs implicated answer functions as the unavoidable answer to the prompt. Here, the obvious implicated response to Jacob's RQ is *No!* which also answers Rachel's exhortative request.[2] With regards to the Relevancy maxim, Jacob's retort RQ is relevant as the inferred answer to Rachel's request is likewise obviously negative. Jacob's answer also follows along the lines of Green's understanding of Garfield's interrogative that "implicates not only 'No,' but also 'as you ought to know.'"[3]

Directional Fit

As I described in my Chapters 1 and 2, an interrogative functioning as a speech act Directive has a world-to-words fit and by uttering this type of IA addressers want the addressees to match the world to their request by doing what was requested. Assertions have words-to-world directional fit as a felicitous utterance must match the current state of affairs. With this in mind, understanding Jacob's interrogative as a genuine question of whether or not he is in the place of God does not satisfactorily match Jacob and Rachel's mutually assumed reality that he is in fact not God. Consequently, the interrogative dimension of this utterance all but disappears and in this instance never arises as a viable option which is confirmed within the narrative as Rachel does not attempt to answer the question. In contrast to the interrogative aspect, the inferred assertion dimension matches a words-to-world directional fit mutually assumed by both Jacob and Rachel.

Through such a pragmatic process, Rachel would mentally infer the Intentional Meaning aspect (*what is meant*) of Jacob's uninformative, retort RQ. She would naturally reverse the polarity of the interrogative and inferentially transform it into the implied exclusive assertion: *No, you are not God who can open my womb!* Due to the uninformative nature of the RQ, this inferred primary Assertive force is weak in this instance which also impacts the strength of the Expressive force. With the

---

2. Moshavi notes that the "RQ as retort does not appear to be manifested in Biblical Hebrew" ("Conducive Questions," 67 n. 5). Granted Jacob's RQ does not precisely match Schaffer's representative examples, Moshavi also mistakenly claims that these RQs *do not* reverse in polarity (see Chapter 2 n. 36) which may be the reason for not locating any such instances.

3. Green, *Pragmatics*, 102.

literal interrogative dimension, Jacob does not appear to cooperate communicatively with Rachel, but with the inferred answer/assertion Jacob successfully communicates as well as directionally matches a words-to-world fit.

Regarding the Initial Perlocutionary goal, Rachel does not disagree or object to the RQ within the narrative. Yet, as an uninformative RQ Rachel would naturally agree with and confirm the inferred answer/assertion. With this type of RQ, Jacob does not persuade or challenge Rachel to rethink her beliefs and commitments about him or God. Thus, she also embraces the Intended Perlocutionary goal without any hesitation or conscious effort. Interestingly, though, the narrative presents Rachel quickly, perhaps even anticipating Jacob's response, offering her own alternative solution to her barrenness (vv. 3–4).

Genesis 50:19 and Other Interrogatives in Genesis

Occurring in the culminating scene within the Joseph narrative (50:15–21), Joseph uses a very similar linguistic interrogative in response to a message sent to him on his father's behalf:

Do not fear!	אל־תיראו
For am I in the place of God?	כי התחת אלהים אני:

As with Jacob's interrogative, most interpreters understand Joseph's here functioning as a RQ. Gordon Wenham apparently understands it as such when he interprets Joseph's words as "Your fears are groundless."[4] Walter Brueggemann explicitly views this interrogative as a RQ while at the same time it is enigmatic and "could hardly have satisfied or reassured the brothers." The RQ "is rather like a rebuke" that echoes Jacob's RQ above.[5] Brueggemann goes on to say that it is probable that the narrator intends the RQ "to be ambiguous to the brothers and to us." On the one hand, it "may be a ploy so that Joseph tells them they will have to deal with God," while on the other, it may be a more direct and personal statement. "Thus Joseph may be asserting that the guilt of his brothers is no proper concern of his." For Brueggemann, Joseph's real speech consists in his exhortation and a "new affirmation that takes the brothers quite by surprise (v. 20)."[6]

---

4. Gordon Wenham, *Genesis 16–50*, WBC 2 (Dallas: Word, 1994), 490; similarly Claus Westermann, *Genesis 37–50: A Commentary*, trans. J. J. Scullion (Minneapolis: Augsburg, 1986), 205.

5. Walter Brueggemann, *Genesis*, Int (Atlanta: John Knox, 1982), 371.

6. Ibid., 372.

Brueggemann supports this latter understanding of Joseph's RQ with Paul A. Riemann's interpretation of Cain's interrogative response to Yahweh in Gen 4:9.[7] Following Cain's killing of his brother, Yahweh asks him:

Where is Abel your brother?	אי הבל אחיך

Cain then responds:

I do not know!	לא ידעתי
Am I my brother's keeper?	השמר אחי אנכי:

Looking at Yahweh's question, Kenneth M. Craig Jr. claims that it "is, of course, rhetorical."[8] Along with a number of interpreters, he also parallels this interrogative with Yahweh's question to Adam in Gen 3:9:

Where are you?	איכה

Although Craig classifies both these interrogatives as rhetorical, he describes how they function in more of a conducive sense by stating that they "invite the guilty to acknowledge responsibility for their deeds."[9] As I described in my Chapter 2, the most prominent Conducive question seeks to confirm a proposition that addressers believe is true such as *She was pushed, wasn't she?* Such Conducive questions match in polarity and intend to confirm the proposition in order to establish a state of agreement between addressers and addressees. Like RQs, this type of question conveys a low degree of informational-elicitation while violating Searle's Preparatory condition as well as the Sincerity/Responsibility condition,

---

7. Paul A. Riemann, "Am I My Brother's Keeper?" *Int* 24 (1970): 482–91.

8. Kenneth M. Craig Jr., "Questions Outside of Eden (Genesis 4.1–16): Yahweh, Cain and Their Rhetorical Interchange," *JSOT* 86 (1999): 121. Craig cites George W. Savran's analysis (*Telling and Retelling: Quotation in Biblical Narrative* [Bloomington: Indiana University Press, 1988], 65) in apparent support of his rhetorical view of Yahweh's interrogative in 4:9 ("Questions," 121 n. 24). Savran categorizes particular biblical texts as "Deceptive Quotation" (pp. 63–65) and within this motif he examines the serpent's quotations in Gen 3:1, 3 and those directed at David by Nathan and Bathsheba in 1 Kgs 1. From here Savran concludes that there are only a "few deceptive questions of any type in biblical narrative." Further and apart from these texts, Savran claims that "in only five instances does a speaker ask a question whose answer she/he already knows: Gen 3:9–10, 4:9, 42:7; 2 Sam 20:9; 2 Kgs 5:25" (*Telling and Retelling*, 65 [pronouns revised]). This is obviously an impossible claim to demonstrate.

9. Craig, "Questions Outside of Eden," 121.

yet while retaining an aspect of interrogativity. The narrative here makes it explicit that Yahweh knows what has happened to Abel in v. 10[10] and thus Yahweh's interrogative is a type of confirming Conducive question that also conveys some *leading* aspects[11] which is the identical type of interrogative Yahweh uses in this same verse:

What have you done? מה עשית

This response is also very similar to Yahweh's question to Eve in 3:13a:

What is this you have done? מה־זאת עשית

This interrogative also functions as a confirming Conducive question as Yahweh explicitly knows what Eve has done based on Adam's previous report (v. 12).[12] Due to the similar circumstances as well as the literary proximity, Yahweh's question to Eve can provide a grid for interpreting his question in 4:10 while Yahweh's question in 4:9 can likewise help in the understanding of his question in 3:9. Yet, none of these interrogatives make contextual sense as RQs when transformed into inferred answers with reversed polarity.[13] The difficulty with Yahweh's question to Adam

---

10. *Pace* John Goldingay, *Old Testament Theology, Volume 1: Israel's Gospel* (Downers Grove: InterVarsity, 2003), 152.

11. Ronald T. Hyman views Gen 3:9 similarly to the "quintessential trap question" מאין באתם "Where have you come from?" asked by Joseph to his brothers in 42:7 ("Questions in the Joseph Story: The Effects and Their Implications for Teaching," *Religious Education* 79 [1984]: 441–43).

12. Wenham views the interrogative in 4:10 as "rhetorical" in light of the intere rogative in 3:13a: (*Genesis 1–15*, 77–78, 107).

13. U. Cassuto understands 3:9 and 4:9 as comparable RQs and illustrates the former with a misbehaving child hiding from her/his father who clearly knows the child's hiding place and calls for her/him to come out and face him (*A Commentary on the Book of Genesis, Part 1: From Adam to Noah*, trans. I. Abrahams (Jerusalem: Magnes, 1961], 155–56). Wenham closely follows Cassuto as he understands 3:9 as inciting the couple to come out and explain their behavior with 4:9 a very close parallel (*Genesis 1–15*, WBC 1 [Waco: Word, 1987], 77). M. D. Gow appeals to both these commentators and identifies 3:9 as a RQ while describing it in a conducive sense, quoting Chrysostom who observes that the question invites the couple "to make admission of their faults" (*Homilies in Genesis* 17.22 cited in Andrew Louth, *Genesis 1–11*, ACCS [Downers Grove: InterVarsity, 2001], 85) ("Fall," in *Dictionary of the Old Testament: Pentateuch*, ed. T. D. Alexander and D. W. Baker [Downers Grove: InterVarsity, 2003], 288). Nahum M. Sarna also sees both interrogatives functioning similarly, without identifying them as RQs, while 4:9 possibly expressing conduciveness by claiming that the question "is a means of opening the conversation,

is that the narrative does not provide the same details about what Yahweh knows as with Cain;[14] although the narrative does state that Yahweh called אל־האדם "to the man" and said לו "to him" (3:9).[15] A more straightforward example of a confirming Conducive question occurs in 3:11b:

המן־העץ אשר צויתיך לבלתי אכל־ממנו אכלת

Have you eaten from the tree which I commanded you not to eat from it?

Here, "God is not seeking new information but rather trying to induce the suspect to confess to an act that He already knows to have taken place."[16]

Cain's interrogative response to Yahweh could also be understood as a confirming Conducive question,[17] but due to Cain's initial response it makes more sense as a RQ with the reversed polarity answer *No!* In further support of this, shepherds like Abel שמר "keep," "watch over," "protect," or "guard" flocks (e.g., Gen 30:31; 1 Sam 17:20; see also Exod 20:9 [Eng. v. 10]) and in effect Cain asks *Am I a shepherd of the shepherd or keeper of the keeper?*[18] Rienmann correctly argues that human beings are not required to שמר other human beings;[19] rather, Yahweh is the one

---

perhaps eliciting confession and contrition" (*Genesis*, JPSTC [Philadelphia: The Jewish Publication Society, 1989], 34); similarly John E. Hartley, *Genesis*, NIBCOT (Peabody: Hendrickson, 2000), 68.

14. Herman Gunkel understands this interrogative as a genuine question (*Genesis*, trans. M. E. Biddle, MLBS [Macon: Mercer University Press, 1997], 19).

15. Cassuto, *Genesis*, 155.

16. Moshavi, "Positive Rhetorical Question," 268. GKC understands this interrogative in an asseverative sense with the translation "*surely thou hast eaten*" (§150e) while, as I noted in my previous chapter, GKC describes this interrogative and other similar ones in a somewhat conducive sense. Wenham identifies this interrogative as rhetorical while also describing it more conducively, but as with 3:9 primarily on theological grounds (*Genesis 1–15*, 77). Joüon-Muraoka view this interrogative as an exclamation (§161b) which I will discuss in more detail below.

17. Sarna apparently understands this interrogative along these lines by claiming that "the obvious fraternal relationship of Cain and Abel emphatically teaches that man is indeed his brother's keeper" (*Genesis*, 34).

18. So Craig, "Questions Outside of Eden," 122–23; Wenham, *Genesis 1–15*, 106.

19. Francis Landy concludes that Cain responds with a RQ to Yahweh's RQ, but then argues without any real substantial evidence that according to the ethics of the Torah it is expected that Cain "*is* his brother's keeper" while his RQ functions as an "apparent disclaimer of responsibility" ("Humour as a Tool for Biblical Exegesis," in *On Humour and the Comic in the Hebrew Bible*, ed. Y. T. Radday and A. Brenner, JSOTSup 92, Bible and Literature Series 23 [Sheffield: Almond Press, 1990], 106–108).

who שמר human beings (e.g., cf. Ps 121:7–8; see also Gen 28:15; Num 6:24). Significantly within the narrative, Yahweh does not provide an answer to Cain's interrogative nor offer any disagreement. In light of all this, Cain already knows the answer to his interrogative which Yahweh the addressee would inferentially agree (Efficiency condition); although there are other familial responsibilities prescribed in the Torah (see Lev 25:25, 47–49; Num 35:12–28). Cain, then, insincerely uses this interrogative (Maxim of Quality and Sincerity/Responsibility) and is not eliciting for some unknown information (Elicitative force) nor arouses any surprise. As with Jacob's response to Rachel, Cain's RQ also functions in a retort sense, though again not in the usual way. While apparently irrelevant[20] it infers that the relevance of his response is that the negative implied answer matches the answer to as well as provides sarcastic and contemptuous justification for his initial lie to Yahweh's Conducive question.

Returning to Joseph's interrogative, Craig argues similarly to Brueggemann that Joseph's RQ is very much like Jacob's and Cain's RQs as they each "attempt to dismiss the point raised while denying all responsibility."[21] Joseph's brothers clearly have every reason to fear: what they had previously done to him, now their father dead, and the position Joseph currently holds in Egypt. Regarding the latter and following Joseph's interpretation of his dreams (41:14–37), the human and divine Pharaoh who occupies the divine throne of Egypt[22] recognizes the uniqueness of Joseph with an interrogative in v. 38:

הנמצא כזה איש אשר רוח אלהים בו:

Can we find a man like this in whom is God's spirit?

The Pharaoh explicitly utters this interrogative to his servants which ultimately functions as an uninformative RQ as the Pharaoh essentially

---

20. Riemann claims that Cain's "question is bold, defiant, and—*irrelevant*" ("Brother's Keeper?" 483; italics mine).

21. Craig, "Questions Outside Eden," 124. Following Rieman's conclusion that only God is a שמר of human beings, Brueggemann states that as Cain poses with his RQ that God is the one who keeps his brother, not him, and likewise Joseph may be asserting that the guilt of his brothers is no proper concern of his (*Genesis*, 372).

22. On the human and divine nature and role of the Pharaoh in Egypt see in particular David P. Silverman, "Divinity and Deities in Ancient Egypt," in *Religion in Ancient Egypt: Gods, Myths, and Personal Practice*, ed. B. E. Shafer (Ithaca: Cornell University Press, 1991), 58–87; see also Marie-Ange Bonhême, "Kingship," in *The Oxford Encyclopedia of Ancient Egypt*, ed. D. B. Redford (Oxford: Oxford University Press, 2001), 2:238–45, cf. 241, 243, 244.

answers it directly to Joseph with the assertion that there is no one like him in discernment and wisdom (v. 39). Based on his conclusions about Joseph, the Pharaoh makes specific Declarative speech acts. In particular, the Pharaoh establishes Joseph second only to himself and places him in a possible type of vizier role over all of Egypt (vv. 40–43),[23] with nothing able to be done without Joseph's consent (v. 44). Based solely on Joseph's delegated pharaonic power, it would be conceivable to take his interrogative as a confirming Conducive question with no reversal of polarity. Accordingly, his brothers do not need to fear, especially due to his current position in Egypt, which make it possible for him to protect them, which they would confirm with a *Yes!* However, this is highly unlikely due to the overall literary context, while also in v. 20 Joseph explicitly attributes his rise to power to אלהים. Following this verse, he virtually reiterates his previous exhortation ועתה אל־תיראו "and now do not fear!" followed by a Declarative speech act promising to take care of them (v. 21a). Literarily, vv. 19–21a form a type of concentric structure:

A   Exhortative assurance (v. 19aα)

    B   Interrogative (v. 19aβ)

        C   Interpretive description of events (v. 20)

A'   Exhortative assurance (v. 21aα)

    B'   Promissory declarative (v. 21aβ)

With this literary structure, the interrogative (B) and promissory Declarative (B') are intentionally set in parallel. This structure points to the former operating as a RQ that likewise conveys a reassuring reason which is enhanced by the כי most naturally functioning in a causal sense.[24] The center of this unit also provides some clarity on who Joseph considers as אלהים in v. 19. Joseph presents the identity of אלהים earlier when he initially discloses his own identity to his brothers. In ch. 45 Joseph makes

---

23. See James K. Hoffmeier, *Israel in Egypt: The Evidence for the Authenticity of the Exodus Tradition* (Oxford: Oxford University Press, 1996), 93–95; K. A. Kitchen, *On the Reliability of the Old Testament* (Grand Rapids: Eerdmans, 2003), 348–50; Wenham, *Genesis 16–50*, 395. For an earlier conclusion on Joseph occupying this role see James H. Breasted, *Ancient Records of Egypt*, 3 vols. (Chicago: University of Chicago Press, 1906), 2:§§671–72. Concerning the issue of the relationship between a vizier and the phrase על־ביתי "over my house" (v. 40a) and its Egyptian equivalent see Roland de Vaux, *Ancient Israel: Its Life and Institutions*, trans. J. McHugh, BRS (Grand Rapids: Eerdmans, 1961), 129–31.

24. On כי introducing causal clauses see Joüon-Muraoka §170d; *IBHS* §38.4.

it clear that אלהים explicitly refers to the *God* of Jacob who has orchestrated his rise to power. He specifically declares three times that it was אלהים who *sent* him, not his brothers (vv. 5b, 7a, 8a), and twice that it was אלהים who *placed* him in his current place of power in Egypt (vv. 8b, 9a). So, with this succinct contextual background information, Joseph's brothers would readily conclude that the אלהים in his interrogative is the *God* of Jacob, Yahweh.

Along with Brueggemann and Craig, I also see some similarities between Joseph's RQ and Jacob's uninformative, retort RQ; however, I do not understand how it infers a rebuke or a dismissive denial of responsibility? The literary parallels suggest otherwise as well as argue against Brueggemann's ambiguous take on the RQ. Regarding his ambiguous interpretation, Brueggemann asserts that in ch. 45 "Joseph claims everything, including the capacity to forgive his brothers," but in ch. 50 now "things are sobered, perhaps more realistic. Joseph now seems aware of the limits of his authority."[25] Brueggemann further states that in ch. 50 the "brothers are not yet rid of their guilt (vv. 15–17). Even though 45:1–15 has already given assurance on this score, the brothers do not know whether the assurance will hold."[26] Clearly Joseph provides assurances to his brothers in ch. 45 (cf. vv. 5–8), but he never explicitly claims here the ability to forgive nor does he extend forgiveness to his brothers. In fact, the only instance where the brothers ask Joseph to forgive them is found in 50:17 which they allege comes from *your father* before his death. Through some intermediary, Jacob pleads twice for Joseph נשׂא "to forgive" his brothers for their פשׁע "crime" (2×) and חטאת "sin" and the רעה "harm" they did to him. Further, through this message Jacob identifies his sons as servants of the *God* of *your father*.[27] What provokes the brothers to send this message is that their father is dead and perhaps Joseph will now take this opportunity to unleash his revenge upon them for all the *harm* they did to him (v. 15). In vv. 19–21a, Joseph responds directly to his father's message, which is prompted by his brother's "guilty fear."[28]

Looking at Joseph's interrogative itself with the above common background in place, Joseph already knows the answer to his interrogative, which his brothers would readily infer (Efficiency condition).

---

25. Brueggemann, *Genesis*, 372.
26. Ibid., 370; see pp. 345–46.
27. Wenham goes so far as to claim that here the brothers "implore Joseph to act like their father's God, who is the one who 'forgives iniquity, transgression [crime], and sin'" (*Genesis 16–50*, 490); however, this is idea is implicit at best.
28. Brueggemann, *Genesis*, 345.

Thus, Joseph insincerely uses this interrogative (Maxim of Quality and Sincerity/Responsibility). Joseph, then, is not eliciting his brothers for some unknown information (Elicitative force) nor does it arouse any surprise. Through these pragmatic processes (*what is implicated*), the brothers would mentally infer from this positive RQ the implied exclusive answer *No, you are not in the place of God!* This answer matches the directional fit of the communicative context of the discourse participants. This answer/assertion is Joseph's intended meaning (*what is meant*) which directly relates to the message relayed to him. Thus Joseph's RQ implicates that he will not function as *God*, executing any vengeance upon his brothers for the transgressing harm they have done to him and consequently they should not fear. Nahum M. Sarna puts it this way while implicitly viewing the interrogative as a RQ: Joseph's brothers "anxiety is allayed at once. Joseph has no interest in seeking revenge because of the very idea offends his personal theology. Man dares not usurp the prerogatives of God to whom alone belongs the right of punitive vindication (cf. Lev. 19:18)."[29] With this RQ, Joseph, then, adds another theological angle to his earlier promises; rather than, as Brueggemann proposes, either implying that the brothers have to deal with God on their own or that Joseph has reevaluated his thinking.

Joseph's RQ, though, is quite complex as it also expresses irony. As I presented above, the אלהים in the RQ would clearly refer to the *God* of Jacob, but Joseph also functions in a type of divine role in Egypt. In fact, the narrator has Judah verbally recognize Joseph's positional status: כמוך כפרעה "you are just like Pharaoh" (44:18b). Through his RQ, Joseph intentionally implicates that he does not occupy the place of the *God* of Jacob which he intends his brothers to infer, but they know that he does exercise divinely empowered pharaonic power. What enhances this irony is how after 39:23 the divine name יהוה all but disappears, just prior to Joseph's rise to pharaonic power, with the generic title/name אלהים predominantly used throughout the remainder of the Joseph narrative. Another aspect of this irony includes Joseph functioning in a comparable role as אלהים granted to him by the divinely enthroned Pharaoh, yet Joseph's rise to this position has been ultimately orchestrated by the אלהים of Jacob. Joseph wields his divine pharaonic power given to him by *God*.[30]

---

29. Sarna, *Genesis*, 350; similarly Hartley, *Genesis*, 367; Hyman, "Joseph Story," 446.

30. Apparently understanding Joseph's interrogative as a RQ, Carolyn J. Sharp concludes: "The implicit claim is that Joseph is not in the place of God, yet the audience knows that he has functioned in a quasi-divine role, omniscient and able

Joseph's RQ, then, displays multifunctionality as Ilie proposes along with what I described in my Introduction with the sentence *I love the sound of your voice* to ironically and sarcastically express displeasure with her/his voice and simultaneously to indirectly ask her/him to stop singing (see also my discussion of Tsohatzidis' observations in Chapter 1). Joseph's ironic RQ also falls somewhere along the degree spectrum of informativity (see Chapter 2 and Figure 2.2). Joseph's RQ is uninformative as he and his brothers would readily confirm that Joseph does not occupy the place of the God of Jacob. Yet, simultaneously the brothers know that Joseph exercises divinely empowered pharaonic power and thus the RQ expresses an aspect of information-providing. The tension between these two informative dimensions as well as the RQ paralleled with the promissory Declarative *centers* on v. 20. Joseph is convinced that what his brothers planned for harm, *God* planned for good for the purpose of preserving life, not taking it.

With the information-providing aspect of this RQ Joseph implies a primary and strong Assertive force along with the Expressive force conveying his attitude specified in the inferred IA. As I described in the previous chapter, with the Expressive force (Austin's Behabitive) addressers express committed psychological attitudes or feelings specified in the sincerity condition about a state of affairs specified in the propositional content. This force relates to both what prompts the interrogative as well as the inferred assertion. With Joseph's RQ, he expresses reassurance in response to his brother's fears and also his sincere conviction about the state of affairs specified in the inferred propositional IA. Thus, Joseph takes the stance that he is not in the place of *God*. Along with the Expressive force, this RQ includes a Commissive whereby Joseph commits himself to not act as *God* in vengeance against his brothers. Thus, with these two forces it appears that his RQ operates in a confessionary sense. Specifically, Joseph's RQ is a self-involved speech act whereby he takes the public *stance* that he is not in the place of God which *entails* that he will not act in judgment against his brothers. While at the same time he commits himself through his parallel promissory Declarative to exert his divinely empowered pharaonic power to preserve and protect the lives and wellbeing of his brothers and their children. Joseph implies through his RQ that his pharaonic power will operate from

to manipulate life-and-death matters unseen. One result is that the relationship between Joseph's pharaonic power and the power of Israel's God is left tensive and problematic" (*Irony and Meaning in the Hebrew Bible*, ISBL [Bloomington: Indiana University Press, 2009], 60).

within the confines of his faithful commitment to his father's *God*. Put another way, his theological perspective constrains him from adopting the position rightfully belonging only to *God*.

Joseph uses the information-providing dimension of his RQ to challenge his brothers to agree with and assent to the inferred answer/assertion and thereby trust him. Due to its irony the interrogative dimension of the RQ would understandably remain for them. The brothers would acknowledge and understand the Initial PE, but with the Intended PE they are challenged to assent to Joseph's intended Assertive force and thereby take the stance in relation to the inferred assertion with the entailments to believe and trust Joseph. Further, they need to remain in Egypt to experience whether or not Joseph will retain his theological stance with its accompanied entailments as well as keep his promissory Declarative.[31] The narrative never explicitly discloses or comments on the brother's response, but it depicts Joseph and Jacob-Israel's household remaining in Egypt as well as implies that Joseph maintained his stance and kept his promise (vv. 22–25).

Exodus 3:11

In response to Yahweh's commission to deliver Israel from Egypt, Moses replies:

Who am I	מי אנכי
that I should go to Pharaoh	כי אלך אל־פרעה
and that I should deliver the people of Israel from Egypt?	וכי אוציא את־בני ישראל ממצרים

Moses' interrogative here occurs within the larger literary unit of 3:1–4:18, which is Yahweh's commission of Moses.[32] This interrogative is located in the first part of this commission (3:1–15) and is specifically a response to

---

31. Although I find certain problems with Dale Patrick's understanding and application of SAT (see Adams, *Performative Nature*, 69–74), his transactional notion appropriately applies here as the brothers must actively engage with the inferred IA in order to experience the reality of its force (*The Rhetoric of Revelation in the Hebrew Bible*, OBT [Minneapolis: Fortress, 1999]).

32. See Thomas B. Dozeman, "The Commission of Moses and the Book of Genesis," in *A Farewell to the Yahwist? The Composition of the Pentateuch in Recent European Interpretation*, ed. Thomas B. Dozeman and K. Schmid, SBLSS 34 (Atlanta: Society of Biblical Literature, 2006), 110–14.

Yahweh's assignment (3:9–10).³³ It also functions as a key interrogative in the Exodus narrative along with 5:2 and 15:11, which I will examine below. There are numerous interrogatives in Exodus, but these three play a crucial interrelated role for the overarching purpose of the narrative as they each connect to the identity and nature of Yahweh.

Moses' response begins with the pronoun מי, which is followed by two כי clauses that essentially reiterate the two aspects of Yahweh's commission which also convey the result of the מי clause.³⁴ These two כי clauses provide indicators that Moses does not inquire about who he is in a philosophical sense, but in regards to his own self-assessment to fulfill Yahweh's delivering task (v. 10). In his analysis on expressions of abasement and insult formulas, George W. Coats includes this interrogative with others as examples of such structural patterns (e.g., Exod 5:2; 16:7; Num 16:11; Judg 9:38; 1 Sam 17:26; 18:18; 2 Sam 9:8; Ps 8:5; Job 3:12; 17:17).³⁵ From a form-critical approach, Coats identifies two structural elements to express either *self-abasement* (first person contexts) or *insult* (second or third person objects) as follows:

a. An introductory question constructed as a noun clause with an interrogative particle (regularly מי or מה) followed by a personal pronoun, a proper name, or a noun.
b. A connecting verbal assertion introduced by a כי or more rarely by an אשר or *waw* consecutive with an imperfect verb (more rarely perfects and participles). The subject or object of the verb has its antecedent in the interrogative clause.

According to Coats, the introductory interrogative abases the noun or pronoun subject by an implied answer to that question. On the basis of this implied answer, the verb in the connecting assertion is negated.³⁶ Coats concludes that with this pattern

---

33. On the genre of Moses' call see Dozeman, "Commission of Moses," 112–13; see also Brevard S. Childs, *The Book of Exodus: A Critical, Theological Commentary*, OTL (Louisville: Westminster, 1974), 53–56; George W. Coats, *Exodus 1–18*, FOTL 2/A (Grand Rapids: Eerdmans, 1999), 34–42; Norman Habel, "The Form and Significance of the Call Narrative," *ZAW* 77 (1965): 297–323, cf. 301–305.

34. Joüon-Muraoka §169e; see also *IBHS* §38.3b.

35. George W. Coats, "Self-Abasement and Insult Formulas," *JBL* 89 (1970): 14–26.

36. Ibid., 14–15, 26.

its setting is basically court or cult, used before someone of higher estate as a self-abasement or an insult for a common enemy. It poses a question in element *a*, then abases the noun or pronoun subject by an implied answer to the question. On the basis of the implied answer, the verb in element *b* is negated.[37]

However, in instances such as Exod 3:11 and Ps 8:5 (see below) Raymond C. Van Leeuwen correctly observes that Coats' last above point misconstrues the idiomatic function of the formula

> by "bleeding" the meaning of the two clauses into one another. It is not true that the formula "negates" the verb in element *b*. Rather, the formula implies that the person in element *a* is unworthy of or unable to do the action in element *b*. The idiom does not imply that the action in element *b* should not be done... Distinguishing the two clauses permits us to explain those cases where only element *a* appears ("Who is X?"), with its implied (or explicit, metaphorical) answer, "nobody." More importantly, this distinction permits us to understand these cases where the verbal action in element *b* is ignored or by-passed, usually by the social superior. In these cases, the negation of the verb in element *b* is not actualized; rather, only the person in the *a* element (the "who-clause") is "negated" with respect to the verbal action in element *b*.[38]

In light of the above analysis as well as the function of the two כי clauses, Moses already knows the answer to his interrogative (Efficiency condition). Thus, Moses insincerely uses this interrogative (Maxim of Quality and Sincerity/Responsibility) and does not elicit from his addressee Yahweh any unknown information (Elicitative force). Moses, then, intends his interrogative to operate as a RQ. Moses' seemingly eager response הנני "Here I am" to Yahweh's initial call (3:4) has now turned into מי אנכי.[39] Yahweh would readily infer from this positive RQ the implied exclusive answer *I am not the person with the necessary capabilities to deliver Israel from Egypt!* Yahweh does not directly answer Moses' question nor does he explicitly display any uncertainty or surprise. Instead, he proceeds with two כי clauses of his own. First a promise of

---

37. Ibid., 26; Waltke/O'Connor utilize Coats' analysis wholesale and directly apply it to Moses' interrogative (*IBHS* §18.2g).

38. Raymond C. Van Leeuwen, "Psalm 8.5 and Job 7.17–18: A Mistaken Scholarly Commonplace?" in *The World of the Aramaeans I*, ed. P. M. Michèle Daviau et al., Festschrift Paul-Eugène Dion, JSOTSup 324 (Sheffield: Sheffield Academic, 2001), 208.

39. Terence E. Fretheim, *Exodus*, Int (Louisville: John Knox, 1991), 61.

his presence כִּי־אֶהְיֶה עִמָּךְ "Certainly I will be with you!" followed by an abbreviated reiteration of his commission כִּי אָנֹכִי שְׁלַחְתִּיךָ "that I myself have sent you" (v. 12), which includes a repeating of the first person pronoun אָנֹכִי. With his own two כִּי clauses and use of אָנֹכִי, Yahweh highlights that the question of Moses' ability is not at issue, but rather the one who is with and has sent Moses.[40] "The inadequacies of Moses' personality profile matter no more than they did in the case of" Ishmael, Abraham, Isaac, and Jacob (Gen 21:20, 22; 26:24; 28:15) with whom Yahweh has also been.[41]

It is important to emphasize that Moses' response of inadequacy directly relates to Yahweh's commission. Moses does offer some specific evidence of his personal inadequacies soon after this episode with his claim of an inability to speak well (4:10). Yet, in light of Egypt as a superpower along with the demonstrated authority of the human and divine Pharaoh, Moses' response makes perfect sense. Thus, Moses may express abasement or unworthiness formulaically, but within this narrative world his response would also be authentic as he has firsthand knowledge of Egypt and its king. Yahweh, though, typically chooses individuals for roles of responsibility who do not have privileged status and/or have character flaws and who do not appear to possess the expected personality traits and/or leadership qualities.[42] Yahweh often selects the ordinary in order to demonstrate his extraordinary power. Coupled with this, in the first part of the Exodus narrative the focus is not concerned in any way with Moses' ability; rather, it centers on and highlights Yahweh and in particular his supreme power displayed through his performance of various signs and wonders in direct challenge to the Pharaoh (9:13–17) and other Egyptian gods (12:12) that ultimately causes the release of Israel from Egyptian slavery.

In light of all of the above, Moses' RQ is uninformative. Both discourse participants share the same knowledge and are committed to the joint mutual understanding that Moses on his own merits does not possess the ability to deliver Israel from the power of the human and divine Pharaoh. With all this, the inferred answer/assertion of the RQ, then, matches the directional fit of the shared knowledge of both Yahweh and Moses.

Although uninformative, Moses' RQ infers a strong primary Assertive force which also includes a strong Behabitive/Expressive force as well as the Commissive. With the Expressive, Moses expresses protest and

---

40. Similarly John I. Durham, *Exodus*, WBC 3 (Waco: Word, 1987), 33.
41. Goldingay, *Israel's Gospel*, 311.
42. See ibid., 540.

inadequacy and also his sincere conviction about the truthfulness specified in his inferred answer/assertion. Thus, Moses takes the stance that he is not the right person for Yahweh's appointed task. With the Commissive force, Moses commits himself to not carry out Yahweh's commission. As such, Moses' RQ is a self-involved speech act. Although Moses does not offer any explicit evidence with his uninformative RQ and unlike Jacob's retort RQ, he does challenge Yahweh that he is not the man for the job. Regarding the PEs of Moses' RQ, Yahweh would recognize and understand Moses' Initial perlocutionary goal and while he would unquestionably agree with the Intended PEs, he obviously rejects assenting to Moses' intended assertion in contrast to Coats' formulaic interpretation. Van Leeuwen puts it this way: "The master is free to sidestep the servant's statement of self-abasement, even when it is factually accurate. While Moses argues for the negation of the verbs in element *b*, Yahweh does not grant it. Moses will go to Pharaoh."[43] This also deviates from how I described the typical function of the Intended PEs. It is not that Yahweh offers a counter answer to the interrogative dimension of Moses' RQ, but rather that Yahweh is committed to use Moses, despite, and more probably because of, his own self-evaluative inadequacies.

Exodus 5:2

Moses ultimately embraces Yahweh's commission and delivers the command of Yahweh, the God of Israel, to the Pharaoh to release his people (v. 1). The Pharaoh responds:

Who is Yahweh	מי יהוה
that I should listen to his voice to release Israel?	אשר אשמע בקלו לשלח את־ישראל
I do not know Yahweh	לא ידעתי את־יהוה
and thus I will not release Israel!	וגם את־ישראל לא אשלח:

Along with many scholars, the initial מי יהוה clause functions as the central question of the Exodus narrative, but ironically the Pharaoh does not appear to use it genuinely. The מי clause resembles Moses', but here אשר is used to convey the result of this clause.[44] The Pharaoh's response also follows Coats' form-critical structural analysis, but he expresses the insult pattern by referring to Yahweh in third person.[45] Moses responds

---

43. Van Leeuwen, "Psalm 8.5," 209.
44. See Joüon-Muraoka §169f; *IBHS* §38.3b.
45. Coats, "Self-Abasement," 21; followed by *IBHS* §18.2g.

to Yahweh's commission with מי אנכי inferring self-assessed inadequacy whereas the Pharaoh responds to Yahweh's request with מי יהוה inferring contemptuous insult.[46] Along with this, the Pharaoh makes it quite clear that he is not sincerely eliciting information about Yahweh from his two addressees (Maxim of Quality and Sincerity/Responsibility; Elicitative force) with his connecting clauses asserting that he does not know or recognize Yahweh as well as his refusal to release Israel. Thus, the Pharaoh already knows the answer to his interrogative (Efficiency condition). The Pharaoh undoubtedly intends his interrogative to function as a RQ which Moses and Aaron would easily infer from this positive RQ the implied exclusive answer/assertion: *Yahweh is not a deity of consequence who I should obey!* This response does not come as a surprise as Yahweh explicitly told Moses and Aaron that he knows the Pharaoh will not immediately release Israel (3:19). Further, based on the common background knowledge concerning the human and divine Pharaoh and the seemingly unrivaled power at his disposal, with some certainty Moses and Aaron would expect such a response from the king of Egypt. Further, unlike the Pharaoh who promoted Joseph, this king of Egypt within the Exodus narrative has had no prior experiential knowledge of Yahweh. Thus, this RQ has all the characteristic markings of an uninformative type.

As with Moses' RQ, the Pharaoh also infers a strong primary Assertive force along with the Behabitive/Expressive and Commissive forces. With the former, the Pharaoh expresses sarcastic disdain regarding Yahweh and also his sincere conviction about the truthfulness specified in his answer/assertion. Thus, the Pharaoh takes the stance of superiority over Yahweh who is not a deity he recognizes as one of any consequence to obey. With the Commissive force, the Pharaoh definitely opposes Yahweh and commits himself to the entailment of not releasing his people Israel, which he makes explicit with his immediately following assertions. Thus, the Pharaoh's RQ here is a self-involved speech act just like Moses' while expressing different stances, but comparable entailments. Moses and Aaron would easily recognize and understand the Initial PEs here. As I described earlier with my spectrum of degrees of informativity (see Chapter 2), although the inferred answer to Pharaoh's uninformative RQ would be quite predictable, Moses and Aaron would not agree that Yahweh is a deity of no consequence or at least they are well on their way to such experiential beliefs. Consequentially, a directional mismatch in fit occurs between the Pharaoh's inferred assertion and Moses and Aaron's

---

46. See Nahum M. Sarna, *Exodus*, JPSTC (Philadelphia: The Jewish Publication Society, 1991), 27.

own beliefs and commitments. With this RQ, the Pharaoh also does not appear to be persuading or challenging his immediate addressees to agree with and to assent to his implied answer. He rather challenges the one who sent Moses and Aaron as he takes a defiant and arrogant stance directly against Yahweh. In this instance, the Intended perlocutionary goal does not become a factor which also displays a variation from my theoretical framework (see Table 2.4) and specifically what one would expect with PEs.

Moses and Pharaoh's RQs are uninformative, with the inferred propositional content expressing their beliefs and commitments. Both of these RQs convey the Behabitive/Expressive and Commissive along with a primary Assertive force with the two former forces typically marking self-involvement. To recall from my Introduction, with self-involvement Briggs states that the addresser takes a stance in the *public domain* which commits her/him to certain forms of positive or negative behavior.[47] With both RQs, the addressers take a stance which includes specific entailments that commit them to particular behavior. Each RQ functions in a confessionary sense in direct relation to Yahweh and his mission to deliver Israel. Moses expresses his self-assessed inadequacy whereas the Pharaoh expresses his self-assessed superiority over Yahweh. Within the Exodus narrative, Moses' inferred inadequacy and the Pharaoh's inferred superiority both in turn highlight Yahweh's supreme and incomparable power.

Exodus 15:11 and Four Psalmic Interrogatives
Conveying Yahweh's Incomparability

Following Yahweh's response to Moses' RQ *I will be with you*, he asks for God's name which he answers with אהיה אשר אהיה "*I will be who I will be,*" which functions as a paronomasia play on the divine name יהוה (3:14).[48] The meaning of his name semantically links to the promise of his presence while his display of power demonstrates the *idem per idem*, idiomatic meaning of his name[49] that *he will be* and *do* whatever he wants

---

47. Briggs, *Words in Action*, 151.
48. E.g., Childs, *Exodus*, 69; Goldingay, *Israel's Gospel*, 336; Donald E. Gowan, *Theology in Exodus: Biblical Theology in the Form of a Commentary* (Louisville: Westminster John Knox, 1994), 84; R. W. L. Moberly, *The Old Testament of the Old Testament: Patriarchal Narratives and Mosaic Yahwism*, OBT (Minneapolis: Fortress, 1992), 21–22.
49. Jack R. Lundbom examines Exod 3:14 and other instances of *idem per idem* forms and concludes that they function rhetorically to terminate a debate ("God's Use of the *Idem per Idem* to Terminate Debate," *HTR* 71 [1978]: 193–201). Although

to do.⁵⁰ Yahweh demonstrates the meaning of his name with a series of Declarative illocutionary forces. With these performative speech acts, Yahweh proclaims a future event that transforms reality by saying that the propositional content matches the world (double directional fit). Yahweh felicitously satisfies these performative speech acts when he subsequently actualizes the propositional content of the respective announcement. Illustrating this with the sign of the insects in 8:16–28 (Eng. 8:20–32), Yahweh declares his action sign ("I will send...") (v. 17) followed by the identity of an area excluded from the plague (a new aspect from the previous signs) with the purpose expressed with the variable refrain typified as תדע כי אני יהוה "you will know that I am Yahweh" (v. 18). Yahweh then states that the sign will occur the next day (v. 19) followed by the narrator explicitly reporting that Yahweh executed the sign (v. 20). The reversal or removal of the plague is also strategically executed by Moses and Yahweh. With this fourth sign and in broad strokes, the Pharaoh asks Moses to remove the plague (v. 21), Moses complies with certain qualifications (vv. 22–23) with the Pharaoh agreeing (v. 24), and Moses prays to Yahweh (vv. 25–26) followed by a narrative report that Yahweh listened to Moses and ended the plague (v. 31).

Yahweh's sign-Declaratives transform the state of affairs in Egypt and directly challenge the gods of Egypt (Exod 12:12; Num 33:4), but primarily the Pharaoh (cf. Exod 8:16)⁵¹ and specifically his royal and divine control of *ma'at* "cosmic order" which is one of his primary duties

---

Lundbom's analysis successfully applies to certain texts (e.g., John 19:22), I agree with Gowan that this expression as it occurs in Exod 3–4 "by no means brings the discussion to an end" (*Theology in Exodus*, 84–85). Rather, analogous *idem per idem* expressions found in the Hebrew Bible provide a more helpful interpretive grid for understanding Yahweh's response (Exod 16:23; 33:19; 1 Sam 23:13; 2 Sam 15:20; 2 Kgs 8:1; Ezek 12:25).

50. Joüon-Muraoka view the *idem per idem* clauses in Exod 33:19; 1 Sam 23:13; 2 Sam 15:20, and 2 Kgs 8:1 expressing "certain nuances of indeterminateness" (§158o). These texts do convey an aspect of indeterminacy, but Exod 33:19 and Ezek 12:25 also clearly show that Yahweh has the freedom to show grace and compassion on whomever he wishes or speak whatever he wants to speak respectively. Likewise, in Exod 16:23 the subject of the clause has the freedom to make her/his own decisions while the expressions in 1 Sam 23:13, 2 Sam 15:20, and 2 Kgs 8:1 also convey such freedom; similarly Gowan, *Theology of Exodus*, 84; see further Goldingay, *Israel's Gospel*, 336–40.

51. See James K. Hoffmeier, "The Arm of God Versus the Arm of Pharaoh in the Exodus Narrative," *Bib* 67 (1986): 378–87; idem, "Egypt, Plagues in," *ABD* 2:376–77.

as king.⁵² With these Declaratives, Yahweh demonstrates his sole ability to manipulate a particular aspect of creation from its original created mode and then subsequently restore it to his intended order.⁵³

These signs and wonders display Yahweh's supreme power with the primary purpose expressed with the "knowing Yahweh" formula. Significantly, this refrain only repeatedly occurs following the Pharaoh's arrogant and defiant RQ. The intended PEs of Yahweh's Declaratives target Israel and, primarily, the Egyptians (7:5, 17; 8:22; 9:14, 29; 10:2; 14:4; 29:46) with the goal for them to experientially *know* that he alone controls the cosmos (9:29) and consequently his incomparability to any other deity (v. 14).⁵⁴ Following Israel's deliverance through the sea and immediately before Moses and Israel's song, the narrator explicitly comments that the Intended PEs of Yahweh's announced and executed signs and wonders have achieved his initial goals: Israel fears Yahweh and believes in him and his servant Moses (14:31).

Yahweh's signs and wonders also answer the interrogative dimension of the Pharaoh's RQ. Yahweh's display of his unparalleled power have created a directional mismatch between the Pharaoh's inferred answer/ assertion and Yahweh's demonstration of the meaning of his name. *Who is Yahweh?* He is a deity who *can be* and *do* whatever he wants to do! Within the narrative world, for Israel, as well as the Egyptians, the Pharaoh's inferred answer/assertion does not match the reality of their

---

52. See Emily Teeter, "Maat," in Redford, ed., *Oxford Encyclopedia*, 2:319; John Baines, "Ancient Egyptian Kingship: Official Forms, Rhetoric, Context," in *King and Messiah in Israel and the Ancient Near East*, ed. J. Day, LHBOTS 270 (London: T&T Clark, 2013), 41–46; John D. Currid, *Ancient Egypt and the Old Testament* (Grand Rapids: Baker, 1997), 113–20; Hoffmeier, *Israel in Egypt*, 149–53.

53. Within the Exodus narrative, along with the staffs turning into serpents episode (7:8–12) the first two signs were duplicated by Pharaoh's magicians (7:22; 8:7); however, they were unable to reverse the plagues while ironically and comically they actually made the conditions in Egypt worse.

54. Marc Vervenne observes that "the expression of the idea 'knowing YHWH' occurs in a variety of patterns employing a particular type of phraseology" while demonstrating that the phrase "is closely associated with the description of divine *actions* in the history of Israel, and in particular with the *announcement* of those *actions* which are going to take place" ("The Phraseology of 'Knowing YHWH' in the Hebrew Bible: A Preliminary Study of its Syntax and Function," in *Studies in the Book of Isaiah*, ed. J. van Ruiten and Marc Vervenne, Festschrift W. A. M. Beuken, BETL 132 [Leuven: Leuven University Press, 1997], 468, italics mine); see also Walther Zimmerli, *I Am Yahweh*, ed. W. Brueggemann, trans. D. W. Stott (Atlanta: John Knox, 1982).

experiential knowledge of Yahweh. Based on the evidence derived from Yahweh's answer, Moses and Israel also provide their own answer to the Pharaoh's interrogative expressed in a series of assertions, confessions, and especially with their own interrogative in their Song of the Sea.

The Exodus narrator identifies the genre of 15:1b–18 as a שירה "song" (v. 1a); however, beyond this general definition interpreters have proposed various genre elements for and within this Song (e.g., a type of Song of Victory or Triumph,[55] a "solo hymn,"[56] praise and thanksgiving to God,[57] a liturgy or litany,[58] and Declarative Praise[59]). From a speech act perspective, though, this Song functions primarily as a self-involved confession.[60] In this Song, Israel expresses its commitment to Yahweh while confessing, describing, declaring, and thanking Yahweh for his triumph over its enemies and safe deliverance. One of the strongest expressions of this commitment is found in the bicolon interrogative in v. 11:

Who is like you among the gods Yahweh?	מי־כמכה באלם יהוה
Who is like you majestic in holiness	מי כמכה נאדר בקדש
awesome in praises, working wonders?	נורא תהלת עשה פלא:

Labuschagne includes these interrogatives with others he identifies as RQs expressing Yahweh's incomparability (Pss 35:10; 71:19; 77:14; 89:9; 113:5; Mic 7:18; Job 36:22; also including Deut 3:24; 4:7). As I presented in my Introduction, Labuschagne views these RQs as "confessions

---

55. E.g., Martin L. Brenner, *The Song of the Sea: Ex 15:1–21*, BZAW 195 (Berlin: de Gruyter, 1991), 36–40; Frank M. Cross and David N. Freedman, *Studies in Ancient Yahwistic Poetry*, BRS (Grand Rapids: Eerdmans, 1975), 31–45; David N. Freedman, *Pottery, Poetry, and Prophecy: Collected Essays on Hebrew Poetry* (Winona Lake: Eisenbrauns, 1980), 132–46; Alan J. Hauser, "Two Songs of Victory: A Comparison of Exodus 15 and Judges 5," in *Directions in Biblical Hebrew Poetry*, ed. E. R. Follis, JSOTSup 40 (Sheffield: Sheffield Academic, 1987), 265–84; Mark S. Smith, "The Poetics of Exodus 15 and Its Position in the Book," in *Imagery and Imagination in Biblical Literature*, ed. L. Boadt and Mark S. Smith, Festschrift Aloysius Fitzgerald, CBQMS 32 (Washington: Catholic Biblical Association, 2001), 24; Sigmund Mowinckel, *The Psalms in Israel's Worship*, trans. D. R. Ap-Thomas, 2 vols. (New York: Abingdon, 1962), 2:26–27.

56. Martin Noth, *Exodus*, trans. J. S. Bowden, OTL (Louisville: Westminster, 1962), 123.

57. Fretheim, *Exodus*, 161.

58. James Muilenburg, "A Liturgy on the Triumphs of Yahweh," in *Studia Biblica et Semitica*, Festschrift T. C. Vriezen (Wageningen: H. Veenman, 1966), 235–36.

59. Claus Westermann, *Praise and Lament in the Psalms*, trans. K. R. Crim and R. N. Soulen (Atlanta: John Knox, 1981), 141.

60. Muilenburg identifies vv. 2–3, 7–8, and 12–14 as Hymnic confessions.

expressing a conviction. Their primary intention is a confession of faith, the driving home of a conviction." I agree with this basic confessionary interpretive view, but Labuschagne never explains how these interrogatives function as RQs or transform into confessions.

Examining this verse, it is composed of two parallel sentences that begin with the pronoun מי as with the above two RQs. Different from these RQs, though, Yahweh is explicitly the addressee who would most assuredly infer the positive answer with *No one is like me!* Moses and Israel, then, already know the answer to this interrogative, with which Yahweh the addressee would obviously agree (Efficiency condition), and would not engage in any pragmatic processes to arrive at the implied answer/assertion. The addressers, then, insincerely use this interrogative (Maxim of Quality and Sincerity/Responsibility) and are not eliciting for some unknown information (Elicitative force). Rather than the addressers persuading the addressee to agree with and assent to an inferred obvious answer, with this particular RQ the addressers confirm their joint mutual knowledge as well as synchronize their beliefs and commitments about Yahweh with Yahweh. Thus, for Yahweh the Initial and Intended PEs do not become factors.

This interrogative, then, operates as an uninformative RQ in the sense of Rohde's narrow definition. But significantly with this RQ, it is Yahweh the addressee who has provided the experiential evidence for the inferred answer/assertion, not the addressers. Because of Yahweh's demonstrated power, both discourse participants share the same knowledge and are committed to the joint mutual belief that no deity compares to Yahweh. The inferred answer/assertion of the RQ, then, matches the directional fit of the shared knowledge of both Yahweh and Moses and Israel. My conclusions here are quite different from what Labuschagne envisions with this and similar RQs. To recall, for Labuschagne because of the "persuasive effect the hearer is not merely listener [*sic*]; she/he is forced to frame the expected answer in her/his mind, and by doing so she/he actually becomes a *co-expressor* of the speaker's conviction."[61] Assuming that Labuschagne's "hearer" and "listener" is the immediate addressee of a particular RQ,[62] in this instance Yahweh is the addressee who is not in any way persuaded and forced to become a co-expressor; rather, Israel expresses an inferred answer/assertion that aligns with Yahweh's own claims about himself.

---

61. Labuschagne, *Incomparability of Yahweh*, 23 (italics mine; pronouns revised).
62. As I noted in my Introduction, Labuschagne does not clearly identify the "hearer" and "listener" of these types of RQs.

The primary inferred Assertive force of this uninformative RQ transforms for the singers into, and counts as, an illocutionary confession: *No other deity compares to the utterly unique Yahweh!* Also, within the Exodus narrative this directly answers the interrogative dimension of the Pharaoh's RQ *Who is Yahweh?* As with Moses and the Pharaoh's self-involved uninformative RQ, this RQ infers a strong Assertive force that functions as a confession that includes the Behabitive/Expressive and Commissive forces. Moses and Israel express their devotion and praise to Yahweh along with their sincere conviction about the truthfulness specified in the inferred propositional IA. As such, the singers take a *stance* regarding Yahweh and all other deities: Yahweh is incomparable. With the Commissive force, they commit themselves to sole allegiance to this God. This *entailment* is later expected with the first command in the Decalogue (Exod 20:3).

Dale Patrick describes how the "Song of the Sea is designed for the readers of the narrative to respond along with the Israel of the narrative world."[63] I agree with this and more specifically, as a reader follows the narrative of Israel's deliverance from Egypt with its focus on exhibiting Yahweh's matchless power unto the Song of the Sea, they are challenged to read/sing along in agreement with the various assertions and confessions expressed. When the reader/singer arrives at the uninformative RQ its hybrid nature even more so implores self-involvement while the interrogative dimension comes back into play and consequently conveys an information-providing aspect. Obviously for Moses and Israel the RQ functions as a confession, but the reader/singer is confronted with the interrogative and the inferred assertion dimensions, with both implicating particular stances and entailments. The *question* the reader/singer is confronted with is does she/he agree with and assent to the exclusive answer/assertion and become a *co-expresser* or more exactly a *co-confessor* with Moses and Israel or will she/he answer the interrogative dimension and offer an unintended contrary answer which would fall more in line with the Pharaoh's inferred answer/assertion to his RQ?

Kuntz identifies four RQs in the Psalms that *explicitly* affirm Yahweh's incomparability which Labuschagne also includes in his list (Pss 35:10; 71:19; 89:7–8 [Eng. vv. 6–7], 9 [v. 8]; 113:5–6). In his analysis of RQs in the Psalms, Kuntz identifies eight different situations involving addressers and addressees along with three main functions. These RQs

---

63. Patrick, *Rhetoric of Revelation*, 44.

occur in his third function which centers on thematic concerns and specifically focusing *"humanity's mind on Yahweh's incomparability."* The former two interrogatives display similarities with Exod 15:11 as Yahweh is also the addressee. In Ps 35, an individual protests and utters an interrogative:

All my bones will say,	כל עצמותי תאמרנה
"Yahweh who is like you	יהוה מי כמוך
one who delivers the weak from someone stronger than him	מציל עני מחזק ממנו
and the weak and needy from someone who robs him?"	ועני ואביון מגזלו:

In Ps 71 the psalmist follows his petitions and trust with:

And your righteousness, God, on high	וצדקתך אלהים עד־מרום
who has done great things;	אשר־עשית גדלות
God, who is like you?	אלהים מי כמוך:

Kuntz claims with the latter interrogative that "Yahweh's saving work is highlighted as that which discloses his incomparability and is celebrated through the *persuasive force* of a rhetorical question."[64] It is unclear, though, who this persuasive force is directed towards in Ps 71 or by association Ps 35. Kuntz recognizes that Yahweh is the addressee with a number of RQs in the Psalter, but does not explore the implications of this fact with these two RQs.[65] Perhaps the persuasive force is for Yahweh, but his above phraseology does not make this exactly clear. Is it rather for the addresser or someone listening to the psalmist? Looking more closely at the RQs, both are expressed by individuals who largely protest and petition Yahweh throughout their respective psalms. Psalm 35 is a more straightforward Protest/Complaint psalm whereas Ps 71 contains more of the same types of expressions to categorize it identically (petition [vv. 1–4, 9, 12–13, 18]; protest/complaint [vv. 10–11]),[66] but its structure is not as refined while including elements of confidence and hope (vv. 5–7, 19–20) along with promises of praise (vv. 8, 14–16, 22–24).[67]

---

64. Kuntz, "Making a Statement," 177 (italics mine).
65. See ibid., 167 and n. 28.
66. So, e.g., Westermann, *Praise and Lament*, 181.
67. Marvin E. Tate concludes that this psalm is "a kind of confident, even jubilant, psalm of lament" (*Psalms 51–100*, WBC 20 [Dallas: Word, 1990], 211); see also

With both RQs the psalmists express confidence and hope in the midst of petition and protest due to their suffering at the hands of others, while Ps 35 presents a far more dire situation. In this psalm, the מי clause is followed by two participle clauses describing the way Yahweh is incomparable. In Ps 71, the psalmist describes Yahweh and his righteous saving acts and then with the final מי clause draws a conclusion about Yahweh's incomparability. Both RQs are uninformative and function very similarly to Exod 15:11, but are used with different intentions.

In Ps 71, the psalmist indirectly confesses with the RQ her/his confidence in Yahweh and takes the stance concerning his incomparability previously demonstrated through his righteous saving acts with the accompanied entailments of placing her/his sole trust in Yahweh to deliver her/him. This RQ directly connects to its previous lines where the psalmist petitions Yahweh to not abandon her/him (v. 18a) until the supplicant declares God's power (v. 18b) and righteous saving acts (v. 19a). The RQ is most naturally included as part of the content of the psalmist's declaration[68] and functions as part of the expressions of promises of praise. As the addressee, Yahweh is left to either agree with the inferred assertion *There is no one like you God!* or answer the interrogative with a counter reply. Yahweh would obviously agree with the exclusive answer/assertion, which is enhanced by the psalmist linking his promised declaration of Yahweh's incomparable "great things" to his *wonders* which he did in Egypt (v. 17b; see Ps 106:21).

In Ps 35, the psalmist begins with a series of petitions to Yahweh to save the supplicant from threatening attacks (vv. 1–8) followed by anticipated praise of Yahweh for his intervention (vv. 9–10). The RQ in v. 10 begins with an introductory speech clause with an imperfect verb identifying what the psalmist's bones *will* say. Specifically and similar to the RQ in Ps 71, the psalmist tells Yahweh that following his salvation the supplicant *will* confess Yahweh's incomparability in relation to his characteristic traits to deliver the powerless and helpless such as the psalmist from oppressors. As with the RQ in Ps 71, Yahweh would without hesitation agree with the answer/assertion of his incomparability (cf. Deut 10:17–18) with the same stance taken with the accompanied entailments. With both RQs and Yahweh's sure agreement and assent, the psalmists challenge Yahweh that without his intervention to deliver, the supplicants

---

Erhard S. Gerstenberger, *Psalms, Part 2, and Lamentations*, FOTL 25 (Grand Rapids: Eerdmans, 2001), 58–64; John Goldingay, *Psalms, Volume 2: Psalms 42–89*, BCOT (Grand Rapids: Baker Academic, 2007), 365–66.

68. So Goldingay, *Psalms 42–89*, 375; see also Gerstenberger, *Psalms, Part 2*, 61–62.

3. The Performative Dimensions of Rhetorical Questions

will be unable to fulfill their promised confessions of praise.[69] Reflected within the Psalter, a "key aspect of the dynamic of Israel's relationship with Yhwh involves Israel praying in the midst of a crisis, Yhwh acting in response to that prayer, and Israel testifying to Yhwh's action"[70] (see, e.g., Ps 9:14–15 [vv. 13–14]). At stake here, Yahweh will not be praised by the respective suppliants while what will remain in *question* is his incomparable reputation of his unmatched power to continue to deliver and how he characteristically delivers the powerless from oppressors. Before moving on, I want to highlight here that in contrast to Eliphaz's initial uninformative RQs (see Chapter 2), both these RQs along with Moses' show how this same type can include a challenging intent accompanied with the agreement and assent of the exclusive answer.

Looking to the next RQs and beginning with Ps 113:

Who is like Yahweh our God	מי כיהוה אלהינו
the one who sits on high	המגביהי לשבת:
the one who makes low to see in the heavens and in the earth?	המשפילי לראות בשמים ובארץ:

For Kuntz, the psalmist uses this RQ "in order to intensify hymnic speech."[71] Earlier in his essay, Kuntz examines a similar incomparable RQ in Ps 77:14b (v. 13b):

Who is a god great as God?	מי־אל גדול כאלהים:

Kuntz, following many English translations that include "our," recognizes that here "the psalmist is not talking to God, but *about* God." The suppliant "is both speaker and addressee." Although Kuntz does not explicitly describe the RQ in Ps 113 as such, it seems clear that the same holds true; however, Kuntz's intensification idea is not as convincing as it is primarily operating in the same sense as the above RQs.

Psalm 113 is a communal Hymn of Praise[72] wherein a group or soloist summons surrounding worshippers identified as *the servants of Yahweh*

---

69. Similarly Goldingay observes in Ps 71 apart from the RQ that the "implicit motivation for God to stay faithful that the suppliant offers to God (vv. 18–19a) is that the pattern of the suppliant's proclamation will then also continue" (*Psalms 42–89*, 374).

70. Goldingay, *Psalms 42–89*, 654.

71. Kuntz, "Making a Statement," 177.

72. See, e.g., Gerstenberger, *Psalms, Part 2*, 277–81; Walter Brueggemann, *The Message of the Psalms: A Theological Commentary* (Minneapolis: Augsburg, 1984), 158, 161–62.

to praise Yahweh and his name (vv. 1–3). Following a testimony about Yahweh (v. 4) and beginning in the exact center, the psalmists use the pronoun מי along with the sole first person plural pronoun. In light of the other RQs expressing Yahweh's incomparability as well the communal "our," what makes it clear that this interrogative intentionally operates as a RQ is that the addressers and addressees are identical. Consequently, the addressers/addressees already know and agree with the inferred answer (Efficiency condition) while not engaging in any pragmatic processes to arrive at the implied answer. Thus, the RQ is naturally uninformative. The addressers/addressees insincerely use this interrogative (Maxim of Quality and Sincerity/Responsibility) and are not eliciting for some unknown information (Elicitative force). Regarding the PEs, the Initial and Intended PEs do not become factors. As with Exod 15:11, the primary inferred Assertive force transforms into and counts as an illocutionary confession: *No one is like Yahweh our God!* This force also includes the Behabitive/Expressive and Commissive forces whereby the psalmist(s) take the self-involving stance concerning Yahweh's uniqueness in relation to his exalted status (v. 4) who lowers himself to concretely transform the hopeless situations of the powerless (vv. 7–9). As Brueggemann observes, the "distinctiveness of Yahweh…is not based on grand cosmic claims," but on concrete "*transformative interventions*" on behalf of the helpless and barren.[73] With the Commissive force, the psalmists commit themselves to allow the exalted Yahweh in his uniqueness to transform the lives of the powerless *on his own* which then gives "reason to praise God."[74] In contrast to the RQs in Pss 35 and 71, this one does not challenge Yahweh; rather, the self-involved confession comes with the entailment that often additionally infers the challenge to solely trust in Yahweh for help and deliverance. Directly derived from the testimony that Yahweh is high above all the nations and the heavens, Erhard S. Gerstenberger claims that with this RQ "the community cries out a challenge to all the world: 'Who is like Yahweh, our God?'"[75] More precisely, the psalmists take a *public* stance through this indirect self-involved confession with the accompanied entailments that inferentially includes the challenge for themselves to solely trust in Yahweh.

In Ps 89, a community of protesters utters two consecutive RQs and first a descriptive type:

---

73. Brueggemann, *Message of the Psalms*, 162.
74. John Goldingay, *Psalms, Volume 3: Psalms 90–150*, BCOT (Grand Rapids: Baker Academic, 2008), 319.
75. Gerstenberger, *Psalms, Part 2*, 279.

3. The Performative Dimensions of Rhetorical Questions 217

For who in the clouds can be likened to Yahweh	כי מי בשחק יערך ליהוה
likens to Yahweh among the sons of God;	ידמה ליהוה בבני אלים:
God inspires awe in the council of holy ones, greatly[76]	אל נערץ בסוד־קדשים רבה
and inspires reverence above all surrounding him?	ונורא על־כל־סביביו:

Followed by a RQ with Yahweh as the addressee:

Yahweh, God of hosts	יהוה אלהי צבאות
who is like you powerful Yah,	מי־כמוך חסין יה
with your faithfulness surrounding you?	ואמונתך סביבותיך:

The former extended RQ does not have an explicit identifiable addressee while describes Yahweh's incomparability in contrast to his council members.[77] In this lengthy eclectic or heterogeneous communal Protest/Complaint psalm,[78] the suppliants begin with praise (vv. 2–3 [vv. 1–2]) and then transition to a reiteration of Yahweh's covenant oath with David (vv. 4–5 [vv. 3–4]). Then from here, the psalmists rehearse in parallel the two terms שמים "heavens" (v. 3b) and the *leitwort* אמונה "faithfulness" (vv. 2b, 3b; אמונה also occurs in vv. 9b, 25a, 34b, 50b) in v. 5 which then leads into the two RQs. With Ballast Variant parallelism in v. 5, the heavens praise Yahweh's *wonders* and his אמונה "in the congregation of holy ones."[79] This motif of Yahweh's council introduced in this verse then becomes the central focus of the first interrogative. This is followed by a second interrogative with Yahweh as the addressee that closely matches the RQs in Exod 15:11 and Pss 35 and 71. This RQ, then, also operates as a self-involved confession while it additionally provides for understanding the previous interrogative as also functioning the same way.

---

76. I am reading the MT here, but רבה is awkward. LXX, Syr, and Vg read רבה with the second colon. However, the use of רבה as an adverb is evidenced in Pss 62:3 and 78:15. Following the Translations, one could read רבה ונורא as a hendiadys "greatly fearful"; but this would perhaps require the masculine רַב as *BHS* suggests. On the adverbial use of Hebrew terms see *IBHS* §39.3.1b.

77. Kuntz, "Making a Statement," 177.

78. On the diverse genres contained in this psalm and the equally diverse genre proposals, see Tate, *Psalms 51–100*, 413–18; see also Gerstenberger, *Psalms, Part 2*, 147–57.

79. I understand שמים here as the subject of the verb ידה similar to how the heavens tell about the glory of God in Ps 19:2 (v. 1). A number of translators see the ב of בקהל קדשים also governing שמים and thereby paralleling these two terms; so e.g., Gerstenberger, *Psalms, Part 2*, 148; Goldingay, *Psalms 42–89*, 670–71.

There is no explicit, internal addressee identified in the first interrogative, but similarly to Ps 77:14b the addressers talk *about* God while implicitly and reflectively address themselves and thus the above interpretive process would also apply here. As an interrogative, the addressers allow for some alternative suggestions, but in the end would conclude that there is no council member who equates to Yahweh. As with the RQs in Pss 35 and 71, Yahweh as the addressee in the concluding RQ would obviously agree with the inferred answer/assertion.

The psalmists do not make it exactly plain as to why they uniquely describe Yahweh's incomparability in relation to his council members. Towards an answer, the heavens are far above the earth and humanity, where Yahweh's throne is located (e.g., Pss 11:4a; 103:19; see also 1 Kgs 8:30; Isa 6:1), and where he rules the cosmos from (e.g., Pss 47:9 [v. 8]; 89:15 [v. 14]) as well as where כל־צבא השמים "all the host of heaven" meet with him (1 Kgs 22:19). In the second RQ, the psalmists characterize Yahweh with power while the term אמונה forms an *inclusio* around the two RQs (vv. 6b, 9b [vv. 5b, 8b]). The purpose, then, of this comparison within this psalm appears to be twofold. First, the closest beings among all creation, especially in the heavens where Yahweh resides (e.g., 1 Kgs 8:27–45), to match his power would be these council members who are not human, but supernatural beings. Yet, even these beings do not equal him either and in fact they are awed by and revere him as well as carry out his deliberated decisions (1 Kgs 22:22–23). Further, Yahweh is אלהי צבאות "God of hosts" with the צבאות identified as his heavenly army (e.g., Josh 5:14–15; 1 Kgs 22:19; see also 2 Kgs 6:16–17). Second, it is these heavenly beings who obey Yahweh and often implement his word and will (Ps 103:20–21). Further, the term אמונה in v. 9b (v. 8b) may also refer to these heavenly beings who surround Yahweh in order to convey the idea that it is these beings who perform his faithfulness.[80] Thus, it is Yahweh alone who ultimately determines when and for whom his faithful power is executed, not his council members.[81] The first RQ, which begins with

---

80. For Walter Brueggemann and William H. Bellinger Jr., Yahweh's faithful character is the primary comparative point with these RQs (*Psalms*, NCBC [Cambridge: Cambridge University Press, 2014], 386).

81. A number of interpreters point to Ps 82 as an illustrative description on how members of Yahweh's council fail in their execution of justice (cf. vv. 2–4) as well as conclude that these beings are divine. However, I consider this psalm functioning as a polemic against other gods and perhaps specifically against the Canaanite pantheon. In support of this interpretive angle, no deliberation concerning an issue occurs nor does God invite any discussion (in contrast, see, e.g., Job 1:6–12; 2:1–6; 1 Kgs 22:19–22). Uniquely here God decides on his own to condemn the entire assembly of

an initial causal כי, gives the reason why the heavens praise Yahweh as there is no one like him in the heavens. The psalmists here present a brief constellation of RQs with the first comparative one providing the premise for drawing the conclusion expressed in the second.

Strategically the psalmists do not immediately reveal the purpose of these two RQs nor their descriptive praise of Yahweh or why they reiterate Yahweh's promises to David and his seed. Following these two RQs, the psalmists continue in their exuberant praise of Yahweh and his power as well as quoting his first person promises to David (vv. 10–38 [vv. 9–37]). Not until v. 39 (v. 38) do the psalmists reveal the reason for their praise, boasts, and reminders to Yahweh, his past חסד "loyalty" and אמונה are not currently being experienced by them (cf. v. 50 [v. 49]). Towards the end of this psalm, the suppliants ask a typical genuine protest question: *How long* Yahweh will hide and continue with his anger? (v. 47 [v. 46]). They plead for Yahweh to remember (v. 48 [v. 47]) and then ask in v. 49 (v. 48):

Who is the man who can live and not see death,	מי גבר יחיה ולא יראה־מות
delivers himself from the power of *Sheol*? *Selah*	ימלט נפשו מיד־שאול סלה:

Yahweh remains the addressee here based on the direct address in the previous genuine question (v. 47). This is another uninformative RQ as both the psalmists and Yahweh share the same common knowledge that no human being on her/his own can escape death. Through this RQ, the commitments of both are synchronized, confirming their joint mutual knowledge about the states of affairs in the world and agreeing upon the

---

gods to die like human beings (82:7a). Further and in direct contrast to the depictions of the divine assemblies in Ugaritic and Mesopotamian literature, the gods are nameless and without any specific assigned roles identified, they do not gather for deliberation, they do not confer authority on another deity, there is no conflict over power among the council members, and the gods do not devise a counter attack to God's condemning decision. In fact, in Ps 82 the gods display no independence from God and are depicted as powerless and utterly subject to his decree. Further, God does not summon or authorize other gods to fulfill the task of executing justice. Using this mythological motif, then, this psalm "announces the permanent adjournment of the assembly and the execution of its constituency: the psalm announces the death of the gods" (James L. Mays, *Psalms*, Int [Louisville: John Knox, 1994], 270); see further Robert P. Gordon, "The Gods Must Die: A Theme in Isaiah and Beyond," in *Isaiah in Context*, ed. M. N. van der Meer et al., Festschrift Arie van der Kooij, VTSup 138 (Leiden: Brill, 2010), 53–55; Patrick D. Miller, *Interpreting the Psalms* (Philadelphia: Fortress, 1989), 120–24; Mark S. Smith, *God in Translation: Deities in Cross-Cultural Discourse in the Biblical World* (Grand Rapids: Eerdmans, 2008), 131–39; Tate, *Psalms 51–100*, 328–42.

exclusive answer/assertion: *No human can deliver her/himself from death!* Functioning within this protest petition section, the intent is for Yahweh to act before the psalmists die so that they will experience his אמונה as he has displayed in the past. Without Yahweh's timely deliverance the psalmists convey that they will be unable to boast anew in Yahweh and thus his promissory oaths of חסד and אמונה to David and his seed and consequently his faithful power will remain in *question*, at least for these psalmists.

Although Ps 89 is more historically and situationally fixed than the other above psalms, contemporary readers/singers can self-involvingly engage with each psalm by assuming the ambiguous personal pronouns.[82] When they reach the RQs they can simultaneously *co-confess* Yahweh's incomparability and challenge him to act based on his uniqueness as well as challenge him to act on their behalf so that in turn they can properly praise him (Pss 35; 71); or praise him for his incomparability with the accompanied inferential challenge to solely trust in Yahweh alone to deliver (Ps 113).

Psalm 88:11–13 (vv. 10–12)

Brueggemann, now famously, contends that "Psalm 88 is an embarrassment to conventional faith."[83] Further, as Goldingay states, it "is astonishing that Book III of the Psalter comes to an end with two psalms that terminate with Yhwh's having abandoned Israel."[84] This poem is truly the most lonely and darkest of all the psalms and is beyond much doubt a Protest/Complaint,[85] but clearly unique among this genre.[86] The poem presents an anonymous voice from *utter darkness* expressing isolation,

---

82. On this notion of others apart from an original speaker or singer adopting literary ambiguous persona see Adams, *Performative Nature*, 87–90.

83. Brueggemann, *Message of the Psalms*, 78.

84. Goldingay, *Psalms 42–89*, 691.

85. E.g., Brueggemann, *Message of Psalms*, 78–81; Gerstenberger, *Psalms, Part 2*, 141–47; Goldingay, *Psalms 42–89*, 644; Frank-Lothar Hossfeld and Erich Zenger, *Psalms 2: A Commentary on Psalms 51–100*, trans. L. M. Maloney, Hermeneia (Minneapolis: Fortress, 2005), 390–91, 393–94; Tate, *Psalms 51–100*, 398–401; Samuel Terrien, *The Psalms: Strophic Structure and Theological Commentary*, ECC (Grand Rapids: Eerdmans, 2003), 626.

86. See Robert C. Culley, "Psalm 88 Among the Complaints," in *Ascribe to the Lord*, ed. L. Eslinger and G. Taylor, Festschrift P. C. Craigie, JSOTSup 67 (Sheffield: JSOT Press, 1988), 289–302.

hopelessness, fear, and protest to a silent and absent God. The experiential situation of the psalmist is plainly some type of severe suffering,[87] but, as Marvin Tate observes, "a specific definition of the distress has the typical elusive quality of descriptive language in the psalms."[88] In contrast to traditional Protest psalms, the psalmist goes from seemingly expressing confidence יהוה אלהי ישועתי "Yahweh, God of my salvation" (v. 2a)[89] to spiraling downward into deeper and deeper despair and depression while ending with a single, lone unconnected word: מחשך "darkness" (v. 19b). Some interpreters do not find any expressions of confidence and trust in this psalm;[90] however, on a linguistic level the opening colon appears to express just that. Based on the remainder of the psalm, though, the psalmist may be wondering if this is in fact true.[91] From a speech act perspective and on the sentence level, this utterance is a self-involved confession whereby the speaker takes a stance with the typical accompanied entailments. However, the psalmist could be uttering an ironic claim in correlation with the other ironies expressed throughout the psalm. As such, the psalmist simultaneously confesses Yahweh as *God of my salvation* as with this poem she/he turns to Yahweh for deliverance while ironically and sarcastically expressing that the suppliant's experience is the exact opposite.

For both individual and communal Protests,[92] form critics have identified common characteristic elements.[93] Claus Westermann has also observed that these typical features naturally group themselves into two

---

87. Mitchell Dahood identifies this psalm as expressions of hopelessness of a mortally ill person (*Psalms II: 51–100*, AB 17 (Garden City: Doubleday, 1968], 302); so also Kraus, *Psalms 60–150*, 192; similarly Artur Weiser, *The Psalms*, trans. H. Hartwell, OTL (Philadelphia: Westminster, 1962), 586.
88. Tate, *Psalms 51–100*, 399.
89. Contra, e.g., Culley, "Psalm 88," 293.
90. E.g., ibid., 293.
91. Goldingay, *Psalms 42–89*, 646.
92. See, e.g., Brueggemann, *Message of the Psalms*, 54–57; Erhard S. Gerstenberger, "Psalms," in *Old Testament Form Criticism*, ed. J. Hayes (San Antonio: Trinity University Press, 1974), 200–207; Claus Westermann, "The Role of the Lament in the Theology of the Old Testament," *Int* 28 (1974): 20–38; idem, *Praise and Lament*, 52–81; idem, *The Psalms: Structure, Content & Message*, trans. R. D. Gehrke (Minneapolis: Augsburg, 1980), 29–45, 53–70.
93. See Gerstenberger, *Psalms Part 1*, 12; see further Westermann, *Praise and Lament*, 52–54, 64–81; see also Brueggemann, *Message of the Psalms*, 54–58; Tremper Longman III, "Lament," in *Cracking Old Testament Codes*, ed. D. B. Sandy and R. L. Giese, Jr. (Nashville: Broadman & Holman, 1995), 199–201.

main categories that express a movement from plea to praise.[94] With this psalm, interpreters have observed the absence of many of the expected genre elements: no confession of guilt or protest of innocence, no description of any enemies, no imprecation against enemies, no vow of praise, no statement of confidence, no certainty of a response from God, no hymnic elements, no anticipated thanksgiving. Most glaringly the psalmist does not express an explicit, developed petition for Yahweh to act. The closest plea interpreters typically identify is v. 3 (v. 2), but still this is merely a general reference to the psalmist's prayer. The other types of petitions consist of reports of what the psalmist has been praying (vv. 2b, 10aβ, b [vv. 1b, 9aβ, b], 14 [v. 13]) including genuine למה "why" bicolon questions (v. 15 [v. 14]).

Most interpreters similarly see a threefold structure in this psalm marked by three pleas (vv. 2b–3, 10aβ, b, 14 [vv. 1b–2, 9aβ, b, 13]) with each followed by expressions of pain (vv. 4–10aα, 11–13, 15–19 [vv. 3–9aα, 10–12, 14–18])[95] and the following center section constitutes a series of interrogatives functioning as one of these complaints:

Do you perform wonders for the dead	הלמתים תעשה־פלא
or do the *R^ephaim* rise up and praise you? *Selah*.	אם־רפאים יקומו יודוך סלה:
Is your loyalty declared in the grave,	היספר בקבר חסדך
your faithfulness in *Abbadon*?	אמונתך באבדון:
Are your wonders known in the darkness	היודע בחשך פלאך
and your righteousness in the land of forgetfulness?	וצדקתך בארץ נשיה:

Kuntz initially claims that the psalmist here "turns to the *efficacy* of interrogative rhetoric to *induce* divine rescue" while subsequently arguing that "these questions sharply intensify the supplicant's plea for divine intervention."[96] Tate similarly claims that these interrogatives function as RQs that "intensify the complaint and add urgency to the speaker's prayer." But Tate then later states that they "*imply* the need of a swift and effective divine intervention."[97] Possibly these interrogatives intensify the supplicant's poem, but I consider that more so Kuntz's inducing idea and Tate's latter conclusion get at what the psalmist intends. Yet how do the interrogatives operate in such a manner?

---

94. According to Westermann, there "is no petition, no pleading from the depths, that did not move at least one step…on the road to praise" (*Praise and Lament*, 154).

95. See, e.g., Brueggemann/Bellinger, *Psalms*, 378–79; Goldingay, *Psalms 42–89*, 644; Hossfeld/Zenger, *Psalms 2*, 301–303; Terrien, *The Psalms*, 626.

96. Kuntz, "Making a Statement," 167, 169 (italics mine).

97. Tate, *Psalms 51–100*, 398, 403 (italics mine).

Right from the beginning of this psalm, the suppliant addresses Yahweh and attests to how she/he has cried out day and night to him. Accordingly, the addressee of these interrogatives is Yahweh. It is possible that these interrogatives are real questions if the psalmist is already among the dead.[98] Clearly the psalmist senses death as an imminent certainty (vv. 4–5), but it is highly unlikely that she/he is truly deceased as the dead do not pray and obviously are unable to petition for deliverance from actual death.

Looking at the content of the interrogatives, the psalmist uses different terms identifying the place where the dead reside: the grave, *Abbadon*, darkness, and the land of forgetfulness. The term *Abbadon* signifies the underworld where the dead go to perish and decay (Prov 15:11; 27:20; Job 26:5–6; 28:22; 31:12) while *Sheol* usually signifies the realm of the dead (e.g., Pss 18:5; 86:13). The psalmist also uses descriptors for the deceased themselves: the dead and *Rᵉphaim* who dwell in *Sheol*. The *Rᵉphaim* can refer to a people group (see Deut 2:10–11; Josh 12:4; 13:12; 15:8; 17:15; 18:16). In this context, though, the *Rᵉphaim* most naturally refer to mythological royal heroes who in the Hebrew Bible are weak and lifeless (Prov 2:18; 21:16) who dwell in *Sheol* (Isa 14:9–10; 26:14, 19; Prov 9:18). The psalmist also describes the inactivity in the realm of the dead and specifically with regards to praise. In the Hebrew Bible, praise is not characteristic of the dead (Pss 6:6; 30:10; 115:17), but of the living (cf. Isa 38:18–19; Pss 118:17; 119:175). "Where death is there is no praise. Where there is life, there is praise."[99] Absolutely nothing happens in *Sheol* as Qoheleth concludes: אין מעשה וחשבון ודעת וחכמה בשאול "there is no activity, planning, knowledge, or wisdom in *Sheol*" (Eccl 9:10bα). *Sheol* and *Abaddon* are before Yahweh (Prov 15:11a) while Yahweh has the ability to go to *Sheol* (e.g., Ps 139:8b; Amos 9:2), but he does not normally act there. Certainly Yahweh has the ability to do whatever he wants to do anywhere including in *Sheol* as he demonstrated his unparalleled *wonders* and power in Egypt, but within the Hebrew Bible worldview usually nothing happens in the realm of the dead.

Prior to and semantically linked to these interrogatives, the suppliant describes that she/he has been forsaken among the *dead*, like one in the *grave* (v. 6a [v. 5a]) who Yahweh no longer remembers (v. 6b [v. 5b]). The psalmist accuses Yahweh of placing her/him במחשכים "in utter darkness" (v. 7 [v. 6]) and removing friends from her/him (v. 9aα [v. 8aα]). In the

---

98. See Goldingay, *Psalms 42–89*, 651–52.
99. Claus Westermann, *The Praise of God in the Psalms*, trans. K. R. Crim (Richmond: John Knox, 1965], 159).

center section, the psalmists asks if Yahweh's *wonders* are *known* (ידע) in the *darkness* (v. 13a [v. 12a]) while ending the complaint accusing Yahweh of removing lover, friend, and "those who *know* me" (מידעי); there is only *darkness* (v. 19 [v. 18]).[100]

Taking all of the above into account, the psalmist already knows the answer to these interrogatives with which Yahweh would agree (Efficiency condition) and would not engage in any pragmatic processes to recognize and infer the implied answers. The addresser, then, insincerely uses these interrogatives (Maxim of Quality and Sincerity/Responsibility) and is not eliciting for some unknown information (Elicitative force). Thus, these lines consist of three parallel RQs and are all uninformative. As such, these RQs are not persuading or challenging Yahweh to agree with and assent to the inferred assertion; rather, both the psalmist and Yahweh's knowledge are synchronized, confirming their joint mutual understanding about the states of affairs in the world and below. Consequently, Yahweh concurs with the goal of the Initial PE. As uninformative RQs, Yahweh would agree with and assent to the exclusive answers and inferentially transform each bicolon RQ collectively into an implied answer: *True, I do not perform salvific wonders in the realm of the dead and consequently the dead do not praise me for such action!* With each parallel RQ, the inferred Assertive force is weak, a factor which also impacts on the strength of the Expressive force while with the latter the psalmist also expresses despair and sarcasm. With the two surrounding RQs, the psalmist also expresses irony regarding whether Yahweh's wonders are done for the *dead* (v. 11a [v. 10a]) and known or experienced in *darkness* (v. 13a [v. 12a]) while the suppliant protests at being currently among the *dead* (v. 6 [v. 5]) and how Yahweh has placed the suppliant in *utter darkness* (v. 7b [v. 6b]) which is also the final isolated term voiced.[101]

For Samuel Terrien, the psalmist has prayed vainly and turns to mock and tease God with the first two interrogatives which he considers to function ironically. "The poet is reaching a theological ultimate when her/his wit implies that God enjoys being praised. It is as if the poet states that the dead become nothing, and she/he is ready to address coarsely the Master of life and death with 'The joke is on thee. Thou art a loser!'"[102] While the psalmist clearly expresses irony with these RQs, I consider them also functioning as the psalmist's key petition as Kuntz and Tate

---

100. See further Irene Nowell, "Psalms 88: A Lesson in Lament," in Boadt and Smith, eds., *Imagery and Imagination*, 111–12.
101. Similarly ibid., 113.
102. Terrien, *Psalms*, 628 (pronouns revised).

point to while a few other scholars similarly agree.¹⁰³ The psalmist's ongoing pleas have apparently fallen on deaf ears and have exhausted the last bit of strength and prayerful strategies and with one final attempt she/he issues these *central* RQs. Although indirectly and in connection to v. 2a, this is the only section where the psalmist utters explicit expressions related to deliverance that reflect Yahweh's salvific activity with Israel (*wonders, righteousness, loyalty, faithfulness*) which are also expressed in the immediate following psalm and directly contrast his inactivity in the realm of the dead. Although the interrogative lines do not precisely match, they form a type of concentric structure:

A   הלמתים תעשׂה־פלא

    B   אם־רפאים יקומו יודוך סלה:

        C   היספר בקבר חסדך

        C'   אמונתך באבדון:

A'   היודע בחשך פלאך

A"   וצדקתך בארץ נשיה:

With a Ballast Variant parallel interrogative in the *center*, the psalmist highlights for Yahweh that in the realm of the dead his *loyalty* and *faithfulness* is not declared.¹⁰⁴ With the use of these two terms, this bicolon RQ creates parallels with Ps 89 and makes explicit what the final RQ in this psalm implicitly conveys: the dead do not praise God. Irene Nowell states that "the description of distress in vv. 4–9—I am like the dead—is linked to the rhetorical questions—Of what use am I to you dead? The grammatical link increases the power of persuasion in the questions."¹⁰⁵ More precisely, Yahweh is not persuaded to agree with these uninformative RQs; rather, the psalmist challenges Yahweh with his unhesitant agreement with and assent to the Intended PE. Consequently, the psalmist

---

103. Hans-Joachim Kraus concludes that the RQs are "pleas, appeals" that "aim to move Yahweh to intervene" (*Psalms 60–150*, trans. H. C. Oswald [Minneapolis: Fortress, 1993], 194). For Goldingay, perhaps "these questions are as near to pleas as the psalm ever gets" (*Psalms 42–89*, 652). See also Frank Crüsemann, "Rhetorische Fragen!? Eine Aufkündigung des Konsenses über Psalm 88:11-13 und Seine BedeuKtung für das Alttestamentliche Reden von Gott und Tod," *BibInt* 11 (2003): 345–60.

104. See Nowell's "chiastic arrangement" of vv. 12–13 ("Psalm 88," 110).

105. Ibid., 112; Culley views these RQs functioning similarly ("Psalm 88," 290–91).

has linguistically and pragmatically painted Yahweh into a corner and now he must make a decision one way or another: either deliver or definitively forget the sufferer and forego her/his praise.

From my analysis, these RQs are not simply complaints of pain and suffering, nor are they "clothed in the form of a humble inquiry."[106] Rather, in a type of reversal of Yahweh's whirlwind barrage of interrogatives to Job, this Job-like sufferer issues a series of RQs that confront and challenge Yahweh to action with the inclusion of the Directive force. As I discussed in my previous chapter, I understand that all RQs convey the Assertive force to one degree or another with the majority of RQs indirectly expressing this force in a primary sense while additional forces may accompany the Assertive simultaneously. Yet, certain RQs can express a different primary force while being accompanied with the Assertive force. To recall, for Searle addressers use genuine Directives to get addressees to do something. Regarding the Directive force, all RQs naturally include this force while some RQs may function as Directives proper in line with Slot's suggestion and exemplified with Searle's Directive RQ *How many times have I told you (must I tell you) not to eat with your fingers?* The inferred Directive here is *Stop eating with your fingers!* which elicits the action to not eat with one's fingers while not conveying much of an Assertive force (see Chapter 2). Other English examples of RQs inferring a primary Directive force include: *Do you want to teach the class today? Do you want to get fired? Why not stop here? Do you want to live at home in the basement for the rest of your life? Do you want to get wet?* Distinct from the above RQs I examined which primarily consist in noun clauses, the RQs here are verbal clauses. Specifically, the psalmist includes verbs concerning Yahweh's delivering actions while in the center verbs of responsive praise for those actions. This corresponds to the sequential pattern of distress, prayer, Yahweh's intervention, followed by praise. Directly related to the psalmists' ironies, the suppliant implicitly includes the Directive force for Yahweh to *perform wonders* for the *dead* psalmist, *make known* his *wonders* in the *darkness* where the psalmist resides. In turn, the psalmist will declare of Yahweh's *loyalty* and *faithfulness* once delivered from the *grave*.

The psalmist's RQs express the seriousness of the situation that faces both the suppliant and Yahweh. For the psalmist, it is a matter of life and death while for Yahweh it is a *question* of being remembered and praised or ironically completely forgotten in the exact same manner as the

---

106. Kraus, *Psalms 60–150*, 194.

psalmist has been experiencing (v. 6).[107] Only with the living is Yahweh remembered and praised. However, if God decides to continue to silently hide the sufferer will likewise forget about and not praise him. Frank-Lothar Hossfeld and Erich Zenger concur and claim that the real point of this central section of RQs is that

> when and where God can no longer be praised, his divinity is in question. That YHWH does not 'remember' his worshipers (v. 6c) has consequences for himself: in such a way he too vanishes from memory. The terrifying image of a 'land of forgetting' with which the section closes, which is meant to move YHWH to a saving intervention, is a threatening possibility for God himself![108]

For the psalmist, then, Yahweh remains hidden and utterly silent and has even forgotten the dead (v. 6aβ [v. 5aβ]) and if God does not decisively act to save, the psalmist challenges Yahweh that her/his death will correspondingly reciprocate, resulting in the memory and praise of Yahweh slipping into the silence of the grave, the land of forgetfulness.

Anyone who finds themselves at some point in utter darkness can assume the identity of this anonymous "I" and express their loneliness and despair while protesting against God and his absent silence. When reading the RQs each suppliant voices them with the intent to confront and challenge God to intervene so that she/he will in turn properly praise God, testify to his faithful wonders, and truthfully confess *God of my salvation!*[109]

Psalm 8:5 (v. 4)

Psalm 8 is a well-known and favorite poem for many, but the bicolon in v. 5 remain extremely difficult to interpret, especially in semantic connection to the framing refrain or *inclusio* in v. 2 and v. 10 (v. 1 and

---

107. Gerhard von Rad claims that "Praise is man's most characteristic mode of existence: praising and not praising stand over against one another like life and death" (*Old Testament Theology, Volume 1*, trans. D. M. G. Stalker [New York: Harper & Row, 1962], 369–70).

108. Hossfeld/Zenger, *Psalms 2*, 396.

109. For examples of applying this psalm see, e.g., Caroline Blyth, "'I Am Alone with My Sickness': Voicing the Experience of HIV- and Aids-Related Stigma Through Psalm 88," *Colloquium* 44 (2012): 149–62; Carleen Mandolfo, "Psalm 88 and the Holocaust: Lament in Search of a Divine Response," *BibInt* 15 (2007): 151–70; Marvin Tate, "Psalm 88," *RevExp* 87 (1990): 91–95.

v. 9) which has resulted in numerous interpretive proposals. Most interpreters correctly identify this psalm as a Hymn of Praise.[110] The issues that arise with this genre classification, though, center on the absence of the usual invitation to praise (e.g., Pss 33:1–3; 96:1–3) and the reason for praise introduced with a causal כי (e.g., Pss 33:4–7; 96:4–6). Also, the psalm uniquely addresses Yahweh alone, which is typical for Protest/Complaint psalms.[111] Yet, despite these anomalies, there are no clear expressions of protest, while the psalmist appears to issue a type of praise in the frame.[112]

With the *inclusio*, the psalmist initially confesses her/his humble submission to God with the phrase יהוה אדנינו "Yahweh our Lord."[113] This is followed by a clause beginning with מה that could be introducing an interrogative or exclamatory praise. Randolph Quirk et al. identify English interrogatives that function as Exclamatives. More technically they claim that "the *exclamatory question* is interrogative in structure, but has the illocutionary force of an exclamatory assertion." These expressions usually occur in negative Yes–No questions such as *Hasn't she grown!* and *Wasn't it a marvelous concert!*[114] These grammarians also include Exclamations along with the other three main clause types (Declaratives, Interrogatives, and Imperatives).[115] Exclamations are therefore a formal categorical sentence type that resemble *wh*-questions beginning with the *wh*-word *What* and *How*.[116]

Joüon-Muraoka describe exclamatory expressions similarly as *exclamatory questions*. Joüon-Muraoka claim that with מה and other biblical Hebrew interrogative markers the "line between a question and an

---

110. E.g., Peter C. Craigie, *Psalms 1–50*, WBC 19 (Waco: Word, 1983), 106; Gerstenberger, *Psalms, Part 1*, 70; Goldingay, *Psalms 1–41*, 154; Kraus, *Psalms 1–59*, 179; Terrien, *Psalms*, 127.

111. Tate observes that this psalm is the only Hymn in the Hebrew Bible composed completely in direct address to God ("An Exposition of Psalm 8," *Perspectives in Religious Studies* 28 [2001]: 344).

112. See further Alter, *Art of Biblical Poetry*, 148–49.

113. Similarly Øystein Lund, "From the Mouth of Babes and Infants You Have Established Strength," *SJOT* 11 (1997): 92; Tate, "Psalm 8," 345.

114. Quirk et al., *Comprehensive Grammar* §11.22 (italics mine).

115. Ibid., §2.46; Jessica Rett argues against viewing the Exclamative as a type of ISA, but instead she considers the expression "as an independent speech act" ("Exclamatives, Degrees and Speech Acts," *Linguist and Philos* 34 [2011]: 413).

116. Quirk et al., *Comprehensive Grammar* §2.57; see further Fabian Beijer, "The Syntax and Pragmatics of Exclamations and Other Expressive/Emotional Utterances," *Working Papers in Linguistics* 2 (2002): 4.

exclamation is often ill-defined." Further, many "interrogative words can be used also as exclamatory words."[117] For example with the English terms *What* and *How*: *What man?* and *What a man!*; *How many are already dead?* and *How many are already dead!*[118] Joüon-Muraoka further support their claims with the English term *How* used to interpret מה (e.g., Num 24:5a; Pss 3:2a [v. 1a]; 36:8aα [v. 7aα]) and אין (e.g., 2 Sam 1:25aα, 27a; Ps 73:19a).[119] For example, the latter term introduces the Exclamative in Isa 1:21a:

How the faithful city has become a harlot!	איכה היתה לזונה קריה נאמנה

and with the former term in Isa 52:7aα:

How lovely on the mountains...!	מה־נאוו על־ההרים

Also according to Joüon-Muraoka, the "adverb הֲ, which is common for questions, sometimes has an exclamatory nuance." Among numerous biblical examples they cite Gen 3:11 and translate "*you have indeed eaten!*"[120] which Moshavi and I myself conclude above is best understood as a confirming Conducive question. Waltke/O'Connor agree with Joüon-Muraoka's exclamatory conclusions and claim that "polar questions with ה can have an exclamatory sense" (cf. Amos 5:25).[121] More explicitly, these two grammarians identify specific examples of "*exclamatory questions*" in the Hebrew Bible (e.g., Gen 27:20; 44:16; Num 23:8; 2 Kgs 4:43; Pss 36:8; 78:40) while including Ps 8:2 in this list.[122]

Conversely, most language specialists agree that interrogatives and Exclamatives are incompatible sentence types with each having entirely different functions and intentions.[123] The difficulty with identifying Exclamatives is that "they do not have a form-type of their own. They look like declaratives or interrogatives."[124] Further, Exclamatives are essentially

---

117. Joüon-Muraoka §162.
118. Joüon-Muraoka §161b n 3.
119. Joüon-Muraoka §162a, b; see also §161b n 3.
120. Joüon-Muraoka §161b.
121. *IBHS* §§40.3b.
122. *IBHS* §18.3f.
123. See Moshavi, "Positive Rhetorical Question," 261 and n. 26.
124. Inger Rosengren, "Expressive Sentence Types – A Contradiction in Terms: The Case of Exclamation," in *Modality in Germanic Languages: Historical and Comparative Perspectives*, ed. T. Swan and O. J. Westvik, TL 99 (Berlin: de Gruyter, 1997), 152.

pragmatic, expressed through a variety of formal structures and grammatical constructions.[125] Along these lines, Rodney Huddleston observes that Exclamatives "normally have the force of exclamatory statements" while bearing "strong formal resemblances to open interrogatives," which is a very widespread phenomenon in the world's languages.[126] Similarly, Rosengren argues that Exclamatives are declarative and interrogative sentence types while inferentially expressing a type of illocutionary act on their own. What specifically characterizes Exclamations is "their expressive directness." Rosengren further observes that Exclamatives are related to Searle's Expressive, but "do not propositionalize the emotive meaning" as this force does.[127] Rather, Exclamatives "express an affective stance towards some propositional content."[128]

As Joüon-Muraoka observe, the English terms *How* and *What* occur with the Exclamative and interrogative. Yet, English Exclamatives are solely marked by these two terms while also expressing a *scalar implicature* of degree or quantity whereas interrogatives rarely function this way and are identified with multiple different terms.[129] Regarding scalar implicature, Exclamatives implicate an unspecified value at the extreme degree of a contextually understood *scale* of other possible alternatives.[130] For example, a surfer exclaims *What a wave!* expressing an affective response about a particular wave implicating that it reaches an extreme degree of flawlessness comparatively greater than any other alternatives

---

125. See, e.g., Beijer, "Pragmatics of Exclamations," 5; König/Siemund, "Speech Act Distinctions," 316–17; Laura A. Michaelis, "Exclamative Constructions," in *Language Typology and Language Universals, Volume 2*, ed. M. Haspelmath et al. (Berlin/New York: de Gruyter, 2001), 1041–42; see also Rodney Huddleston, "On Exclamatory-Inversion Sentences in English," *Lingua* 90 (1993): 259–69.

126. Huddleston, "Clause Type," 922; so also, e.g., Sadock/Zwicky, "Speech Act Distinctions," 162.

127. Rosengren, "Case of Exclamation," 179–80; Beijer concludes that in general Exclamatives "are similar to Searle's Expressives..., but they are not identical to them" ("Pragmatics of Exclamations," 6). König/Siemund do not see Exclamatives are not a type included in Searle's typology ("Speech Act Distinctions," 316).

128. Laura A. Michaelis and Knud Lambrecht, "The Exclamative Sentence Type in English," in *Conceptual Structure, Discourse and Language*, ed. A. E. Goldberg (Stanford: CSLI, 1996), 378.

129. Peter Collins, "Exclamative Clauses in English," *Word* 56 (2005): 6–7; Huddleston, "Clause Type," 918.

130. Michaelis/Lambrecht observe that the "degree of the scalar property in question is unusually high" ("Exclamative Sentence," 378).

under consideration.[131] In connection to this implicature, some specialists identify surprise as the primary characteristic response of Exclamations;[132] however, most properly broaden their function to include astonishment, remarkableness, appreciation, admiration, disapproval, degradation, condemnation, and even vehemence.[133]

In addition to all this, Exclamatives do not correspond to the normally obligatory subject-auxiliary inversion as with interrogatives: e.g., Exclamative: *What a mistake they made!*; Open Interrogative: *What mistake did they make?*[134] Thus according to Huddleston, "the exclamatory statement force has been grammaticalized: in spite of the resemblance, exclamatives are grammatically distinct from open interrogatives…and they do not belong in the semantic category of question [*sic*]." However, Closed interrogatives such as *Wasn't it a disaster!* or *Did she hate it!* can commonly express exclamatory statements. This force, though, is indirectly and pragmatically conveyed whereas "at the direct level, they are questions."[135] A number of specialists also include that Exclamatives are "inherently factive."[136] That is, as Peter Siemund states, "the truth of

---

131. See, e.g., Collins, "Exclamative Clauses," 5; Peter Siemund, "Exclamative Clauses in English and their Relevance for Theories of Clause Types," *Studies in Language* 39 (2015): 703; Raffaella Zanuttini and Paul Portner, "Exclamative Clauses: At the Syntax-Semantics Interface," *Language* 79 (2003): 47.

132. E.g., König/Siemund, "Speech Act Distinctions," 316; Michaelis, "Exclamative Constructions," 1039; Michaelis/Lambrecht, "Exclamative Sentences," 378; Rett, "Exclamatives."

133. Moshavi also notes how surprise is too narrow a conception for understanding exclamatives and provides an example of vehemence with *What a pain the neck you are!* which was personally communicated by Richard Steiner (Moshavi, "Positive Rhetorical Question," 262 n. 28). See also Nadia Amin Hasan, "Exclamations in English and Arabic: A Contrastive Study," *International Journal of Science Commerce and Humanities* 2 (2014): 174–98.

134. Huddleston, "Clause Type," 920, 922; see also, e.g., Klaus Abels, "Factivity in Exclamatives is a Presupposition," *Studia Linguistica* 64 (2010): 141; Beijer, "Exclamations," 3; Dale E. Elliot, "Toward a Grammar of Exclamations," *Foundations of Language* 11 (1974): 233–34.

135. Huddleston, "Clause Type," 922–23. See also e.g., idem, "On Exclamatory-Inversion Sentences," 231–46.

136. See Jane Grimshaw, "Complement Selection and the Lexicon," *Linguistic Inquiry* 10 (1979): 285; Abels, "Factivity in Exclamatives," 141–57; Zanuttini/Portner, "Exclamative Clauses," 46–47; see also Huddleston, "Clause Type," 922; *pace* Elliot, "Grammar of Exclamations," 239–40.

the proposition expressed is presupposed, though not the evaluation."[137] Without explicitly including this categorical descriptor, Huddleston similarly concludes that "because the statement component is background it is presented as uncontroversial, not at issue. Thus one normally doesn't envisage disagreement, dispute."[138] As such, in contrast to genuine questions Exclamatives do not display addresser ignorance and consequently do not elicit unknown information.[139] Thus, the Exclamative does not introduce a genuine question nor does it function as answers to questions.[140] Along these lines, Jessica Rett observes that "the utterance of an exclamation expresses a violation of the speaker's expectation,"[141] which corresponds with the response of surprise, astonishment, regret, dismay, etc.

It is quite understandable how the above Hebrew grammarians and others either describe or categorize Exclamatives as *exclamatory questions* as such expressions often use the interrogative sentence form as well as the terms *What* and *How*. Further, Exclamatives do not have a distinct sentence form or constitute a sentence type.[142] Also, interrogatives do not normally express scalar implicature. Focusing on this latter characteristic and specifically regarding the so-called exclamatory nuance of the adverb ה, Moshavi concludes that a "glance at the verses cited by Joüon-Muraoka [Gen 3:11; Num 20:10; 31:15; 1 Sam 2:27; 1 Kgs 18:17; 21:19; 22:3; Jer 7:9; Amos 5:25; Jonah 4:4; Hag 2:19; Ruth 1:19[143]] shows that they do not involve scalar values, and therefore cannot be expressed by syntactically exclamative clauses. Without the analogy to the exclamative clause, there is little evidence for asserting that interrogative clauses in Biblical Hebrew can have exclamatory meaning."[144] Regarding the particle מה,

---

137. Siemund, "Exclamative Clauses," 702–703.

138. Huddleston, "Clause Type," 922; see also Sadock/Zwicky, "Speech Act Distinctions," 162.

139. Grimshaw, "Complement Selection," 283.

140. E.g., Collins, "Exclamative Clauses," 4; Grimshaw, "Complement Selection," 321; Huddleston, "Clause Type," 922; Siemund, "Exclamative Clauses," 703; Zanuttini/Portner, "Exclamative Clauses," 47–49.

141. Rett, "Exclamatives," 412–16.

142. Rosengren concedes that the Exclamative "is probably the most prominent candidate for recognition as a sentence type in grammar on a par with the three major types," but in the end he concludes it is not a distinct sentence type ("Case of Exclamation," 152; see also cf. 153, 175, 179–80); see also König/Siemund, "Speech Act Distinctions," 317.

143. See further Joüon-Muraoka §161b.

144. Moshavi, "Positive Rhetorical Question," 263.

what becomes evident in the Hebrew Bible in correspondence with numerous global languages is that the particle distinctly functions with either interrogative clauses (e.g., Gen 31:36b; 32:28a [v. 27a]; 1 Sam 20:1b; 29:3a) or Exclamative clauses as displayed above (also, e.g., Gen 27:20a; Num 23:8a; 24:5a; 2 Kgs 4:43a; Pss 36:8a; 78:40a).[145]

To summarize the above and in order to distinguish the Exclamative, the following characteristics include:

- express a strong emotional reaction
- convey scalar implicature
- inability to function as genuine questions or as answers to questions
- violate addressers' expectations
- inherent factivity

Even with this criteria, Peter Collins highlights that in certain instances and contexts, a pragmatic similarity between two possible interpretations can occur which still makes it difficult to determine which is the appropriate intended meaning. He illustrates this with

> the indirect complaint force of *How inconsiderate are you!* relates on one reading to its question force as an interrogative (albeit a rhetorical question, to which only an uncooperative addressee would be tempted to supply an answer), and on another to its exclamatory force as an exclamative (the speaker's disapproval stemming from the assessment that the addressee's degree of inconsiderateness was extraordinary).[146]

Turning to the initial and final מה clauses in Ps 8, the psalmist voices:

| What/How majestic is your name in all the earth?! | מה־אדיר שמך בכל־הארץ |

Framing this Hymn of Praise as well as immediately following a humble submissive confession *Yahweh, our Lord*, the psalmist does not elicit for unknown information and does not display ignorance. Thus, the psalmist is not asking a genuine question. The truth of the sentence is presupposed (factive) while conveying a scalar implicature. The psalmist affective response concerning Yahweh's name implicates that it reaches an extreme

---

145. Moshavi also notes the distinct exclamatory use of מה in biblical Hebrew (see ibid., 261 n. 26) as well as in the Haggadah and Mishnah as observed by Richard C. Steiner, "On the Original Structure and Meanings of *Mah Nishtannah* and the History of its Reinterpretation," *Jewish Studies: An Internet Journal* 7 (2008): 184–85.

146. Collins, "Exclamative Clauses," 9.

degree of magnificence comparatively greater than any other alternative names and/or deities under consideration. Finally, the sentence conveys an aspect of the violation of the psalmist's expectations which is also reflected in the body of the psalm. With all this, the framing מה clauses do not introduce interrogatives, but Exclamatives which should then be translated *How majestic is your name in all the earth!* as with most all Translations and interpreters.

In the fifth line of the ten, the exact center of this poem the psalmist voices two parallel colons:

How/What is a frail human being that you consider it or a child of humanity that you care for it!?	מה־אנוש כי־תזכרנו ובן־אדם כי תפקדנו:

With these lines and in contrast to the other poetic lines, the "semantic movement is slowed to allow for the strong, stately emphasis of virtual synonymity, noun for noun and verb for verb in the same syntactical order."[147] Because of this and the precise placement of the bicolon, the psalmist further highlights them as the thematic *center* of this poem.[148]

This thematic role is enhanced further with the repetition of the particle מה followed by an initial א consonant:

How majestic	מה־אדיר
How/What is a frail human being	מה־אנוש
How majestic	מה־אדיר

The frame exclamatorily praises Yahweh while with the center bicolon the psalmist continues to address Yahweh. Unlike the incomparable RQs with psalmists describing and confessing about God, the poet here contemplatively reflects in praise about human beings in relation to God. Because of the poetic play with the pronouns and consonants and the relatively clear exclamatory function of the framing מה clauses, the reader/singer would understandably assume that the center מה clauses express the same emotive response.[149] However, as illustrated above by Collins, is this how these lines are functioning? Or do they express a genuine or rhetorical question?

Interpreters propose that the center bicolon functions in either of these ways. James L. Mays appears to understand this parallel interrogative as

---

147. Alter, *Biblical Poetry*, 150.
148. See also Tate, "Psalm 8," 347–48.
149. For additional poetic features used by this psalmist see Alter, *Biblical Poetry*, 148–50.

a genuine question which he specifically identifies as the "man question" that concerns humanity's relation to God as well as its nature and purpose.[150] Øystein Lund similarly assumes that "v. 5 stands as a central question in the psalm."[151] Goldingay identifies the lines as a question that perhaps "like a lament...functions to give people opportunity to articulate their uncertainties about their positions as human beings in the world, before drawing them into statements of faith."[152] Yet, when he comments on Ps 144:3–4 Goldingay explicitly identifies Ps 8:5 as a RQ.[153] Robert Alter coins this as a "famous cry of amazement over God's singling out of man."[154] Brueggemann/Bellinger quote Alter here while at the same time they state that vv. 3–4 "constitute a remarkable piece of biblical faith and raise *questions* about the place of humans in relationship with God."[155] Tate similarly identifies v. 5 as a "question" whereby the psalmist "asks in astonished fashion."[156] While others view this bicolon functioning as a parallel RQ.[157] Kraus explicitly identifies v. 5 as a RQ that "should certainly be understood to be an *exclamation* of amazement."[158] Kuntz confesses his doubts concerning its rhetorical function, but similarly concludes that this bicolon "may be construed as an *exclamation*, this does not disqualify it as a rhetorical question, for on occasion such interrogatives facilitate exclamatory speech."[159] What Kuntz, along with Kraus, appear to propose is that these lines could function as exclamatory RQs.

Raffaella Zanuttini and Paul Portner describe how RQs like *Who could be cuter than you?* cannot function as a proper Exclamative. In brief, they show how this interrogative introduces a question and thus is not factive. Because the RQ can be answered it does not operate as an Exclamative. Finally, these two specialists could not construct any examples to test for scalar implicature with this RQ.[160] In addition, in contrast to Exclamatives

---

150. Mays, *Psalms*, 66–68; similarly Gerstenberger, *Psalms, Part 1*, 69.
151. Lund, "Mouth of Babes," 97.
152. John Goldingay, *Psalms, Volume 1: Psalms 1–41*, BCOT (Grand Rapids: Baker Academic, 2006), 159; see also Gerstenberger, *Psalms Part 1*, 71–72.
153. Goldingay, *Psalms 90–150*, 685.
154. Alter, *Biblical Poetry*, 150; similarly Terrien, *Psalms*, 129–30; Gerald H. Wilson, *Psalms, Volume 1*, NIVAC (Grand Rapids: Zondervan, 2002), 204–205.
155. Brueggemann/Bellinger, *Psalms*, 59 (italics mine).
156. Tate, "Psalm 8," 354.
157. Craigie, *Psalms 1–50*, 108; *IBHS* §18.3g.
158. Hans-Joachim Kraus, *Psalms 1–59*, trans. H. C. Oswald (Minneapolis: Augsburg, 1988), 179 (italics mine); see also p. 182.
159. Kuntz, "Making a Statement," 160.
160. See Zanuttin/Portner, "Exclamative Clauses," 47–49.

and as Ilie observed, RQs can function as valid answers to genuine questions[161] as exemplified with RQs-as-retort. With this in mind, can one legitimately view certain interrogatives operating as exclamatory RQs?

Looking at the immediate context of the interrogatives in this psalm, following the opening verses of praise (vv. 2–3) a singular ambiguous "I" appears who begins with a כי like other such Hymns, but here introduces a temporal bicolon clause.[162] The psalmist prefaces the center lines with a description of whenever she/he looks up and reflects upon the heavens during the night (v. 4 [v. 3]). With the observations portrayed, the psalmist then voices the two parallel lines that closely resemble Ps 144:3 as well as Job 7:17–18 (see below). In light of the night sky, the psalmist depicts the proportional disparity between humanity and the vast heavens with the moon and stars and even more so the immensity of their Creator. Specifically, the poet reflects on Yahweh and uniquely describes the heavens and their hosts as מעשי אצבעתיך "the works of your fingers" while also employing the term אנוש which often indicates the frailty and weakness of humanity.[163] The semantic parallels between the *inclusio* and the center lines further highlight the differences between the *majestic* (אדיר) name of Yahweh and the *mortal* (אנוש) nature of humanity.[164] As the psalmist reflects on the night sky and wonders about humanity, comparatively humankind is miniscule and frail. Craigie aptly puts it this way: "In contrast to God, the heavens are tiny, pushed and prodded into shape by the divine digits; but in contrast to the heavens which seem so vast in the human perception, it is mankind that is tiny."[165]

---

161. *What Else Can I Tell You?*, 49–51, 64.

162. On כי introducing temporal clauses see Joüon-Muraoka §166o; *IBHS* §38.7.

163. So also, e.g., Brueggemann/Bellinger, *Psalms*, 59; Goldingay, *Psalms 1–41*, 158; Wilson, *Psalms, Volume 1*, 204. אנוש directly relates to the verb I אנש which means "weak, sick, feeble" (*HALOT* 73). The verb occurs once in the niphal in 2 Sam 12:15 and in all other instances as a qal passive participle meaning "incurable" (see Isa 17:11; Jer 15:18; 17:9; 30:12, 15). Obviously it is an interpretive fallacy to assume that אנוש always means "frailty, weakness" etc. in each of its occurrences, especially when the term often in poetry parallels אדם as it is here in Ps 8 (Victor P. Hamilton, "אנש," *NIDOTE* 1:454). However, in the overall context of Pss 8 and 144 אנוש does appear to express frailty, mortality which the vast majority of scholars agree (see also, e.g., Pss 90:3; 103:15). It is quite interesting that אנוש occurs first in the parallel with אדם which is most directly related to the previous comparative reflection of God and the heavens while in Ps 144 אנוש occurs second immediately followed by clear expressions of humanity's (אדם) brevity (v. 4).

164. Similarly Lund, "Mouths of Babes," 97.

165. Craigie, *Psalms 1–50*, 108.

These two center מה clauses are very similar to Moses' RQ in Exod 3:11, with the two כי clauses also expressing result.[166] Clearly Yahweh is the sole addressee of this psalm and is the only possible antecedent subject of the second person singular verbs in the bicolon. However, the psalmist reflectively and descriptively praises Yahweh, and in particular the majesty of his name. With the center lines, the psalmist self-reflects and contemplates about the status of humanity in relation to God; not directly addressing Yahweh in order to prompt a response as in the above psalms.

Distinct from the frame lines, the parallel center מה lines do not properly function as Exclamatives. With the above criteria in mind, these lines appear to express some type of emotional reaction based on an aspect of violating the psalmist's expectations. Still and in direct contrast to the frame Exclamative, the bicolon מה lines do not convey a scalar implicature, especially with the inclusion of the two כי result clauses. The interrogative dimension can be answered and because of this it is not factive. Following the literary sequencing of the poem, the psalmist's center lines are a direct response to her/his own contemplative and comparative heavenly observations. Thus, the poet already knows the answer to her/his interrogative (Efficiency condition). The psalmist, then, insincerely uses this interrogative (Maxim of Quality and Sincerity/Responsibility) while she/he is not eliciting for some unknown information (Elicitative force). Thus, these parallel interrogatives best operate as a bicolon RQ which infers a negative illocutionary assertion: *Human beings are nothing special for Yahweh to pay such conscientious attention to!* This obvious and exclusive answer matches the directional fit of the literary context that human beings are of no significance in comparison to immense heavens and even more so their massive creator who in fact pays careful attention to humanity. This parallel RQ is essentially uninformative as the psalmist contemplatively reflects on her/his own knowledge and beliefs. As such, both the Initial and Intended PEs do not become a factor.

The inferred answer/assertion of the parallel RQ includes a primary strong Assertive force accompanied by a strong Expressive. As I described in my last chapter, with the Expressive force addressers express committed psychological attitudes or feelings specified in the sincerity condition about the state of affairs identified in the propositional content. With RQs, I suggest viewing this force in relation to both what prompts the interrogative as well as the inferred IA. The psalmist here expresses her/his sincere conviction about the truthfulness specified in the inferred answer/assertion.

---

166. Both Joüon-Muraoka (§169e) and Waltke/O'Connor (*IBHS* §38.3b) explicitly include Ps 8:5 as an example of this function.

In addition to this, the psalmist expresses amazement and wonder along with this force based on her/his heavenly observations. To recall from above, Rosengren understands the Exclamative closest to the Expressive but does "not propositionalize the emotive meaning" as this force does. Rather, Exclamatives "express an affective stance towards some propositional content."[167] Although he does not refer to the Expressive category and as I quoted in my Introduction, Schmidt-Radefeldt similarly describes how RQs "*express* a propositional attitude of the speaker (e.g., reproach, indignation, protest, *wonder*, perplexity or dismay, or emphasis)."[168] It appears to me that this is exactly what the psalmist does here with the inferred answer/assertion also prompted by her/his observations of the night sky. Thus, as Kraus and especially Kuntz point to, through this parallel RQ the psalmist uninformatively infers a primary Assertive force asserting the frail and minuteness of humanity while simultaneously with the Expressive conveys an exclamatory emotional outburst of amazement at Yahweh's conscientious attentiveness. The bicolon RQ implies a primary Assertive force whereby the psalmist adopts an exclamatory stance of amazement based on the inferred assertion itself, but also prompted by the vast night sky. The psalmist self-reflectively expresses a strong self-involving assertion and thereby takes the *stance* that humanity is insignificant and frail with the derived *entailments* of humility and gratitude.[169] This RQ, then, exemplifies that although RQs are not Exclamatives in a proper sense, they can indirectly express this force or emotion.[170]

Coats understands these interrogatives as well as the parallel in Ps 144:3 and Job 7:17–18 functioning as RQs within his formulaic pattern of abasement that includes both the abasing of the human being along with a subtle aspect of self-defense. As I presented above, with his formulaic pattern, the psalmist poses a question in element *a* and then abases the pronoun subject with the implied answer with the verb in element *b* is negated. Thus, Coats's inferred answer here in Ps 8:5 is "Because man is man, you [Yahweh] *should not do* these things."[171] Thus, this answer "does

---

167. Michaelis argues that an "exclamation count as an assertion," but then similarly describes the function of the Exclamative as addressers express an "affective stance toward the propositional content" ("Exclamative Constructions," 1041).

168. Schmidt-Radefeldt, "Rhetorical Questions," 389 (italics mine).

169. Similarly Wilson, *Psalms, Volume 1*, 205.

170. Anzilotti suggests that RQs express a "exclamatory performative layer" along with the declarative and imperative with the examples *What's to be done?* or *May God, what's going to happen?* ("Rhetorical Question," 290, 299).

171. Coats, "Self-Abasement," 24 (italics mine).

not present an admiring grateful response to God's visit, but suggests," because of the nature of humanity "in comparison to the rest of creation, that God should not visit him."[172] Coats' interpretive conclusion appears to be the result of his formulaic pattern which does not mechanistically apply in each of his suggested examples. Conversely, van Leeuwen's revising adjustment properly applies in this instance here as well as with Exod 3:11. Rather than the formula implying that the action in the second element should not be done, the psalmist implies that the human being in the first element is unworthy of the action done by Yahweh in the second element. Here in Ps 8, with the Expressive force the psalmist exclamatorily expresses amazement that God does in fact pay conscientious attention to human beings despite their comparable insignificance.

The psalmist does not stop with humanity's insignificance but continues to contemplate upon humanity with reflections closely resembling Gen 1:26–30. Specifically, the psalmist describes Yahweh creating humanity מעט מאלהים "a little lower than God" (v. 6a), a little less than divine,[173] while at the same time crowned with royal status (v. 6b).[174] Further, Yahweh has made human beings to rule במעשי ידיך "over the works of your hands" (vv. 7–9). There is nothing in these reflections, though, that negates the comparative inferred answer/assertion to the parallel RQ; rather, both reflections are true. The content of the psalmist's latter reflections derive from the only first person speech in Gen 1:1–2:4a (cf. vv. 26, 29) which also contributes to the depicted uniqueness of human beings in this Genesis text. As the psalmist obviously plays with the particle מה and somewhat along the lines of several interpreters who see a genuine question here, it is as if the psalmist takes it upon her/himself to provide an answer for Yahweh to the interrogative dimension of the RQ. In v. 4 the psalmist comparatively describes humanity in relation to God from the perspective of the human being *looking up* while in vv. 6–9 the psalmist describes the nature, status, and responsibilities of human beings from the perspective of the *transcendent* God. In contrast to the above psalms, the poet here is not confessing about Yahweh's uniqueness or challenging him to act; rather, the psalmist is exclamatorily praising Yahweh for his name and for his unfathomable attentiveness to human

---

172. Ibid., 25.

173. The term אלהים here could be translated as "divine beings," "gods," or "God" referring to Yahweh as I have taken it. The latter makes the most sense especially when the psalmist is reflecting on Gen 1:1–2:4a as a large number of interpreters concur; see Tate's discussion in particular ("Psalm 8," 354–55).

174. On the royal terms used for humanity in this psalm see in particular Tate, "Psalm 8," 348.

beings as well as for the nature of humanity and for the reasons he has created it. As such, the psalmist engages with the hybrid nature of her/his parallel RQs, but does not counter the inferred assertion; rather, provides evidence for why God does in fact pay attention to human beings. The psalmist is not only responding to and answering the God who addressed Israel and humanity in the Torah and elsewhere in Scripture as Eugene H. Peterson perceptively depicted the use of the Psalms,[175] but here is also answering *for* God as she/he echoes God's first person speech in Gen 1. With these reflections, the psalmist has created a tension with v. 5 at the *center* of this tension. In v. 4, human beings are small and frail in comparison to Yahweh and *the works of your fingers* while at the same time Yahweh has made human beings to rule over *the works of your hands*. In this way, the exclamatory force of the RQ is prompted by the previous and following propositional contents.[176] This exclamatory expression of wonder *centers* on the tension between humanity's frail insignificance in comparison to Yahweh and his heavenly creation and Yahweh's conscientious attentiveness as well as elevated significance of humanity within his earthly creation.[177]

Drawing my analysis together, the bicolon RQ is directly linked to the confessionary submission expressed in the first part of the *inclusio* which then moves to exclamatory praise. With the parallel RQ, the psalmist continues with expressions of submission and exclamation. Embracing the self-reflective inferred answer/assertion keeps the psalmist in a proper tension of submissive humility and gratitude while engaging in the delegated royal privileges and responsibilities.[178] This tension is also structurally displayed in this psalm as humanity in v. 5 stands *below* Yahweh and the heavens in v. 4 and who is made a *little lower than God* (v. 6a) while *above* the living creatures which Yahweh has placed *under* humanity's feet in vv. 7b–9.[179] Through this bicolon RQ, self-involving readers/singers assume the ambiguous "I" and contemplate along with the original psalmist and adopt the safeguards of humble self-perception

---

175. Eugene H. Peterson, *Answering God: The Psalms as Tools for Prayer* (New York: HarperCollins, 1989), cf. 5–6

176. Similarly Lund, "Mouths of Babes," 97; followed by Tate, "Psalm 8," 348.

177. Van Leeuwen states that the formulaic pattern provides a clue as to how the surprising element of vv. 6–9 is possible: "The divine sovereign overrides human inadequacy and unworthiness to bestow grace, the gift of life, dignity, and responsible work in the cosmos ("Psalm 8.5," 213); see also Goldingay, *Psalms 1–41*, 161.

178. Similarly Weiser, *Psalms*, 143.

179. Similarly Lund, "Mouth of Babes," 99.

while acknowledging her/his unique nature and status within creation as well as engaging in the royal responsibilities—all while in submission to *Yahweh, our Lord*.

Psalm 144:3–4 and Job 7:17–18

In Ps 144, the psalmist addresses Yahweh:

Yahweh what is humankind that you acknowledge it,	יהוה מה־אדם ותדעהו
a child of a frail human being that you think of it?	בן־אנוש ותחשבהו:
Humanity resembles breath	אדם להבל דמה
its days are like a passing shadow.	ימיו כצל עובר:

The suppliant here, quite possibly a king, begins the poem with an implicit reference to Ps 8 by reflecting on how Yahweh has trained אצבעותי "my fingers" (v. 1) as the canonically prior psalmist comparatively reflects on the works of Yahweh's *fingers* (v. 4a). Following a number of self-involved confessionary assertions (v. 2), the psalmist closely recites the parallel RQ in Ps 8 which is also an uninformative parallel RQ with Yahweh as the addressee. Also, instead of two כי clauses the psalmist uses two *wayyiqtol* result clauses.[180] As with Ps 8:5 and in contrast to Coats' view that Yahweh should not do the two result clauses,[181] van Leeuwen's adjustment also fits best here: frail humanity is unworthy of Yahweh's acknowledgement. With this RQ, the psalmist infers a weak Assertive and Expressive while also expressing lament. The psalmist also exclaims amazement at Yahweh's thoughtfulness for frail humanity while enhancing the fragileness of the human being with the subsequent lines. Simultaneously and in connection to the following petitions (vv. 5–8, 11), the psalmist reflects on as well as reminds Yahweh of his acknowledged thoughtfulness which then also conveys a Directive force. Brueggemann/Bellinger state that "it is as if the king in Jerusalem acknowledges the limit, if not the futility, of his own military capacity. Human (royal) capacity is fragile and vulnerable."[182] The suppliant, though, does not merely resign himself to these facts, but also includes the verbal actions of Yahweh's acknowledgement and thoughtfulness towards humanity. Whereas the psalmist of Ps 8 solely reflects in exclamatory amazement, the psalmist here additionally challenges Yahweh to acknowledge the suppliant's transience and vulnerability in close connection to the described

---

180. Joüon-Muraoka §161m (also n. 4); 169e; *IBHS* §33.3.4c.
181. Coats, "Self-Abasement," 26.
182. Brueggemann/Bellinger, *Psalms*, 600.

threatening situation and therefore thoughtfully act in deliverance. Along these lines, Leo G. Perdue states that the psalmist "uses the tradition of the exaltation of undeserving humanity to remind God of the frailty of the human condition and therefore his own, and *to move* the Divine Warrior to come in judgment to destroy his enemies and deliver him form the distress of chaos."[183]

In Job's second speech (6:1–7:21) he reflects upon and adapts the bicolon RQ in Ps 8[184] in the second part (7:1–21) wherein he predominantly speaks directly to God:

What is a frail human being that you magnify it	מה־אנוש כי תגדלנו
and that you pay attention to it	וכי־תשית אליו לבך:
that you examine it every morning	ותפקדנו לבקרים
and every moment you test it?	לרגעים תבחננו:

Similarly to Ps 8,[185] Job here also begins with מה followed by two כי result clauses.[186] As with the psalmist, Job addresses God, with exclamatory praise but also in a protesting and contemptuous way. Based on Job's experience and his use of Ps 8, he already knows the answer to the interrogative (Efficiency condition). Job is using it insincerely (Maxim of Quality and Sincerity/Responsibility) and does not elicit God for some unknown information (Elicitative force) nor does this arouse any uncertainty. Thus, this interrogative operates as a RQ which infers a negative illocutionary assertion very similarly to Ps 8:5: *Human beings are nothing special for Yahweh to scrupulously examine and test!*

Most interpreters view Job's lines here as some type of parody or ironic play on Ps 8,[187] but not necessarily a RQ. It appears that Coats understands Job here expressing a RQ and views him parodying vv. 6–9, but not v. 5.

---

183. Perdue, *Wisdom in Revolt*, 130 (italics mine).

184. Despite Paul E. Dion's warnings that even "when Job is ironically distorting pious expressions which we know from the canonical writings, it never seems possible…to demonstrate that the statement taken to task was unique to one specific song of the Israelites" ("Formulaic Language in the Book of Job: International Background and Ironical Distortions," *SR* 16 [1987]: 192), it remains clear that Job adapts for his own purposes the hymnic lines found in Ps 8:5 as most all scholars concur.

185. See Habel, *Book of Job*, 164–65.

186. Joüon-Muraoka §169e.

187. E.g., Clines, *Job 1–20*, 192–93; Michael Fishbane, *Biblical Interpretation in Ancient Israel* (Oxford: Clarendon, 1985), 285–86; Habel, *Book of Job*, 164–65; idem, *Book of Job*, 151; Perdue, *Wisdom in Revolt*, 130–31; idem, *Wisdom Literature*, 106; idem, "Metaphorical Theology in the Book of Job: Theological Anthropology in the First Cycle of Job's Speeches (Job 3; 6–7; 9–10)," in Beuken, ed., *The Book of Job*, 152; Pope, *Job*, 62.

Job "does not ridicule or poke comic satire at the formula." Consequently, both texts "are remarkably parallel in both form and content" while also present "a common view of" humanity.[188] With his revisions of Coats, van Leeuwen similarly claims that although the literary context can change the effect of the formula, by itself in Pss 8:5, 144:3, and Job 7:17–18 the pattern "functions in an entirely traditional way: to indicate human lowliness vis-à-vis God."[189] For Coats, as with Pss 8 and 144, the verb in element *b* is negated and thus God should not do these things. Van Leeuwen understands Job inferring that humanity is "'nobody,' unworthy of God's attention."[190] That said, he understands Job's use of the formula "far more traditional than is Psalm 8."[191] In the end, van Leeuwen's adjustment of Coats' pattern is important for Exod 3, Ps 8, and Ps 144, but here aspects of Coats' original understanding of the pattern *ironically* applies.

"In every respect the language of the psalm is reapplied ironically by Job."[192] In concert with the psalmist, Job begins by exclamatorily describing how God *magnifies, exalts* (גדל) frail humanity. In contrast, Job views God's conscientious attentiveness to humanity as a harassing and oppressive examination and testing. As Perdue concludes, "Job also speaks of God's exaltation of humans, not to rule over all creation, but to become the target of divine assault."[193] More specifically, as John Hartley describes, "Job experiences God's vigilance as unrelenting oppression. So he turns these hymnic lines inside out. Instead of praising God with them Job uses them as a complaint against God's continual effort to find and punish his every flaw."[194] Job uses this RQ with multidimensional forces and in a multifunctional way. Job infers strong Assertive and Expressive forces that human beings are too insignificant for God to exalt and pay such careful attention to them, while with the Expressive also includes irony whereby Job sarcastically protests God's "unrelenting tyrannical spying on" humanity.[195] Like the RQs in Ps 88, Job also includes the Directive force, but more explicitly and with the interrogatives formed only with Yahweh as the subject of the verbs acting in certain ways towards

188. Coats, "Self-Abasement," 25.
189. Van Leeuwen, "Psalm 8.5," 211.
190. Ibid.
191. Ibid., 212.
192. Clines, *Job 1–20*, 192.
193. Perdue, "Metaphorical Theology," 152; see also W. A. M. Beuken, "Job's Imprecation as the Cradle of a New Religious Discourse: The Perplexing Impact of the Semantic Correspondence between Job 3, Job 4–5 and Job 6–7," in Beuken, ed., *The Book of Job*, 63.
194. Hartley, *Book of Job*, 151.
195. Dion, "Formulaic Language," 190.

humanity. With the initial line introduced by the first כי, Job includes a verb with Yahweh as the subject while expressing amazement along with the psalmist in Ps 8. With the following lines introduced by the second כי, Job uses additional verbal clauses with Yahweh also as the subject, but here acting in objectionable ways. Similarly, van Leeuwen concludes that "Job's irony is that he wishes to be left alone by his master."[196] A certain amount of Job's irony centers on the term פקד, which displays a wide range of meaning.[197] The verb can convey in certain contexts "to care, show concern, protect, attend to, help" (e.g., Gen 50:24, 25; Exod 3:16; 4:31; Jer 15:15; Zeph 2:7; Ps 80:15 [v. 14]; Ruth 1:6) whereas in other contexts means "punishment" especially of the wicked (Exod 20:5; Lev 18:25; 1 Sam 15:2; Isa 13:11; Jer 6:15; Hos 4:14; Ps 17:3). Thus, more precisely the irony here is that where the psalmist exclaims about Yahweh's *conscientious attentiveness* (פקד) despite the comparable insignificance of humanity, for Job human insignificance should cause God to not pay such *scrutinizing attentiveness* (פקד) to humanity and specifically to him![198] Job matches the psalmist's use of two כי clauses and with the first infers the Assertive and Expressive forces while mirroring the psalmist's exclamatory view of exalted humanity whereas with the second he continues with these forces while inferring a primary Directive for God to stop his harassing examination, or, as in Coats' terms, he "should not do these things."

Job's response is also an information-providing type of RQ. Both Yahweh and Job would agree that humanity is frail and insignificant, but not necessarily that they would agree that this should cause him to therefore stop examining human beings. Job, then, expresses his own beliefs and commitments to challenge God to agree with and assent to his inferred exclusive answer. With this hybrid expression and as Job is left to either agree or disagree with Eliphaz's information-providing RQ in 15:9 (see Chapter 2), so Yahweh is here left to do the same. With the Initial PE, God would recognize the intended meaning of Job's RQ while God is left with the option to either agree with and assent to the Intended PE and follow the indirect Directive or answer the interrogative dimension with a counter assertion and thereby reject Job's challenge to stop paying such close, scrutinizing attention to him.

---

196. Van Leeuwen, "Psalm 8.5," 211.
197. See, e.g., *HALOT* 955–58.
198. See Tyler F. Williams, "פקד," *NIDOTE* 3:657–63, cf. 659; Perdue, *Wisdom in Revolt*, 130.

Psalm 27:1

These parallel lines begin a Psalm of Confidence/Trust and Petition:[199]

Yahweh, my light and my salvation!	יהוה אורי וישעי
From among whom should I fear?	ממי אירא
Yahweh, protector of my life!	יהוה מעוז־חיי
From among whom should I be afraid?	ממי אפחד:

As I proposed in my Introduction, the two confessionary assertions about Yahweh provide contextual indicators that the psalmist does not pose genuine questions. What further demonstrates this conclusion is the use of similar declarations of trust/confidence in v. 3, especially the first bicolon:

If an army should encamp against me	אם־תחנה עלי מחנה
my heart will not fear	לא־יירא לבי
If a war should arise against me,	אם־תקום עלי מלחמה
in this I trust.	בזאת אני בוטח:

Looking at the first bicolon, the second line semantically parallels the first interrogative with the repeated term ירא "to fear." With this colon, the psalmist proposes a hypothetical scenario followed by a self-involved speech act that includes the Behabitive/Expressive and Commissive forces. With this speech act, the psalmist commits to not fearing in the face of an encamped enemy.

Kuntz identifies the two interrogatives in v. 1 as RQs which occur in the situation of others hearing the psalmist (his sixth configuration) and within his second main function which he describes as often "presenting themselves as exclamatory utterance that is either for or against something, *rhetorical questions in the Psalms show a proclivity to intensify the discourse in which they appear.*" In this function and more specifically, certain RQs "unmask certain propositional attitudes of the psalmist toward God." With 27:1 along with Pss 118:6b and 56:5c (v. 4c) "the psalmist is poised to confess her/his trust in a God to whom she/he may to turn for help in times of acute adversity" which is obviously set forth

---

199. Beginning with Gunkel, this psalm has often been understood as two completely separate psalms: Psalm of Confidence or Trust (vv. 1–6) and an Individual Complaint (vv. 7–14); see, e.g., Weiser, *Psalms*, 244–55. Although, there are clearly two distinct sections within this Psalm, most modern interpreters treat it as a literary whole; see, e.g., Brueggemann, *Message of the Psalms*, 152–54; Brueggemann/Bellinger, *Psalms*, 137–42; Craigie, *Psalms 1–50*, 228–35; Goldingay, *Psalms 1–41*, 389–401; Gerstenberger, *Psalms Part 1*, 124–27; Kraus, *Psalms 1–59*, 330–37.

with these RQs.²⁰⁰ In addition, the two parallel assertions "are truly *reinforced* by this pair of rhetorical questions."²⁰¹ In his configuration, Kuntz understands the psalmist voicing these lines "to an assembled body of worshippers" with the intent of inviting the listeners "to assume her/his propositional attitude as their own." Then he claims that each assertion "*evokes*" the parallel RQs.²⁰²

Examining these two interrogatives, both begin with the preposition מ followed by the pronoun מי and a verb. Along with the interpretive help of the two parallel assertions and subsequent proclamations, what makes it clear that these two interrogatives intentionally operate as RQs is that the addresser and addressee are identical. Thus, the pragmatic procedure I presented with Ps 113 also applies here. Along with this, what the psalmist makes clear in this Psalm is that the reason for fear is authentic.²⁰³ Coupled with the expressions of confidence and trust the addresser identifies threatening evildoers, adversaries (vv. 2–3), enemies (v. 6), and foes (v. 11). In addition, the psalmist reiterates a request to dwell in the safety of the house of Yahweh (vv. 4–6), petitions for Yahweh to listen and not abandon her/him (vv. 7–12), and uses a series of self-exhortative verbs to wait for Yahweh (2×), to be strong, and for the heart to take courage (v. 14).²⁰⁴ Viewed as a whole, the psalm's purpose centers on the suppliant's anticipated attacks expressed in the second part, while in the first part the psalmist does ponder future trouble (vv. 3, 8). In the first section, the psalmist gives testimony about Yahweh's past protection along with expressions of confidence and trust which then introduce and provide the basis for the suppliant's urgent pleas to Yahweh for future protection while also encouraging oneself to be strong. Thus, although the addresser/addressee would naturally agree with and assent to the Intended PE, these two RQs convey a challenging dimension for the addresser/addressee in light of anticipated trouble.

The two parallel assertions in v. 1 are undeniably self-involved confessions whereby the addresser takes a public stance concerning Yahweh as her/his light, salvation, and protector with accompanied entailments.

200. Kuntz, "Making a Statement," 171 (pronouns revised).
201. Ibid., 172 (italics mine).
202. Ibid., 167 (pronouns revised; italics mine).
203. So, e.g., Brueggemann, *Psalms*, 154; Goldingay, *Psalms 1–41*, 392; Patrick D. Miller, *They Cried to the Lord: The Form and Theology of Biblical Prayer* (Minneapolis: Fortress, 1994), 230.
204. Understanding the three volitional verbs in v. 14 as self-addressed so also Goldingay, *Psalms 1–41*, 400; Weiser, *Psalms*, 254; contra Brueggemann, *Psalms*, 154.

One could draw some general, implicit entailments, but the explicit entailments are immediately found with the following parallel RQs. In the Hebrew Bible, RQs can reinforce or intensify closely connected statements (e.g., Jer 17:9)[205] and it is plausible to see an aspect of this function with the psalmist's RQs here as Kuntz suggests. Still, I consider Kuntz's *evoking* view gets closer to the intended function of the RQs which has affinities with my entailment suggestion.[206]

With the two RQs, the entailed inferred answer is *I will fear no one!* The inferred answer is typically reconstructed by interpreters as an assertion such as *No one!* or *Nobody!*, but should reflect the verbal nature of the literal interrogatives. Thus, the inferred answer expresses an Assertive force, but not in a primary way. As I presented above, Kuntz claims that with these RQs the psalmist displays her/his *propositional* attitude toward God as well as *confesses* her/his trust in God. But, the inferred answers here do not on their own express such confessions of trust in Yahweh; rather, these RQs involve more of a type of action in contrast to the typical noun clause RQs like the above incomparability RQs that infer a primary Assertive force. Any expressions of confession and trust here derives from the previous and related self-involved assertions. Based on their verbal nature and understood within the larger psalm, these RQs express a Directive that functions as the primary force with an accompanied Assertive force.

Entailed from the parallel assertions, the psalmist infers through the two RQs the Directive force for her/him to not fear anyone when faced with trouble. Thus, the two RQs function as self-addressed Directive entailments of the stances taken with the parallel assertions: *Yahweh is my light, salvation, and protector and **therefore** I will fear no one!* As the psalmist exhorts the self to wait on Yahweh, be strong, and take courage (v. 14), so here with these RQs the suppliant issues a Directive to not fear when anticipated attacks become reality. Understood this way, the opening RQs and the closing self-exhortations form an *inclusio* for this psalm which may provide another reason for understanding this psalm as a literary unit.

---

205. See Moshavi, "What Can I Say?" 98–108; see also, e.g., James L. Crenshaw, "Impossible Questions, Sayings, and Tasks," *Semeia* 17 (1980): 26; Johnson, "Rhetorical Question," 105; J. F. J. van Rensburg, "Wise Men Saying Things by Asking Questions: The Function of the Interrogative in Job 3 and 14," *Old Testament Essays* 4 (1991): 233–36, 245.

206. Similarly Goldingay, *Psalms 1–41*, 392; Kraus, *Psalms 1–59*, 333; Weiser, *Psalms*, 246.

This psalm is dominated by first person language with the psalmist describing, addressing, and pleading to Yahweh throughout, and it is beyond plausible that psalmists sang this psalm in front of others;[207] however, it remains unclear that the psalm was intended to be sung in front of other worshippers. Further, with the RQs the addresser does not express a propositional attitude for the listeners to adopt as their own as Kuntz contends. More conceivable and similar to the Song of the Sea, throughout the historical use of the Psalter a person would read/sing this psalm while assuming the identity of the ambiguous literary first person "I." Any self-involved reader/singer would begin with the assertions and thereby become a co-confessor taking a public stance concerning Yahweh as Light, Savior, and Protector. With the entailed pair of RQs, the reader/singer then exhorts her/himself with an indirect Directive to not fear anyone in times of trouble.

Isaiah 40:12–31

Do you not know? Do you not hear? Continuing with the several unidentified voices in the Prologue for chs. 40–55 (vv. 1–11),[208] another ambiguous voice appears and remains throughout the second section of this first chapter (vv. 12–31). Although this voice is never explicitly identified here nor throughout the second literary section in Isaiah, it is presumably that of the prophet. In this latter section of ch. 40 a first person voice appears once, a voice which would naturally belong to Yahweh, the Holy One (v. 25) in close proximity to the lone quoted complaint of Jacob-Israel (v. 27). Interpreters generally agree with the form-critical classification of a Disputation as the overarching genre for this section.[209] Westermann concurs while seeing v. 27 introducing the true disputation

---

207. Kuntz, "Making a Statement," 167. Craigie proposes that this psalm is a Royal Psalm possibly used during the coronation of a new king (*Psalms 1–50*, 228–35). For Brueggemann, the imperatives in v. 14 "are addressed to the cohorts of the speaker, to get them to trust the relationship" (*Psalms*, 154); similarly Brueggemann/Bellinger, *Psalms*, 141.

208. See Roy F. Melugin, *The Formation of Isaiah 40–55*, BZAW 141 (Berlin: de Gruyter, 1976), 82–86.

209. See in particular Jan L. Koole, *Isaiah Part 3, Volume 1: Isaiah 40–48*, trans. A. P. Runia, HCOT (Kampen: KOK Pharos, 1997), 86–87; Melugin, *Formation of Isaiah 40–55*, 31–36; Antoon Schoors, *I Am God Your Savior: A Form-Critical Study of the Main Genres in Is. XL–LV*, VTSup 24 (Leiden: Brill, 1973), 247–59; Bruce D. Naidoff, "The Rhetoric of Encouragement in Isaiah 40 12–31: A Form-Critical Study," *ZAW* 93 (1981): 62–76; Marvin A. Sweeney, *Isaiah 40–66*, FOTL (Grand Rapids: Eerdmans, 2016), 59–60.

of vv. 28–31.²¹⁰ There is no denying that throughout this pericope the prophet interrogates, makes arguments, confronts, and challenges an exilic addressee explicitly identified as Jacob-Israel. The prophet also encourages his audience towards the end of this section while throughout he utilizes different genre elements and strategically employs various types of interrogatives and other linguistic strategies all centering around Yahweh's incomparability.²¹¹ How to conceive the structure of this section is where interpreters diverge. In broad strokes, vv. 12–31 neatly divide into vv. 12–26 and 27–31, marked by the first appearance of Jacob-Israel in v. 27 in these chapters, the switch to the singular addressee, and the MT caesura ס.²¹² Scholars remain puzzled about identifying any progression of thought in vv. 12–26,²¹³ but two parallel sequences appear with Yahweh depicted as inactive in the first (vv. 12–20) and active in the second (vv. 21–26),²¹⁴ indicated in part by the first person pronouns in v. 25.

As I presented in my Introduction, the two parallel interrogatives of *knowing* and *hearing* occur twice within this literary unit (v. 21aα; v. 28a). The first instance occurs with plural imperfect verbs:

Do you not know?	הלוא תדעו
Do you not hear?	הלוא תשמעו

While the second occurs with singular perfects:

Have you not known?	הלוא ידעת
or have you not heard?	אם־לא שמעת

These parallel interrogatives occur in close connection with the specific theme of Yahweh's incomparability found throughout chs. 40–48, which is highlighted by two other paired interrogatives in this same section (vv. 18, 25):

210. Claus Westermann, *Isaiah 40–66*, trans. D. M. G. Stalker (Philadelphia: Westminster, 1969), 48.

211. According to Kuntz, the interrogatives in vv. 12–14 and vv. 18 and 25 "collectively remind us that Deutero-Isaiah relies heavily on rhetorical questions as he rigorously puts forward his case defending Yahweh's uniqueness" ("Rhetorical Questions," 135).

212. Sweeney sees a threefold structure: vv. 12–20, 21–26, 27–31 (*Isaiah 40–66*, 52–59).

213. See Roy F. Melugin, "Deutero-Isaiah and Form Criticism," *VT* 21 (1971): 326–37.

214. See John Goldingay, *The Message of Isaiah 40–55: A Literary-Theological Commentary* (London/New York: T&T Clark, 2005), 33–34; see also Schoors, *I Am God Your Savior*, 259.

| And to whom do you liken God | ואל־מי תדמיון אל |
| or what form can you compare to him? | ומה־דמות תערכו לו׃ |

| And to whom do you liken me and I thus be equated | ואל־מי תדמיוני ואשוה |
| says the Holy One? | יאמר קדוש׃ |

These incomparability interrogatives directly preface a sarcastic polemic (vv. 19–20) and descriptions of the all-powerful Yahweh (v. 26), respectively. Interestingly, though, the claims that follow each of these interrogatives add and elaborate on proceeding ones: vv. 22–24 correspond to and elaborate upon vv. 12–17 while v. 26 does the same with vv. 19–20.[215] The first *knowing/hearing* interrogative directly follows the first incomparability interrogative and polemic while the second follows Jacob-Israel's complaint and also prefaces a description of Yahweh (vv. 28b–31).

Scholars are also divided on how to interpretively understand each of the interrogatives found in vv. 12–31. For a number of interpreters, all but v. 27 should be understood as RQs. However, as Bruce D. Naidoff warns, it "is important to distinguish between those questions which are truly rhetorical (i.e., those to which the answer is obvious) and those which, on the surface at least, appear to reflect a genuine dispute."[216] Naidoff agrees with Westermann that v. 27 reflects this latter category while he extends this classification to the incomparable interrogatives. All three interrogatives, then, "are not, in the strictest sense, rhetorical, but argumentative." Yet, at the same time, Naidoff interprets the incomparable interrogatives as RQs with the obvious answer *No!* These interrogatives are apparently not *true* RQs because they "envisage the unnamed opponents as actually seeking to make a comparison with God."[217] Goldingay similarly concludes that the "not-really-so-rhetorical question presupposes that actually there *were* images with which people could compare Yhwh." Then he subsequently concludes that the "question 'With whom can we compare El?' is open to a number of theologically correct or incorrect answers, but *rhetorically* the only correct answer is 'No one,' the same answer as that required by the questions in vv. 13–14 and by many of the 'Who' questions in Isa. 40–55."[218] Perhaps Naidoff and Goldingay recognize here the hybrid nature of RQs as well as something along the lines of a degrees of informativity? In contrast to Naidoff, Westermann views the *knowing/ hearing* interrogatives functioning identically as v. 27 and thus are not

215. See Goldingay, *Isaiah 40–55*, 53, 58–59.
216. Naidoff, "Rhetoric of Encouragement," 67.
217. Ibid., 67, 68.
218. Goldingay, *Isaiah 40–55*, 46, 47 (italics mine); see further pp. 45–46.

rhetorical, but "true questions expecting an answer."[219] Nevertheless, the overwhelming majority of interpreters consider these parallel interrogatives operating as RQs.[220] Viewed this way, these negative interrogatives would infer the obvious reversed polarity answer of *Of course we know and hear!* But within chs. 40–55, does Jacob-Israel actually correctly *know*? Is the nation even able to *hear*?

The prophet begins his argumentative confrontation with a barrage of interrogatives (vv. 12–14) which also recall Yahweh answering Job that correspondingly many scholars identify as RQs. If functioning as such, then the inferred answer would be *No one!* or *No human being!*[221] or perhaps more contextually appropriate *No deity!* Marvin A. Sweeney understands the interrogatives in vv. 12–14 as RQs that he appears to synonymously categorize as "rhetorical assertions." Klaus Baltzer proposes two possible answers *Yahweh!* or *No human being!* for the RQs in vv. 12–14, while both "answers do not have to be mutually exclusive," but in the end he seems to prefer the former.[222] For Sweeney, the "first *rhetorical assertion* of YHWH's role as creator appears in 40:12," while the RQs in vv. 13–14 infers the answer "no one."[223] Kuntz concurs that the answer to the RQ of v. 12 is "Yahweh alone," while the only answer to the following RQs in vv. 13–14 is "nobody."[224] Most all interpreters agree that each of these interrogatives operate as RQs while, as John N. Oswalt similarly concludes, "it seems best to allow different answers in v. 12 and in vv. 13–14,"[225] which also begins to address Naidoff's warning.

---

219. Westermann, *Isaiah 40–66*, 55.

220. E.g., Klaus Baltzer, *Deutero-Isaiah*, trans. M. Kohl, Hermeneia (Minneapolis: Fortress, 2001), 78; Joseph Blenkinsopp, *Isaiah 40–55*, AB 19A (New York: Doubleday, 2002), 194; Koole, *Isaiah 40–48*, 106–108, 122–24; Kuntz, "Rhetorical Questions," 133; John N. Oswalt, *The Book of Isaiah Chapters 40–66*, NICOT (Grand Rapids: Eerdmans, 1998), 66–67, 73; Shalom M. Paul, *Isaiah 40–66*, ECC (Grand Rapids: Eerdmans, 2012), 148–49, 154; Sweeney, *Isaiah 40–66*, 57–59; *IBHS* §40.3b; Westermann, *Isaiah 40–66*, 55.

221. John L. McKenzie, *Second Isaiah*, AB 20 (Garden City: Doubleday, 1968), 23; Westermann, *Isaiah 40–66*, 50–51.

222. Baltzer, *Deutero-Isaiah*, 67–70; similarly Brevard S. Childs, *Isaiah*, OTL (Louisville: Westminster John Knox, 2001), 308–309; Goldingay, *Isaiah 40–55*, 35; Koole, *Isaiah 40–48*, 88–90; R. N. Whybray, *Isaiah 40–66*, NCBC (Grand Rapids: Eerdmans, 1975), 53; Schoors, *God your Saviour*, 251.

223. Sweeney, *Isaiah 40–66*, 55, 56 (italics mine); similarly Blenkinsopp, *Isaiah 40–55*, 190–91; Walter Brueggemann, *Isaiah 40–66* (Louisville: Westminster John Knox, 1998), 23; Paul, *Isaiah 40–66*, 138–43.

224. Kuntz, "Rhetorical Questions," 131.

225. Oswalt, *Isaiah 40–66*, 59.

The interrogatives in v. 12 prefaced by מי could be understood as genuine questions whereas those in vv. 13–14 beginning with the same pronoun are clearly RQs with the inferred answer of *No one!* Along with the majority of interpreters, the prophet would not conceivably entertain any human being or idol-god directing the spirit of Yahweh or providing Yahweh with counsel and understanding. Regarding v. 12, the four verbs of measurement as well as the references to the principle and foundational elements of creation (waters, heavens, earth, mountains and hills) point to Israel's deeply rooted traditions that Yahweh alone is the creator of the cosmos who is thereby sovereign over all his creation (e.g., Gen 1:1–2:4a; Pss 33; 74; 104; Job 38–41).[226] Consequently, I agree with most interpreters that the intended answer to the interrogatives in v. 12 is Yahweh, but how RQs characteristically operate does not allow for such an inferred answer. Understanding v. 12 as consisting of RQs, Oswalt proposes that the inferred answer is "none *but God*."[227] This interpretation makes contextual sense, but obviously adds an inferential linguistic element.

The interrogatives in v. 12 clearly express a low degree of information-elicitation as they violate Searle's Preparatory and the Sincerity/ Responsibility conditions. Yet, rather than understood as RQs these interrogatives more appropriately correspond to confirming type Conducive questions. Accordingly, the prophet opens his arguments with Conducive questions to intentionally lead and elicit Jacob-Israel to verbally confirm the intended, expected answer that it is Yahweh alone who is the creator of the heavens and the earth. As the prophet continues the discourse, his specificity increases, eventually making it quite clear that the only possible antecedent of מי is Yahweh.

These different types of opening interrogatives are immediately followed by assertions (vv. 15–17) that continue with the ambiguity of v. 12. Here the prophet compares the nations to a third masculine singular pronoun, with the only logical referent again being Yahweh. The prophet follows these assertions with the first incomparable interrogative, which contains a key verb דמה "resemble, be like" (see Ps 89:7 above)[228] that

---

226. See Paul, *Isaiah 40–66*, 138–42; Goldingay, *Isaiah 40–55*, 35–41.
227. Oswalt, *Isaiah Chapters 40–66*, 59 (italics mine).
228. Labuschagne overstates that the term דמה "is used in connection with Yahweh *only* to express His incomparability" (*Incomparability of Yahweh*, 29 [italics mine]). The verb occurs some 30 times in the Hebrew Bible with only a few instances used in direct connection to Yahweh.

the prophet here uses four times and exclusively in reference to Yahweh's incomparability to idol-gods.²²⁹ The verb occurs in both of the incomparable interrogatives in ch. 40 and twice in 46:5:

To whom would you liken me and equate	למי תדמיוני ותשוו
and compare me that we may be alike?	ותמשלוני ונדמה

This interrogative virtually mirrors the previous ones while being placed within a similar description of the helplessness and worthlessness of idol-gods (46:1–7). In fact, chs. 40–46 present a concentration of polemics against idol-gods in direct comparison to the unique Yahweh.²³⁰

All three of these interrogatives obviously correspond closely to the incomparable RQs I analyzed above, but in contrast Jacob-Israel is the addressee with the prophet as the addresser in the first one with Yahweh speaking in first person in the latter two. Following along similar pragmatic processes I also outlined previously, the prophet and Yahweh already know the answer to these interrogatives (Efficiency condition) and thus they insincerely use them (Maxim of Quality and Sincerity/Responsibility) while not eliciting for some unknown information (Elicitative force). Thus, each of these interrogatives function as RQs as most interpreters conclude. To persuasively lead the addressee to pragmatically infer and assent to the intended answer, the prophet immediately follows the initial incomparable interrogatives with a sarcastic polemic of human beings manufacturing deities (vv. 19–20), something which is later expanded in 44:9–20. With the second, and in contrast to the psalmist voluntarily looking up in amazement to the heavens in Ps 8, here the prophet exhorts the addressees to lift up *your eyes* on high and *see* מי *created* (ברא) as well as guides and calls the unidentified hosts in the heavens by name (v. 26). Due to all this, along with the regular use of incomparable RQs in the ANE and especially in Mesopotamian literature,²³¹ Jacob-Israel would readily recognize the prophet and Yahweh's insincere use of these

---

229. Similarly Goldingay, *Isaiah 40–55*, 46; see also Isa 14:14; Ps 50:21.
230. See in particular Richard J. Clifford, "The Function of Idol Passages in Second Isaiah," *CBQ* 42 (1980): 450–64; Knut Holter, *Second Isaiah's Idol-Fabrication Passages*, BBET 28 (Frankfurt: Lang, 1995); Hendrik C. Spykerboer, *The Structure and Composition of Deutero-Isaiah with Special Reference to the Polemics Against Idolatry* (Meppel: Krips, 1976); Rikki E. Watts, "Consolation or Confrontation? Isaiah 40–55 and the Delay of the New Exodus," *TynBul* 41 (1990): 31–59; Westermann, *Isaiah 40–66*, 15–17.
231. See Labuschagne, *Incomparability of Yahweh*, 31–63.

interrogatives and infer collectively the obvious answer/assertion: *No idol-god can compare to unique Yahweh!* As with the other incomparable RQs, these infer a strong primary Assertive along with the Behabitive/ Expressive and Commissive forces. With the Intended PEs, the prophet challenges Jacob-Israel to agree with and assent to the inferred answer/ assertion and thereby mentally confess that no image along with the representative deity compares or equates to Yahweh. Accompanying this stance is the entailment of committing to serve and worship Yahweh alone. In contrast to the incomparable RQs *about* Yahweh often being with him as the addressee, these are information-providing RQs and corresponding more along the lines of Labuschagne's *co-expresser* notion. Both Yahweh and the prophet are utterly committed to the exclusive inferred answer/ assertion, but does Jacob-Israel agree? A directional mismatch exists between the addressee's experiential world and this inferred answer/assertion. Jacob-Israel seriously *questions* Yahweh's sovereign power in light of the current desolation of Jerusalem and its exilic existence (44:26–28). The city's destruction demonstrates for Jacob-Israel that Yahweh is in fact no match for the Babylonians and their gods. As I summarized with my degrees of informativity notion, what licenses interrogatives to operate as felicitous RQs is the shared mutual knowledge about the world between the communicative participants. However, both do not need to be committed to those same beliefs and values while the obvious and exclusive answer is already known and/or readily inferable by the addressee. With any type of RQ, the ultimate intention aims at synchronizing the beliefs and commitments of both conversational participants. Jacob-Israel would recognize the intended answer/assertion, but agreeing with and assenting to it is another *question* altogether.

In the book of Isaiah, eyes and ears are naturally necessary for seeing, listening, and comprehension, but in chs. 40–48 servant Jacob-Israel is self-inflicted with *blindness* and *deafness* (42:19) and *no knowledge* due to its *objects* of worship (cf. 45:20; see also, e.g., 40:18–20; 42:17; 44:9–20; 45:20; 46:1–7). Consequently, even though Yahweh does not *weary* (יגע) or tire (40:28a) Jacob-Israel has grown *weary* (יגע) of Yahweh and thus no longer calls upon him (43:22). Israel is Israel in name only (48:1) and because of its stubbornness and rebelliousness God's people would quickly assign any act of power to any other idol-god rather than Yahweh (vv. 4–5).[232] Because of all this, Jacob-Israel would unsurprisingly counter the inferred answers to the incomparable RQs that Naidoff

---

232. See Adams, *Performative Nature*, 97–99.

and Goldingay point to by answering the interrogative dimension and offering the identities of other deities that the nation considers comparable and/or superior to Yahweh.

The first instance of the *knowing/hearing* interrogatives in Isa 40 is followed by two interrogatives beginning with exact same particle:

Has it not been declared to you from the beginning?	הלוא הגד מראש לכם
Have you not understood from the foundations of the earth?	הלוא הבינתם מוסדות הארץ

These interrogatives are quite vague, but in one sense denote what Jacob-Israel's traditions refer to as the *beginning* of creation (Gen 1:1; Prov 8:23), the *foundations of the earth* (see Pss 24:2; 89:11 [v. 12]; 104:5; Prov 8:29), both of which relate back to v. 12 and are specified in v. 26. Towards clarifying this creation theme, the prophet immediately follows them with a description of the transcendent massiveness and supreme power of Yahweh in comparison to the cosmos and its inhabitants (vv. 22–24). In another sense, these lines correlate with the prophet's focus on Yahweh's sovereignty over history which also links back to vv. 15–17. In particular, Yahweh orchestrates the *beginning* of historical events (41:4a, 26a; 48:16).[233] As the prophet's words unfold, the chief concern of chs. 40–48 is the claim that Yahweh alone has *declared* from the *beginning*,[234] not predicted, the coming of Cyrus to conquer Babylon and save Israel (cf. 41:26).[235] In direct connection to historical events in general and specifically with Cyrus, Yahweh strategically asserts about himself in the beginning, middle, and end of chs. 40–48: אני ראשון ואני אחרון "I am the *first* and the last" (41:4b; 44:6b; 48:12b).[236] As the above interrogatives point to similar creation motifs found in v. 12, they may

---

233. See Goldingay, *Isaiah 40–55*, 53–55.

234. Yahweh's actual Declarative of the Cyrus event is not explicitly expressed in chs. 40–48. In this section, Yahweh's performative speech act is presented as already beginning to take place, but not yet fully realized. Yahweh claims throughout these chapters that he declared it from the beginning, in former times, from beforehand, from old (see 41:21–29; 43:8–13). These expressions correspond to Yahweh's Declarative of the overthrow of Babylon through other prophets (e.g., Jer 51) and specifically through Isaiah ben Amoz's declaration that the Medes will conquer the city (13:17–19); see further Adams, *Performative Nature*, 135–36.

235. See ibid., 131–33.

236. Rosario P. Merendino, *Der Erste und der Letzte: Eine Untersuchung von Jes 40–48*, VTSup 31 (Leiden: Brill, 1981), cf. 7–8.

appear to function as confirming Conducive questions with the match polarity answer of *No, it has not been declared nor understood!* However, Jacob-Israel's traditions are clear that Yahweh is creator of the cosmos and thereby sovereign over creation and history. Taking all of the above into account, these interrogatives are best viewed operating as RQs. The prophet already knows that Jacob-Israel has been told and has theoretically understood its traditions and claims about Yahweh (Efficiency condition). He insincerely uses these parallel interrogatives (Maxim of Quality and Sincerity/Responsibility) and does not elicit for information (Elicitative force). The prophet does not explicitly answer the parallel interrogatives with vv. 22–24 like he does elsewhere (e.g., 41:26),[237] but he certainly descriptively rehearses *who* Yahweh is to remind and reaffirm for Jacob-Israel of its own traditional claims. Jacob-Israel would recognize the prophet's insincere use of these interrogatives and infer the obvious answer/assertion: *It has been declared to you and understood from the beginning!*

Moshavi identifies the particle הלא as synchronically distinct from the combination of the interrogative ה and the negative לא. According to Moshavi, this non-interrogative, non-negative הלא belongs to the syntactic class of other clausal adverbs that includes other adverbs such as הנה "behold," לכן "therefore," and אולם "whereas." The clausal adverb הלא pragmatically functions in discourse contexts such as answers to questions, announcements, predictions, and most often with justifications. As such, הלא does not express an interrogative nor is asseverative; rather, it functions as a presentative particle for assertions that closely resembles clauses prefaced with הנה.[238] Applying her analysis here, these above clauses would be interpreted accordingly:

> הלוא it has been declared to you from the beginning!
> הלוא you have understood from the foundations of the earth!

Understood this way, these parallel clauses essentially convey the exact same inferred answers/assertions if taken as RQs. I prefer understanding these interrogatives as RQs, though, due to my above analysis as well as the overarching argumentative and challenging intent of the prophet in

---

237. Contra Sweeney, *Isaiah 40–66*, 57.

238. See Moshavi, "הלא as a Discourse Marker of Justification in Biblical Hebrew," *HS* 48 (2007): 177–86; idem, "Syntactic Evidence for a Clausal Adverb הלא in Biblical Hebrew," *JNWSL* 33 (2007): 51–63; idem, "The Rhetorical Question or Assertion? The Pragmatics of הלא in Biblical Hebrew," *JANES* 32 (2011): 91–105.

this literary unit.²³⁹ The prophet, then, begins this section with the parallel *knowing/hearing* interrogatives and then uses these two linguistically similar RQs to function as a direct response which further introduces descriptions about the incomparable Yahweh.

Beginning the second part of this larger literary unit, the prophet quotes Jacob-Israel's complaint of Yahweh's hidden disregard with the genuine question in v. 27:

Why do you say Jacob and speak Israel	למה תאמר יעקב ותדבר ישׂראל
My way is hidden from Yahweh	נסתרה דרכי מהוה
and my cause is disregarded by my God?	ומאלהי משפטי יעבור:

The prophet initially responds to this complaint with the second *knowing/hearing* interrogatives. These are then promptly followed by the prophet asserting that Yahweh is אלהי עולם יהוה בורא קצות הארץ "the eternal God, Yahweh, the creator of the ends of the earth" (v. 28aβ) along with descriptions of his tireless power which he gives to those who wait on him (vv. 28b–31). This initial assertion directly links to the second incomparable interrogative and specifically with the immediately following descriptions of Yahweh (v. 26) and the second use of ברא as well as it further specifies the מי of vv. 12 and 26. The prophet has been *questioning* what Jacob-Israel *knows* and *hears* while in the parallel interrogatives he recollects what it *has known* and *heard*. Yet, this quoted complaint displays that it does not *know* or *hear!* Moreover, Yahweh's blind and deaf servant does not apparently possess the capacity to *know* and *hear!*

Joüon-Muraoka view all of the examples of the singular perfect הראית "Do you see? (1 Kgs 20:13; 21:29; Jer 3:6; Ezek 8:12, 15, 17; 47:6) and the plural perfect הראיתם "Do you see?" (1 Sam 10:24; 17:25; 2 Kgs 6:32) as expressing the exclamatory force. Joüon-Muraoka also understand "Do you know?" in 1 Kgs 22:3 likewise (§161b) while GKC interprets this verse as an asseverative (§150e). As I discussed above with Ps 8:5 and 1 Sam 10:24 (see Chapter 2), the above biblical texts do not match the criteria of proper Exclamatives or expressing asseveration, but rather

---

239. Moshavi observes how "it is generally not clear when הלא is the clausal adverb marking an explicit assertion, as opposed to the interrogative-negative combination marking a rhetorical question implying the same assertion" as with Gen 43:22. For Moshavi, the clausal adverb הלא is best identified in contexts atypical for RQs that characteristically involve the inference of obvious answers and used as a persuasive device ("Rhetorical Question or Assertion?" 94–95).

are most appropriately understood as confirming Conducive questions.²⁴⁰ Although not explicitly described by Joüon-Muraoka or GKC, these negated *knowing/hearing* interrogatives do not function as Exclamatives while possibly expressing an asseverative sense: *You certainly do not know! You certainly do not hear!* These interrogatives could also function as genuine questions,²⁴¹ but the prophet does not convey much information-elicitative force, as Kuntz indicates while viewing them as RQs.²⁴² As with the interrogatives in v. 12, these also violate Searle's Preparatory condition as well as the Sincerity/Responsibility condition like RQs. In contrast to the similarly formed interrogatives in v. 21aβ–b, though, with the *knowing/hearing* interrogatives the prophet already knows that Jacob-Israel is blind and deaf and not knowing and thus understanding them as RQs implying a positive, obvious answer/assertion is not contextually viable. Understanding הלוא functioning as a presentative clausal adverb, these two clauses would be interpreted as הלוא *you know!* הלוא *you hear!* closely corresponding to the inferred assertions if taken as RQs which again does not fit the overall context of Isa 40–55. Taking all of this into account, these *knowing/hearing* interrogatives are best understood as Conducive questions, but here the type that expresses an aspect of surprise which also matches in polarity. As I described in my previous chapter, this type of conduciveness displays a discrepancy between addressers' anticipated or assumed disagreement and the actual affirmative answer as with *Did your children really go to school today?* These types also include negative-oriented interrogatives that often include critique, disappointment, disapproval, annoyance etc., such as with *Can't you drive straight?* or *Aren't you ashamed of yourself?* while the above interrogative in this category additionally conveys such negative connotations.²⁴³ Sweeney identifies these interrogatives in v. 21 and v. 28 as RQs, with the function of the former to shame "the audience into *admitting* that they know of YHWH's power."²⁴⁴ Sweeney's reverses

---

240. So Moshavi, "Positive Rhetorical Question," 271–72; see also idem, "Conducive Questions," 73–74.

241. David J. A. Clines presumably understands the interrogatives in v. 21aα as RQs while acknowledging that what is not specified "is *when* Israel's coming to know and hearing is supposed to have taken place" ("The Parallelism of Greater Precision: Notes from Isaiah 40 for a Theory of Hebrew Poetry," in *Directions of Biblical Hebrew Poetry*, ed. E. R. Follis, JSOTSup 40 [Sheffield; Sheffield Academic Press, 1987], 81–82).

242. Kuntz, "Rhetorical Questions," 133.

243. See further Moshavi, "Conducive Questions," 74–76.

244. Sweeney, *Isaiah 40–66*, 57, 63 (italics mine).

the polarity of the interrogatives correctly if RQs, but then describes their function somewhat conducively.²⁴⁵ Both the *knowing/hearing* interrogatives are properly understood as Conducive questions which the prophet uses to surprisingly and disapprovingly elicit an affirmative answer from Jacob-Israel that in fact it does not know or hear. These interrogatives understood as RQs do not contextually make sense while asseveratives do not typically convey negative critique.²⁴⁶ So again, why does Israel not know or hear? Because the nation worships idol-gods who cannot see, hear, speak, move, or know anything. Thus, the prophet uses these low information-eliciting interrogatives to lead Jacob-Israel to admit that it incorrectly *knows* and is *blind* and *deaf*, which Yahweh intentionally infers soon after with another RQ (42:19). As the prophet's words unfold throughout chs. 41–48, the irony expressed with these interrogatives becomes more and more apparent. In particular with the parallel RQs in v. 21aβ–b, Jacob-Israel would agree and assent to the inferred assertions of being told and understanding: "Israel *has* heard. It *has* been told."²⁴⁷ However, Jacob-Israel cannot know or hear because no idol-god can *declare* nor can its words be *heard* (41:26b). The nation does not truly know or accurately hear, which the prophet intentionally leads the nation to admit with the *knowing/hearing* interrogatives.

In this section, the prophet uses several types of interrogatives to develop his arguments to challenge and encourage Jacob-Israel. With the confirming Conducive questions in v. 12 the prophet opens his arguments with the intent to lead the nation to verbally confirm that Yahweh alone is the creator of the cosmos and thus all-powerful. In the following RQs (vv. 13–14), the prophet challenges Jacob-Israel to agree with and assent that no other possible being and specifically idol-god has directed Yahweh's spirit or has counseled Yahweh in the way of wisdom and knowledge. The intention of this inferred answer/assertion is for the nation to mentally confess that Yahweh alone directs his own spirit and that he does not need an advisor in the way of justice and understanding. With the incomparable RQs (40:18, 25; 46:5), the prophet and Yahweh

---

245. Goldingay also identifies these interrogatives as RQs while taking "a different form from those in vv. 12–14, but they are equally designed to make a strong statement about something that ought to be uncontroversial, by putting it in the form of an incredulous question" (*Isaiah 40–55*, 53).

246. Oswalt views the *knowing/hearing* interrogatives as RQs in correspondence to v. 12, but then identifies the subsequent interrogatives in v. 21aβ–b as "questions of fact" (*Isaiah Chapters 40–66*, 66) without actually defining what he means by this.

247. Kuntz, "Rhetorical Questions," 133.

also challenge Jacob-Israel to agree with and assent that no image and its representative deity compares to Yahweh. The intention of this inferred assertion is for God's people to mentally confess that Yahweh alone is God and thereby serve and worship him exclusively. To dissent from the inferred exclusive assertion and provide a counter answer to the interrogative dimension of the RQs, Jacob-Israel alternatively places its trust and hope in deities who cannot see, hear, know, speak, move and especially cannot save (45:20). While Jacob-Israel would agree that it has been told and understood that Yahweh is sovereign over creation and history (v. 21aβ–b), with the *knowing/hearing* interrogatives (40:21aα, 28a) the prophet disapprovingly, sarcastically, and ironically leads Jacob-Israel to verbally admit it does not correctly know and hear.

Yahweh remains committed, though, to blind and deaf Jacob-Israel by appointing his servant another task: to witness to itself that he alone is God (43:8–13). The Cyrus event will provide this proof (see 41:21–29; 44:28; 45:1–7); Yahweh claims that it is him alone who has *declared*, saved, and *proclaimed* (שמע) (43:12aα). Yahweh appoints his servant as his witnesses with the purpose that through his Declarative of the Cyrus event Jacob-Israel will *know* (ידע), believe, and *understand* (בין) that he alone is God (v. 10b).[248] In connection to the incomparable RQs (also 44:7–8), Yahweh's absolute uniqueness will be demonstrated through his Declarative of the Cyrus event similar to what he did in Egypt. The evidence for Jacob-Israel's old indirect confession anticipated to be verbalized afresh, its new Song (42:10), is the quickly approaching overthrow of and Israel's deliverance from Babylon which Yahweh declared long before (13:17–19). The realization of Yahweh's Declarative intends to quash any directional mismatch between Yahweh's claims about himself and the idol-gods appealed to by Jacob-Israel. Throughout chs. 40–48 the prophet reminds Jacob-Israel as well as tells the nations (cf. 45:20–25) of Yahweh's former Declarative, and thus they have now *heard* which they will all witness to with their *eyes*. The realization of Yahweh's Declarative demonstrates his incomparability. The perlocutionary goal aims at anyone among Jacob-Israel and the nations to know and testify that Yahweh alone is God. By embracing this goal, she/he will swear sole allegiance to Yahweh (cf. 44:5) and thereby include her/himself into the confessional community identified as Yahweh's servant/s.[249]

---

248. See Adams, *Performative Nature*, 100–103.
249. See ibid., 115–16; see also Joseph Blenkinsopp, "Second Isaiah—Prophet of Universalism," *JSOT* 41 (1988): 83–103, esp. 86.

Conclusion

Do you not know? Do you not hear? I ended my Introduction with a brief look at these interrogatives and then finished my select analysis of RQs with a more comprehensive examination of their function in their literary setting. One of the objectives of my research was to provide supplemental ways for *knowing* a RQ when we *hear* or *see* one as well as for identifying other similar interrogatives and expressions. Most Isaianic interpreters view these *knowing/hearing* interrogatives as RQs, but I suggest that they properly function as Conducive questions and in particular the type with matched polarity expressing surprise and disapproval. This unit in Isaiah highlights how genre, literary context, and background information play crucial roles for identifying the function of diverse types of interrogatives. Similarly and regarding the incomparability RQs, all of them infer confessionary illocutions while some contextually include a challenging dimension (e.g., Pss 35; 71; Isa 40; 46) whereas others do not (e.g., Exod 15). Primarily based on literary context, many scholars incorrectly identify a number of interrogatives as RQs while often times correctly interpreting them with matched polarity and/or in a conducive sense. As I described, Conducive questions function very similarly to RQs as both imply a specific intended answer expected or predetermined by addressers. Yet while the former retains a dimension of interrogativity whereas the latter intentionally and pragmatically transform into obvious and exclusive answers. Also, RQs characteristically reverse in polarity and in contrast the two types of Conducive questions I examined in the Hebrew Bible match in polarity.

The overarching intent of my research centered on providing additional criteria for identifying and interpreting the performative dimensions of RQs along with some of the other types of interrogatives spread throughout the pages of the Bible. As I presented in Chapter 2 and attempted to demonstrate in Chapter 3,

> RQs consist of a hybrid expression that includes a literal interrogative and an intentionally inferred answer, often an assertion that *counts as* an IA. Addressers imply an exclusive answer characteristically in the reverse polarity of the interrogative which addressees recognize through pragmatic

processes. Addressers intend addressees to mentally and self-involvingly agree with, assent to, or confirm this inferred answer which sometimes elicits a particular responsive action while addressees retain the option to respond to the interrogative dimension with a counter answer and/or opinion. RQs operate along a degrees of informativity spectrum with information-providing at one end and uninformative at the other with others lying in-between. RQs are *multidimensional* that infer multiple illocutionary forces and often times with the Assertive force primary, but sometimes other forces can function in a primary way accompanied by the Assertive conveyed to one degree or another. RQs are also *multifunctional* that infer the propositional attitudes and feelings of addressers and sometimes several emotive expressions simultaneously. What licenses interrogatives to operate as felicitous RQs is that both communicative participants share a specific knowledge about the other's beliefs and values regarding the real world. Addressees may or may not be committed to the same beliefs and values held by addressers. Addressees already know and/or can readily infer the obvious and exclusive answers that addressers imply and are utterly committed to. With any type of RQ, the ultimate intention aims at synchronizing the beliefs and commitments of both addressers and addressees.

My above analysis of RQs provides some nuances to this summary. For instance, when addressers and addressees are identical (e.g., Pss 27; 113). Or with several of the incomparable RQs (e.g., Exod 15) when the addressee (Yahweh) initiates and demonstrates the evidence for the inferred, exclusive answer that addressers then imply.

To expand upon my summary, I suggest that the primary interpretive grid for understanding the nature of RQs is to categorize them as types of ISAs which also provides ways to recognize their performative function. Although my central aim for presenting the various views of ISAs in my first chapter was to then apply that analysis for understanding RQs, I also hope that my descriptions of indirect statements will contribute towards identifying and interpreting such expressions in the biblical text as illustrated with Eliphaz's indirect claims in Job 15:10. As a type of ISA, RQs simultaneously express a linguistic interrogative while pragmatically infer an intended meaning. This incompatible inferred meaning is an obvious and exclusive answer implied by addressers and inferred by addressees through pragmatic processes. Accordingly, as highlighted by Schmidt-Radafeldt as well as Ilie, RQs are hybrid expressions. Addressees are faced with a question to answer as well as an obvious answer to infer with the intention for them to agree with, assent to, or confirm that answer. This hybrid form prompts the immediate self-involvement of addressees as RQs often provoke thoughtful engagement, contemplation, and possible counter answers and/or opinions. With the inferred answer of RQs, addressers convey their attitudinal stances while due to the multifunctionality character of RQs they can sometimes express several emotive responses simultaneously.

RQs are also often multidimensional as they convey various illocutionary forces at the same time. As interrogatives, RQs imply an overarching Directive force intending for addressees to respond. In contrast to many language specialists, Ilie demonstrates that RQs in fact do expect a response, not a verbal one, but a mental response, i.e., mental answer-eliciting. Through pragmatic processes, addressees recognize addresser's implied meaning while addressers intend agreement with and assent to that meaning. Yet, addressees can counter that intended answer with a response of their own to the interrogative dimension of the RQ. The intended answer of RQs often infers a primary Assertive force that simultaneously includes the Expressive and sometimes the Commissive forces. Thus, RQs usually infer an assertion with the Expressive related to what prompted the RQ initially as well as the inferred assertion itself. All RQs infer an Assertive force to one degree or another, but sometimes another force such as the Directive will function in a primary sense, as displayed with the RQs in Job 7 and Ps 27. With these particular RQs, the literal interrogative consists principally of verbal clauses in contrast to many RQs formed as noun clauses. As such, reconstructing the inferred propositional content should properly reflect the verbal nature of the interrogatives.

As I described in detail in Chapter 2, Ilie identified five characteristics of RQs:

- The discrepancy between the interrogative form of the RQ and its communicative function as a statement
- The polarity shift between the RQ and its implied answer
- The implicitness and the exclusiveness of the answer to the RQ
- The addresser's firm commitment to the implicit answer of the RQ
- The multifunctionality of the RQ

With certain qualifications and adjustments, these syntactico-semantic and pragmatic descriptions are key for distinguishing how interrogatives characteristically and intentionally operate as RQs. Ilie, though, does not expand in much detail on exactly *how* addressees infer an intended meaning from a linguistic interrogative. As I discussed with ISAs, this inferred area of meaning is what Grice and numerous language specialists have focused on with the concept of pragmatic processes and specifically the notion of *implicature*. Within Ilie's theoretical frame and related descriptions (see Chapter 2 and Table 2.2) I find her mistakenly bypassing the Gricean implicature dimension or pragmatic processes that Vanderveken and van Eemeren/Grootendort explicitly include in their inferential notions for ISAs, while Slot employs the latter's scheme for RQs. Where I also differ from Ilie centers on her two-fold perlocutionary goals. I wholeheartedly concur with Ilie that PEs should be conceptually incorporated into the performative function of RQs, I would also argue along the lines of van Eemeren/Grootendort, but more correspondingly with how these two specialists conceive PEs as functioning in ways that closely correlate to other speech act theorists and in particular Gu. Thus, I also propose a two-fold perlocutionary scheme, but contrastingly my Initial and Intended PEs are triggered by the inferred answer recognized through pragmatic processes while ultimately realized by addressees.

Within my proposed framework I attempt to follow a theoretical sequence of the characteristics and interpretation of RQs that also reflects their hybrid nature:

1. Literal Illocutionary Interrogative (*what is said*)
2. Inferred Illocutionary Answer
   - Implicature aspect (*what is implicated*)
   - Intentional Meaning aspect (*what is meant*)
3. Perlocutionary Effects
   - Initial Perlocutionary goal
   - Intended Perlocutionary goal (for the details of my framework see Table 2.4)

Addressees will typically understand a literal interrogative while in particular communicative contexts it may not appear that addressers elicit for some unknown information. Consequently, the literal speech act violates the communicative principles of rational conversational engagement. Addressees, though, assume addressers are conversationally cooperating and thus they are doing something different with the interrogative which addresses recognize.

Various communicative rules and felicity conditions along with the violation of some of these conditions trigger addressees' recognition that addressers are doing something beyond the literal interrogative. Towards identifying and interpreting the Inferred Illocutionary Answer and specifically the Implicature aspect, I propose the following conditions and characteristics:

- Maxim of Relevance
- Efficiency condition
- Maxim of Quality and Sincerity/Responsibility
- Elicitative Force
- Degrees on Informativity
- Directional Fit

Following van Eemeren/Grootendorst and Slot, a sequential order of conditions occurs that addressees interpretively engage with and follow: Efficiency, Quality and Sincerity/Responsibility, and Elicitative Force. Along with these, I propose other conditions that provide supplemental and complimentary criteria for identifying and interpreting RQs. In particular, through my analysis of Ilie and Rhode, I suggest viewing RQs operating along a degrees of informativity spectrum. Almost all biblical interpreters follow numerous language specialists who contrast genuine questions that *seek for information* (high information-elicitative) with RQs that conversely *provide information* (zero information-elicitation). However, Rhode argues that all RQs are *uninformative* that synchronize confirmed joint mutual beliefs and commitments of the discourse participants and thus are redundant interrogatives. As I attempted to demonstrate, not all RQs are uninformative nor are they all information-providing. Thus, as reflected in Ilie's own work, I suggest that RQs range in degree from information-providing to uninformative with others operating along this spectrum.

In an attempt to sharpen Rhode's uninformative thesis, I propose that what licenses felicitous RQs is that both discourse participants share a specific knowledge about each others' beliefs and values regarding the real world while addressees may or may not be committed to those same beliefs and values with the implied obvious and exclusive answer already known and/or readily inferable which addressers are utterly committed to. Along with this, each type of RQ can persuasively challenge addressees, but in general the more information-providing the higher degree of persuasion or challenge the answer conveys which addressees are intended to infer and ultimately agree with and assent to whereas uninformative RQs typically confirm or reinforce already mutually shared and committed beliefs and values. In Job 15, Eliphaz uses several uninformative RQs that in-and-of themselves do not convey any persuasive aspect. With Eliphaz's initial RQs (vv. 7–9), both he and Job share identical beliefs in relation to the inferred answer which also does not arouse any uncertainty and/or surprise; the implied answer is completely predictable. Thus, the RQs are not individually providing any information nor persuasively challenging

Job in any way. Yet, collectively, Eliphaz employs these RQs to set up his following claims for Job to draw specific conclusions in order to concede and assent to Eliphaz's goal. Still, as displayed with Moses' RQ as well as those in Ps 88, particular uninformative RQs can include a challenging intent while certain information-providing RQs may reinforce mutually shared beliefs and values.

Incomparability RQs are salient examples of multidimensional force and multifunctional RQs. Searle described indirect Directives and Commissive speech acts (see Chapter 1 and Table 1.3), but neither him nor any other speech act theorist to my knowledge has discussed RQs inferring illocutionary forces in any detail other than Searle's brief examples and Slot's passing claims. Although not identified as IAs, Ilie along with Schmidt-Radefeldt highlight how RQs can express diverse emotive responses as the inferred answer displays the propositional attitude of addressers. In most of the incomparability RQs I analyzed, Yahweh is the addressee while addressers speak about him. Labuschagne focuses on these types of interrogatives, which he views as persuasively effecting an addressee with the goal of becoming a *co-expresser* of an addresser's intended answer. However, with the incomparable RQs in Exod 15 and the Psalms, the inferred answer consists more in the confirmation type assertions about Yahweh which he has already previously demonstrated for the addressers. In the case of the RQ in the Song of the Sea, Yahweh is not in any way compelled to become a *co-expresser*; rather, Israel expresses an inferred answer/assertion that aligns with Yahweh's own claims about himself. Thus, this RQ is an uninformative type that does not persuade Yahweh in any way while it infers a primary Assertive force that transforms into and *counts as* an illocutionary confession. Along with the Assertive force, this RQ includes Behabitive/Expressive and Commissive forces whereby the self-involved addressers take a stance about Yahweh with accompanied entailments. Some of the Psalms I analyzed similarly infer confessionary assertions and other expressions about Yahweh, but the psalmists use their RQs with the additional contextual goal of challenging Yahweh to action (Pss 35; 71; 89). With all of these poems, contemporary readers/singers can self-involvingly engage with each by joining the identified or assume the ambiguous personal pronouns. When they reach the RQs they can simultaneously *co-confess* Yahweh's incomparability while in some instances challenge him to act based on his uniqueness so that in turn she/he can properly praise him.

Almost all RQs are multifunctional as Ilie suggests, while several of the ones I examined particularly include irony. Joseph's RQ and the ones in Ps 88 express irony primarily in relation to the surrounding literary context, whereas Job directly reflects and adapts the bicolon RQ in Ps 8 ironically. The poet in this psalm also displays with the interrogative the multidimensional nature of RQs. Accordingly, the psalmist employs multiple forces with the bicolon RQ that includes a strong primary Assertive force as well as the Expressive. RQs cannot function as genuine Exclamatives, but can indirectly infer this force in association with the Expressive force. With the bicolon RQ in Ps 8, the psalmist adopts an exclamatory stance of amazement based on the inferred assertion itself, but also prompted by the vast night sky as well as with subsequent propositions that echo Yahweh's first person speech in Gen 1. Through this bicolon RQ, self-involving readers/singers contemplate along with the original psalmist and adopt the safeguards of humble self-perception while acknowledging her/his unique nature and status within creation as well as engaging in the royal responsibilities—all while in submission to *Yahweh, our Lord*.

Returning to the incomparability RQs in Isa 40–46, these challenge the addressee Jacob-Israel in obvious distinction to those addressing Yahweh. These RQs are information-providing, inferring an obvious assertion, but not one that Jacob-Israel would readily accept. By agreeing with and assenting to the inferred assertion, Jacob-Israel mentally confesses that Yahweh alone is God. This thereby entails serving and worshipping him exclusively which, matches the nation's foundational uninformative confessionary RQ about Yahweh following its deliverance through the sea. To dissent and offer a counter answer to the interrogative dimension of the RQs, Jacob-Israel alternatively places its trust and hope in certain idol-gods who do not compare to Yahweh, who uniquely sees, hears, speaks, knows, moves, and especially saves (45:21b).

Bibliography

Abels, Klaus. "Factivity in Exclamatives is a Presupposition." *Studia Linguistica* 64 (2010): 141–57.
Abrams, M. H. *A Glossary of Literary Terms*. New York: Holt, Rinehart & Winston, 1985.
Adams, Jim W. *The Performative Nature and Function of Isaiah 40–55*. LHBOTS 448. New York/London: T&T Clark, 2006.
Alston, William P. "Illocutionary Acts and Linguistic Meaning." Pages 29–49 in *Foundations of Speech Act Theory: Philosophical and Linguistic Perspectives*. Edited by Savas L. Tsohatzidis. London/New York: Routledge, 1994.
Alston, William P. *Illocutionary Acts and Sentence Meaning*. Ithaca, NY/London: Cornell University Press, 2000.
Alston, William P. "Matching Illocutionary Act Types." Pages 151–63 in *On Being and Saying*. Edited by Judith J. Thompson. Cambridge, MA: MIT, 1987.
Alston, William P. "Searle on Illocutionary Acts." Pages 57–80 in *John Searle and His Critics*. Edited by Ernest Lepore and Robert Van Gulick. Oxford: Blackwell, 1991.
Alston, William P. "Sentence Meaning and Illocutionary Act Potential." *Philosophical Exchange* 2 (1977): 17–35.
Alter, Robert. *The Art of Biblical Poetry*. Revised and updated ed. New York: Basic, 2011.
Anzilotti, Gloria I. "The Rhetorical Question as an Indirect Speech Device in English and Italian." *Canadian Modern Language Review* 38 (1982): 290–302.
Asher, Nicholas, and Alex Lascarides. "Indirect Speech Acts." *Synthese* 128 (2001): 183–228.
Asher, Nicholas, and Alex Lascarides. "Questions in Dialogue." *Linguistics and Philosophy* 21 (1998): 237–309.
Atlas, Jay D. *Logic, Meaning, and Conversation: Semantical Underdeterminacy, Implicature, and their Interface*. New York: Oxford University Press, 2005.
Austin, J. L. *How to Do Things with Words*. 2nd ed. Edited by J. O. Urmson and Marina Sbisà. Cambridge, MA: Harvard University Press, 1975.
Bach, Kent. "Conversational Impliciture." *Mind and Language* 9 (1994): 124–62.
Bach, Kent. "Impliciture vs Explicature: What's the Difference?" Pages 126–37 in *Explicit Communication: Robyn Carston's Pragmatics*. Edited by B. Soria and E. Romero. Basingstoke: Palgrave Macmillan, 2010.
Bach, Kent. "Pragmatics and the Philosophy of Language." Pages 463–87 in *The Handbook of Pragmatics*. Edited by L. R. Horn and G. Ward. Oxford: Blackwell, 2004.
Bach, Kent. "Semantic Slack: What Is Said and More." Pages 267–91 in *Foundations of Speech Act Theory*. Edited by S. L. Tsohatzidis. London: Routledge, 1994.
Bach, Kent. "The Semantics-Pragmatics Distinction: What It Is and Why It Matters." Pages 65–84 in *The Semantic/Pragmatics Interface from Different Points of View*. Edited by Ken Turner. Oxford: Elsevier, 1999.

Bach, Kent. "Speech Acts and Pragmatics." Pages 147–67 in *Blackwell Guide to the Philosophy of Language*. Edited by M. Devitt and R. Hanley. Oxford: Blackwell, 2006.
Bach, Kent. "Standardization Revisited." Pages 712–22 in *Pragmatics: Critical Concepts, Volume 4: Presuppositions, Implicature and Indirect Speech Acts*. Edited by A. Kasher. London/New York: Routledge, 1998.
Bach, Kent. "You Don't Say." *Synthese* 128 (2001): 15–44.
Bach, Kent, and Robert M. Harnish. "How Performatives Really Work: A Reply to Searle." *Linguistics and Philosophy* 15 (1992): 93–110.
Bach, Kent, and Robert M. Harnish. *Linguistic Communication and Speech Acts*. Cambridge, MA: MIT, 1979.
Baines, John. "Ancient Egyptian Kingship: Official Forms, Rhetoric, Context." Pages 16–53 in *King and Messiah in Israel and the Ancient Near East*. LHBOTS 270. Edited by J. Day. London: T&T Clark, 2013.
Baltzer, Klaus. *Deutero-Isaiah: A Commentary on Isaiah 40–55*. Translated by Margaret Kohl. Hermeneia. Minneapolis: Fortress, 2001.
Banuazizi, Antissa, and Cassandre Creswell. "Is that a Real Question? Final Rises, Final Falls and Discourse Function in Yes–No Question Intonation." *CLS* 35 (1999): 1–14.
Beckson, Karl, and Arthur Ganz. *Literary Terms: A Dictionary*. London: André Deutsch, 1990.
Beekman, John. "Analyzing and Translating the Questions in the New Testament." *Notes on Translation* 44 (1972): 3–21.
Beekman, John, and John Callow. *Translating the Word of God*. Grand Rapids: Zondervan, 1974.
Beijer, Fabian. "The Syntax and Pragmatics of Exclamations and Other Expressive/ Emotional Utterances." *Working Papers in Linguistics* 2 (2002): 1–21.
Bell, Martin. "Questioning." *PhQ* 25 (1975): 193–21.
Bertolet, Rod. "Are There Indirect Speech Acts?" Pages 335–49 in *Foundations of Speech Act Theory*. Edited by S. L. Tsohatzidis. London: Routledge, 1994.
Beuken, W. A. M. "Job's Imprecation as the Cradle of a New Religious Discourse: The Perplexing Impact of the Semantic Correspondence between Job 3, Job 4–5 and Job 6–7." Pages 41–78 in *The Book of Job*. BETL 114. Edited by W. A. M. Beuken. Leuven: Leuven University Press, 1994.
Bianchi, Claudia, ed. *The Semantics/Pragmatics Distinction*. Stanford, CA: CSLI, 2004.
Black, Edwin. *Rhetorical Questions: Studies in Public Discourse*. Chicago/London: Chicago University Press, 1992.
Blenkinsopp, Joseph. *Isaiah 40–55*. AB 19A. New York: Doubleday, 2002.
Blenkinsopp, Joseph. "Second Isaiah—Prophet of Universalism." *JSOT* 41 (1988): 83–103.
Blyth, Caroline. "'I am Alone with My Sickness': Voicing the Experience of HIV- and Aids-Related Stigma Through Psalm 88." *Colloquium* 44 (2012): 149–62.
Bolinger, Dwight L. *Interrogative Structures of American English (The Direct Question)*. Publication of the American Dialect Society 28. Alabama: University of Alabama Press, 1957.
Bolinger, Dwight L. "Yes–No Questions are not Alternative Questions." Pages 87–105 in *Questions*. Edited by H. Hiz. Dordrecht/Boston: D. Reidel Publishing, 1978.
Bonhême, Marie-Ange. "Kingship." Pages 238–45 in vol. 2 in *The Oxford Encyclopedia of Ancient Egypt*. Edited by D. B. Redford. Oxford: Oxford University Press, 2001.
Borkin, Ann. "Polarity Items in Questions." *CLS* 7 (1971): 53–62.
Braun, David. "Implicating Questions." *Mind & Language* 26 (2011): 574–95.

Breasted, James H. *Ancient Records of Egypt*. 3 vols. Chicago: University of Chicago Press, 1906–1907.
Brenner, Martin L. *The Song of the Sea: Ex 15:1–21*. BZAW 195. Berlin: de Gruyter, 1991.
Briggs, Richard S. *Words in Action: Speech Act Theory and Biblical Interpretation. Toward a Hermeneutic of Self-Involvement*. Edinburgh: T. & T. Clark, 2001.
Brown, Penelope, and Stephen C. Levinson. *Politeness: Some Universals in Language Usage*. Studies in Interactional Sociolinguistics 4. Cambridge: Cambridge University Press, 1987.
Brueggemann, Walter. *Genesis*. Int. Atlanta: John Knox, 1982.
Brueggemann, Walter. *Isaiah 40–66*. Louisville: Westminster John Knox, 1998.
Brueggemann, Walter. "Jeremiah's Use of Rhetorical Questions." *JBL* 92 (1973): 358–74.
Brueggemann, Walter. *The Message of the Psalms: A Theological Commentary*. Minneapolis: Augsburg, 1984.
Brueggemann, Walter, and William H. Bellinger, Jr. *Psalms*. NCBC. Cambridge: Cambridge University Press, 2014.
Bublitz, Wolfram. "Conducive Yes–No Questions in English." *Linguistics* 19 (1981): 851–70.
Carston, Robyn. "Linguistic Meaning, Communicated Meaning and Cognitive Pragmatics." *Mind & Language* 17 (2002): 127–48.
Carston, Robyn. "Implicature, Explicature, and Truth-Theoretic Semantics." Pages 155–81 in *Mental Representations: The Interface between Language and Reality*. Edited by R. M. Kempson. Cambridge: Cambridge University Press, 1988.
Carston, Robyn. "Relevance Theory and the Saying/Implicating Distinction." Pages 633–56 in *The Handbook of Pragmatics*. Edited by L. R. Horn and G. Ward. Oxford: Blackwell, 2004.
Carston, Robyn. "Word Meaning, What Is Said and Explicature." Pages 175–203 in *What Is Said and What Is Not: The Semantics/Pragmatics Interface*. Edited by C. Penco and F. Domaneschi. Stanford: CSLI Publications, 2013.
Cassuto, U. *A Commentary on the Book of Genesis. Part One: From Adam to Noah*. Translated by I. Abrahams. Jerusalem: Magnes, 1961.
Chafe, Wallace L. *Meaning and the Structure of Language*. Chicago: University of Chicago Press, 1970.
Childs, Brevard S. *The Book of Exodus: A Critical, Theological Commentary*. OTL. Louisville: Westminster, 1974.
Childs, Brevard S. *Isaiah*. OTL. Louisville: Westminster John Knox, 2001.
Chisholm Jr., William S., ed. *Interrogativity: A Colloquium on the Grammar, Typology and Pragmatics of Questions in Seven Diverse Languages*. Typological Studies in Language 4. Amsterdam/Philadelphia: John Benjamins Publishing, 1984.
Clark, Donald L. *Rhetoric in Greco-Roman Education*. Morningside Heights, New York: Columbia University Press, 1957.
Clifford, Richard J. "The Function of Idol Passages in Second Isaiah." *CBQ* 42 (1980): 450–64.
Clines, David J. A. *Job 1–20*. WBC 17. Dallas: Word, 1989.
Clines, David J. A. "The Parallelism of Greater Precision: Notes form Isaiah 40 for a Theory of Hebrew Poetry." Pages 77–100 in *Directions of Biblical Hebrew Poetry*. Edited by E. R. Follis. JSOTSup 40. Sheffield: Sheffield Academic, 1987.
Coats, George W. *Exodus 1–18*. FOTL 2/A. Grand Rapids: Eerdmans, 1999.
Coats, George W. "Self-Abasement and Insult Formulas." *JBL* 89 (1970): 14–26.

Cohen, Felix S. "What Is a Question?" *The Monist* 39 (1929): 350–64.
Cohen, Philip R., and Hector J. Levesque. "Rational Interaction as the Basis for Communication." Pages 221–55 in *Intentions in Communication*. Edited by P. R. Cohen et al. Cambridge, MA: MIT, 1990.
Cohen, Philip R., and Hector J. Levesque. "Speech Acts and the Recognition of Shared Plans." Pages 263–71 in *Proceedings of the Third Biennial Conference of the Canadian Society for Computational Studies of Intelligence*. Victoria, BC: University of Victoria, 1980.
Cole, Peter. "The Synchronic and Diachronic Status of Conversational Implicature." Pages 257–88 in *Syntax and Semantics 3: Speech Acts*. Edited by P. Cole and J. L. Morgan. New York: Academic, 1975.
Collins, Peter. "Exclamative Clauses in English." *Word* 56 (2005): 1–17.
Conant, James. "Wittgenstein on Meaning and Use." *Philosophical Investigations* 21 (1998): 222–50.
Cope, E. M. *An Introduction to Aristotle's Rhetoric*. London: Macmillan, 1867.
Craig Jr., Kenneth M. "Questions Outside of Eden (Genesis 4.1–16): Yahweh, Cain and their Rhetorical Interchange." *JSOT* 86 (1999): 107–28.
Craigie, Peter C. *Psalms 1–50*. WBC 19. Waco: Word, 1983.
Crenshaw, James L. "Impossible Questions, Sayings, and Tasks." *Semeia* 17 (1980): 19–34.
Cross, Frank M., and David N. Freedman. *Studies in Ancient Yahwistic Poetry*. BRS. Grand Rapids: Eerdmans, 1975.
Crüsemann, Frank. "Rhetorische Fragen!? Eine Aufkündigung des Konsenses über Psalm 88:11–13 und Seine Bedeutung für das Alttestamentliche Reden von Gott und Tod." *BibInt* 11 (2003): 345–60.
Cuddon, J. A. *The Penguin Dictionary of Literary Terms and Literary Theory*. Revised by C. E. Preston. Oxford: Blackwell, 1998.
Culley, Robert C. "Psalm 88 Among the Complaints." Pages 289–302 in *Ascribe to the Lord: Biblical and Other Essays in Memory of P. C. Craigie*. JSOTSup 67. Edited by L. Eslinger and G. Taylor. Sheffield: JSOT, 1988.
Currid, John D. *Ancient Egypt and the Old Testament*. Grand Rapids: Baker, 1997.
Dahood, Mitchell. *Psalms II: 51–100*. AB 17. Garden City: Doubleday, 1968.
Dascal, Marcelo. "Speech Act Theory and Gricean Pragmatics: Some Differences of Detail that Make a Difference." Pages 323–34 in *Foundations of Speech Act Theory: Philosophical and Linguistic Perspectives*. Edited by Savas L. Tsohatzidis. London/ New York: Routledge, 1994.
Davison, Alice. "Indirect Speech Acts and What to Do with Them." Pages 143–85 in *Syntax and Semantics 3: Speech Acts*. Edited by P. Cole and J. L. Morgan. New York: Academic, 1975.
de Regt, Lénart J. "Discourse Implications of Rhetorical Questions in Job, Deuteronomy and the Minor Prophets." Pages 51–78 in *Literary Structure and Rhetorical Strategies in the Hebrew Bible*. Edited by Lénart J. de Regt, J. de Waard, and J. P. Fokkelman. Assen: Van Gorcum, 1996.
de Regt, Lénart J. "Implications of Rhetorical Questions in Strophes in Job 11 and 15." Pages 321–28 in *The Book of Job*. BETL 114. Edited by W. A. M. Beuken. Leuven: Leuven University Press, 1994.
Dion, P. E. "Formulaic Language in the Book of Job: International Background and Ironical Distortions." *SR* 16 (1987): 187–9.

Dozeman, Thomas B. "The Commission of Moses and the Book of Genesis." Pages 107–29 in *A Farewell to the Yahwist? The Composition of the Pentateuch in Recent European Interpretation*. SBLSS 34. Edited by Thomas B. Dozeman and K. Schmid. Atlanta: Society of Biblical Literature, 2006.

Durham, John I. *Exodus*. WBC 3. Waco: Word, 1987.

Elliott, Dale E. "Toward a Grammar of Exclamations." *Foundations of Language* 11 (1974): 231–46.

Ene (Ilie), Cornelia. "Rhetorical Questions within the Theory of Speech Acts." *Cahiers de Linguistique Théorique et Appliqué* 20 (1983): 35–54.

Ene (Ilie), Cornelia. "Text Analysis of Rhetorical Questions." *Rêvue Roumaine de Linguistique* 28 (1983): 307–16.

Evans, Donald D. *The Logic of Self-Involvement: A Philosophical Study of Everyday Language with Special Reference to the Christian Use of Language about God as Creator*. London: SCM, 1963.

Fiengo, Robert. *Asking Questions: Using Meaningful Structures to Imply Ignorance*. Oxford: Oxford University Press, 2007.

Fishbane, Michael. *Biblical Interpretation in Ancient Israel*. Oxford: Clarendon, 1985.

Frank, Jane. "You Call that a Rhetorical Question?" *JP* 14 (1970): 723–38.

Frápolli, María J., and Robyn Carston. "Introduction: Representation and Metarepresentation." Pages 1–17 in *Saying, Meaning and Referring*. Palgrave Studies in Pragmatic, Language and Cognition. Edited by M. J. Frápolli. New York: Palgrave Macmillan, 2007.

Freedman, David N. *Pottery, Poetry, and Prophecy: Studies in Early Hebrew Poetry*. Winona Lake: Eisenbrauns, 1980.

Fretheim, Terence E. *Exodus*. Interpretation. Louisville: John Knox, 1991.

Garcìa-Carpintero, Manuel. "Explicit Performatives, What Is Said, and the Social Character of Assertion." Pages 99–126 in *What Is Said and What Is Not: The Semantics/Pragmatics Interface*. CSLI Lecture Notes 207. Edited by C. Penco and F. Domaneschi. Stanford: CSLI, 2013.

Gazdar, Gerald. "Speech Act Assignment." Pages 64–83 in *Elements of Discourse Understanding*. Edited by A. K. Joshi et al. Cambridge: Cambridge University Press, 1981.

Geis, Michael L. *Speech Acts and Conversational Interaction: Toward a Theory of Conversational Competence*. Cambridge: Cambridge University Press, 1995.

Gerstenberger, Erhard S. "Psalms." Pages 179–223 in *Old Testament Form Criticism*. Edited by J. H. Hayes. San Antonio: Trinity University Press, 1974.

Gerstenberger, Erhard S. *Psalms, Part 2 and Lamentations*. FOTL 15. Grand Rapids: Eerdmans, 2001.

Goldingay, John. *The Message of Isaiah 40–55: A Literary-Theological Commentary*. London/New York: T&T Clark, 2005.

Goldingay, John. *Old Testament Theology, Volume 1: Israel's Gospel*. Downers Grove: InterVarsity, 2003.

Goldingay, John. *Psalms, Volume 1: Psalms 1–41*. BCOT. Grand Rapids: Baker Academic, 2006.

Goldingay, John. *Psalms, Volume 2: Psalms 41–89*. BCOT. Grand Rapids: Baker Academic, 2007.

Goldingay, John. *Psalms, Volume 3: Psalms 90–150*. BCOT. Grand Rapids: Baker Academic, 2008.

Gordis, Robert. "A Rhetorical Use of Interrogative Sentences in Biblical Hebrew." *AJSL* 49 (1932/33): 212–17.

Gordon, David, and George Lakoff. "Conversational Postulates." Pages 83–106 in *Syntax and Semantics 3: Speech Acts*. Edited by P. Cole and J. L. Morgan. New York: Academic, 1975.

Gordon, Robert P. "The Gods Must Die: A Theme in Isaiah and Beyond." Pages 45–61 in *Isaiah in Context: Studies in Honour of Arie van der Kooij on the Occasion of his Sixty-Fifth Birthday*. Edited by Michael N. van der Meer et al. VTSup 138. Leiden: Brill, 2010.

Gow, M. D. "Fall." Pages 285–91 in *Dictionary of the Old Testament: Pentateuch*. Edited by T. D. Alexander and D. W. Baker. Downers Grove: Intervarsity, 2003.

Gowan, Donald E. *Theology in Exodus: Biblical Theology in the Form of a Commentary*. Louisville: Westminster John Knox, 1994.

Green, Georgia M. "How to Get People to Do Things with Words: The Whimperative Question." Pages 107–41 in *Syntax and Semantics 3: Speech Acts*. Edited by P. Cole and J. L. Morgan. New York: Academic, 1975.

Green, Georgia M. *Pragmatics and Natural Language Understanding*. 2nd ed. New York/ London: Routledge, 1996.

Green, Georgia M. "The Universality of Gricean Interpretation." *Berkeley Linguistics Society* 16 (1990): 411–28.

Grice, H. P. "Logic and Conversation." Pages 41–58 in *Syntax and Semantics 3: Speech Acts*. Edited by P. Cole and J. L. Morgan. New York: Academic, 1975.

Grice, H. P. "Meaning." Pages 39–48 in *Philosophical Logic*. Edited by P. F. Strawson. Oxford: Oxford University Press, 1971.

Grice, H. P. *Studies in the Way of Words*. Cambridge, MA/London: Harvard University Press, 1989.

Grimshaw, Jane. "Complement Selection and the Lexicon." *Linguistic Inquiry* 10 (1979): 279–326.

Gu, Yueguo. "The Impasse of Perlocution." *JP* 20 (1993): 405–32.

Gunkel, Hermann. *Genesis*. MLBS. Translated by M. E. Biddle. Macon: Mercer University Press, 1997.

Gunlogson, Christine. "True to Form: Rising and Falling Declaratives as Questions in English." PhD diss., University of California, 2001.

Habel, Norman C. *The Book of Job*. OTL. Philadelphia: Westminster, 1985.

Habel, Norman C. "The Form and Significance of the Call Narrative." *ZAW* 77 (1965): 297–323.

Han, Chung-hye. "Deriving the Interpretation of Rhetorical Questions." *Proceedings of the 16th West Coast Conference on Formal Linguistics* 16 (1978): 1–17.

Han, Chung-hye. "Interpreting Interrogatives as Rhetorical Questions." *Lingua* 112 (2002): 201–29.

Hancher, Michael. "The Classification of Cooperative Illocutionary Acts." *Language and Society* 8 (1979): 1–14.

Hartley, John E. *The Book of Job*. NICOT. Grand Rapids: Eerdmans, 1988.

Hartley, John E. *Genesis*. NIBCOT. Peabody: Hendrickson, 2000.

Hasan, Nadia Amin. "Exclamation in English and Arabic: A Contrastive Study." *International Journal of Science Commerce and Humanities* 2 (2014): 174–98.

Hauser, Alan J. "Two Songs of Victory: A Comparison of Exodus 15 and Judges 5." Pages 265–84 in *Directions in Biblical Hebrew Poetry*. Edited by E. R. Follis. JSOTSup 40. Sheffield: Sheffield Academic, 1987.

Higginbotham, James. "The Semantics of Questions." Pages 361–83 in *The Handbook of Contemporary Semantic Theory*. Blackwell Handbooks in Linguistics. Edited by S. Lappin. Oxford: Blackwell, 1996.

Hoffmeier, James K. "The Arm of God Versus the Arm of Pharaoh in the Exodus Narrative." *Bib* 67 (1986): 378–87.

Hoffmeier, James K. "Egypt, Plagues in." *ABD* 2:374–78.

Hoffmeier, James K. *Israel in Egypt: The Evidence for the Authenticity of the Exodus Tradition*. Oxford: Oxford University Press, 1996.

Holdcroft, David. "Indirect Speech Acts and Propositional Content." Pages 350–64 in *Foundations of Speech Act Theory*. Edited by S. L. Tsohatzidis. London: Routledge, 1994.

Holroyd, Kristofer. *A (S)word Against Babylon: An Examination of the Multiple Speech Acts Layers within Jeremiah 50–51*. Siphrut 22. Winona Lake: Eisenbrauns, 2017.

Holter, Knut. *Second Isaiah's Idol-Fabrication Passages*. BBET 28. Frankfurt: Peter Lang, 1995.

Horn, Laurence R. "Implicature." Pages 3–28 in *The Handbook of Pragmatics*. Edited by Laurence R. Horn and G. Ward. Oxford: Blackwell Publishing, 2004.

Horn, Laurence R. "Postscript (1995): Neg-Raising Revisited: Tinkering with the Short-Circuit." Pages 676–81 in *Pragmatics: Critical Concepts. Volume 4: Presuppositions, Implicature and Indirect Speech Acts*. Edited by A. Kasher. London/New York: Routledge, 1998.

Horn, Laurence R. "Pragmatic Theory." Pages 113–45 in *Linguistics: The Cambridge Survey, Volume 1: Linguistic Theory: Foundations*. Edited by F. J. Newmeyer. Cambridge: Cambridge University Press, 1988.

Horn, Laurence R., and Samuel Bayer. "Short-Circuited Implicature: A Negative Contribution." Pages 658–76 in *Pragmatics: Critical Concepts, Volume 4: Presuppositions, Implicature and Indirect Speech Acts*. Edited by A. Kasher. London/New York: Routledge, 1998. Reprint of "Short-Circuited Implicature: A Negative Contribution." *Linguistics and Philosophy* 7 (1984): 397–414.

Horn, Laurence R., and Gregory Ward, eds. *The Handbook of Pragmatics*. Oxford: Blackwell, 2004.

Hornsby, Jennifer. "Illocution and its Significance." Pages 187–207 in *Foundations of Speech Act Theory: Philosophical and Linguistic Perspectives*. Edited by S. L. Tsohatzidis. New York/London: Routledge, 1994.

Hossfeld, Frank-Lothar, and Erich Zenger. *Psalms 2: A Commentary on Psalms 51–100*. Hermeneia. Translated by L. M. Maloney. Minneapolis: Fortress, 2005.

Huang, Yan. *Pragmatics*. Oxford Textbooks in Linguistics. Oxford: Oxford University Press, 2007.

Huang, Yan. "Speech Acts." Pages 656–65 in vol. 11 of *The Encyclopedia of Language and Linguistics*. 14 vols. 2d ed. Edited by K. Brown. New York: Elsevier Science, 2006.

Huddleston, Rodney. "Clause Type and Illocutionary Force." Pages 851–945 in *The Cambridge Grammar of the English Language*. Edited by Rodney Huddleston and G. K. Pullman in Collaboration with Laurie Bauer et al. Cambridge: Cambridge University Press, 2002.

Huddleston, Rodney. "On Exclamatory-Inversion Sentences in English." *Lingua* 90 (1993): 259–69.

Hudson, Richard A. "The Meaning of Questions." *Language* 51 (1975): 1–31.

Hungerland, Isabel C. "Contextual Implication." *Inquiry* 3 (1960): 211–58.

Hyman, Ronald T. "Questions in the Joseph Story: The Effects and Their Implications for Teaching." *Religious Education* 79 (1984): 437–55.
Ilie, Cornelia. "Rhetorical Questions." Pages 405–407 in *The Routledge Pragmatics Encyclopedia*. Edited by Louise Cummings. London/New York: Routledge, 2013.
Ilie, Cornelia. *What Else Can I Tell You? A Pragmatic Study of English Rhetorical Questions as Discursive and Argumentative Acts*. Stockholm Studies in English 82. Stockholm: Almqvist & Wiksell International, 1994.
Janzen, J. Gerald. *Job*. Int. Atlanta: John Knox Press, 1985.
Jaszczolt, K. M. "Default Semantics, Pragmatics, and Intentions." Pages 200–203 in *The Semantic/Pragmatics Interface from Different Points*. Edited by K. Turner. Oxford: Elsevier, 1999.
Johnson, Jr., Raymond E. "The Rhetorical Question as a Literary Device in Ecclesiastes." PhD diss., The Southern Baptist Theological Seminary, 1986.
Kiefer, Ferenc. "Yes–No Questions as Wh-Questions." Pages 97–119 in *Speech Act Theory and Pragmatics*. Texts and Studies in Linguistics and Philosophy 10. Edited by J. R. Searle, Ferenc Kiefer, and M. Bierwisch. Dordrecht: Reidel, 1980.
Kitchen, K. A. *On the Reliability of the Old Testament*. Grand Rapids: Eerdmans, 2003.
König, Ekkehard, and Peter Siemund. "Speech Act Distinctions in Grammar." Pages 276–324 in *Language Typology and Syntactic Description, Volume 1: Clause Structure*. 2nd ed. Edited by T. Shopen. Cambridge: Cambridge University Press, 2007.
Koole, Jan L. *Isaiah Part 3, Volume 1: Isaiah 40–48*. HCOT. Translated by A. P. Runia. Kampen: KOK Pharos Publishing House, 1997.
Koops, Robert. "Rhetorical Questions and Implied Meaning in the Book of Job." *BT* 39 (1988): 415–23.
Korta, Kepa, and John Perry. "How to Say Things with Words." Pages 169–89 in *John Searle's Philosophy of Language: Force, Meaning and Mind*. Edited by S. L. Tsohatzidis. Cambridge: Cambridge University Press, 2007.
Korta, Kepa, and John Perry. "Three Demonstrations and a Funeral." *Mind & Language* 21 (2006): 168.
Kraus, Hans-Joachim. *Psalms 1–59*. Translated by H. C. Oswald. Minneapolis: Augsburg, 1988.
Kraus, Hans-Joachim. *Psalms 60–150*. Translated by H. C. Oswald. Minneapolis: Fortress, 1993.
Kuntz, J. Kenneth. "The Form, Location, and Function of Rhetorical Questions in Deutero-Isaiah." Pages 121–41 in vol. 1 of *Writing and Reading the Scroll of Isaiah*. VTSup 70. Edited by C. C. Broyles and C. A. Evans. Leiden: Brill, 1997.
Kuntz, J. Kenneth. "Making a Statement: Rhetorical Questions in the Hebrew Psalter." Pages 156–78 in *Probing the Frontiers of Biblical Studies*. PTMS. Edited by J. H. Ellens and J. T. Greene. Eugene, OR: Pickwick, 2009.
Labuschagne, C. J. *The Incompatibility of Yahweh in the Old Testament*. Pretoria Oriental Series 5. Leiden: Brill, 1966.
Landy, Francis. "Humour as a Tool for Biblical Exegesis." Pages 99–115 in *On Humour and the Comic in the Hebrew Bible*. JSOTSup 92. Bible and Literature Series 23. Edited by Y. T. Radday and A. Brenner. Sheffield: Almond, 1990.
Larkin, Don, and Michael H. O'Malley. "Declarative Sentences and the Rule-of-Conversation Hypothesis." *CLS* 9 (1973): 306–19.
Leech, Geoffrey N. *A Linguistic Guide to English Poetry*. London: Longman, 1973.
Leech, Geoffrey N. *Principles of Pragmatics*. London/New York: Longman, 1983.

Levinson, Stephen C. *Pragmatics*. Cambridge Textbooks in Linguistics. Cambridge: Cambridge University Press, 1983.
Levinson, Stephen C. *Presumptive Meanings: The Theory of Generalized Conversational Implicature*. Cambridge, MA: MIT, 2000.
Llewelyn, John E. "What Is a Question." *The Australian Journal of Philosophy* 42 (1964): 69–85.
Loar, Brian. "Language, Thought, and Meaning." Pages 77–90 in *The Blackwell Guide to the Philosophy of Language*. Edited by M. Devitt and R. Hanley. Oxford: Blackwell, 2006.
Longman III, Tremper. "Lament." Pages 197–215 in *Cracking Old Testament Codes*. Edited by D. B. Sandy and R. L. Giese, Jr. Nashville: Broadman & Holman, 1995.
Louth, Andrew, ed. *Genesis 1–11*. ACCS. Downers Grove: InterVarsity, 2001.
Lund, Øystein. "From the Mouth of Babes and Infants you have Established Strength." *Scandinavian Journal of the Old Testament* 11 (1997): 78–99.
Lundbom, Jack R. "God's Use of the Idem per Idem to Terminate Debate." *HTR* 71 (1978): 193–201.
Lycan, William G. *Logical Form in Natural Language*. Cambridge, MA: MIT, 1984.
Mandolfo, Carleen. "Psalm 88 and the Holocaust: Lament in Search of a Divine Response." *BibInt* 15 (2007): 151–70.
Mays, James L. *Psalms*. Int. Louisville: John Knox, 1994.
McKenzie, John L. *Second Isaiah*. AB 20. Garden City: Doubleday, 1968.
Meibauer, Jörg. *Rhetorische Fragen*. Tübingen: Max Niemeyer, 1986.
Melugin Roy F. "Deutero-Isaiah and Form Criticism." *VT* 21 (1971): 326–37.
Melugin Roy F. *The Formation of Isaiah 40–55*. BZAW 141. Berlin: de Gruyter, 1976.
Merendino, Rosario P. *Der Erste und der Letzte: Eine Untersuchung von Jes 40–48*. VTSup 31. Leiden: Brill, 1981.
Mettinger, T. N. D. *The Eden Narrative: A Literary and Religio-historical Study of Genesis 2–3*. Winona Lake: Eisenbrauns, 2007.
Mettinger, T. N. D. *King and Messiah: The Civil and Sacral Legitimation of the Israelite Kings*. ConBOT 8. Lund: Gleerup, 1976.
Meulen ter, Alice. "Linguistics and the Philosophy of Language." Pages 430–46 in *Linguistics: The Cambridge Survey, Volume 1: Linguistics Theory: Foundations*. Edited by F. J. Newmeyer. Cambridge: Cambridge University Press, 1988.
Michaelis, Laura A. "Exclamative Constructions." Pages 1038–50 in *Language Typology and Language Universals, Volume 2*. Edited by M. Haspelmath et al. Berlin/New York: de Gruyter, 2001.
Michaelis, Laura A., and Knud Lambrecht. "The Exclamative Sentence Type in English." Pages 375–89 in *Conceptual Structure, Discourse and Language*. Edited by A. E. Goldberg. Stanford: CSLI, 1996.
Miller, Patrick D. *Interpreting the Psalms*. Philadelphia: Fortress, 1989.
Miller, Patrick D. *They Cried to the Lord: The Form and Theology of Biblical Prayer*. Minneapolis: Fortress, 1994.
Moberly, R. W. L. *The Old Testament of the Old Testament: Patriarchal Narratives and Mosaic Yahwism*. OBT. Minneapolis: Fortress, 1992.
Morgan, J. L. "Conversational Postulates Revisited." *Language* 53 (1977): 277–84.
Morgan, J. L. "Two Types of Convention in Indirect Speech Acts." Pages 261–80 in *Syntax and Semantics 9: Pragmatics*. Edited by P. Cole. New York: Academic, 1978.
Moshavi, Adina. "הלא as a Discourse Marker of Justification in Biblical Hebrew." *HS* 48 (2007): 171–86.

Moshavi, Adina. "Can a Positive Rhetorical Question have a Positive Answer in the Bible?" *JSS* 56 (2011): 253–73.
Moshavi, Adina. "'Is That Your Voice, My Son David?' Conducive Questions in Biblical Hebrew." *JNSL* 36 (2010): 65–81.
Moshavi, Adina. "Rhetorical Question or Assertion? The Pragmatics of הלא in Biblical Hebrew." *JNES* 32 (2011): 91–105.
Moshavi, Adina. "Syntactic Evidence for a Clausal Adverb הלא in Biblical Hebrew." *JNSL* 33 (2007): 51–63.
Moshavi, Adina. "Two Types of Argumentation Involving Rhetorical Questions in Biblical Hebrew Dialogue." *Bib* 90 (2009): 32–46.
Moshavi, Adina. "What Can I Say? Implications and Communicative Functions of Rhetorical 'WH' Questions in Classical Biblical Hebrew Prose." *VT* 64 (2014): 93–108.
Mowinckel, Sigmund. *The Psalms in Israel's Worship*. 2 vols. Translated by D. R. Ap-Thomas. New York: Abingdon, 1962.
Muilenburg, James. "A Liturgy on the Triumphs of Yahweh." Pages 233–51 in *Studia Biblica et Semitica*. Festschrift T. C. Vriezen. Wageningen: H. Veenman, 1966.
Mullen, E. Theodore, Jr. *The Divine Council in Canaanite and Early Hebrew Literature*. HSM 24. Chico: Scholars Press, 1980.
Naidoff, Bruce D. "The Rhetoric of Encouragement in Isaiah 40 12–31: A Form-Critical Study." *ZAW* 93 (1981): 62–76.
Nida, E. A., et al. *Style and Discourse: With Special Reference to the Text of the Greek New Testament*. Cape Town: Bible Society, 1983.
Noth, Martin. *Exodus*. Translated by J. S. Bowden. OTL. Philadelphia: Westminster, 1962.
Nowell, Irene. "Psalms 88: A Lesson in Lament." Pages 105–18 in *Imagery and Imagination in Biblical Literature*. Festschrift Aloysius Fitzgerald. CBQMS 32. Edited by L. Boadt and M. S. Smith. Washington: Catholic Biblical Association, 2001.
Oswalt, John N. *The Book of Isaiah, Chapters 40–66*. NICOT. Grand Rapids: Eerdmans, 1998.
Patrick, Dale. *The Rhetoric of Revelation in the Hebrew Bible*. OBT. Minneapolis: Fortress, 1999.
Paul, Shalom M. *Isaiah 40–66: Translation and Commentary*. ECC. Grand Rapids: Eerdmans, 2012.
Penco, Carlo, and Filippo Domaneschi. "What Is Said: A Short History in Quotes." Pages 1–12 in *What Is Said and What Is Not: The Semantic/Pragmatics Interface*. CSLI Lecture Notes Number 207. Edited by Carlo Penco and Filippo Domaneschi. Stanford: CSLI, 2013.
Perdue, Leo G. "Metaphorical Theology in the Book of Job: Theological Anthropology in the First Cycle of Job's Speeches (Job 3; 6–7; 9–10)." Pages 129–56 in *The Book of Job*. BETL 114. Edited by W. A. M. Beuken. Leuven: Leuven University Press, 1994.
Perdue, Leo G. *Wisdom & Creation: The Theology of Wisdom Literature*. Nashville: Abingdon, 1994.
Perdue, Leo G. *Wisdom in Revolt: Metaphorical Theology in the Book of Job*. JSOTSup 112. Sheffield: JSOT Press, 1991.
Perdue, Leo G. *Wisdom Literature: A Theological History*. Louisville: Westminster John Knox, 2007.
Perrault, C. Raymond. "An Application of Default Logic to Speech Act Theory." Pages 161–85 in *Intentions in Communication*. Edited by P. R. Cohen et al. Cambridge, MA: MIT, 1990.

Peterson, Eugene H. *Answering God: The Psalms as Tools for Prayer*. New York: HarperCollins, 1989.
Piazza, Robert. "The Pragmatic of Conducive Questions in Academic Discourse." *JP* 34 (2002): 509–27.
Pope, Emily Norwood. *Questions and Answers in English*. The Hague/Paris: Mouton, 1976.
Pope, Marvin H. *Job*. AB 15. New York: Doubleday, 1973.
Quintilian. *The Institutio Oratoria of Quintilian*. Translated by H. E. Butler. Cambridge, MA: Harvard University Press, 1943.
Quirk, R., S. Greenbaum, G. Leech, and J. Svartyik. *A Grammar of Contemporary English*. London: Longman, 1974.
Quirk, R., S. Greenbaum, G. Leech, and J. Svartvik. *A Comprehensive Grammar of the English Language*. London/New York: Longman, 1985.
Rad, Gerhard von. *Old Testament Theology, Volume 1*. Translated by D. M. G. Stalker. New York: Harper & Row, 1962.
Rad, Gerhard von. *Wisdom in Israel*. Translated by J. D. Martin. Valley Forge: Trinity Press International, 1972.
Rakić, Stanimir. "Serbo-Croatian Yes/No-Questions and Speech Acts." *JP* 8 (1984): 693–713.
Reboul, Olivier. *Introduction à la rhétorique*. Paris: Presses Universitaires de France, 1991.
Récanati, François. "The Alleged Priority of Literal Interpretation." *Cognitive Science* 19 (1995): 207–32.
Récanati, François. "Contextualism and Anti-Contextualism in the Philosophy of Language." Pages 156–66 in *Foundations of Speech Act Theory: Philosophical and Linguistic Perspectives*. Edited by Savas L. Tsohatzidis. London/New York: Routledge, 1994.
Récanati, François. *Direct Reference: From Language to Thought*. Oxford: Blackwell, 1993.
Récanati, François. "Does Linguistic Communication Rest on Inference." *Mind & Language* 17 (2002): 105–26.
Récanati, François. "The Limits of Expressibility." Pages 189–213 in *John Searle*. Contemporary Philosophy in Focus. Edited by B. Smith. Cambridge: Cambridge University Press, 2003.
Récanati, François. *Literal Meaning*. Cambridge: Cambridge University Press, 2004.
Récanati, François. "Literal/Nonliteral." *Midwest Studies in Philosophy* 25 (2001): 264–74.
Récanati, François. *Meaning and Force: The Pragmatics of Performative Utterances*. Cambridge: Cambridge University Press, 1987.
Récanati, François. *Oratio Obliqua, Oratio Recta: An Essay on Metarepresentation*. Cambridge, MA: MIT, 2000.
Récanati, François. "Pragmatics and Semantics." Pages 442–62 in *The Handbook of Pragmatics*. Edited by L. R. Horn and G. Ward. Oxford: Blackwell, 2004.
Récanati, François. "The Pragmatics of What Is Said." *Mind and Language* 4 (1989): 295–329.
Récanati, François. "Some Remarks on Explicit Performatives, Indirect Speech Acts, Locutionary Meaning and Truth-Value." Pages 205–20 in *Speech Act Theory and Pragmatics*. Texts and Studies in Linguistics and Philosophy 10. Edited by John R. Searle, Ferenc Kiefer, and Manfred Bierwisch. Dordrecht: Reidel, 1980.

Récanati, François. "What Is Said." *Synthese* 128 (2001): 75–91.
Récanati, François. "'What Is Said' and the Semantics/Pragmatics Distinction." Pages 45–64 in *The Semantics/Pragmatics Distinction*. Edited by Claudia Bianchi. Stanford, CA: CSLI, 2004.
Rett, Jessica. "Exclamatives, Degrees and Speech Acts." *Linguist and Philos* 34 (2011): 411–42.
Riemann, Paul A. "Am I My Brother's Keeper?" *Int* 24 (1970): 482–91.
Rosengren, Inger. "Expressive Sentence Types—A Contradiction in Terms. The Case of Exclamation." Pages 151–84 in *Modality in Germanic Languages: Historical and Comparative Perspectives*. Trends in Linguistics: Studies and Monographs 99. Edited by T. Swan and O. J. Westvik. Berlin: de Gruyter, 1997.
Rohde, Hannah. "Rhetorical Questions as Redundant Interrogatives." *San Diego Linguistics Papers* 2 (2006): 134–68.
Sadock, Jerrold M. "On Testing for Conversational Implicature." Pages 281–97 in *Syntax and Semantics 9: Pragmatics*. Edited by P. Cole. New York: Academic Press, 1978.
Sadock, Jerrold M. "Queclaratives." *Papers from the Seventh Regional Meeting of the Chicago Linguistic Society* 7 (1971): 223–31.
Sadock, Jerrold M. "Speech Act Idioms." *CLS* (1972): 329–39.
Sadock, Jerrold M. "Speech Acts." Pages 53–73 in *The Handbook of Pragmatics*. Edited by L. R. Horn and G. Ward. Oxford: Blackwell, 2004.
Sadock, Jerrold M. "Toward a Grammatically Realistic Typology of Speech Acts." Pages 393–406 in *Foundations of Speech Act Theory: Philosophical and Linguistic Perspectives*. Edited by Savas L. Tsohatzisis. London/New York: Routledge, 1994.
Sadock, Jerrold M. *Toward a Linguistic Theory of Speech Acts*. New York: Academic, 1974.
Sadock, Jerrold M., and Arnold M. Zwicky. "Speech Act Distinctions in Syntax." Pages 155–96 in *Language Typology and Syntactic Description, Volume 1: Clause Structure*. Edited by Timothy Shopen. Cambridge: Cambridge University Press, 1985.
Salmon, Nathan. "The Pragmatic Fallacy." *Philosophical Studies* 63 (1991): 83–97.
Salmon, Nathan. "Two Conceptions of Semantics." Pages 317–28 in *Semantics vs. Pragmatics*. Edited by Z. G. Szabó. Oxford: Clarendon Press, 2005.
Sarna, Nahum M. *Exodus*. The JPS Torah Commentary. Philadelphia: Jewish Publication, 1991.
Sarna, Nahum M. *Genesis*. The JPS Torah Commentary. Philadelphia: Jewish Publication, 1989.
Savran, George W. *Telling and Retelling: Quotation in Biblical Narrative*. Bloomington: Indiana University Press, 1988.
Schaffer, Deborah. "Can Rhetorical Questions Function as Retorts? Is the Pope Catholic?" *JP* 37 (2005): 433–60.
Schmidt-Radefeldt, Jürgen. "On So-Called 'Rhetorical' Questions." *JP* 1 (1977): 375–92.
Schoors, Antoon. *I Am God Your Savior: A Form-Critical Study of the Main Genres in Is. XL–LV*. VTSup 24. Leiden: Brill, 1973.
Searle, John R. "The Background of Meaning." Pages 221–32 in *Speech Act Theory and Pragmatics*. Texts and Studies in Linguistics and Philosophy 10. Edited by John R. Searle, Ferenc Kiefer, and Manfred Bierwisch. Dordrecht: Springer Netherlands, 1980.
Searle, John R. "Indirect Speech Acts." Pages 30–57 in *Expression and Meaning*. Cambridge: Cambridge University Press, 1979. Reprint of "Indirect Speech Acts." Pages 59–82 in *Speech Acts: Syntax and Semantics 3*. Edited by P. Cole and J. L. Morgan. New York: Academic, 1975.

Searle, John R. *Expression and Meaning: Studies in the Theory of Speech Acts*. Cambridge: Cambridge University Press, 1979.

Searle, John R. "How Performatives Work." Pages 85–107 in *Essays in Speech Act Theory*. Pragmatics & Beyond New Series 77. Edited by Daniel Vanderveken and Susumu Kubo. Amsterdam/Philadelphia: John Benjamins, 2002. Reprint of "How Performatives Work." *Linguistics and Philosophy* 12 (1989): 535–58.

Searle, John R. *Speech Acts: An Essay in the Philosophy of Language*. Cambridge: Cambridge University Press, 1969.

Searle, John R. "What Is a Speech Act?" Pages 39–53 in *Philosophy of Language*. Edited by John R. Searle. Oxford: Oxford University Press, 1971. Reprint of "What Is a Speech Act?" Pages 221–39 in *Philosophy in America*. Edited by M. Black. Ithaca, NY: Cornell University Press, 1965.

Searle, John R., Ferenc Kiefer, and Manfred Bierwisch, "Introduction." Pages vii–xii in *Speech Act Theory and Pragmatics*. Edited by John R. Searle. Texts and Studies in Linguistics and Philosophy 10. Dordrecht: Reidel, 1980.

Searle, John R., and Daniel Vanderveken. *Foundations of Illocutionary Logic*. Cambridge: Cambridge University Press, 1985.

Siemund, Peter. "Exclamative Clauses in English and their Relevance for Theories of Clause Types." *Studies in Language* 39 (2015): 697–727.

Siemund, Peter. "Interrogative Constructions." Pages 1010–28 in *Language Typology and Language Universals, Volume 2*. Edited by M. Haspelmath et al. Berlin/New York: de Gruyter, 2001.

Sharp, Carolyn J. *Irony and Meaning in the Hebrew Bible*. ISBL. Bloomington: Indiana University Press, 2009.

Shipley, Joseph T. *Dictionary of World Literary Terms*. London: George Allen & Unwin, 1955.

Silverman, David P. "Divinity and Deities in Ancient Egypt." Pages 7–87 in *Religion in Ancient Egypt: Gods, Myths, and Personal Practice*. Edited by B. E. Shafer. Ithaca: Cornell University Press, 1991.

Slot, Pauline. *How Can You Say That? Rhetorical Questions in Argumentative Texts*. Studies in Language and Language Use 2. Amsterdam: IFOTT, 1993.

Slot, Pauline. Review of Cornelia Ilie, *What Else Can I Tell You? A Pragmatic Study of English Rhetorical Questions as Discursive and Argumentative Acts*. Argumentation 11 (1997): 383–86.

Smith, Mark S. *God in Translation: Deities in Cross-Cultural Discourse in the Biblical World*. Grand Rapids: Eerdmans, 2008.

Smith, Mark S. "The Poetics of Exodus 15 and Its Position in the Book." Pages 23–34 in *Imagery and Imagination in Biblical Literature: Festschrift Aloysius Fitzgerald*. CBQMS 32. Edited by L. Boadt and Mark S. Smith. Washington: Catholic Biblical Association, 2001.

Soames, Scott. *Philosophical Essays, Volume 1: Natural Language: What It Means and How We Use It*. Princeton: Princeton University Press, 2009.

Soames, Scott. *Philosophical Essays, Volume 2: The Philosophical Significance of Language*. Princeton: Princeton University Press, 2009.

Soames, Scott. *Philosophy of Language*. Princeton Foundations of Contemporary Philosophy. Princeton: Princeton University Press, 2010.

Sperber, Dan, and Deirdre Wilson. "Loose Talk." *Proceedings of the Aristotelian Society* 86 (1985–86): 153–71.

Sperber, Dan, and Deirdre Wilson. "The Mapping between the Mental and the Public Lexicon." Pages 52–70 in *Pragmatics II: Critical Concepts in Linguistics, Volume 2*. Edited by A. Kasher. London: Routledge, 2012. Reprint of "The Mapping Between the Mental and the Public Lexicon." Pages 184–200 in *Language and Thought: Interdisciplinary Themes*. Edited by P. Carruthers and J. Boucher. Cambridge: Cambridge University Press, 1998.

Sperber, Dan, and Deirdre Wilson. "Pragmatics, Modularity, and Mind-Reading." *Mind & Language* 17 (2002): 3–23.

Sperber, Dan, and Deirdre Wilson. "Précis of Relevance: Communication and Cognition." *Behavioral and Brain Sciences* 10 (1987): 697–754.

Sperber, Dan, and Deirdre Wilson. *Relevance: Communication and Cognition*. Oxford: Blackwell, 1986.

Spykerboer, Hendrik C. *The Structure and Composition of Deutero-Isaiah with Special Reference to the Polemics Against Idolatry*. Meppel: Krips, 1976.

Stampe, Dennis W. "Meaning and Truth in the Theory of Speech Acts." Pages 1–39 in *Syntax and Semantics 3: Speech Acts*. Edited by P. Cole and J. L. Morgan. New York: Academic, 1975.

Steiner, Richard C. "On the Original Structure and Meanings of *Mah Nishtannah* and the History of its Reinterpretation." *Jewish Studies: An Internet Journal* 7 (2008): 163–204.

Stenström, Anna-Brita. *Questions and Responses in English Conversation*. Lund Studies in English. Lund: Liber Förlag. Malmö: CWK Gleerup, 1984.

Strawson, P. F. "Intention and Convention in Speech Acts." Pages 23–38 in *The Philosophy of Language*. Edited by John R. Searle. Oxford: Oxford University Press, 1971. Reprint of "Intention and Convention in Speech Acts." Pages 380–400 in *Symposium on J. L. Austin*. Edited by K. T. Fann. London: Routledge & Kegan Paul, 1969. Reprint of "Intention and Convention in Speech Acts." *Philosophical Review* 73 (1964): 439–60.

Sweeney, Marvin A. *Isaiah 40–66*. FOTL. Grand Rapids: Eerdmans, 2016.

Szabó, Zoltán G. "Introduction." Pages 1–14 in *Semantics vs. Pragmatics*. Edited by Zoltán G. Szabó. Oxford: Clarendon, 2005.

Szabó, Zoltán G., ed. *Semantics vs. Pragmatics*. Oxford: Clarendon, 2005.

Tate, Marvin E. "An Expositions of Psalm 8." *Perspectives in Religious Studies* 28 (2001): 343–59.

Tate, Marvin E. "Psalm 88." *RevExp* 87 (1990): 91–95.

Tate, Marvin E. *Psalms 51–100*. WBC 20. Dallas: Word, 1990.

Teeter, Emily. "Maat." Pages 319–21 in volume 2 of *The Oxford Encyclopedia of Ancient Egypt*. Edited D. B. Redford. Oxford: Oxford University Press, 2001.

Terkourafi, Marina. "Conventionality." Pages 79–81 in *The Routledge Pragmatics Encyclopedia*. Edited by L. Cummings. London/New York: Routledge, 2010.

Terrien, Samuel. *The Psalms: Strophic Structure and Theological Commentary*. Grand Rapids: Eerdmans, 2003.

Thiselton, A. C. "Communicative Action and Promise in Interdisciplinary, Biblical, and Theological Hermeneutics." Pages 133–239 in *The Promise of Hermeneutics*. Roger Lundin, Clarence Walhout, and A. C. Thiselton. Grand Rapids: Eerdmans/Carlisle: Paternoster, 1999.

Thiselton, A. C. *New Horizons in Hermeneutics: The Theory and Practice of Transforming Biblical Reading*. Grand Rapids: Zondervan, 1992.

Tsohatzidis, Savas L. "Speaker Meaning, Sentence Meaning and Metaphor." Pages 365–73 in *Foundations of Speech Act Theory: Philosophical and Linguistic Perspectives*. Edited by Savas L. Tsohatzidis. London/New York: Routledge, 1994.

Turner, K. ed. *The Semantics/Pragmatics Interface from Different Points of View*. Oxford: Elsevier, 1999.

Van Eemeren, Frans H., and Rob Grootendorst. *Argumentation, Communication and Fallacies: A Pragma-Dialectical Perspective*. Hillsdale: Lawrence Erlbaum, 1992.

Van Eemeren, Frans H., and Rob Grootendorst. "Speech Act Conditions as Tools for Reconstructing Argumentative Discourse." *Argumentation* 3 (1989): 367–83.

Van Eemeren, Frans H., and Rob Grootendorst. *Speech Acts in Argumentative Discussions: A Theoretical Model for the Analysis of Discussions Directed towards Solving Conflicts of Opinion*. Studies of Argumentation in Pragmatics and Discourse Analysis. Dordrecht: Publications, 1984.

Van Eemeren, Frans H., Rob Grootendorst, and Francisca S. Henkemans. *Fundamentals of Argumentation Theory: A Handbook of Historical Backgrounds and Contemporary Developments*. New York/London: Routledge, 1996.

Van Leeuwen, Raymond C. "Psalm 8.5 and Job 7.17–18: A Mistaken Scholarly Commonplace?" Pages 205–15 in *The World of the Aramaeans I: Biblical Studies in Honor of Paul-Eugène Dion*. JSOTSup 324. Edited by P. M. Michèle Daviau et al. Sheffield: Sheffield Academic, 2001.

Van Rensburg, J. F. J. "Wise Men Saying Things by Asking Questions: The Function of the Interrogative in Job 3 and 14." *Old Testament Essays* 4 (1991): 227–47.

Van Rooy, Robert. "Negative Polarity Items in Questions: Strength as Relevance." *Journal of Semantics* 20 (2003): 239–73.

Vanderveken, Daniel. "A Complete Formulation of a Simple Logic of Elementary Illocutionary Acts." Pages 99–131 in *Foundations of Speech Act Theory: Philosophical and Linguistic Perspectives*. Edited by Savas L. Tsohatzidis. London/New York: Routledge, 1994.

Vanderveken, Daniel. *Meaning and Speech Acts, Volume 1: Principles of Language Use*. Cambridge: Cambridge University Press, 1990.

Vanderveken, Daniel. "Non-Literal Speech Acts and Conversational Maxims." Pages 371–84 in *John Searle and his Critics*. Edited by Ernest Lepore and Robert van Gulick. Oxford: Blackwell, 1991.

Vanderveken, Daniel. "Universal Grammar and Speech Act Theory." Pages 25–62 in *Essays in Speech Act Theory*. Pragmatics & Beyond New Series 77. Edited by Daniel Vanderveken and Susumu Kubo. Amsterdam/Philadelphia: John Benjamins, 2002.

Vanderveken, Daniel, and Susumu Kubo, eds. *Essays in Speech Act Theory*. Pragmatics & Beyond New Series 77. Amsterdam/Philadelphia: John Benjamins, 2002.

Vaux, Roland de. *Ancient Israel: Its Life and Institutions*. BRS. Translated by J. McHugh. Grand Rapids: Eerdmans, 1961.

Vervenne, Marc. "The Phraseology of 'Knowing YHWH' in the Hebrew Bible: A Preliminary Study of its Syntax and Function." Pages 467–92 in *Studies in the Book of Isaiah*. Festschrift W. A. M. Beuken. Edited by J. van Ruiten and Marc Vervenne. BETL 132. Leuven: Leuven University Press, 1997.

Wales, Katie. *A Dictionary of Stylistics*. London: Longman, 1989.

Warnock, G. J. "Some Types of Performative Utterance." Pages 69–89 in *Essays on J. L. Austin*. Edited by Isaiah Berlin et al. Oxford: Clarendon, 1973.

Watson, Wilfred G. E. *Classical Hebrew Poetry*. JSOTSup 26. Sheffield: Sheffield Academic, 1986.

Watts, Rikki E. "Consolation or Confrontation? Isaiah 40–55 and the Delay of the New Exodus." *TynBul* 41 (1990): 31–59.
Weinberg, Howard I., John Wadsworth, and Robert S. Baron. "Demand and the Impact of Leading Questions on Eyewitness Testimony." *Memory & Cognition* 11 (1983): 101–104.
Weiser, Artur. *The Psalms*. Old Testament Library. Translated by H. Hartwell. Philadelphia: Westminster, 1962.
Wendland, Ernst. "Linear and Concentric Patterns in Malachi." *BT* 36 (1985): 108–21.
Wenham, Gordon. *Genesis 1–15*. WBC 1. Waco: Word, 1987.
Wenham, Gordon. *Genesis 16–50*. WBC 2. Dallas: Word, 1994.
Westermann, Claus. *Genesis 37–50: A Commentary*. Translated by J. J. Scullion. Minneapolis: Augsburg, 1986.
Westermann, Claus. *Isaiah 40–66*. Translated by D. M. G. Stalker. Philadelphia: Westminster, 1969.
Westermann, Claus. *Praise and Lament in the Psalms*. Translated by K. R. Crim and R. N. Soulen. Atlanta: John Knox, 1981.
Westermann, Claus. *The Praise of God in the Psalms*. Translated by K. R. Crim. Richmond: John Knox, 1965.
Westermann, Claus. *The Psalms: Structure, Content & Message*. Translated by R. D. Gehrke. Minneapolis: Augsburg, 1980.
Westermann, Claus. "The Role of the Lament in the Theology of the Old Testament." *Int* 28 (1974): 20–38.
Wharton, Tim. "Speech Act Theory." Pages 452–56 in *The Routledge Pragmatics Encyclopedia*. Edited by L. Cummings. London/New York: Routledge, 2010.
Whybray, R. N. *The Heavenly Counsellor in Isaiah 13–14: A Study of the Sources of the Theology of Deutero-Isaiah*. Cambridge: Cambridge University Press, 1971.
Whybray, R. N. *Isaiah 40–66*. NCBC. Grand Rapids: Eerdmans, 1975.
Wilson, Deirdre. "Relevance Theory." Pages 393–99 in *The Routledge Pragmatics Encyclopedia*. Edited by Louise Cummings. London/New York: Routledge, 2010.
Wilson, Deirdre, and Dan Sperber. "On Grice's Theory of Conversation." Pages 347–68 in *Pragmatics: Critical Concepts, Volume 4: Presuppositions, Implicature, and Indirect Speech Acts*. Edited by Asa Kasher. London/New York: Routledge, 1998.
Wilson, Deirdre, and Dan Sperber. "Relevance Theory." Pages 607–32 in *The Handbook of Pragmatics*. Edited by L. R. Horn and G. Ward. Oxford: Blackwell, 2004.
Wilson, Gerald H. *Psalms, Volume 1*. NIVAC. Grand Rapids: Zondervan, 2002.
Wittgenstein, Ludwig. *Philosophical Investigations*. 3rd ed. Translated by G. E. M. Anscombe. Englewood Cliffs, NJ: Prentice Hall, 1958.
Wunderlich, Dieter. "Methodological Remarks on Speech Act Theory." Pages 291–312 in *Speech Act Theory and Pragmatics*. Texts and Studies in Linguistics and Philosophy 10. Edited by John R. Searle, Ferenc Kiefer, and Manfred Bierwisch. Dordrecht: Reidel, 1980.
Young, Richard A. "A Classification of Conditional Sentences Based on Speech Act Theory." *Grace Theological Journal* 10 (1989): 29–49.
Yule, George. *Pragmatics*. Oxford Introductions to Language Study. Oxford: Oxford University Press, 1996.
Zanuttini, Raffaella, and Paul Portner. "Exclamative Clauses: At the Syntax-Semantics Interface." *Language* 79 (2003): 39–81.
Zimmerli, Walther. *I am Yahweh*. Edited by W. Brueggemann. Translated by D. W. Stott. Atlanta: John Knox, 1982.

Index of References

Hebrew Bible/ Old Testament		41:19	197	3:12	204
		41:20	197	3:14	207
Genesis		41:21	197	3:16	244
1	240, 267	41:38	196	3:19	206
1:1–2:4	239, 252	41:39	197	4:10	204
1:1	255	41:40–43	197	4:31	244
1:26–30	239	41:44	197	5:1	205
3:1	193	42:7	193	5:2	202, 205
3:3	193	43:22	257	7:5	209
3:9–10	193	44:16	229	7:8–12	209
3:9	193–95	44:18	199	7:17	209
3:10	194	45	197, 198	7:22	209
3:11	137, 195, 229, 232	45:1–15	198	8:7	209
		45:5–8	198	8:16–28	208
3:12	194	45:5	198	8:16	208
3:13	194	45:7	198	8:17	208
4:9	193, 194	45:8	198	8:18	208
4:10	194	45:9	198	8:19	208
21:20	204	50	198	8:20–32 Eng.	208
21:22	204	50:15–21	192	8:20	208
26:24	204	50:15–17	198	8:21	208
27:20	229, 233	50:15	198	8:22–23	208
27:24	6	50:17	198	8:22	209
27:36	137	50:19–21	198	8:24	208
28:15	196, 204	50:20	192, 200	8:25–26	208
29:15	137	50:22–25	201	8:31	208
30	188	50:24	244	9:13–17	204
30:1	188	50:25	244	9:14	209
30:2	188			9:24	209
30:3–4	192	Exodus		9:29	209
30:31	195	3–4	208	10:2	209
31:36	233	3	243	12:12	204, 208
32:27 Eng.	233	3:1–4:18	201	14:4	209
32:28	233	3:1–15	201	14:31	209
39:23	199	3:9–10	202	15	261, 262, 266
41:14–37	196	3:11	203, 237, 239		
41:19–21	197			15:1–18	210

Index of References

15:1	210	18:16	223	22:19–23	175
15:2–3	210			22:19–22	218
15:7–8	210	*Judges*		22:19	218
15:10	202	4:6	137	22:22–23	218
15:11	14, 202, 207, 210, 213, 214, 216, 217	9:38	202		
		18:14	140	*2 Kings*	
				2:3	140
		Ruth		4:43	229, 233
15:12–14	210	1:6	244	5:25	193
16:7	202	1:19	232	6:16–17	218
16:23	208			6:32	257
20:3	212	*1 Samuel*		8:1	208
20:5	244	2:27	137, 232		
20:9	195	10:24	136, 141, 257	*Job*	
20:10 Eng.	195			1:1	186
29:46	209	10:25	142	1:6–12	175, 218
33:19	208	15:2	244	1:8	186
		17:20	195	2:1–6	175, 218
Leviticus		17:25	142, 257	2:3	186
18:25	244	17:26	202	2:10	6
19:18	199	18:18	202	3:12	202
25:25	196	20:1	233	4:2–5:27	177
25:47–49	196	20:37	137	6:1–7:21	242
		23:13	208	6:26	136
Numbers		29:3	233	6:30	186
6:24	196			7	263
16:11	202	*2 Samuel*		7:1–21	242
20:10	232	1:25	229	7:17–18	236, 238, 241
23:8	229, 233	1:27	229		
24:5	229, 233	6	4	8:8–9	178
31:15	232	9:8	202	9:15	186
33:4	208	12:15	236	10:9	6
35:12–28	196	15:20	208	12:1–14:22	177
		20:9	193	12:2–6	186
Deuteronomy				12:2–3	173
2:10–11	223	*1 Kings*		12:7–12	173
3:24	14, 210	1	193	12:12	178
4:7	14, 210	6–7	4	13:1–2	173
10:17–18	214	8:27–45	218	13:25	136
11:30	137	8:30	218	15	155, 173, 175, 265
		18:17	232		
Joshua		20:13	142, 257	15:2–16	173
5:14–15	218	21:19	232	15:7–10	173, 179, 186
12:4	223	21:29	257		
13:12	223	22:3–4	142	15:7–9	265
15:8	223	22:3	137, 232, 257	15:7–8	156, 173, 176, 186
17:15	223				

2 Kings (cont.)		9:14–15	215	71:10–11	213		
15:7	173, 176	11:4	218	71:12–13	213		
15:8	176	17:3	244	71:14–16	213		
15:9	177–79, 186, 244	18:5	223	71:17	214		
		19:1 Eng.	217	71:18–19	215		
15:10	178, 179, 186, 262	19:2	217	71:18	213, 214		
		24:2	255	71:19–20	213		
15:11	136, 186	27	3, 15, 262, 263	71:19	14, 210, 212, 214		
17:17	202						
20:4	137	27:1–6	245	71:22–24	213		
26:5–6	223	27:1	245	73:19	229		
28:22	223	27:2–3	246	74	252		
31:12	223	27:3	245, 246	77:13 Eng.	215		
36:22	14, 210	27:4–6	246	77:14	14, 210, 215, 218		
38–41	252	27:6	246				
42:7–8	186	27:7–14	245	78:15	217		
		27:7–12	246	78:40	229, 233		
Psalms		27:8	246	80:14 Eng.	244		
3:1 Eng.	229	27:11	246	80:15	244		
3:2	229	27:14	246, 247	82	218		
6:6	223	30:10	223	82:2–4	218		
8	233, 236, 239, 241–44, 253, 267	33	252	82:7	219		
		33:1–3	228	86:13	223		
		33:4–7	228	88	220, 225, 266, 267		
		35	213, 214, 216–18, 220, 261, 266				
8:1 Eng.	228			88::2	222		
8:2–3	236			88:1 Eng.	222		
8:2	227, 229			88:1–2 Eng.	222		
8:3 Eng.	236	35:1–8	214	88:2	221, 225		
8:3–4	235	35:9–10	214	88:2 Eng.	222		
8:4	236, 239, 240	35:10	14, 210, 212, 214	88:2–3	222		
				88:3–9 Eng.	222		
8:4 Eng.	227	36:7 Eng.	229	88:3	222		
8:5	202, 203, 227, 235, 237, 238, 240–43, 257	36:8	229, 233	88:4–10	222		
		47:8 Eng.	218	88:4–9	225		
		47:9	218	88:5 Eng.	223, 224, 227		
		50:21	253				
		56:4 Eng.	245	88:6	223, 224, 227		
8:6–9	239, 240, 242	56:5	245				
		62:3	217	88:6 Eng.	223, 224		
8:6	239, 240	71	213–18, 220, 261, 266	88:7	223, 224		
8:7–9	239, 240			88:8 Eng.	223		
8:9 Eng.	228			88:9	223		
8:10	227	71:1–4	213	88:9 Eng.	222		
8:26	239	71:5–7	213	88:10	222		
8:29	239	71:8	213	88:10 Eng.	224		
9:13–14 Eng.	215	71:9	213	88:10–12 Eng.	220, 222		

Index of References

88:11–13	220, 222	89:49 Eng.	219	*Ecclesiastes*	
88:11	224	89:50	217, 219	9:10	223
88:12 Eng.	224	90:3	236		
88:12–13	225	96:1–3	228	*Isaiah*	
88:13	224	96:4–6	228	1:21	229
88:13 Eng.	222	103:15	236	6:1	218
88:14	222	103:19	218	13:11	244
88:14 Eng.	222	103:20–21	218	13:17–19	255, 260
88:14–18 Eng.	222	104	252	14:9–10	223
88:15–19	222	104:5	255	14:14	253
88:15	222	106:21	214	17:11	236
88:18 Eng.	224	113	215, 220,	26:14	223
88:19	221, 224		246, 262	26:19	223
89	216, 220,	113:1–3	216	38:18–19	223
	266	113:4	216	40–55	18, 248,
89:1–2 Eng.	217	113:5–6	212		250, 251
89:2–3	217	113:5	14, 210	40–48	18, 19,
89:2	217	113:7–9	216		249, 254,
89:3–4 Eng.	217	115:17	223		255, 260
89:3	217	118:6	245	40–46	253, 267
89:4–5	217, 223	118:17	223	40	253, 255,
89:5	217	119:175	223		261
89:5 Eng.	218	121:7–8	196	40:1–11	18, 248
89:6–7 Eng.	212	139:8	223	40:1–8	175
89:6	218	144	236, 241,	40:10	260
89:7–8	212		243	40:12–31	18, 19,
89:7	252	144:1	241		248–50
89:8 Eng.	212, 218	144:2	241	40:12–26	249
89:9–37 Eng.	219	144:3–4	235, 241	40:12–20	249
89:9	14, 210,	144:3	236, 238,	40:12–17	250
	212, 217,		243	40:12–14	249, 251
	218	144:4	236, 241	40:12	251, 252,
89:10–38	219	144:5–8	241		255,
89:11	255	144:11	241		257–59
89:12 Eng.	255			40:13–14	250–52,
89:14 Eng.	218	*Proverbs*			259
89:15	218	2:18	223	40:15–17	252, 255
89:25	217	8:22–31	174	40:18–20	19, 254
89:34	217	8:23	255	40:18	249, 259
89:38 Eng.	219	8:25	174	40:19–20	250, 253
89:39	219	8:29	255	40:21–26	249
89:46 Eng.	219	9:18	223	40:21	18, 249,
89:47	219	15:11	223		258–60
89:47 Eng.	219	21:16	223	40:22–24	250, 255,
89:48	219	27:20	223		256
89:48 Eng.	219			40:25	248, 249,
89:49	219				259

Isaiah (cont.)
40:26	250, 257	46	261	*Hosea*	
40:27–31	249	46:1–7	19, 253, 254	4:14	244
40:27	248–50, 257	46:5	253, 259	*Amos*	
		46:12–14	259	5:25	229, 232
40:28–31	249, 250, 257	48:1	254	9:2	223
		48:4–5	254		
40:28	18, 249, 254, 257, 258, 260	48:12	255	*Jonah*	
		48:16	255	4:4	232
		52:7	229		
41–48	259	53:1	4	*Micah*	
41:4	255	53:11	4	3:1	137
41:21–29	255, 260			7:18	14, 210
41:26	255, 256, 259	*Jeremiah*		*Zephaniah*	
		3:6	257	2:7	244
42:10	260	6:15	244		
42:17	19, 254	7:9	232	*Haggai*	
42:19	19, 254, 259	15:15	244	2:19	232
		15:18	236		
43:8–13	255, 260	17:9	236, 247	**NEW TESTAMENT**	
43:12	260	23:18	175	*John*	
43:22	254	23:21–22	175	19:22	208
44:5	260	30:12	236		
44:6	255	30:15	236		
44:7–8	260	50–51	21	**CLASSICAL AND ANCIENT**	
44:9–20	19, 253, 254	51	255	**CHRISTIAN WRITINGS**	
				Chrysostom	
44:26–28	254	*Ezekiel*		*Homily on Genesis*	
44:28	260	8:12	257	17:22	194
45:1–7	260	8:15	257		
45:20–25	260	8:17	257		
45:20	19, 254, 260	12:25	208		
		47:6	257		
45:21	267				

Index of Authors

Abels, K. 231
Abrams, M. H. 127
Adams, J. W. 12, 13, 21, 33, 35, 40, 43, 58, 85, 163, 165, 186, 201, 220, 254, 260
Alston, W. P. 36, 37, 39, 56
Alter, R. 173, 228, 234, 235
Anzilotti, G. I. 8, 13, 127, 238
Asher, N. 41
Atlas, J. D. 49
Austin, J. L. 29–31, 34, 38, 60, 165, 166

Bach, K. 10, 22–27, 40, 45, 51–53, 55, 69–74, 76, 81, 104, 112, 117, 118, 152
Baines, J. 209
Baltzer, K. 251
Banuazizi, A. 6
Baron, R. D. 134
Bayer, S. 68, 109
Beckson, K. 127
Beekman, J. 7, 126, 145
Beijer, F. 228, 230, 231
Bell, M. 6
Bellinger, W. H., Jr. 218, 222, 235, 236, 241, 245, 248
Bertolet, R. 44–46, 81–83
Beuken, W. A. M. 243
Bianchi, C. 24
Black, E. 8
Blenkinsopp, J. 251, 260
Blyth, C. 227
Bolinger, D. L. 137, 138
Bonhême, M.-A. 196
Borkin, A. 7
Braun, D. 169
Breasted, J. H. 197
Brenner, M. L. 210
Briggs, R. S. 13, 14, 34–36, 43, 163, 166, 186, 207

Brown, P. 8, 127, 168
Brueggemann, W. 3, 192, 196, 198, 216, 218, 220–22, 235, 236, 241, 245, 246, 248, 251
Bublitz, W. 134, 135, 137, 139, 140, 142

Callow, J. C. 7, 126
Carston, R. 23, 115, 116
Cassuto, U. 194, 195
Chafe, W. L. 7
Childs, B. S. 202, 207, 251
Chisholm Jr., W. S. 137
Clark, D. L. 2
Clifford, R. J. 253
Clines, D. J. A. 174, 175, 177, 178, 242, 243, 258
Coats, G. W. 202, 203, 205, 238, 239, 241, 243
Cohen, F. S. 6
Cohen, P. R. 52
Cole, P. 47, 109
Collins, P. 230–33
Conant, J. 24
Cope, E. M. 1
Craig, K. M., Jr. 193, 195, 196
Craigie, P. C. 228, 235, 236, 245, 248
Crenshaw, J. L. 247
Creswell, C. 6
Cross, F. M. 210
Crüsemann, F. 225
Cuddon, J. A. 127
Culley, R. C. 220, 221, 225
Currid, J. D. 209

Dahood, M. J. 221
Dascal, M. 80
Davison, A. 48, 66, 144
de Regt, L. J. 6, 136, 156, 186
Dion, P. E. 242, 243

Domaneschi, F. 23, 24
Dozeman, T. B. 201, 202
Durham, J. I. 204

Elliott, D. E. 231
Ene (Ilie), C. 8, 130, 133, 146, 147
Evans, D. D. 13, 165, 166

Fiengo, R. 5, 7, 127, 132
Fishbane, M. 242
Frápolli, M. J. 23
Frank, J. 1, 12
Freedman, D. N. 210
Fretheim, T. E. 203, 210

Ganz, A. 127
Garcia-Carpintero, M. 112, 169
Gazdar, G. 43
Geis, M. L. 46, 48, 65, 66, 68, 108
Gerstenberger, E. S. 214–17, 220, 221, 228, 235, 245
Goldingay, J. 194, 204, 207, 208, 214–17, 220, 221, 223, 225, 228, 235, 236, 240, 245–47, 249–53, 255, 259
Gordis, R. 108, 136
Gordon, D. 46–48
Gordon, R. P. 219
Gow, M. D. 194
Gowan, D. E. 207, 208
Green, G. M. 21, 48, 49, 51–53, 78, 79, 109, 119, 120, 145, 170, 178, 191
Greenbaum, S. 127
Grice, H. P. 27, 48, 50–60, 67, 80, 100, 109, 112, 114, 117, 120
Grimshaw, J. 231, 232
Grootendorst, R. 9, 91–98, 149, 153, 154, 179
Gu, Y. 40
Gunkel, H. 195
Gunlogson, C. 171

Habel, N. C. 173, 175, 176, 202, 242
Hamilton, V. P. 236
Han, C.-h. 7, 127, 131
Hancher, M. 34
Harnish, R. M. 45, 52, 53, 69–74, 76, 81
Hartley, J. E. 174, 175, 195, 199, 243
Hasan, N. A. 231
Hauser, A. J. 210
Henkemans, F. S. 9, 179

Higginbotham, J. 5
Hoffmeier, J. K. 197, 208, 209
Holdcroft, D. 31, 88–90
Holroyd, K. 21
Holter, K. 253
Horn, L. R. 24, 40, 41, 51, 52, 55, 68, 81, 109, 118, 119
Hornsby, J. 76, 77
Hossfeld, F.-L. 220, 227
Huang, Y. 21, 22, 24–26, 28, 39, 43–46, 49, 50, 52, 54, 55, 57, 65, 103, 114, 118, 121, 154
Huddleston, R. 5, 6, 135, 140, 230–32
Hudson, R. A. 17, 134, 140
Hungerland, I. C. 27
Hyman, R. T. 194, 199

Ilie, C. 3, 7, 11, 12, 16–18, 126, 128–31, 133–35, 138, 139, 143–52, 155, 158, 163, 164, 172, 173, 236

Janzen, J. G. 175
Jaszczolt, K. M. 24
Johnson, R. E., Jr. 15, 247

Kiefer, F. 127, 139, 144
Kitchen, K. A. 197
Koole, J. L. 248, 251
Koops, R. 155, 156
König, E. 4–6, 230–32
Korta, K. 27, 28, 80
Kraus, H.-J. 221, 225, 226, 228, 235, 245, 247
Kuntz, J. K. 7, 15, 19, 213, 215, 217, 222, 235, 246, 248, 249, 251, 258, 259

Labuschagne, C. J. 15, 211, 252, 253
Lakoff, G. 46–48, 108
Lambrecht, K. 230, 231
Landy, F. 195
Larkin, D. 79
Lascarides, A. 41
Leech, G. N. 66, 127
Levesque, H. J. 52
Levinson, S. C. 8, 9, 11, 34, 43–47, 50, 54, 55, 57, 119, 127, 155, 168
Llewelyn, J. E. 6
Loar, B. 23, 24, 56
Longman III, T. 221
Louth, A. 194

Lund, Ø. 228, 235, 236, 240
Lundbom, J. R. 207
Lycan, W. G. 46, 47, 68, 108

Mandolfo, C. 227
Mays, J. L. 219, 235
McKenzie, J. L. 251
Meibauer, J. 8
Melugin, R. F. 248, 249
Merendino, R. P. 255
Mettinger, T. N. D. 142, 175
Meulen ter, A. 23
Michaelis, L. A. 230, 231, 238
Miller, P. D. 219, 246
Moberly, R. W. L. 207
Morgan, J. L. 45, 47, 48, 67–69, 108, 132
Moshavi, A. 15, 132, 135–37, 140–42, 179, 191, 195, 229, 231–33, 247, 256–58
Mowinckel, S. 210
Muilenburg, J. 210
Mullen, E. T., Jr. 175

Naidoff, B. D. 248, 250
Nida, E. A. 7
Noth, M. 210
Nowell, I. 224, 225

O'Malley, M. H. 79
Oswalt, J. N. 251, 252, 259

Patrick, D. 201, 212
Paul, S. M. 251, 252
Penco, C. 23, 24
Perdue, L. G. 174, 176, 178, 242–44
Perrault, C. R. 52
Perry, J. 27, 28, 80
Peterson, E. H. 240
Piazza, R. 134
Pope, E. 127, 132, 134, 159, 160
Pope, M. H. 175, 242
Portner, P. 231, 232, 235

Quirk, R. S. 126, 127, 134, 135, 140, 228

Rad, G. von 3, 227
Rakić, S. 8, 12, 13, 18, 137, 140, 141, 160, 185
Reboul, O. 127

Récanati, F. 8, 23–25, 27, 29, 33, 99–106, 113, 116, 121
Rett, J. 228, 231, 232
Riemann, P. A. 193, 196
Rohde, H. 7, 170–72, 190
Rosengren, I. 229, 230, 232

Sadock, J. M. 4, 6, 7, 22, 32, 34, 38, 41, 44–49, 54, 69, 80, 81, 83, 127, 133, 137, 154, 162, 230, 232
Salmon, N. 24, 26, 118
Sarna, N. M. 195, 199, 206
Savran, G. W. 193
Schaffer, D. 131, 132
Schmidt-Radefeldt, J. 6, 16, 17, 238
Schoors, A. 248, 249, 251
Searle, J. R. 11, 30–33, 35, 38, 39, 42, 45, 47, 58, 60–65, 74–76, 80, 81, 85, 89, 148, 163, 165, 166
Sharp, C. J. 200
Shipley, J. T. 127
Siemund, P. 4–6, 230–32
Silverman, D. P. 196
Slot, P. 8, 98, 126, 153, 157–62
Smith, M. S. 210, 219
Soames, S. 23, 24, 59, 110, 111
Sperber, D. 49, 51, 104, 114–16
Spykerboer, H. C. 253
Stampe, D. W. 78
Steiner, R. C. 233
Stenström, A.-B. 17, 133–35, 138, 141, 162
Strawson, P. F. 69
Svartyk, J. 127
Sweeney, M. A. 248, 249, 251, 256, 258
Szabó, Z. G. 27, 28, 58

Tate, M. E. 213, 217, 219–22, 227, 228, 234, 235, 239, 240
Teeter, E. 209
Terkourafi, M. 157
Terrien, S. 220, 222, 224, 228, 235
Thiselton, A. C. 13, 34–36
Tsohatzidas, S. L. 67
Turner, K. 24

Van Eemeren, F. H. 9, 91–98, 149, 153, 154, 179
Van Leeuwen, R. C. 203, 205, 240, 243, 244

Van Rensburg, J. F. J. 247
Van Rooy, R. 17, 127, 171
Vanderveken, D. 30, 35, 75, 84–88, 124, 163, 165
Vaux, R. de 197
Vervenne, M. 209

Wadsworth, J. 134
Wales, K. 127
Ward, G. 24
Warnock, G. J. 35, 74
Watson, W. G. E. 15
Watts, R. E. 253
Weinberg, H. I. 134
Weiser, A. 221, 240, 245–47
Wendland, E. 3
Wenham, G. 192, 194, 195, 197, 198

Westermann, C. 192, 210, 213, 221–23, 249, 251, 253
Wharton, T. 22, 154
Whybray, R. N. 174, 251
Williams, T. F. 244
Wilson, D. 49, 51, 104, 114–16
Wilson, G. H. 235, 236, 238
Wittgenstein, L. 24
Wunderlich, D. 34

Young, R. A. 21
Yule. G. 50

Zanuttini, R. 231, 232, 235
Zenger, E. 220, 227
Zimmerli, W. 209
Zwicky, A. M. 4, 6, 137, 230, 232

www.ingramcontent.com/pod-product-compliance
Lightning Source LLC
Chambersburg PA
CBHW072124290426
44111CB00012B/1771